THE POETRY OF ROBERT FROST

THE POETRY
OF
ROBERT FROST

THE COLLECTED POEMS

EDITED BY

EDWARD CONNERY LATHEM

HENRY HOLT AND COMPANY

NEW YORK

Henry Holt and Company, LLC
Publishers since 1866
175 Fifth Avenue
New York, New York 10010
enryholt.com

Henry Holt® and ® are registered trademarks
of Henry Holt and Company, LLC.

PUBLISHER'S NOTE
This book contains those poems which, on documentary and other evidence,
it is believed Robert Frost himself would have chosen to represent his poetic
achievement had he lived to supervise a comprehensive edition of his work. He
left at this death in 1963 no unpublished, completed poems that there is
definite reason to believe he would have included in such a collection as this.
The time will come for a variorum of definitive edition in which it will be
appropriate to print every scrap of verse that can be attributed to Frost, but the
materials are not yet adequately in hand.

Library of Congress Cataloging-in-Publication Data
Frost, Robert.
The Poetry of Robert Frost.
ISBN-13: 978-0-8050-0502-8
ISBN-10: 0-8050-0502-1
I. Lathem, Edward Connery.
PS3511.R94   1979   811'.52—dc20   68-24759

Henry Holt books are available for special promotions and
premiums. For details contact: Director, Special Markets.

Designed by Rudolph Ruzicka

Printed in the United States of America
41   43   45   44   42

WEST-RUNNING BROOK

xi

A FURTHER RANGE

xvi

The Poetry of Robert Frost

PHOTOGRAPH BY CLARA E. SIPPRELL

THE PASTURE

I'm going out to clean the pasture spring;
I'll only stop to rake the leaves away
(And wait to watch the water clear, I may):
I shan't be gone long.—You come too.

I'm going out to fetch the little calf
That's standing by the mother. It's so young
It totters when she licks it with her tongue.
I shan't be gone long.—You come too.

A Boy's Will

: 1913 :

INTO MY OWN

One of my wishes is that those dark trees,
So old and firm they scarcely show the breeze,
Were not, as 'twere, the merest mask of gloom,
But stretched away unto the edge of doom.

I should not be withheld but that some day   5
Into their vastness I should steal away,
Fearless of ever finding open land,
Or highway where the slow wheel pours the sand.

I do not see why I should e'er turn back,
Or those should not set forth upon my track   10
To overtake me, who should miss me here
And long to know if still I held them dear.

They would not find me changed from him they knew—
Only more sure of all I thought was true.

GHOST HOUSE

I dwell in a lonely house I know
That vanished many a summer ago,
    And left no trace but the cellar walls,
    And a cellar in which the daylight falls
And the purple-stemmed wild raspberries grow.   5

O'er ruined fences the grapevines shield
The woods come back to the mowing field;
    The orchard tree has grown one copse

5

Of new wood and old where the woodpecker chops;
The footpath down to the well is healed.   10

I dwell with a strangely aching heart
In that vanished abode there far apart
    On that disused and forgotten road
    That has no dust-bath now for the toad.
Night comes; the black bats tumble and dart;   15

The whippoorwill is coming to shout
And hush and cluck and flutter about:
    I hear him begin far enough away
    Full many a time to say his say
Before he arrives to say it out.   20

It is under the small, dim, summer star.
I know not who these mute folk are
    Who share the unlit place with me—
    Those stones out under the low-limbed tree
Doubtless bear names that the mosses mar.   25

They are tireless folk, but slow and sad—
Though two, close-keeping, are lass and lad—
    With none among them that ever sings,
    And yet, in view of how many things,
As sweet companions as might be had.   30

MY NOVEMBER GUEST

My Sorrow, when she's here with me,
    Thinks these dark days of autumn rain
Are beautiful as days can be;
She loves the bare, the withered tree;
    She walks the sodden pasture lane.   5

6

Her pleasure will not let me stay.
    She talks and I am fain to list:
She's glad the birds are gone away,
She's glad her simple worsted gray
    Is silver now with clinging mist.   10

The desolate, deserted trees,
    The faded earth, the heavy sky,
The beauties she so truly sees,
She thinks I have no eye for these,
    And vexes me for reason why.   15

Not yesterday I learned to know
    The love of bare November days
Before the coming of the snow,
But it were vain to tell her so,
    And they are better for her praise.   20

LOVE AND A QUESTION

A Stranger came to the door at eve,
    And he spoke the bridegroom fair.
He bore a green-white stick in his hand,
    And, for all burden, care.
He asked with the eyes more than the lips   5
    For a shelter for the night,
And he turned and looked at the road afar
    Without a window light.

The bridegroom came forth into the porch
    With, "Let us look at the sky,   10
And question what of the night to be,
    Stranger, you and I."
The woodbine leaves littered the yard,

7

The woodbine berries were blue,
Autumn, yes, winter was in the wind;   15
"Stranger, I wish I knew."

Within, the bride in the dusk alone
　Bent over the open fire,
Her face rose-red with the glowing coal
　And the thought of the heart's desire.   20
The bridegroom looked at the weary road,
　Yet saw but her within,
And wished her heart in a case of gold
　And pinned with a silver pin.

The bridegroom thought it little to give   25
　A dole of bread, a purse,
A heartfelt prayer for the poor of God,
　Or for the rich a curse;
But whether or not a man was asked
　To mar the love of two   30
By harboring woe in the bridal house,
　The bridegroom wished he knew.

A LATE WALK

When I go up through the mowing field,
　The headless aftermath,
Smooth-laid like thatch with the heavy dew,
　Half closes the garden path.

And when I come to the garden ground,   5
　The whir of sober birds
Up from the tangle of withered weeds
　Is sadder than any words.

A tree beside the wall stands bare,
But a leaf that lingered brown,   10
Disturbed, I doubt not, by my thought,
Comes softly rattling down.

I end not far from my going forth,
By picking the faded blue
Of the last remaining aster flower   15
To carry again to you.

STARS

How countlessly they congregate
O'er our tumultuous snow,
Which flows in shapes as tall as trees
When wintry winds do blow!—

As if with keenness for our fate,   5
Our faltering few steps on
To white rest, and a place of rest
Invisible at dawn—

And yet with neither love nor hate,
Those stars like some snow-white   10
Minerva's snow-white marble eyes
Without the gift of sight.

STORM FEAR

When the wind works against us in the dark,
And pelts with snow
The lower-chamber window on the east,
And whispers with a sort of stifled bark,
The beast,   5

9

"Come out! Come out!"—
It costs no inward struggle not to go,
Ah, no!
I count our strength,
Two and a child,   10
Those of us not asleep subdued to mark
How the cold creeps as the fire dies at length—
How drifts are piled,
Dooryard and road ungraded,
Till even the comforting barn grows far away,   15
And my heart owns a doubt
Whether 'tis in us to arise with day
And save ourselves unaided.

WIND AND WINDOW FLOWER

Lovers, forget your love,
    And list to the love of these,
She a window flower,
    And he a winter breeze.

When the frosty window veil   5
    Was melted down at noon,
And the cagèd yellow bird
    Hung over her in tune,

He marked her through the pane,
    He could not help but mark,   10
And only passed her by
    To come again at dark.

He was a winter wind,
    Concerned with ice and snow,

Dead weeds and unmated birds,   15
  And little of love could know.

But he sighed upon the sill,
  He gave the sash a shake,
As witness all within
  Who lay that night awake.   20

Perchance he half prevailed
  To win her for the flight
From the firelit looking-glass
  And warm stove-window light.

But the flower leaned aside   25
  And thought of naught to say,
And morning found the breeze
  A hundred miles away.

TO THE THAWING WIND

Come with rain, O loud Southwester!
Bring the singer, bring the nester;
Give the buried flower a dream;
Make the settled snowbank steam;
Find the brown beneath the white;   5
But whate'er you do tonight,
Bathe my window, make it flow,
Melt it as the ice will go;
Melt the glass and leave the sticks
Like a hermit's crucifix;   10
Burst into my narrow stall;
Swing the picture on the wall;
Run the rattling pages o'er;

Scatter poems on the floor;
Turn the poet out of door. 15

A PRAYER IN SPRING

Oh, give us pleasure in the flowers today;
And give us not to think so far away
As the uncertain harvest; keep us here
All simply in the springing of the year.

Oh, give us pleasure in the orchard white, 5
Like nothing else by day, like ghosts by night;
And make us happy in the happy bees,
The swarm dilating round the perfect trees.

And make us happy in the darting bird
That suddenly above the bees is heard, 10
The meteor that thrusts in with needle bill,
And off a blossom in mid-air stands still.

For this is love and nothing else is love,
The which it is reserved for God above
To sanctify to what far ends He will, 15
But which it only needs that we fulfill.

FLOWER-GATHERING

I left you in the morning,
And in the morning glow
You walked a way beside me
To make me sad to go.
Do you know me in the gloaming, 5

12

Gaunt and dusty gray with roaming?
Are you dumb because you know me not,
Or dumb because you know?

All for me? And not a question
For the faded flowers gay   10
That could take me from beside you
For the ages of a day?
They are yours, and be the measure
Of their worth for you to treasure,
The measure of the little while   15
That I've been long away.

ROSE POGONIAS

A saturated meadow,
    Sun-shaped and jewel-small,
A circle scarcely wider
    Than the trees around were tall;
Where winds were quite excluded,   5
    And the air was stifling sweet
With the breath of many flowers—
    A temple of the heat.

There we bowed us in the burning,
    As the sun's right worship is,   10
To pick where none could miss them
    A thousand orchises;
For though the grass was scattered,
    Yet every second spear
Seemed tipped with wings of color   15
    That tinged the atmosphere.

13

We raised a simple prayer
Before we left the spot,
That in the general mowing
That place might be forgot;   20
Or if not all so favored,
Obtain such grace of hours
That none should mow the grass there
While so confused with flowers.

WAITING

Afield at dusk

What things for dream there are when specter-like,
Moving among tall haycocks lightly piled,
I enter alone upon the stubble field,
From which the laborers' voices late have died,
And in the antiphony of afterglow   5
And rising full moon, sit me down
Upon the full moon's side of the first haycock
And lose myself amid so many alike.

I dream upon the opposing lights of the hour,
Preventing shadow until the moon prevail;   10
I dream upon the nighthawks peopling heaven,
Each circling each with vague unearthly cry,
Or plunging headlong with fierce twang afar;
And on the bat's mute antics, who would seem
Dimly to have made out my secret place,   15
Only to lose it when he pirouettes,
And seek it endlessly with purblind haste;
On the last swallow's sweep; and on the rasp
In the abyss of odor and rustle at my back,
That, silenced by my advent, finds once more,   20

14

After an interval, his instrument,
And tries once—twice—and thrice if I be there;
And on the worn book of old-golden song
I brought not here to read, it seems, but hold
And freshen in this air of withering sweetness;   25
But on the memory of one absent, most,
For whom these lines when they shall greet her eye.

IN A VALE

When I was young, we dwelt in a vale
    By a misty fen that rang all night,
And thus it was the maidens pale
I knew so well, whose garments trail
    Across the reeds to a window light.   5

The fen had every kind of bloom,
    And for every kind there was a face,
And a voice that has sounded in my room
Across the sill from the outer gloom.
    Each came singly unto her place,   10

But all came every night with the mist;
    And often they brought so much to say
Of things of moment to which, they wist,
One so lonely was fain to list,
    That the stars were almost faded away   15

Before the last went, heavy with dew,
    Back to the place from which she came—
Where the bird was before it flew,
Where the flower was before it grew,
    Where bird and flower were one and the same.   20

15

And thus it is I know so well
Why the flower has odor, the bird has song.
You have only to ask me, and I can tell.
No, not vainly there did I dwell,
Nor vainly listen all the night long.   25

A DREAM PANG

I had withdrawn in forest, and my song
Was swallowed up in leaves that blew alway;
And to the forest edge you came one day
(This was my dream) and looked and pondered long,
But did not enter, though the wish was strong: 5
You shook your pensive head as who should say,
"I dare not—too far in his footsteps stray—
He must seek me would he undo the wrong."

Not far, but near, I stood and saw it all,
Behind low boughs the trees let down outside;   10
And the sweet pang it cost me not to call
And tell you that I saw does still abide.
But 'tis not true that thus I dwelt aloof,
For the wood wakes, and you are here for proof.

IN NEGLECT

They leave us so to the way we took,
    As two in whom they were proved mistaken,
That we sit sometimes in the wayside nook,
With mischievous, vagrant, seraphic look,
    And *try* if we cannot feel forsaken.   5

16

THE VANTAGE POINT

If tired of trees I seek again mankind,
  Well I know where to hie me—in the dawn,
  To a slope where the cattle keep the lawn.
There amid lolling juniper reclined,
Myself unseen, I see in white defined   5
  Far off the homes of men, and farther still,
  The graves of men on an opposing hill,
Living or dead, whichever are to mind.

And if by noon I have too much of these,
  I have but to turn on my arm, and lo,   10
  The sunburned hillside sets my face aglow,
My breathing shakes the bluet like a breeze,
  I smell the earth, I smell the bruisèd plant,
  I look into the crater of the ant.

MOWING

There was never a sound beside the wood but one,
And that was my long scythe whispering to the ground.
What was it it whispered? I knew not well myself;
Perhaps it was something about the heat of the sun,
Something, perhaps, about the lack of sound—   5
And that was why it whispered and did not speak.
It was no dream of the gift of idle hours,
Or easy gold at the hand of fay or elf:
Anything more than the truth would have seemed too weak
To the earnest love that laid the swale in rows,   10
Not without feeble-pointed spikes of flowers
(Pale orchises), and scared a bright green snake.
The fact is the sweetest dream that labor knows.
My long scythe whispered and left the hay to make.

17

GOING FOR WATER

The well was dry beside the door,
  And so we went with pail and can
Across the fields behind the house
  To seek the brook if still it ran;

Not loth to have excuse to go, 5
  Because the autumn eve was fair
(Though chill), because the fields were ours,
  And by the brook our woods were there.

We ran as if to meet the moon
  That slowly dawned behind the trees, 10
The barren boughs without the leaves,
  Without the birds, without the breeze.

But once within the wood, we paused
  Like gnomes that hid us from the moon,
Ready to run to hiding new 15
  With laughter when she found us soon.

Each laid on other a staying hand
  To listen ere we dared to look,
And in the hush we joined to make
  We heard, we knew we heard the brook. 20

A note as from a single place,
  A slender tinkling fall that made
Now drops that floated on the pool
  Like pearls, and now a silver blade.

REVELATION

We make ourselves a place apart
  Behind light words that tease and flout,
But oh, the agitated heart
  Till someone really find us out.

'Tis pity if the case require   5
  (Or so we say) that in the end
We speak the literal to inspire
  The understanding of a friend.

But so with all, from babes that play
  At hide-and-seek to God afar,   10
So all who hide too well away
  Must speak and tell us where they are.

THE TRIAL BY EXISTENCE

Even the bravest that are slain
  Shall not dissemble their surprise
On waking to find valor reign,
  Even as on earth, in paradise;
And where they sought without the sword   5
  Wide fields of asphodel fore'er,
To find that the utmost reward
  Of daring should be still to dare.

The light of heaven falls whole and white
  And is not shattered into dyes,   10
The light forever is morning light;
  The hills are verdured pasturewise;

19

The angel hosts with freshness go,
    And seek with laughter what to brave—
And binding all is the hushed snow   15
    Of the far-distant breaking wave.

And from a cliff top is proclaimed
    The gathering of the souls for birth,
The trial by existence named,
    The obscuration upon earth.   20
And the slant spirits trooping by
    In streams and cross- and counter-streams
Can but give ear to that sweet cry
    For its suggestion of what dreams!

And the more loitering are turned   25
    To view once more the sacrifice
Of those who for some good discerned
    Will gladly give up paradise.
And a white shimmering concourse rolls
    Toward the throne to witness there   30
The speeding of devoted souls
    Which God makes His especial care.

And none are taken but who will,
    Having first heard the life read out
That opens earthward, good and ill,   35
    Beyond the shadow of a doubt;
And very beautifully God limns,
    And tenderly, life's little dream,
But naught extenuates or dims,
    Setting the thing that is supreme.   40

Nor is there wanting in the press
    Some spirit to stand simply forth,

Heroic in its nakedness,
    Against the uttermost of earth.
The tale of earth's unhonored things   45
    Sounds nobler there than 'neath the sun;
And the mind whirls and the heart sings,
    And a shout greets the daring one.

But always God speaks at the end:
    "One thought in agony of strife   50
The bravest would have by for friend,
    The memory that he chose the life;
But the pure fate to which you go
    Admits no memory of choice,
Or the woe were not earthly woe   55
    To which you give the assenting voice."

And so the choice must be again,
    But the last choice is still the same;
And the awe passes wonder then,
    And a hush falls for all acclaim.   60
And God has taken a flower of gold
    And broken it, and used therefrom
The mystic link to bind and hold
    Spirit to matter till death come.

'Tis of the essence of life here,   65
    Though we choose greatly, still to lack
The lasting memory at all clear,
    That life has for us on the wrack
Nothing but what we somehow chose;
    Thus are we wholly stripped of pride   70
In the pain that has but one close,
    Bearing it crushed and mystified.

THE TUFT OF FLOWERS

I went to turn the grass once after one
Who mowed it in the dew before the sun.

The dew was gone that made his blade so keen
Before I came to view the leveled scene.

I looked for him behind an isle of trees;   5
I listened for his whetstone on the breeze.

But he had gone his way, the grass all mown,
And I must be, as he had been—alone,

"As all must be," I said within my heart,
"Whether they work together or apart."   10

But as I said it, swift there passed me by
On noiseless wing a bewildered butterfly,

Seeking with memories grown dim o'er night
Some resting flower of yesterday's delight.

And once I marked his flight go round and round,   15
As where some flower lay withering on the ground.

And then he flew as far as eye could see,
And then on tremulous wing came back to me.

I thought of questions that have no reply,
And would have turned to toss the grass to dry;   20

But he turned first, and led my eye to look
At a tall tuft of flowers beside a brook,

A leaping tongue of bloom the scythe had spared
Beside a reedy brook the scythe had bared.

The mower in the dew had loved them thus,   25
By leaving them to flourish, not for us,

Nor yet to draw one thought of ours to him,
But from sheer morning gladness at the brim.

The butterfly and I had lit upon,
Nevertheless, a message from the dawn,   30

That made me hear the wakening birds around,
And hear his long scythe whispering to the ground,

And feel a spirit kindred to my own;
So that henceforth I worked no more alone;

But glad with him, I worked as with his aid,   35
And weary, sought at noon with him the shade;

And dreaming, as it were, held brotherly speech
With one whose thought I had not hoped to reach.

"Men work together," I told him from the heart,
"Whether they work together or apart."   40

PAN WITH US

Pan came out of the woods one day—
His skin and his hair and his eyes were gray,
The gray of the moss of walls were they—
    And stood in the sun and looked his fill
    At wooded valley and wooded hill.   5

He stood in the zephyr, pipes in hand,
On a height of naked pasture land;
In all the country he did command

23

He saw no smoke and he saw no roof.
That was well! and he stamped a hoof.   10

His heart knew peace, for none came here
To this lean feeding, save once a year
Someone to salt the half-wild steer,
    Or homespun children with clicking pails
    Who see so little they tell no tales.   15

He tossed his pipes, too hard to teach
A new-world song, far out of reach,
For a sylvan sign that the blue jay's screech
    And the whimper of hawks beside the sun
    Were music enough for him, for one.   20

Times were changed from what they were:
Such pipes kept less of power to stir
The fruited bough of the juniper
    And the fragile bluets clustered there
    Than the merest aimless breath of air.   25

They were pipes of pagan mirth,
And the world had found new terms of worth.
He laid him down on the sunburned earth
    And raveled a flower and looked away.
    Play? Play?—What should he play?   30

THE DEMIURGE'S LAUGH

It was far in the sameness of the wood;
    I was running with joy on the Demon's trail,
Though I knew what I hunted was no true god.
    It was just as the light was beginning to fail
That I suddenly heard—all I needed to hear: 5

24

It has lasted me many and many a year.

The sound was behind me instead of before,
  A sleepy sound, but mocking half,
As of one who utterly couldn't care.
  The Demon arose from his wallow to laugh,   10
Brushing the dirt from his eye as he went;
And well I knew what the Demon meant.

I shall not forget how his laugh rang out.
  I felt as a fool to have been so caught,
And checked my steps to make pretense   15
  It was something among the leaves I sought
(Though doubtful whether he stayed to see).
Thereafter I sat me against a tree.

NOW CLOSE THE WINDOWS

Now close the windows and hush all the fields:
  If the trees must, let them silently toss;
No bird is singing now, and if there is,
  Be it my loss.

It will be long ere the marshes resume,   5
  It will be long ere the earliest bird:
So close the windows and not hear the wind,
  But see all wind-stirred.

IN HARDWOOD GROVES

The same leaves over and over again!
They fall from giving shade above,
To make one texture of faded brown

And fit the earth like a leather glove.

Before the leaves can mount again   5
To fill the trees with another shade,
They must go down past things coming up.
They must go down into the dark decayed.

They *must* be pierced by flowers and put
Beneath the feet of dancing flowers.   10
However it is in some other world
I know that this is the way in ours.

A LINE-STORM SONG

The line-storm clouds fly tattered and swift.
    The road is forlorn all day,
Where a myriad snowy quartz-stones lift,
    And the hoofprints vanish away.
The roadside flowers, too wet for the bee,   5
    Expend their bloom in vain.
Come over the hills and far with me,
    And be my love in the rain.

The birds have less to say for themselves
    In the wood-world's torn despair   10
Than now these numberless years the elves,
    Although they are no less there:
All song of the woods is crushed like some
    Wild, easily shattered rose.
Come, be my love in the wet woods, come,   15
    Where the boughs rain when it blows.

There is the gale to urge behind
    And bruit our singing down,

And the shallow waters aflutter with wind
    From which to gather your gown.   20
What matter if we go clear to the west,
    And come not through dry-shod?
For wilding brooch, shall wet your breast
    The rain-fresh goldenrod.

Oh, never this whelming east wind swells   25
    But it seems like the sea's return
To the ancient lands where it left the shells
    Before the age of the fern;
And it seems like the time when, after doubt,
    Our love came back amain.   30
Oh, come forth into the storm and rout
    And be my love in the rain.

OCTOBER

O hushed October morning mild,
Thy leaves have ripened to the fall;
Tomorrow's wind, if it be wild,
Should waste them all.
The crows above the forest call;   5
Tomorrow they may form and go.
O hushed October morning mild,
Begin the hours of this day slow.
Make the day seem to us less brief.
Hearts not averse to being beguiled,   10
Beguile us in the way you know.
Release one leaf at break of day;
At noon release another leaf;
One from our trees, one far away.
Retard the sun with gentle mist;   15

27

Enchant the land with amethyst.
Slow, slow!
For the grapes' sake, if they were all,
Whose leaves already are burnt with frost,
Whose clustered fruit must else be lost—   20
For the grapes' sake along the wall.

MY BUTTERFLY

Thine emulous fond flowers are dead, too,
And the daft sun-assaulter, he
That frighted thee so oft, is fled or dead:
Save only me
(Nor is it sad to thee!)—   5
Save only me
There is none left to mourn thee in the fields.

The gray grass is scarce dappled with the snow;
Its two banks have not shut upon the river;
But it is long ago—   10
It seems forever—
Since first I saw thee glance,
With all thy dazzling other ones,
In airy dalliance,
Precipitate in love,   15
Tossed, tangled, whirled and whirled above,
Like a limp rose-wreath in a fairy dance.

When that was, the soft mist
Of my regret hung not on all the land,
And I was glad for thee,   20
And glad for me, I wist.

Thou didst not know, who tottered, wandering on high,

That fate had made thee for the pleasure of the wind,
With those great careless wings,
Nor yet did I.   25

And there were other things:
It seemed God let thee flutter from His gentle clasp,
Then fearful He had let thee win
Too far beyond Him to be gathered in,
Snatched thee, o'ereager, with ungentle grasp.   30

Ah! I remember me
How once conspiracy was rife
Against my life—
The languor of it and the dreaming fond;
Surging, the grasses dizzied me of thought,   35
The breeze three odors brought,
And a gem-flower waved in a wand!

Then when I was distraught
And could not speak,
Sidelong, full on my cheek,   40
What should that reckless zephyr fling
But the wild touch of thy dye-dusty wing!

I found that wing broken today!
For thou art dead, I said,
And the strange birds say.   45
I found it with the withered leaves
Under the eaves.

RELUCTANCE

Out through the fields and the woods
And over the walls I have wended;

I have climbed the hills of view
    And looked at the world, and descended;
I have come by the highway home,   5
    And lo, it is ended.

The leaves are all dead on the ground,
    Save those that the oak is keeping
To ravel them one by one
    And let them go scraping and creeping   10
Out over the crusted snow,
    When others are sleeping.

And the dead leaves lie huddled and still,
    No longer blown hither and thither;
The last lone aster is gone;   15
    The flowers of the witch hazel wither;
The heart is still aching to seek,
    But the feet question "Whither?"

Ah, when to the heart of man
    Was it ever less than a treason   20
To go with the drift of things,
    To yield with a grace to reason,
And bow and accept the end
    Of a love or a season?

North of Boston

: 1914 :

MENDING WALL

Something there is that doesn't love a wall,
That sends the frozen-ground-swell under it
And spills the upper boulders in the sun,
And makes gaps even two can pass abreast.
The work of hunters is another thing: 5
I have come after them and made repair
Where they have left not one stone on a stone,
But they would have the rabbit out of hiding,
To please the yelping dogs. The gaps I mean,
No one has seen them made or heard them made,   10
But at spring mending-time we find them there.
I let my neighbor know beyond the hill;
And on a day we meet to walk the line
And set the wall between us once again.
We keep the wall between us as we go.   15
To each the boulders that have fallen to each.
And some are loaves and some so nearly balls
We have to use a spell to make them balance:
"Stay where you are until our backs are turned!"
We wear our fingers rough with handling them.   20
Oh, just another kind of outdoor game,
One on a side. It comes to little more:
There where it is we do not need the wall:
He is all pine and I am apple orchard.
My apple trees will never get across   25
And eat the cones under his pines, I tell him.
He only says, "Good fences make good neighbors."

Spring is the mischief in me, and I wonder
If I could put a notion in his head:
"*Why* do they make good neighbors? Isn't it   30
Where there are cows? But here there are no cows.
Before I built a wall I'd ask to know
What I was walling in or walling out,
And to whom I was like to give offense.
Something there is that doesn't love a wall,   35
That wants it down." I could say "Elves" to him,
But it's not elves exactly, and I'd rather
He said it for himself. I see him there,
Bringing a stone grasped firmly by the top
In each hand, like an old-stone savage armed.   40
He moves in darkness as it seems to me,
Not of woods only and the shade of trees.
He will not go behind his father's saying,
And he likes having thought of it so well
He says again, "Good fences make good neighbors."   45

THE DEATH OF THE HIRED MAN

Mary sat musing on the lamp-flame at the table,
Waiting for Warren. When she heard his step,
She ran on tiptoe down the darkened passage
To meet him in the doorway with the news
And put him on his guard. "Silas is back."   5
She pushed him outward with her through the door
And shut it after her. "Be kind," she said.
She took the market things from Warren's arms
And set them on the porch, then drew him down
To sit beside her on the wooden steps.   10

"When was I ever anything but kind to him?

But I'll not have the fellow back," he said.
"I told him so last haying, didn't I?
If he left then, I said, that ended it.
What good is he? Who else will harbor him   15
At his age for the little he can do?
What help he is there's no depending on.
Off he goes always when I need him most.
He thinks he ought to earn a little pay,
Enough at least to buy tobacco with,   20
So he won't have to beg and be beholden.
'All right,' I say, 'I can't afford to pay
Any fixed wages, though I wish I could.'
'Someone else can.' 'Then someone else will have to.'
I shouldn't mind his bettering himself   25
If that was what it was. You can be certain,
When he begins like that, there's someone at him
Trying to coax him off with pocket money—
In haying time, when any help is scarce.
In winter he comes back to us. I'm done."   30

"Sh! not so loud: he'll hear you," Mary said.

"I want him to: he'll have to soon or late."

"He's worn out. He's asleep beside the stove.
When I came up from Rowe's I found him here,
Huddled against the barn door fast asleep,   35
A miserable sight, and frightening, too—
You needn't smile—I didn't recognize him—
I wasn't looking for him—and he's changed.
Wait till you see."
                    "Where did you say he'd been?"

"He didn't say. I dragged him to the house,   40

35

And gave him tea and tried to make him smoke.
I tried to make him talk about his travels.
Nothing would do: he just kept nodding off."

"What did he say? Did he say anything?"

"But little."

    "Anything? Mary, confess   45
He said he'd come to ditch the meadow for me."

"Warren!"

    "But did he? I just want to know."

"Of course he did. What would you have him say?
Surely you wouldn't grudge the poor old man
Some humble way to save his self-respect.   50
He added, if you really care to know,
He meant to clear the upper pasture, too.
That sounds like something you have heard before?
Warren, I wish you could have heard the way
He jumbled everything. I stopped to look   55
Two or three times—he made me feel so queer—
To see if he was talking in his sleep.
He ran on Harold Wilson—you remember—
The boy you had in haying four years since.
He's finished school, and teaching in his college.   60
Silas declares you'll have to get him back.
He says they two will make a team for work:
Between them they will lay this farm as smooth!
The way he mixed that in with other things.
He thinks young Wilson a likely lad, though daft   65
On education—you know how they fought
All through July under the blazing sun,
Silas up on the cart to build the load,

Harold along beside to pitch it on."

"Yes, I took care to keep well out of earshot."   70

"Well, those days trouble Silas like a dream.
You wouldn't think they would. How some things linger!
Harold's young college-boy's assurance piqued him.
After so many years he still keeps finding
Good arguments he sees he might have used.   75
I sympathize. I know just how it feels
To think of the right thing to say too late.
Harold's associated in his mind with Latin.
He asked me what I thought of Harold's saying
He studied Latin, like the violin,   80
Because he liked it—that an argument!
He said he couldn't make the boy believe
He could find water with a hazel prong—
Which showed how much good school had ever done him.
He wanted to go over that. But most of all   85
He thinks if he could have another chance
To teach him how to build a load of hay——"

"I know, that's Silas' one accomplishment.
He bundles every forkful in its place,
And tags and numbers it for future reference,   90
So he can find and easily dislodge it
In the unloading. Silas does that well.
He takes it out in bunches like big birds' nests.
You never see him standing on the hay
He's trying to lift, straining to lift himself."   95

"He thinks if he could teach him that, he'd be
Some good perhaps to someone in the world.
He hates to see a boy the fool of books.
Poor Silas, so concerned for other folk,

And nothing to look backward to with pride,   100
And nothing to look forward to with hope,
So now and never any different."

Part of a moon was falling down the west,
Dragging the whole sky with it to the hills.
Its light poured softly in her lap. She saw it   105
And spread her apron to it. She put out her hand
Among the harplike morning-glory strings,
Taut with the dew from garden bed to eaves,
As if she played unheard some tenderness
That wrought on him beside her in the night.   110
"Warren," she said, "he has come home to die:
You needn't be afraid he'll leave you this time."

"Home," he mocked gently.

                "Yes, what else but home?
It all depends on what you mean by home.
Of course he's nothing to us, any more   115
Than was the hound that came a stranger to us
Out of the woods, worn out upon the trail."

"Home is the place where, when you have to go there,
They have to take you in."

                "I should have called it
Something you somehow haven't to deserve."   120

Warren leaned out and took a step or two,
Picked up a little stick, and brought it back
And broke it in his hand and tossed it by.
"Silas has better claim on us you think
Than on his brother? Thirteen little miles   125
As the road winds would bring him to his door.
Silas has walked that far no doubt today.

Why doesn't he go there? His brother's rich,
A somebody—director in the bank."

"He never told us that."

                              "We know it, though."   130

"I think his brother ought to help, of course.
I'll see to that if there is need. He ought of right
To take him in, and might be willing to—
He may be better than appearances.
But have some pity on Silas. Do you think   135
If he had any pride in claiming kin
Or anything he looked for from his brother,
He'd keep so still about him all this time?"

"I wonder what's between them."

                              "I can tell you.
Silas is what he is—we wouldn't mind him—   140
But just the kind that kinsfolk can't abide.
He never did a thing so very bad.
He don't know why he isn't quite as good
As anybody. Worthless though he is,
He won't be made ashamed to please his brother."   145

"*I* can't think Si ever hurt anyone."

"No, but he hurt my heart the way he lay
And rolled his old head on that sharp-edged chair-back.
He wouldn't let me put him on the lounge.
You must go in and see what you can do.   150
I made the bed up for him there tonight.
You'll be surprised at him—how much he's broken.
His working days are done; I'm sure of it."

"I'd not be in a hurry to say that."

"I haven't been. Go, look, see for yourself.   155
But, Warren, please remember how it is:
He's come to help you ditch the meadow.
He has a plan. You mustn't laugh at him.
He may not speak of it, and then he may.
I'll sit and see if that small sailing cloud   160
Will hit or miss the moon."

                        It hit the moon.
Then there were three there, making a dim row,
The moon, the little silver cloud, and she.

Warren returned—too soon, it seemed to her—
Slipped to her side, caught up her hand and waited.   165

"Warren?" she questioned.

                    "Dead," was all he answered.

THE MOUNTAIN

The mountain held the town as in a shadow.
I saw so much before I slept there once:
I noticed that I missed stars in the west,
Where its black body cut into the sky.
Near me it seemed: I felt it like a wall   5
Behind which I was sheltered from a wind.
And yet between the town and it I found,
When I walked forth at dawn to see new things,
Were fields, a river, and beyond, more fields.
The river at the time was fallen away,   10
And made a widespread brawl on cobblestones;
But the signs showed what it had done in spring:
Good grassland gullied out, and in the grass
Ridges of sand, and driftwood stripped of bark.

I crossed the river and swung round the mountain.   15
And there I met a man who moved so slow
With white-faced oxen, in a heavy cart,
It seemed no harm to stop him altogether.

"What town is this?" I asked.

                         "This? Lunenburg."

Then I was wrong: the town of my sojourn,   20
Beyond the bridge, was not that of the mountain,
But only felt at night its shadowy presence.
"Where is your village? Very far from here?"

"There is no village—only scattered farms.
We were but sixty voters last election.   25
We can't in nature grow to many more:
That thing takes all the room!" He moved his goad.
The mountain stood there to be pointed at.
Pasture ran up the side a little way,
And then there was a wall of trees with trunks;   30
After that only tops of trees, and cliffs
Imperfectly concealed among the leaves.
A dry ravine emerged from under boughs
Into the pasture.

                   "That looks like a path.
Is that the way to reach the top from here?—   35
Not for this morning, but some other time:
I must be getting back to breakfast now."

"I don't advise your trying from this side.
There is no proper path, but those that *have*
Been up, I understand, have climbed from Ladd's.   40
That's five miles back. You can't mistake the place:
They logged it there last winter some way up.

I'd take you, but I'm bound the other way."

"You've never climbed it?"

                        "I've been on the sides,   45
Deer-hunting and trout-fishing. There's a brook
That starts up on it somewhere—I've heard say
Right on the top, tip-top—a curious thing.
But what would interest you about the brook,
It's always cold in summer, warm in winter.
One of the great sights going is to see   50
It steam in winter like an ox's breath,
Until the bushes all along its banks
Are inch-deep with the frosty spines and bristles—
You know the kind. Then let the sun shine on it!"

"There ought to be a view around the world   55
From such a mountain—if it isn't wooded
Clear to the top." I saw through leafy screens
Great granite terraces in sun and shadow,
Shelves one could rest a knee on getting up—
With depths behind him sheer a hundred feet—   60
Or turn and sit on and look out and down,
With little ferns in crevices at his elbow.

"As to that I can't say. But there's the spring,
Right on the summit, almost like a fountain.
That ought to be worth seeing."

                              "If it's there.   65
You never saw it?"

                     "I guess there's no doubt
About its being there. I never saw it.
It may not be right on the very top:
It wouldn't have to be a long way down

To have some head of water from above,   70
And a *good distance* down might not be noticed
By anyone who'd come a long way up.
One time I asked a fellow climbing it
To look and tell me later how it was."

"What did he say?"

                    "He said there was a lake   75
Somewhere in Ireland on a mountain top."

"But a lake's different. What about the spring?"

"He never got up high enough to see.
That's why I don't advise your trying this side.
He tried this side. I've always meant to go   80
And look myself, but you know how it is:
It doesn't seem so much to climb a mountain
You've worked around the foot of all your life.
What would I do? Go in my overalls,
With a big stick, the same as when the cows   85
Haven't come down to the bars at milking time?
Or with a shotgun for a stray black bear?
'Twouldn't seem real to climb for climbing it."

"I shouldn't climb it if I didn't want to—
Not for the sake of climbing. What's its name?"   90

"We call it Hor: I don't know if that's right."

"Can one walk around it? Would it be too far?"

"You can drive round and keep in Lunenburg,
But it's as much as ever you can do,
The boundary lines keep in so close to it.   95
Hor is the township, and the township's Hor—
And a few houses sprinkled round the foot,

Like boulders broken off the upper cliff,
Rolled out a little farther than the rest."

"Warm in December, cold in June, you say?"   100

"I don't suppose the water's changed at all.
You and I know enough to know it's warm
Compared with cold, and cold compared with warm.
But all the fun's in how you say a thing."

"You've lived here all your life?"

                                      "Ever since Hor   105
Was no bigger than a——" What, I did not hear.
He drew the oxen toward him with light touches
Of his slim goad on nose and offside flank,
Gave them their marching orders and was moving.

A HUNDRED COLLARS

Lancaster bore him—such a little town,
Such a great man. It doesn't see him often
Of late years, though he keeps the old homestead
And sends the children down there with their mother
To run wild in the summer—a little wild.   5
Sometimes he joins them for a day or two
And sees old friends he somehow can't get near.
They meet him in the general store at night,
Preoccupied with formidable mail,
Rifling a printed letter as he talks.   10
They seem afraid. He wouldn't have it so:
Though a great scholar, he's a democrat,
If not at heart, at least on principle.

Lately when coming up to Lancaster,
His train being late, he missed another train   15

And had four hours to wait at Woodsville Junction
After eleven o'clock at night. Too tired
To think of sitting such an ordeal out,
He turned to the hotel to find a bed.

"No room," the night clerk said. "Unless———"   20

Woodsville's a place of shrieks and wandering lamps
And cars that shock and rattle—and *one* hotel.

"You say 'unless.'"

        "Unless you wouldn't mind
Sharing a room with someone else."

                "Who is it?"

"A man."

        "So I should hope. What kind of man?"   25

"I know him: he's all right. A man's a man.
Separate beds, of course, you understand."
The night clerk blinked his eyes and dared him on.

"Who's that man sleeping in the office chair?
Has he had the refusal of my chance?"   30

"He was afraid of being robbed or murdered.
What do you say?"

        "I'll have to have a bed."

The night clerk led him up three flights of stairs
And down a narrow passage full of doors,
At the last one of which he knocked and entered.   35
"Lafe, here's a fellow wants to share your room."

"Show him this way. I'm not afraid of him.
I'm not so drunk I can't take care of myself."

The night clerk clapped a bedstead on the foot.
"This will be yours. Good-night," he said, and went.   40

"Lafe was the name, I think?"

                             "Yes, *Lay*fayette.
You got it the first time. And yours?"

                                    "Magoon.
Doctor Magoon."

                    "A Doctor?"

                                 "Well, a teacher."

"Professor Square-the-circle-till-you're-tired?
Hold on, there's something I don't think of now   45
That I had on my mind to ask the first
Man that knew anything I happened in with.
I'll ask you later—don't let me forget it."

The Doctor looked at Lafe and looked away.
A man? A brute. Naked above the waist,   50
He sat there creased and shining in the light,
Fumbling the buttons in a well-starched shirt.
"I'm moving into a size-larger shirt.
I've felt mean lately; mean's no name for it.
I just found what the matter was tonight: 55
I've been a-choking like a nursery tree
When it outgrows the wire band of its name tag.
I blamed it on the hot spell we've been having.
'Twas nothing but my foolish hanging back,
Not liking to own up I'd grown a size.   60
Number eighteen this is. What size do you wear?"

The Doctor caught his throat convulsively.
"Oh—ah—fourteen—fourteen."

                              "Fourteen! You say so!
I can remember when I wore fourteen.
And come to think I must have back at home   65
More than a hundred collars, size fourteen.
Too bad to waste them all. You ought to have them.
They're yours and welcome; let me send them to you.—
What makes you stand there on one leg like that?
You're not much furtherer than where Kike left you.   70
You act as if you wished you hadn't come.
Sit down or lie down, friend; you make me nervous."

The Doctor made a subdued dash for it,
And propped himself at bay against a pillow.

"Not that way, with your shoes on Kike's white bed.   75
You can't rest that way. Let me pull your shoes off."

"Don't touch me, please—I say, don't touch me, please.
I'll not be put to bed by you, my man."

"Just as you say. Have it your own way, then.
'My man' is it? You talk like a professor.   80
Speaking of who's afraid of who, however,
I'm thinking I have more to lose than you
If anything should happen to be wrong.
Who wants to cut your number fourteen throat!
Let's have a showdown as an evidence   85
Of good faith. There is ninety dollars.
Come, if you're not afraid."
                              "I'm not afraid.
There's five: that's all I carry."
                              "I can search you?
Where are you moving over to? Stay still.
You'd better tuck your money under you   90

                         47

And sleep on it, the way I always do
When I'm with people I don't trust at night."

"Will you believe me if I put it there
Right on the counterpane—that I do trust you?"

"You'd say so, Mister Man.—I'm a collector.   95
My ninety isn't mine—you won't think that.
I pick it up a dollar at a time
All round the country for the *Weekly News*,
Published in Bow. You know the *Weekly News*?"

"Known it since I was young."

                              "Then you know me.   100
Now we are getting on together—talking.
I'm sort of Something for it at the front.
My business is to find what people want:
They pay for it, and so they ought to have it.
Fairbanks, he says to me—he's editor—   105
'Feel out the public sentiment'—he says.
A good deal comes on me when all is said.
The only trouble is we disagree
In politics: I'm Vermont Democrat—
You know what that is, sort of double-dyed;   110
The *News* has always been Republican.
Fairbanks, he says to me, 'Help us this year,'
Meaning by us their ticket. 'No,' I says,
'I can't and won't. You've been in long enough:
It's time you turned around and boosted us.   115
You'll have to pay me more than ten a week
If I'm expected to elect Bill Taft.
I doubt if I could do it anyway.' "

"You seem to shape the paper's policy."

"You see I'm in with everybody, know 'em all.
I almost know their farms as well as they do."

"You drive around? It must be pleasant work."

"It's business, but I can't say it's not fun.
What I like best's the lay of different farms,
Coming out on them from a stretch of woods,   125
Or over a hill or round a sudden corner.
I like to find folks getting out in spring,
Raking the dooryard, working near the house.
Later they get out further in the fields.
Everything's shut sometimes except the barn;   130
The family's all away in some back meadow.
There's a hay load a-coming—when it comes.
And later still they all get driven in:
The fields are stripped to lawn, the garden patches
Stripped to bare ground, the maple trees   135
To whips and poles. There's nobody about.
The chimney, though, keeps up a good brisk smoking.
And I lie back and ride. I take the reins
Only when someone's coming, and the mare
Stops when she likes: I tell her when to go.   140
I've spoiled Jemima in more ways than one.
She's got so she turns in at every house
As if she had some sort of curvature,
No matter if I have no errand there.
She thinks I'm sociable. I maybe am.   145
It's seldom I get down except for meals, though.
Folks entertain me from the kitchen doorstep,
All in a family row down to the youngest."

"One would suppose they might not be as glad
To see you as you are to see them."

49

Because I want their dollar? I don't want
Anything they've not got. I never dun.
I'm there, and they can pay me if they like.
I go nowhere on purpose: I happen by.—
Sorry there is no cup to give you a drink. 155
I drink out of the bottle—not your style.
Mayn't I offer you——?"

                "No, no, no, thank you."

"Just as you say. Here's looking at you, then.—
And now I'm leaving you a little while.
You'll rest easier when I'm gone, perhaps— 160
Lie down—let yourself go and get some sleep.
But first—let's see—what was I going to ask you?
Those collars—who shall I address them to,
Suppose you aren't awake when I come back?"

"Really, friend, I can't let you. You—may need them." 165

"Not till I shrink, when they'll be out of style."

"But really I—I have so many collars."

"I don't know who I rather would have have them.
They're only turning yellow where they are.
But you're the doctor, as the saying is. 170
I'll put the light out. Don't you wait for me:
I've just begun the night. You get some sleep.
I'll knock so-fashion and peep round the door
When I come back, so you'll know who it is.
There's nothing I'm afraid of like scared people. 175
I don't want you should shoot me in the head.—
What am I doing carrying off this bottle?—
There now, you get some sleep."

He shut the door.
The Doctor slid a little down the pillow.

HOME BURIAL

He saw her from the bottom of the stairs
Before she saw him. She was starting down,
Looking back over her shoulder at some fear.
She took a doubtful step and then undid it
To raise herself and look again. He spoke   5
Advancing toward her: "What is it you see
From up there always?—for I want to know."
She turned and sank upon her skirts at that,
And her face changed from terrified to dull.
He said to gain time: "What is it you see?"   10
Mounting until she cowered under him.
"I will find out now—you must tell me, dear."
She, in her place, refused him any help,
With the least stiffening of her neck and silence.
She let him look, sure that he wouldn't see,   15
Blind creature; and awhile he didn't see.
But at last he murmured, "Oh," and again, "Oh."

"What is it—what?" she said.

                         "Just that I see."

"You don't," she challenged. "Tell me what it is."

"The wonder is I didn't see at once.   20
I never noticed it from here before.
I must be wonted to it—that's the reason.
The little graveyard where my people are!
So small the window frames the whole of it.
Not so much larger than a bedroom, is it?   25

51

There are three stones of slate and one of marble,
Broad-shouldered little slabs there in the sunlight
On the sidehill. We haven't to mind *those*.
But I understand: it is not the stones,
But the child's mound——"

                              "Don't, don't, don't,
    don't," she cried.   30

She withdrew, shrinking from beneath his arm
That rested on the banister, and slid downstairs;
And turned on him with such a daunting look,
He said twice over before he knew himself:
"Can't a man speak of his own child he's lost?"   35

"Not you!—Oh, where's my hat? Oh, I don't need it!
I must get out of here. I must get air.—
I don't know rightly whether any man can."

"Amy! Don't go to someone else this time.
Listen to me. I won't come down the stairs."   40
He sat and fixed his chin between his fists.
"There's something I should like to ask you, dear."

"You don't know how to ask it."

                              "Help me, then."

Her fingers moved the latch for all reply.

"My words are nearly always an offense.   45
I don't know how to speak of anything
So as to please you. But I might be taught,
I should suppose. I can't say I see how.
A man must partly give up being a man
With womenfolk. We could have some arrangement   50
By which I'd bind myself to keep hands off

Anything special you're a-mind to name.
Though I don't like such things 'twixt those that love.
Two that don't love can't live together without them.
But two that do can't live together with them."   55
She moved the latch a little. "Don't—don't go.
Don't carry it to someone else this time.
Tell me about it if it's something human.
Let me into your grief. I'm not so much
Unlike other folks as your standing there   60
Apart would make me out. Give me my chance.
I do think, though, you overdo it a little.
What was it brought you up to think it the thing
To take your mother-loss of a first child
So inconsolably—in the face of love.   65
You'd think his memory might be satisfied——"

"There you go sneering now!"

                                       "I'm not, I'm not!
You make me angry. I'll come down to you.
God, what a woman! And it's come to this,
A man can't speak of his own child that's dead."   70

"You can't because you don't know how to speak.
If you had any feelings, you that dug
With your own hand—how could you?—his little grave;
I saw you from that very window there,
Making the gravel leap and leap in air,   75
Leap up, like that, like that, and land so lightly
And roll back down the mound beside the hole.
I thought, Who is that man? I didn't know you.
And I crept down the stairs and up the stairs
To look again, and still your spade kept lifting.   80
Then you came in. I heard your rumbling voice

53

Out in the kitchen, and I don't know why,
But I went near to see with my own eyes.
You could sit there with the stains on your shoes
Of the fresh earth from your own baby's grave   85
And talk about your everyday concerns.
You had stood the spade up against the wall
Outside there in the entry, for I saw it."

"I shall laugh the worst laugh I ever laughed.
I'm cursed. God, if I don't believe I'm cursed."   90

"I can repeat the very words you were saying:
'Three foggy mornings and one rainy day
Will rot the best birch fence a man can build.'
Think of it, talk like that at such a time!
What had how long it takes a birch to rot   95
To do with what was in the darkened parlor?
You *couldn't* care! The nearest friends can go
With anyone to death, comes so far short
They might as well not try to go at all.
No, from the time when one is sick to death,   100
One is alone, and he dies more alone.
Friends make pretense of following to the grave,
But before one is in it, their minds are turned
And making the best of their way back to life
And living people, and things they understand.   105
But the world's evil. I won't have grief so
If I can change it. Oh, I won't, I won't!"

"There, you have said it all and you feel better.
You won't go now. You're crying. Close the door.
The heart's gone out of it: why keep it up?   110
Amy! There's someone coming down the road!"

"*You*—oh, you think the talk is all. I must go—

54

Somewhere out of this house. How can I make you——"

"If—you—do!" She was opening the door wider.
"Where do you mean to go? First tell me that.   115
I'll follow and bring you back by force. I *will!*—"

THE BLACK COTTAGE

We chanced in passing by that afternoon
To catch it in a sort of special picture
Among tar-banded ancient cherry trees,
Set well back from the road in rank lodged grass,
The little cottage we were speaking of,   5
A front with just a door between two windows,
Fresh painted by the shower a velvet black.
We paused, the minister and I, to look.
He made as if to hold it at arm's length
Or put the leaves aside that framed it in.   10
"Pretty," he said. "Come in. No one will care."
The path was a vague parting in the grass
That led us to a weathered windowsill.
We pressed our faces to the pane. "You see," he said,
"Everything's as she left it when she died.   15
Her sons won't sell the house or the things in it.
They say they mean to come and summer here
Where they were boys. They haven't come this year.
They live so far away—one is out West—
It will be hard for them to keep their word.   20
Anyway they won't have the place disturbed."
A buttoned haircloth lounge spread scrolling arms
Under a crayon portrait on the wall,
Done sadly from an old daguerreotype.
"That was the father as he went to war.   25

She always, when she talked about the war,
Sooner or later came and leaned, half knelt,
Against the lounge beside it, though I doubt
If such unlifelike lines kept power to stir
Anything in her after all the years.   30
He fell at Gettysburg or Fredericksburg,
I ought to know—it makes a difference which:
Fredericksburg wasn't Gettysburg, of course.
But what I'm getting to is how forsaken
A little cottage this has always seemed;   35
Since she went, more than ever, but before—
I don't mean altogether by the lives
That had gone out of it, the father first,
Then the two sons, till she was left alone.
(Nothing could draw her after those two sons.   40
She valued the considerate neglect
She had at some cost taught them after years.)
I mean by the world's having passed it by—
As we almost got by this afternoon.
It always seems to me a sort of mark   45
To measure how far fifty years have brought us.
Why not sit down if you are in no haste?
These doorsteps seldom have a visitor.
The warping boards pull out their own old nails
With none to tread and put them in their place.   50
She had her own idea of things, the old lady.
And she liked talk. She had seen Garrison
And Whittier, and had her story of them.
One wasn't long in learning that she thought,
Whatever else the Civil War was for,   55
It wasn't just to keep the States together,
Nor just to free the slaves, though it did both.
She wouldn't have believed those ends enough

56

To have given outright for them all she gave.
Her giving somehow touched the principle   60
That all men are created free and equal.
And to hear her quaint phrases—so removed
From the world's view today of all those things.
That's a hard mystery of Jefferson's.
What did he mean? Of course the easy way   65
Is to decide it simply isn't true.
It may not be. I heard a fellow say so.
But never mind, the Welshman got it planted
Where it will trouble us a thousand years.
Each age will have to reconsider it.   70
You couldn't tell her what the West was saying,
And what the South, to her serene belief.
She had some art of hearing and yet not
Hearing the latter wisdom of the world.
White was the only race she ever knew.   75
Black she had scarcely seen, and yellow never.
But how could they be made so very unlike
By the same hand working in the same stuff?
She had supposed the war decided that.
What are you going to do with such a person?   80
Strange how such innocence gets its own way.
I shouldn't be surprised if in this world
It were the force that would at last prevail.
Do you know but for her there was a time
When, to please younger members of the church,   85
Or rather say non-members in the church,
Whom we all have to think of nowadays,
I would have changed the Creed a very little?
Not that she ever had to ask me not to;
It never got so far as that; but the bare thought   90
Of her old tremulous bonnet in the pew,

And of her half asleep, was too much for me.
Why, I might wake her up and startle her.
It was the words 'descended into Hades'
That seemed too pagan to our liberal youth.   95
You know they suffered from a general onslaught.
And well, if they weren't true why keep right on
Saying them like the heathen? We could drop them.
Only—there was the bonnet in the pew.
Such a phrase couldn't have meant much to her.   100
But suppose she had missed it from the Creed,
As a child misses the unsaid Good-night
And falls asleep with heartache—how should *I* feel?
I'm just as glad she made me keep hands off,
For, dear me, why abandon a belief   105
Merely because it ceases to be true.
Cling to it long enough, and not a doubt
It will turn true again, for so it goes.
Most of the change we think we see in life
Is due to truths being in and out of favor.   110
As I sit here, and oftentimes, I wish
I could be monarch of a desert land
I could devote and dedicate forever
To the truths we keep coming back and back to.
So desert it would have to be, so walled   115
By mountain ranges half in summer snow,
No one would covet it or think it worth
The pains of conquering to force change on.
Scattered oases where men dwelt, but mostly
Sand dunes held loosely in tamarisk   120
Blown over and over themselves in idleness.
Sand grains should sugar in the natal dew
The babe born to the desert, the sandstorm

Retard mid-waste my cowering caravans—

"There are bees in this wall." He struck the clapboards, 125
Fierce heads looked out; small bodies pivoted.
We rose to go. Sunset blazed on the windows.

BLUEBERRIES

"You ought to have seen what I saw on my way
To the village, through Patterson's pasture today:
Blueberries as big as the end of your thumb,
Real sky-blue, and heavy, and ready to drum
In the cavernous pail of the first one to come!   5
And all ripe together, not some of them green
And some of them ripe! You ought to have seen!"

"I don't know what part of the pasture you mean."

"You know where they cut off the woods—let me see—
It was two years ago—or no!—can it be   10
No longer than that?—and the following fall
The fire ran and burned it all up but the wall."

"Why, there hasn't been time for the bushes to grow.
That's always the way with the blueberries, though:
There may not have been the ghost of a sign   15
Of them anywhere under the shade of the pine,
But get the pine out of the way, you may burn
The pasture all over until not a fern
Or grass-blade is left, not to mention a stick,
And presto, they're up all around you as thick   20
And hard to explain as a conjuror's trick."

"It must be on charcoal they fatten their fruit.
I taste in them sometimes the flavor of soot.

And after all, really they're ebony skinned:
The blue's but a mist from the breath of the wind,   25
A tarnish that goes at a touch of the hand,
And less than the tan with which pickers are tanned."

"Does Patterson know what he has, do you think?"

"He may and not care, and so leave the chewink
To gather them for him—you know what he is.   30
He won't make the fact that they're rightfully his
An excuse for keeping us other folk out."

"I wonder you didn't see Loren about."

"The best of it was that I did. Do you know,
I was just getting through what the field had to show   35
And over the wall and into the road,
When who should come by, with a democrat-load
Of all the young chattering Lorens alive,
But Loren, the fatherly, out for a drive."

"He saw you, then? What did he do? Did he frown?"   40

"He just kept nodding his head up and down.
You know how politely he always goes by.
But he thought a big thought—I could tell by his eye—
Which being expressed, might be this in effect:
'I have left those there berries, I shrewdly suspect,   45
To ripen too long. I am greatly to blame.'"

"He's a thriftier person than some I could name."

"He seems to be thrifty; and hasn't he need,
With the mouths of all those young Lorens to feed?
He has brought them all up on wild berries, they say,   50
Like birds. They store a great many away.
They eat them the year round, and those they don't eat

60

They sell in the store and buy shoes for their feet."

"Who cares what they say? It's a nice way to live,
Just taking what Nature is willing to give,   55
Not forcing her hand with harrow and plow."

"I wish you had seen his perpetual bow—
And the air of the youngsters! Not one of them turned,
And they looked so solemn-absurdly concerned."

"I wish I knew half what the flock of them know   60
Of where all the berries and other things grow,
Cranberries in bogs and raspberries on top
Of the boulder-strewn mountain, and when they will crop.
I met them one day and each had a flower
Stuck into his berries as fresh as a shower;   65
Some strange kind—they told me it hadn't a name."

"I've told you how once, not long after we came,
I almost provoked poor Loren to mirth
By going to him of all people on earth
To ask if he knew any fruit to be had   70
For the picking. The rascal, he said he'd be glad
To tell if he knew. But the year had been bad.
There *had* been some berries—but those were all gone.
He didn't say where they had been. He went on:
'I'm sure—I'm sure'—as polite as could be.   75
He spoke to his wife in the door, 'Let me see,
Mame, *we* don't know any good berrying place?'
It was all he could do to keep a straight face."

"If he thinks all the fruit that grows wild is for him,
He'll find he's mistaken. See here, for a whim,   80
We'll pick in the Pattersons' pasture this year.
We'll go in the morning, that is, if it's clear,

And the sun shines out warm: the vines must be wet.
It's so long since I picked I almost forget
How we used to pick berries: we took one look round, 85
Then sank out of sight like trolls underground,
And saw nothing more of each other, or heard,
Unless when you said I was keeping a bird
Away from its nest, and I said it was you.
'Well, one of us is.' For complaining it flew 90
Around and around us. And then for a while
We picked, till I feared you had wandered a mile,
And I thought I had lost you. I lifted a shout
Too loud for the distance you were, it turned out,
For when you made answer, your voice was as low 95
As talking—you stood up beside me, you know."

"We shan't have the place to ourselves to enjoy—
Not likely, when all the young Lorens deploy.
They'll be there tomorrow, or even tonight.
They won't be too friendly—they may be polite— 100
To people they look on as having no right
To pick where they're picking. But we won't complain.
You ought to have seen how it looked in the rain,
The fruit mixed with water in layers of leaves,
Like two kinds of jewels, a vision for thieves." 105

A SERVANT TO SERVANTS

I didn't make you know how glad I was
To have you come and camp here on our land.
I promised myself to get down some day
And see the way you lived, but I don't know!
With a houseful of hungry men to feed 5
I guess you'd find. . . . It seems to me

I can't express my feelings, any more
Than I can raise my voice or want to lift
My hand (oh, I can lift it when I have to).
Did ever you feel so? I hope you never. 10
It's got so I don't even know for sure
Whether I *am* glad, sorry, or anything.
There's nothing but a voice-like left inside
That seems to tell me how I ought to feel,
And would feel if I wasn't all gone wrong. 15
You take the lake. I look and look at it.
I see it's a fair, pretty sheet of water.
I stand and make myself repeat out loud
The advantages it has, so long and narrow,
Like a deep piece of some old running river 20
Cut short off at both ends. It lies five miles
Straightaway through the mountain notch
From the sink window where I wash the plates,
And all our storms come up toward the house,
Drawing the slow waves whiter and whiter and whiter. 25
It took my mind off doughnuts and soda biscuit
To step outdoors and take the water dazzle
A sunny morning, or take the rising wind
About my face and body and through my wrapper,
When a storm threatened from the Dragon's Den, 30
And a cold chill shivered across the lake.
I see it's a fair, pretty sheet of water,
Our Willoughby! How did you hear of it?
I expect, though, everyone's heard of it.
In a book about ferns? Listen to that! 35
You let things more like feathers regulate
Your going and coming. And you like it here?
I can see how you might. But I don't know!
It would be different if more people came,

63

For then there would be business. As it is, 40
The cottages Len built, sometimes we rent them,
Sometimes we don't. We've a good piece of shore
That ought to be worth something, and may yet.
But I don't count on it as much as Len.
He looks on the bright side of everything, 45
Including me. He thinks I'll be all right
With doctoring. But it's not medicine—
Lowe is the only doctor's dared to say so—
It's rest I want—there, I have said it out—
From cooking meals for hungry hired men 50
And washing dishes after them—from doing
Things over and over that just won't stay done.
By good rights I ought not to have so much
Put on me, but there seems no other way.
Len says one steady pull more ought to do it. 55
He says the best way out is always through.
And I agree to that, or in so far
As that I can see no way out but through—
Leastways for me—and then they'll be convinced.
It's not that Len don't want the best for me. 60
It was his plan our moving over in
Beside the lake from where that day I showed you
We used to live—ten miles from anywhere.
We didn't change without some sacrifice,
But Len went at it to make up the loss. 65
His work's a man's, of course, from sun to sun,
But he works when he works as hard as I do—
Though there's small profit in comparisons.
(Women and men will make them all the same.)
But work ain't all. Len undertakes too much. 70
He's into everything in town. This year
It's highways, and he's got too many men

Around him to look after that make waste.
They take advantage of him shamefully,
And proud, too, of themselves for doing so.   75
We have four here to board, great good-for-nothings,
Sprawling about the kitchen with their talk
While I fry their bacon. Much they care!
No more put out in what they do or say
Than if I wasn't in the room at all.   80
Coming and going all the time, they are:
I don't learn what their names are, let alone
Their characters, or whether they are safe
To have inside the house with doors unlocked.
I'm not afraid of them, though, if they're not   85
Afraid of me. There's two can play at that.
I have my fancies: it runs in the family.
My father's brother wasn't right. They kept him
Locked up for years back there at the old farm.
I've been away once—yes, I've been away.   90
The State Asylum. I was prejudiced;
I wouldn't have sent anyone of mine there;
You know the old idea—the only asylum
Was the poorhouse, and those who could afford,
Rather than send their folks to such a place,   95
Kept them at home; and it does seem more human.
But it's not so: the place is the asylum.
There they have every means proper to do with,
And you aren't darkening other people's lives—
Worse than no good to them, and they no good   100
To you in your condition; you can't know
Affection or the want of it in that state.
I've heard too much of the old-fashioned way.
My father's brother, he went mad quite young.
Some thought he had been bitten by a dog,   105

Because his violence took on the form
Of carrying his pillow in his teeth;
But it's more likely he was crossed in love,
Or so the story goes. It was some girl.
Anyway all he talked about was love. 110
They soon saw he would do someone a mischief
If he wa'n't kept strict watch of, and it ended
In father's building him a sort of cage,
Or room within a room, of hickory poles,
Like stanchions in the barn, from floor to ceiling— 115
A narrow passage all the way around.
Anything they put in for furniture
He'd tear to pieces, even a bed to lie on.
So they made the place comfortable with straw,
Like a beast's stall, to ease their consciences. 120
Of course they had to feed him without dishes.
They tried to keep him clothed, but he paraded
With his clothes on his arm—all of his clothes.
Cruel—it sounds. I s'pose they did the best
They knew. And just when he was at the height, 125
Father and mother married, and mother came,
A bride, to help take care of such a creature,
And accommodate her young life to his.
That was what marrying father meant to her.
She had to lie and hear love things made dreadful 130
By his shouts in the night. He'd shout and shout
Until the strength was shouted out of him,
And his voice died down slowly from exhaustion.
He'd pull his bars apart like bow and bowstring,
And let them go and make them twang, until 135
His hands had worn them smooth as any oxbow.
And then he'd crow as if he thought that child's play—
The only fun he had. I've heard them say, though,

They found a way to put a stop to it.
He was before my time—I never saw him; 140
But the pen stayed exactly as it was,
There in the upper chamber in the ell,
A sort of catchall full of attic clutter.
I often think of the smooth hickory bars.
It got so I would say—you know, half fooling— 145
"It's time I took my turn upstairs in jail"—
Just as you will till it becomes a habit.
No wonder I was glad to get away.
Mind you, I waited till Len said the word.
I didn't want the blame if things went wrong. 150
I was glad though, no end, when we moved out,
And I looked to be happy, and I was,
As I said, for a while—but I don't know!
Somehow the change wore out like a prescription.
And there's more to it than just window views 155
And living by a lake. I'm past such help—
Unless Len took the notion, which he won't,
And I won't ask him—it's not sure enough.
I s'pose I've got to go the road I'm going:
Other folks have to, and why shouldn't I? 160
I almost think if I could do like you,
Drop everything and live out on the ground—
But it might be, come night, I shouldn't like it,
Or a long rain. I should soon get enough,
And be glad of a good roof overhead. 165
I've lain awake thinking of you, I'll warrant,
More than you have yourself, some of these nights.
The wonder was the tents weren't snatched away
From over you as you lay in your beds.
I haven't courage for a risk like that. 170
Bless you, of course you're keeping me from work,

But the thing of it is, I need to *be* kept.
There's work enough to do—there's always that;
But behind's behind. The worst that you can do
Is set me back a little more behind.   175
I shan't catch up in this world, anyway.
I'd *rather* you'd not go unless you must.

AFTER APPLE-PICKING

My long two-pointed ladder's sticking through a tree
Toward heaven still,
And there's a barrel that I didn't fill
Beside it, and there may be two or three
Apples I didn't pick upon some bough.   5
But I am done with apple-picking now.
Essence of winter sleep is on the night,
The scent of apples: I am drowsing off.
I cannot rub the strangeness from my sight
I got from looking through a pane of glass   10
I skimmed this morning from the drinking trough
And held against the world of hoary grass.
It melted, and I let it fall and break.
But I was well
Upon my way to sleep before it fell,   15
And I could tell
What form my dreaming was about to take.
Magnified apples appear and disappear,
Stem end and blossom end,
And every fleck of russet showing clear.   20
My instep arch not only keeps the ache,
It keeps the pressure of a ladder-round.
I feel the ladder sway as the boughs bend.

And I keep hearing from the cellar bin
The rumbling sound   25
Of load on load of apples coming in.
For I have had too much
Of apple-picking: I am overtired
Of the great harvest I myself desired.
There were ten thousand thousand fruit to touch,   30
Cherish in hand, lift down, and not let fall.
For all
That struck the earth,
No matter if not bruised or spiked with stubble,
Went surely to the cider-apple heap   35
As of no worth.
One can see what will trouble
This sleep of mine, whatever sleep it is.
Were he not gone,
The woodchuck could say whether it's like his   40
Long sleep, as I describe its coming on,
Or just some human sleep.

THE CODE

There were three in the meadow by the brook
Gathering up windrows, piling cocks of hay,
With an eye always lifted toward the west
Where an irregular sun-bordered cloud
Darkly advanced with a perpetual dagger   5
Flickering across its bosom. Suddenly
One helper, thrusting pitchfork in the ground,
Marched himself off the field and home. One stayed.
The town-bred farmer failed to understand.

"What is there wrong?"

"What did I say?"

"About our taking pains."

"To cock the hay?—because it's going to shower?
I said that more than half an hour ago.
I said it to myself as much as you."

"You didn't know. But James is one big fool.   15
He thought you meant to find fault with his work.
That's what the average farmer would have meant.
James would take time, of course, to chew it over
Before he acted: he's just got round to act."

"He *is* a fool if that's the way he takes me."   20

"Don't let it bother you. You've found out something.
The hand that knows his business won't be told
To do work better or faster—those two things.
I'm as particular as anyone:
Most likely I'd have served you just the same.   25
But I know you don't understand our ways.
You were just talking what was in your mind,
What was in all our minds, and you weren't hinting.
Tell you a story of what happened once:
I was up here in Salem, at a man's   30
Named Sanders, with a gang of four or five
Doing the haying. No one liked the boss.
He was one of the kind sports call a spider,
All wiry arms and legs that spread out wavy
From a humped body nigh as big's a biscuit.   35
But work! that man could work, especially
If by so doing he could get more work
Out of his hired help. I'm not denying

70

He was hard on himself. I couldn't find
That he kept any hours—not for himself. 40
Daylight and lantern-light were one to him:
I've heard him pounding in the barn all night.
But what he liked was someone to encourage.
Them that he couldn't lead he'd get behind
And drive, the way you can, you know, in mowing— 45
Keep at their heels and threaten to mow their legs off.
I'd seen about enough of his bulling tricks
(We call that bulling). I'd been watching him.
So when he paired off with me in the hayfield
To load the load, thinks I, Look out for trouble. 50
I built the load and topped it off; old Sanders
Combed it down with a rake and says, 'O.K.'
Everything went well till we reached the barn
With a big jag to empty in a bay.
You understand that meant the easy job 55
For the man up on top, of throwing *down*
The hay and rolling it off wholesale,
Where on a mow it would have been slow lifting.
You wouldn't think a fellow'd need much urging
Under those circumstances, would you now? 60
But the old fool seizes his fork in both hands,
And looking up bewhiskered out of the pit,
Shouts like an army captain, 'Let her come!'
Thinks I, D'ye mean it? 'What was that you said?'
I asked out loud, so's there'd be no mistake, 65
'Did you say, "Let her come"?' 'Yes, let her come.'
He said it over, but he said it softer.
Never you say a thing like that to a man,
Not if he values what he is. God, I'd as soon
Murdered him as left out his middle name. 70
I'd built the load and knew right where to find it.

71

Two or three forkfuls I picked lightly round for
Like meditating, and then I just dug in
And dumped the rackful on him in ten lots.
I looked over the side once in the dust   75
And caught sight of him treading-water-like,
Keeping his head above. 'Damn ye,' I says,
'That gets ye!' He squeaked like a squeezed rat.
That was the last I saw or heard of him.
I cleaned the rack and drove out to cool off.   80
As I sat mopping hayseed from my neck,
And sort of waiting to be asked about it,
One of the boys sings out, 'Where's the old man?'
'I left him in the barn under the hay.
If ye want him, ye can go and dig him out.'   85
They realized from the way I swabbed my neck
More than was needed, something must be up.
They headed for the barn; I stayed where I was.
They told me afterward. First they forked hay,
A lot of it, out into the barn floor.   90
Nothing! They listened for him. Not a rustle.
I guess they thought I'd spiked him in the temple
Before I buried him, or I couldn't have managed.
They excavated more. 'Go keep his wife
Out of the barn.' Someone looked in a window,   95
And curse me if he wasn't in the kitchen
Slumped way down in a chair, with both his feet
Against the stove, the hottest day that summer.
He looked so clean disgusted from behind
There was no one that dared to stir him up,   100
Or let him know that he was being looked at.
Apparently I hadn't buried him
(I may have knocked him down); but my just trying
To bury him had hurt his dignity.

He had gone to the house so's not to meet me.   105
He kept away from us all afternoon.
We tended to his hay. We saw him out
After a while picking peas in his garden:
He couldn't keep away from doing something."

"Weren't you relieved to find he wasn't dead?"   110

"No! and yet I don't know—it's hard to say.
I went about to kill him fair enough."

"You took an awkward way. Did he discharge you?"

"Discharge me? No! He knew I did just right."

THE GENERATIONS OF MEN

A governor it was proclaimed this time,
When all who would come seeking in New Hampshire
Ancestral memories might come together.
And those of the name Stark gathered in Bow,
A rock-strewn town where farming has fallen off,   5
And sprout-lands flourish where the ax has gone.
Someone had literally run to earth
In an old cellar hole in a byroad
The origin of all the family there.
Thence they were sprung, so numerous a tribe   10
That now not all the houses left in town
Made shift to shelter them without the help
Of here and there a tent in grove and orchard.
They were at Bow, but that was not enough:
Nothing would do but they must fix a day   15
To stand together on the crater's verge
That turned them on the world, and try to fathom
The past and get some strangeness out of it.

But rain spoiled all. The day began uncertain,   ¹⁹
With clouds low-trailing and moments of rain that misted.
The young folk held some hope out to each other
Till well toward noon, when the storm settled down
With a swish in the grass. "What if the others
Are there," they said. "It isn't going to rain."
Only one from a farm not far away   ²⁵
Strolled thither, not expecting he would find
Anyone else, but out of idleness.
One, and one other, yes, for there were two.
The second round the curving hillside road
Was a girl; and she halted some way off   ³⁰
To reconnoiter, and then made up her mind
At least to pass by and see who he was,
And perhaps hear some word about the weather.
This was some Stark she didn't know. He nodded.
"No fête today," he said.

                            "It looks that way."   ³⁵
She swept the heavens, turning on her heel.
"I only idled down."

                    "I idled down."

Provision there had been for just such meeting
Of stranger-cousins, in a family tree
Drawn on a sort of passport with the branch   ⁴⁰
Of the one bearing it done in detail—
Some zealous one's laborious device.
She made a sudden movement toward her bodice,
As one who clasps her heart. They laughed together.

"Stark?" he inquired. "No matter for the proof."   ⁴⁵

"Yes, Stark. And you?"

                    "I'm Stark." He drew his passport.

"You know we might not be and still be cousins:
The town is full of Chases, Lowes, and Baileys,
All claiming some priority in Starkness.
My mother was a Lane, yet might have married   50
Anyone upon earth and still her children
Would have been Starks, and doubtless here today."

"You riddle with your genealogy,
Like a Viola. I don't follow you."

"I only mean my mother was a Stark   55
Several times over, and by marrying father
No more than brought us back into the name."

"One ought not to be thrown into confusion
By a plain statement of relationship,
But I own what you say makes my head spin.   60
You take my card—you seem so good at such things—
And see if you can reckon our cousinship.
Why not take seats here on the cellar wall
And dangle feet among the raspberry vines?"

"Under the shelter of the family tree."   65

"Just so—that ought to be enough protection."

"Not from the rain. I think it's going to rain."

"It's raining."

              "No, it's misting; let's be fair.
Does the rain seem to you to cool the eyes?"

The situation was like this: the road   70
Bowed outward on the mountain halfway up,
And disappeared and ended not far off.

                        75

No one went home that way. The only house
Beyond where they were was a shattered seedpod.
And below roared a brook hidden in trees,   75
The sound of which was silence for the place.
This he sat listening to till she gave judgment.

"On father's side, it seems, we're—let me see——"

"Don't be too technical.—You have three cards."

"Four cards: one yours, three mine (one for each branch
Of the Stark family I'm a member of)."   81

"D'you know a person so related to herself
Is supposed to be mad."

                    "I may be mad."

"You look so, sitting out here in the rain
Studying genealogy with me   85
You never saw before. What will we come to
With all this pride of ancestry, we Yankees?
I think we're all mad. Tell me why we're here,
Drawn into town about this cellar hole
Like wild geese on a lake before a storm?   90
What do we see in such a hole, I wonder."

"The Indians had a myth of Chicamoztoc,
Which means The-Seven-Caves-that-We-Came-Out-of.
This is the pit from which we Starks were digged."

"You must be learned. That's what you see in it?"   95

"And what do you see?"

                    "Yes, what *do* I see?
First let me look. I see raspberry vines——"

"Oh, if you're going to use your eyes, just hear

What *I* see. It's a little, little boy,
As pale and dim as a match flame in the sun;   100
He's groping in the cellar after jam—
He thinks it's dark, and it's flooded with daylight."

"He's nothing. Listen. When I lean like this
I can make out old Grandsir Stark distinctly—
With his pipe in his mouth and his brown jug—   105
Bless you, it isn't Grandsir Stark, it's Granny;
But the pipe's there and smoking, and the jug.
She's after cider, the old girl, she's thirsty;
Here's hoping she gets her drink and gets out safely."

"Tell me about her. Does she look like me?"   110

"She should, shouldn't she?—you're so many times
Over descended from her. I believe
She does look like you. Stay the way you are.
The nose is just the same, and so's the chin—
Making allowance, making due allowance."   115

"You poor, dear, great, great, great, great Granny!"

"See that you get her greatness right. Don't stint her."

"Yes, it's important, though you think it isn't.
I won't be teased. But see how wet I am."

"Yes, you must go; we can't stay here forever.   120
But wait until I give you a hand up.
A bead of silver water more or less,
Strung on your hair, won't hurt your summer looks.
I wanted to try something with the noise
That the brook raises in the empty valley.   125
We have seen visions—now consult the voices.
Something I must have learned riding in trains

77

When I was young. I used to use the roar
To set the voices speaking out of it,
Speaking or singing, and the band-music playing. 130
Perhaps you have the art of what I mean.
I've never listened in among the sounds
That a brook makes in such a wild descent.
It ought to give a purer oracle."

"It's as you throw a picture on a screen: 135
The meaning of it all is out of you;
The voices give you what you wish to hear."

"Strangely, it's anything they wish to give."

"Then I don't know. It must be strange enough.
I wonder if it's not your make-believe. 140
What do you think you're like to hear today?"

"From the sense of our having been together—
But why take time for what I'm like to hear?
I'll tell you what the voices really say.
You will do very well right where you are 145
A little longer. I mustn't feel too hurried,
Or I can't give myself to hear the voices."

"Is this some trance you are withdrawing into?"

"You must be very still; you mustn't talk."

"I'll hardly breathe."

     "The voices seem to say——" 150

"I'm waiting."

    "Don't! The voices seem to say:
Call her Nausicaä, the unafraid
Of an acquaintance made adventurously."

78

"I let you say that—on consideration."

"I don't see very well how you can help it.   155
You want the truth. I speak but by the voices.
You see they know I haven't had your name,
Though what a name should matter between us——"

"I shall suspect——"

                    "Be good. The voices say:
Call her Nausicaä, and take a timber   160
That you shall find lies in the cellar, charred
Among the raspberries, and hew and shape it
For a doorsill or other corner piece
In a new cottage on the ancient spot.
The life is not yet all gone out of it.   165
And come and make your summer dwelling here,
And perhaps she will come, still unafraid,
And sit before you in the open door
With flowers in her lap until they fade,
But not come in across the sacred sill——"   170

"I wonder where your oracle is tending.
You can see that there's something wrong with it,
Or it would speak in dialect. Whose voice
Does it purport to speak in? Not old Grandsir's
Nor Granny's, surely. Call up one of them.   175
They have best right to be heard in this place."

"You seem so partial to our great-grandmother
(Nine times removed. Correct me if I err.)
You will be likely to regard as sacred
Anything she may say. But let me warn you,   180
Folks in her day were given to plain speaking.
You think you'd best tempt her at such a time?"

"It rests with us always to cut her off."

"Well then, it's Granny speaking: 'I dunnow!
Mebbe I'm wrong to take it as I do.   185
There ain't no names quite like the old ones, though,
Nor never will be to my way of thinking.
One mustn't bear too hard on the newcomers,
But there's a dite too many of them for comfort.
I should feel easier if I could see   190
More of the salt wherewith they're to be salted.
Son, you do as you're told! You take the timber—
It's as sound as the day when it was cut—
And begin over——' There, she'd better stop.
You can see what is troubling Granny, though.   195
But don't you think we sometimes make too much
Of the old stock? What counts is the ideals,
And those will bear some keeping still about."

"I can see we are going to be good friends."

"I like your 'going to be.' You said just now   200
It's going to rain."

                    "I know, and it was raining.
I let you say all that. But I must go now."

"You let me say it? on consideration?
How shall we say good-by in such a case?"

"How shall we?"

                    "Will you leave the way to me?"   205

"No, I don't trust your eyes. You've said enough.
Now give me your hand up.—Pick me that flower."

"Where shall we meet again?"

80

"Nowhere but here
Once more before we meet elsewhere."

"In rain?"

"It ought to be in rain. Sometime in rain.   210
In rain tomorrow, shall we, if it rains?
But if we must, in sunshine." So she went.

THE HOUSEKEEPER

I let myself in at the kitchen door.

"It's you," she said. "I can't get up. Forgive me
Not answering your knock. I can no more
Let people in than I can keep them out.
I'm getting too old for my size, I tell them.   5
My fingers are about all I've the use of
So's to take any comfort. I can sew:
I help out with this beadwork what I can."

"That's a smart pair of pumps you're beading there.
Who are they for?"

"You mean?—oh, for some miss.   10
I can't keep track of other people's daughters.
Lord, if I were to dream of everyone
Whose shoes I primped to dance in!"

"And where's John?"

"Haven't you seen him? Strange what set you off
To come to his house when he's gone to yours.   15
You can't have passed each other. I know what:
He must have changed his mind and gone to Garland's.
He won't be long in that case. You can wait.
Though what good you can be, or anyone—

It's gone so far. You've heard? Estelle's run off."

"Yes, what's it all about? When did she go?"

"Two weeks since."

                "She's in earnest, it appears."

"I'm sure she won't come back. She's hiding somewhere.
I don't know where myself. John thinks I do.
He thinks I only have to say the word,
And she'll come back. But, bless you, I'm her mother—
I can't talk to her, and, Lord, if I could!"

"It will go hard with John. What will he do?
He can't find anyone to take her place."

"Oh, if you ask me that, what *will* he do?
He gets some sort of bakeshop meals together,
With me to sit and tell him everything,
What's wanted and how much and where it is.
But when I'm gone—of course I can't stay here:
Estelle's to take me when she's settled down.
He and I only hinder one another.
I tell them they can't get me through the door, though:
I've been built in here like a big church organ.
We've been here fifteen years."

                        "That's a long time
To live together and then pull apart.
How do you see him living when you're gone?
Two of you out will leave an empty house."

"I don't just see him living many years,
Left here with nothing but the furniture.
I hate to think of the old place when we're gone,
With the brook going by below the yard,

20

25

30

35

40

45

82

And no one here but hens blowing about.
If he could sell the place, but then, he can't:
No one will ever live on it again.
It's too run down. This is the last of it.   50
What I think he will do, is let things smash.
He'll sort of swear the time away. He's awful!
I never saw a man let family troubles
Make so much difference in his man's affairs.
He's just dropped everything. He's like a child.   55
I blame his being brought up by his mother.
He's got hay down that's been rained on three times.
He hoed a little yesterday for me:
I thought the growing things would do him good.
Something went wrong. I saw him throw the hoe   60
Sky-high with both hands. I can see it now—
Come here—I'll show you—in that apple tree.
That's no way for a man to do at his age:
He's fifty-five, you know, if he's a day."

"Aren't you afraid of him? What's that gun for?"   65

"Oh, that's been there for hawks since chicken-time.
John Hall touch me! Not if he knows his friends.
I'll say that for him, John's no threatener
Like some menfolk. No one's afraid of him;
All is, he's made up his mind not to stand   70
What he has got to stand."
                              "Where is Estelle?
Couldn't one talk to her? What does she say?
You say you don't know where she is."
                                        "Nor want to!
She thinks if it was bad to live with him,
It must be right to leave him."

"Yes, but he should have married her."

                              "I know."

"The strain's been too much for her all these years:
I can't explain it any other way.
It's different with a man, at least with John:
He knows he's kinder than the run of men.   80
Better than married ought to be as good
As married—that's what he has always said.
I know the way he's felt—but all the same!"

"I wonder why he doesn't marry her
And end it."

                  "Too late now: she wouldn't have him.   85
He's given her time to think of something else.
That's his mistake. The dear knows my interest
Has been to keep the thing from breaking up.
This is a good home: I don't ask for better.
But when I've said, Why shouldn't they be married?   90
He'd say, Why should they?—no more words than that."

"And after all why should they? John's been fair
I take it. What was his was always hers.
There was no quarrel about property."

"Reason enough, there was no property.   95
A friend or two as good as own the farm,
Such as it is. It isn't worth the mortgage."

"I mean Estelle has always held the purse."

"The rights of that are harder to get at.
I guess Estelle and I have filled the purse.   100
'Twas we let him have money, not he us.

John's a bad farmer. I'm not blaming him.
Take it year in, year out, he doesn't make much.
We came here for a home for me, you know,
Estelle to do the housework for the board   105
Of both of us. But look how it turns out:
She seems to have the housework, and besides,
Half of the outdoor work, though as for that,
He'd say she does it more because she likes it.
You see our pretty things are all outdoors.   110
Our hens and cows and pigs are always better
Than folks like us have any business with.
Farmers around twice as well off as we
Haven't as good. They don't go with the farm.
One thing you can't help liking about John,   115
He's fond of nice things—too fond, some would say.
But Estelle don't complain: she's like him there.
She wants our hens to be the best there are.
You never saw this room before a show,
Full of lank, shivery, half-drowned birds   120
In separate coops, having their plumage done.
The smell of the wet feathers in the heat!
You spoke of John's not being safe to stay with.
You don't know what a gentle lot we are:
We wouldn't hurt a hen! You ought to see us   125
Moving a flock of hens from place to place.
We're not allowed to take them upside down,
All we can hold together by the legs.
Two at a time's the rule, one on each arm,
No matter how far and how many times   130
We have to go."

           "You mean that's John's idea."

"And we live up to it; or I don't know

What childishness he wouldn't give way to.
He manages to keep the upper hand
On his own farm. He's boss. But as to hens: 135
We fence our flowers in and the hens range.
Nothing's too good for them. We say it pays.
John likes to tell the offers he has had,
Twenty for this cock, twenty-five for that.
He never takes the money. If they're worth   140
That much to sell, they're worth as much to keep.
Bless you, it's all expense, though. Reach me down
The little tin box on the cupboard shelf—
The upper shelf, the tin box. That's the one.
I'll show you. Here you are."

                "What's this?"

                        "A bill—   145
For fifty dollars for one Langshang cock—
Receipted. And the cock is in the yard."

"Not in a glass case, then?"

                   "He'd need a tall one:
He can eat off a barrel from the ground.
He's been in a glass case, as you may say,   150
The Crystal Palace, London. He's imported.
John bought him, and we paid the bill with beads—
Wampum, I call it. Mind, we don't complain.
But you see, don't you, we take care of him."

"And like it, too. It makes it all the worse."   155

"It seems as if. And that's not all: he's helpless
In ways that I can hardly tell you of.
Sometimes he gets possessed to keep accounts
To see where all the money goes so fast.

You know how men will be ridiculous.   160
But it's just fun the way he gets bedeviled—
If he's untidy now, what will he be——?"

"It makes it all the worse. You must be blind."

"Estelle's the one. You needn't talk to me."

"Can't you and I get to the root of it?   165
What's the real trouble? What will satisfy her?"

"It's as I say: she's turned from him, that's all."

"But why, when she's well off? Is it the neighbors,
Being cut off from friends?"
                          "We have our friends.
That isn't it. Folks aren't afraid of us."   170

"She's let it worry her. You stood the strain,
And you're her mother."
                          "But I didn't always.
I didn't relish it along at first.
But I got wonted to it. And besides—
John said I was too old to have grandchildren.   175
But what's the use of talking when it's done?
She won't come back—it's worse than that—she can't."

"Why do you speak like that? What do you know?
What do you mean?—she's done harm to herself?"

"I mean she's married—married someone else."   180

"Oho, oho!"
          "You don't believe me."
                          "Yes, I do,
Only too well. I knew there must be something!

87

So that was what was back. She's bad, that's all!"

"Bad to get married when she had the chance?" 184

"Nonsense! See what she's done! But who, but who———?"

"Who'd marry her straight out of such a mess?
Say it right out—no matter for her mother.
The man was found. I'd better name no names.
John himself won't imagine who he is."

"Then it's all up. I think I'll get away. 190
You'll be expecting John. I pity Estelle;
I suppose she deserves some pity, too.
You ought to have the kitchen to yourself
To break it to him. You may have the job."

"You needn't think you're going to get away. 195
John's almost here. I've had my eye on someone
Coming down Ryan's Hill. I thought 'twas him.
Here he is now. This box! Put it away.
And this bill."

    "What's the hurry? He'll unhitch."

"No, he won't, either. He'll just drop the reins 200
And turn Doll out to pasture, rig and all.
She won't get far before the wheels hang up
On something—there's no harm. See, there he is!
My, but he looks as if he must have heard!"

John threw the door wide but he didn't enter. 205
"How are you, neighbor? Just the man I'm after.
Isn't it Hell?" he said. "I want to know.
Come out here if you want to hear me talk.—
I'll talk to you, old woman, afterward.—
I've got some news that maybe isn't news. 210

88

What are they trying to do to me, these two?"

"Do go along with him and stop his shouting."
She raised her voice against the closing door:
"Who wants to hear your news, you—dreadful fool?"

THE FEAR

A lantern-light from deeper in the barn
Shone on a man and woman in the door
And threw their lurching shadows on a house
Nearby, all dark in every glossy window.
A horse's hoof pawed once the hollow floor,   5
And the back of the gig they stood beside
Moved in a little. The man grasped a wheel.
The woman spoke out sharply, "Whoa, stand still!—
I saw it just as plain as a white plate,"
She said, "as the light on the dashboard ran   10
Along the bushes at the roadside—a man's face.
You *must* have seen it too."

                    "I didn't see it.
Are you sure——"

                 "Yes, I'm sure!"

                         "—it was a face?"

"Joel, I'll have to look. I can't go in,
I can't, and leave a thing like that unsettled.   15
Doors locked and curtains drawn will make no difference.
I always have felt strange when we came home
To the dark house after so long an absence,
And the key rattled loudly into place
Seemed to warn someone to be getting out   20
At one door as we entered at another."

What if I'm right, and someone all the time——
Don't hold my arm!"

            "I say it's someone passing."

"You speak as if this were a traveled road.
You forget where we are. What is beyond   25
That he'd be going to or coming from
At such an hour of night, and on foot too?
What was he standing still for in the bushes?"

"It's not so very late—it's only dark.
There's more in it than you're inclined to say.   30
Did he look like——?"

            "He looked like anyone.
I'll never rest tonight unless I know.
Give me the lantern."

            "You don't want the lantern."

She pushed past him and got it for herself.

"You're not to come," she said. "This is my business. 35
If the time's come to face it, I'm the one
To put it the right way. He'd never dare——
Listen! He kicked a stone. Hear that, hear that!
He's coming towards us. Joel, *go in*—please.
Hark!—I don't hear him now. But please go in."   40

"In the first place you can't make me believe it's——"

"It is—or someone else he's sent to watch.
And now's the time to have it out with him
While we know definitely where he is.
Let him get off and he'll be everywhere   45
Around us, looking out of trees and bushes
Till I shan't dare to set a foot outdoors.

And I can't stand it. Joel, let me go!"

"But it's nonsense to think he'd care enough."

"You mean you couldn't understand his caring.   50
Oh, but you see he hadn't had enough—
Joel, I won't—I won't—I promise you.
We mustn't say hard things. You mustn't either."

"I'll be the one, if anybody goes!
But you give him the advantage with this light.   55
What couldn't he do to us standing here!
And if to see was what he wanted, why,
He has seen all there was to see and gone."

He appeared to forget to keep his hold,
But advanced with her as she crossed the grass.   60

"What do you want?" she cried to all the dark.
She stretched up tall to overlook the light
That hung in both hands, hot against her skirt.

"There's no one; so you're wrong," he said.

                                        "There is.—
What do you want?" she cried, and then herself   65
Was startled when an answer really came.

"Nothing." It came from well along the road.

She reached a hand to Joel for support:
The smell of scorching woolen made her faint.
"What are you doing round this house at night?"   70

"Nothing." A pause: there seemed no more to say.

And then the voice again: "You seem afraid.
I saw by the way you whipped up the horse.
I'll just come forward in the lantern-light

91

And let you see."

"Yes, do.—Joel, go back!" 75

She stood her ground against the noisy steps
That came on, but her body rocked a little.

"You see," the voice said.

"Oh." She looked and looked.

"You don't see—I've a child here by the hand.
A robber wouldn't have his family with him." 80

"What's a child doing at this time of night——?"

"Out walking. Every child should have the memory
Of at least one long-after-bedtime walk.
What, son?"

"Then I should think you'd try to find 84
Somewhere to walk——"

"The highway, as it happens—
We're stopping for the fortnight down at Dean's."

"But if that's all—Joel—you realize—
You won't think anything. You understand?
You understand that we have to be careful.
This is a very, very lonely place.— 90
Joel!" She spoke as if she couldn't turn.
The swinging lantern lengthened to the ground,
It touched, it struck, it clattered and went out.

THE SELF-SEEKER

"Willis, I didn't want you here today:
The lawyer's coming for the company.
I'm going to sell my soul, or rather, feet.

92

Five hundred dollars for the pair, you know."

"With you the feet have nearly been the soul;   5
And if you're going to sell them to the devil,
I want to see you do it. When's he coming?"

"I half suspect you knew, and came on purpose
To try to help me drive a better bargain."

"Well, if it's true! Yours are no common feet.   10
The lawyer don't know what it is he's buying:
So many miles you might have walked you won't walk.
You haven't run your forty orchids down.
What does he think?—How *are* the blessèd feet?
The doctor's sure you're going to walk again?"   15

"He thinks I'll hobble. It's both legs and feet."

"They must be terrible—I mean, to look at."

"I haven't dared to look at them uncovered.
Through the bed blankets I remind myself
Of a starfish laid out with rigid points."   20

"The wonder is it hadn't been your head."

"It's hard to tell you how I managed it.
When I saw the shaft had me by the coat,
I didn't try too long to pull away,
Or fumble for my knife to cut away,   25
I just embraced the shaft and rode it out—
Till Weiss shut off the water in the wheel pit.
That's how I think I didn't lose my head.
But my legs got their knocks against the ceiling."

"Awful. Why didn't they throw off the belt   30
Instead of going clear down in the wheel pit?"

"They say some time was wasted on the belt—
Old streak of leather—doesn't love me much
Because I make him spit fire at my knuckles,
The way Ben Franklin used to make the kite string.   35
That must be it. Some days he won't stay on.
That day a woman couldn't coax him off.
He's on his rounds now with his tail in his mouth,
Snatched right and left across the silver pulleys.
Everything goes the same without me there.   40
You can hear the small buzz saws whine, the big saw
Caterwaul to the hills around the village
As they both bite the wood. It's all our music.
One ought as a good villager to like it.
No doubt it has a sort of prosperous sound,   45
And it's our life."

                    "Yes, when it's not our death."

"You make that sound as if it wasn't so
With everything. What we live by we die by.—
I wonder where my lawyer is. His train's in.
I want this over with; I'm hot and tired."   50

"You're getting ready to do something foolish."

"Watch for him, will you, Will? You let him in.
I'd rather Mrs. Corbin didn't know;
I've boarded here so long, she thinks she owns me.
You're bad enough to manage, without her."   55

"I'm going to be worse instead of better.
You've got to tell me how far this is gone:
Have you agreed to any price?"

                    "Five hundred.
Five hundred—five—five! One, two, three, four, five.

You needn't look at me."

                      "I don't believe you."   60

"I told you, Willis, when you first came in.
Don't you be hard on me. I have to take
What I can get. You see they have the feet,
Which gives them the advantage in the trade.
I can't get back the feet in any case."   65

"But your flowers, man, you're selling out your flowers."

"Yes, that's one way to put it—all the flowers
Of every kind everywhere in this region
For the next forty summers—call it forty.
But I'm not selling those, I'm giving them;   70
They never earned me so much as one cent:
Money can't pay me for the loss of them.
No, the five hundred was the sum they named
To pay the doctor's bill and tide me over.
It's that or fight, and I don't want to fight—   75
I just want to get settled in my life,
Such as it's going to be, and know the worst,
Or best—it may not be so bad. The firm
Promise me all the shooks I want to nail."

"But what about your flora of the valley?"   80

"You have me there. But that—you didn't think
That was worth money to me? Still I own
It goes against me not to finish it
For the friends it might bring me. By the way,
I had a letter from Burroughs—did I tell you?—   85
About my *Cypripedium reginæ*;
He says it's not reported so far north.—
There! there's the bell. He's rung. But you go down

And bring him up, and don't let Mrs. Corbin.—
Oh, well, we'll soon be through with it. I'm tired."   90

Willis brought up besides the Boston lawyer
A little barefoot girl, who in the noise
Of heavy footsteps in the old frame house,
And baritone importance of the lawyer,
Stood for a while unnoticed, with her hands   95
Shyly behind her.

        "Well, and how is Mister . . . ?"
The lawyer was already in his satchel
As if for papers that might bear the name
He hadn't at command. "You must excuse me,
I dropped in at the mill and was detained."   100

"Looking round, I suppose," said Willis.

            "Yes,
Well, yes."

      "Hear anything that might prove useful?"

The Broken One saw Anne. "Why, here is Anne.
What do you want, dear? Come, stand by the bed;
Tell me what is it?"

        Anne just wagged her dress,   105
With both hands held behind her. "Guess," she said.

"Oh, guess which hand? My, my! Once on a time
I knew a lovely way to tell for certain
By looking in the ears. But I forget it.
Er, let me see. I think I'll take the right.   110
That's sure to be right, even if it's wrong.
Come, hold it out. Don't change.—A Ram's Horn orchid!
A Ram's Horn! What would I have got, I wonder,

If I had chosen left. Hold out the left.
Another Ram's Horn! Where did you find those,   115
Under what beech tree, on what woodchuck's knoll?"

Anne looked at the large lawyer at her side,
And thought she wouldn't venture on so much.

"Were there no others?"

                      "There were four or five.
I knew you wouldn't let me pick them all."   120

"I wouldn't—so I wouldn't. You're the girl!
You see Anne has her lesson learned by heart."

"I wanted there should be some there next year."

"Of course you did. You left the rest for seed,
And for the backwoods woodchuck. You're the girl!   125
A Ram's Horn orchid seedpod for a woodchuck
Sounds something like. Better than farmer's beans
To a discriminating appetite,
Though the Ram's Horn is seldom to be had
In bushel lots—doesn't come on the market.   130
But, Anne, I'm troubled; have you told me all?
You're hiding something. That's as bad as lying.
You ask this lawyer man. And it's not safe
With a lawyer at hand to find you out.
Nothing is hidden from some people, Anne.   135
You don't tell me that where you found a Ram's Horn
You didn't find a Yellow Lady's Slipper.
What did I tell you? What? I'd blush, I would.
Don't you defend yourself. If it was there,
Where is it now, the Yellow Lady's Slipper?"   140

"Well, wait—it's common—it's too *common*."

                                    "Common?

The Purple Lady's Slipper's commoner."

"I didn't bring a Purple Lady's Slipper.
To *You*—to you I mean—they're both too common."

The lawyer gave a laugh among his papers   145
As if with some idea that she had scored.

"I've broken Anne of gathering bouquets.
It's not fair to the child. It can't be helped, though:
Pressed into service means pressed out of shape.
Somehow I'll make it right with her—she'll see.   150
She's going to do my scouting in the field,
Over stone walls and all along a wood
And by a river bank for water flowers,
The Floating Heart, with small leaf like a heart,
And at the sinus under water a fist   155
Of little fingers all kept down but one,
And that thrust up to blossom in the sun
As if to say, 'You! You're the Heart's desire.'
Anne has a way with flowers to take the place
Of what she's lost: she goes down on one knee   160
And lifts their faces by the chin to hers
And says their names, and leaves them where they are."

The lawyer wore a watch the case of which
Was cunningly devised to make a noise
Like a small pistol when he snapped it shut   165
At such a time as this. He snapped it now.

"Well, Anne, go, dearie. Our affair will wait.
The lawyer man is thinking of his train.
He wants to give me lots and lots of money
Before he goes, because I hurt myself,   170
And it may take him I don't know how long.

98

But put our flowers in water first.—Will, help her:
The pitcher's too full for her.—There's no cup?
Just hook them on the inside of the pitcher.
Now run.—Get out your documents! You see   175
I have to keep on the good side of Anne.
I'm a great boy to think of number one.
And you can't blame me in the place I'm in.
Who will take care of my necessities
Unless I do?"

              "A pretty interlude,"   180
The lawyer said. "I'm sorry, but my train—
Luckily terms are all agreed upon.
You only have to sign your name. Right—there."

"You, Will, stop making faces. Come round here
Where you can't make them. What is it you want?   185
I'll put you out with Anne. Be good or go."

"You don't mean you will sign that thing unread?"

"Make yourself useful, then, and read it for me.—
Isn't it something I have seen before?"

"You'll find it is. Let your friend look at it."   190

"Yes, but all that takes time, and I'm as much
In haste to get it over with as you.—
But read it, read it.—That's right, draw the curtain:
Half the time I don't know what's troubling me.—
What do you say, Will? Don't you be a fool,   195
You, crumpling folks's legal documents.
Out with it if you've any real objection."

"Five hundred dollars!"

              "What would you think right?"

"A thousand wouldn't be a cent too much;
You know it, Mr. Lawyer. The sin is   200
Accepting anything before he knows
Whether he's ever going to walk again.
It smells to me like a dishonest trick."

"I think—I think—from what I heard today—
And saw myself—he would be ill-advised——"   205

"What did you hear, for instance?" Willis said.

"Now, the place where the accident occurred——"

The Broken One was twisted in his bed.
"This is between you two apparently.
Where I come in is what I want to know.   210
You stand up to it like a pair of cocks.
Go outdoors if you want to fight. Spare me.
When you come back, I'll have the papers signed.
Will pencil do? Then, please, your fountain pen.
One of you hold my head up from the pillow."   215

Willis flung off the bed. "I wash my hands—
I'm no match—no, and don't pretend to be——"

The lawyer gravely capped his fountain pen.
"You're doing the wise thing: you won't regret it.
We're very sorry for you."
                               Willis sneered: 220
"Who's *we*?—some stockholders in Boston?
I'll go outdoors, by gad, and won't come back."

"Willis, bring Anne back with you when you come.
Yes. Thanks for caring.—Don't mind Will: he's savage.
He thinks you ought to pay me for my flowers.   225
You don't know what I mean about the flowers.

Don't stop to try to now. You'll miss your train.
Good-by." He flung his arms around his face.

THE WOOD-PILE

Out walking in the frozen swamp one gray day,
I paused and said, "I will turn back from here.
No, I will go on farther—and we shall see."
The hard snow held me, save where now and then
One foot went through. The view was all in lines   5
Straight up and down of tall slim trees
Too much alike to mark or name a place by
So as to say for certain I was here
Or somewhere else: I was just far from home.
A small bird flew before me. He was careful   10
To put a tree between us when he lighted,
And say no word to tell me who he was
Who was so foolish as to think what *he* thought.
He thought that I was after him for a feather—
The white one in his tail; like one who takes   15
Everything said as personal to himself.
One flight out sideways would have undeceived him.
And then there was a pile of wood for which
I forgot him and let his little fear
Carry him off the way I might have gone,   20
Without so much as wishing him good-night.
He went behind it to make his last stand.
It was a cord of maple, cut and split
And piled—and measured, four by four by eight.
And not another like it could I see.   25
No runner tracks in this year's snow looped near it.
And it was older sure than this year's cutting,
Or even last year's or the year's before.

The wood was gray and the bark warping off it
And the pile somewhat sunken. Clematis   30
Had wound strings round and round it like a bundle.
What held it, though, on one side was a tree
Still growing, and on one a stake and prop,
These latter about to fall. I thought that only
Someone who lived in turning to fresh tasks   35
Could so forget his handiwork on which
He spent himself, the labor of his ax,
And leave it there far from a useful fireplace
To warm the frozen swamp as best it could
With the slow smokeless burning of decay.   40

GOOD HOURS

I had for my winter evening walk—
No one at all with whom to talk,
But I had the cottages in a row
Up to their shining eyes in snow.

And I thought I had the folk within: 5
I had the sound of a violin;
I had a glimpse through curtain laces
Of youthful forms and youthful faces.

I had such company outward bound.
I went till there were no cottages found.   10
I turned and repented, but coming back
I saw no window but that was black.

Over the snow my creaking feet
Disturbed the slumbering village street
Like profanation, by your leave,   15
At ten o'clock of a winter eve.

Mountain Interval

: 1916 :

THE ROAD NOT TAKEN

Two roads diverged in a yellow wood,
And sorry I could not travel both
And be one traveler, long I stood
And looked down one as far as I could
To where it bent in the undergrowth;   5

Then took the other, as just as fair,
And having perhaps the better claim,
Because it was grassy and wanted wear;
Though as for that, the passing there
Had worn them really about the same,   10

And both that morning equally lay
In leaves no step had trodden black.
Oh, I kept the first for another day!
Yet knowing how way leads on to way,
I doubted if I should ever come back.   15

I shall be telling this with a sigh
Somewhere ages and ages hence:
Two roads diverged in a wood, and I—
I took the one less traveled by,
And that has made all the difference.   20

CHRISTMAS TREES

A Christmas circular letter

The city had withdrawn into itself
And left at last the country to the country;

When between whirls of snow not come to lie
And whirls of foliage not yet laid, there drove
A stranger to our yard, who looked the city,   5
Yet did in country fashion in that there
He sat and waited till he drew us out,
A-buttoning coats, to ask him who he was.
He proved to be the city come again
To look for something it had left behind   10
And could not do without and keep its Christmas.
He asked if I would sell my Christmas trees;
My woods—the young fir balsams like a place
Where houses all are churches and have spires.
I hadn't thought of them as Christmas trees.   15
I doubt if I was tempted for a moment
To sell them off their feet to go in cars
And leave the slope behind the house all bare,
Where the sun shines now no warmer than the moon.
I'd hate to have them know it if I was.   20
Yet more I'd hate to hold my trees, except
As others hold theirs or refuse for them,
Beyond the time of profitable growth—
The trial by market everything must come to.
I dallied so much with the thought of selling.   25
Then whether from mistaken courtesy
And fear of seeming short of speech, or whether
From hope of hearing good of what was mine,
I said, "There aren't enough to be worth while."

"I could soon tell how many they would cut,   30
You let me look them over."

                          "You could look.
But don't expect I'm going to let you have them."

Pasture they spring in, some in clumps too close
That lop each other of boughs, but not a few
Quite solitary and having equal boughs   35
All round and round. The latter he nodded "Yes" to,
Or paused to say beneath some lovelier one,
With a buyer's moderation, "That would do."
I thought so too, but wasn't there to say so.
We climbed the pasture on the south, crossed over,   40
And came down on the north.

                                He said, "A thousand."

"A thousand Christmas trees!—at what apiece?"

He felt some need of softening that to me:
"A thousand trees would come to thirty dollars."

Then I was certain I had never meant   45
To let him have them. Never show surprise!
But thirty dollars seemed so small beside
The extent of pasture I should strip, three cents
(For that was all they figured out apiece)—
Three cents so small beside the dollar friends   50
I should be writing to within the hour
Would pay in cities for good trees like those,
Regular vestry-trees whole Sunday Schools
Could hang enough on to pick off enough.

A thousand Christmas trees I didn't know I had!   55
Worth three cents more to give away than sell,
As may be shown by a simple calculation.
Too bad I couldn't lay one in a letter.
I can't help wishing I could send you one
In wishing you herewith a Merry Christmas.   60

AN OLD MAN'S WINTER NIGHT

All out-of-doors looked darkly in at him
Through the thin frost, almost in separate stars,
That gathers on the pane in empty rooms.
What kept his eyes from giving back the gaze
Was the lamp tilted near them in his hand. 5
What kept him from remembering what it was
That brought him to that creaking room was age.
He stood with barrels round him—at a loss.
And having scared the cellar under him
In clomping here, he scared it once again 10
In clomping off—and scared the outer night,
Which has its sounds, familiar, like the roar
Of trees and crack of branches, common things,
But nothing so like beating on a box.
A light he was to no one but himself 15
Where now he sat, concerned with he knew what,
A quiet light, and then not even that.
He consigned to the moon—such as she was,
So late-arising—to the broken moon,
As better than the sun in any case 20
For such a charge, his snow upon the roof,
His icicles along the wall to keep;
And slept. The log that shifted with a jolt
Once in the stove, disturbed him and he shifted,
And eased his heavy breathing, but still slept. 25
One aged man—one man—can't keep a house,
A farm, a countryside, or if he can,
It's thus he does it of a winter night.

THE EXPOSED NEST

You were forever finding some new play.
So when I saw you down on hands and knees
In the meadow, busy with the new-cut hay,
Trying, I thought, to set it up on end,
I went to show you how to make it stay,   5
If that was your idea, against the breeze,
And, if you asked me, even help pretend
To make it root again and grow afresh.
But 'twas no make-believe with you today,
Nor was the grass itself your real concern,   10
Though I found your hand full of wilted fern,
Steel-bright June-grass, and blackening heads of clover.
'Twas a nest full of young birds on the ground
The cutter bar had just gone champing over
(Miraculously without tasting flesh)   15
And left defenseless to the heat and light.
You wanted to restore them to their right
Of something interposed between their sight
And too much world at once—could means be found.
The way the nest-full every time we stirred   20
Stood up to us as to a mother-bird
Whose coming home has been too long deferred,
Made me ask would the mother-bird return
And care for them in such a change of scene,
And might our meddling make her more afraid.   25
That was a thing we could not wait to learn.
We saw the risk we took in doing good,
But dared not spare to do the best we could
Though harm should come of it; so built the screen
You had begun, and gave them back their shade.   30
All this to prove we cared. Why is there then

No more to tell? We turned to other things.
I haven't any memory—have you?—
Of ever coming to the place again
To see if the birds lived the first night through,   35
And so at last to learn to use their wings.

A PATCH OF OLD SNOW

There's a patch of old snow in a corner,
    That I should have guessed
Was a blow-away paper the rain
    Had brought to rest.

It is speckled with grime as if   5
    Small print overspread it,
The news of a day I've forgotten—
    If I ever read it.

IN THE HOME STRETCH

She stood against the kitchen sink, and looked
Over the sink out through a dusty window
At weeds the water from the sink made tall.
She wore her cape; her hat was in her hand.
Behind her was confusion in the room,   5
Of chairs turned upside down to sit like people
In other chairs, and something, come to look,
For every room a house has—parlor, bedroom,
And dining room—thrown pell-mell in the kitchen.
And now and then a smudged, infernal face   10
Looked in a door behind her and addressed
Her back. She always answered without turning.

"Where will I put this walnut bureau, lady?"

110

"Put it on top of something that's on top
Of something else," she laughed. "Oh, put it where   15
You can tonight, and go. It's almost dark;
You must be getting started back to town."

Another blackened face thrust in and looked
And smiled, and when she did not turn, spoke gently,
"What are you seeing out the window, *lady*?"   20

"Never was I beladied so before.
Would evidence of having been called lady
More than so many times make me a lady
In common law, I wonder."

                                    "But I ask,
What are you seeing out the window, lady?"   25

"What I'll be seeing more of in the years
To come as here I stand and go the round
Of many plates with towels many times."

"And what is that? You only put me off."

"Rank weeds that love the water from the dishpan   30
More than some women like the dishpan, Joe;
A little stretch of mowing field for you;
Not much of that until I come to woods
That end all. And it's scarce enough to call
A view."

                    "And yet you think you like it, dear?"   35

"That's what you're so concerned to know! You hope
I like it.—Bang goes something big away
Off there upstairs. The very tread of men
As great as those is shattering to the frame
Of such a little house. Once left alone,   40
You and I, dear, will go with softer steps

111

Up and down stairs and through the rooms, and none
But sudden winds that snatch them from our hands
Will ever slam the doors."
                              "I think you see
More than you like to own to out that window."   45

"No; for besides the things I tell you of,
I only see the years. They come and go
In alternation with the weeds, the field,
The wood."
              "What kind of years?"
                                        "Why, latter years—
Different from early years."
                              "I see them, too.   50
You didn't count them?"
                          "No, the further off
So ran together that I didn't try to.
It can scarce be that they would be in number
We'd care to know, for we are not young now.—
And bang goes something else away off there.   55
It sounds as if it were the men went down,
And every crash meant one less to return
To lighted city streets we, too, have known,
But now are giving up for country darkness."

"Come from that window where you see too much,   60
And take a livelier view of things from here.
They're going. Watch this husky swarming up
Over the wheel into the sky-high seat,
Lighting his pipe now, squinting down his nose
At the flame burning downward as he sucks it."   65

"See how it makes his nose-side bright, a proof

How dark it's getting. Can you tell what time
It is by that? Or by the moon? The new moon!
What shoulder did I see her over? Neither.
A wire she is of silver, as new as we   70
To everything. Her light won't last us long.
It's something, though, to know we're going to have her
Night after night and stronger every night
To see us through our first two weeks. But, Joe,
The stove! Before they go! Knock on the window;   75
Ask them to help you get it on its feet.
We stand here dreaming. Hurry! Call them back!"

"They're not gone yet."

        "We've got to have the stove,
Whatever else we want for. And a light.
Have we a piece of candle if the lamp   80
And oil are buried out of reach?"

              Again
The house was full of tramping, and the dark,
Door-filling men burst in and seized the stove.
A cannon-mouth-like hole was in the wall,
To which they set it true by eye; and then   85
Came up the jointed stovepipe in their hands,
So much too light and airy for their strength
It almost seemed to come ballooning up,
Slipping from clumsy clutches toward the ceiling.
"A fit!" said one, and banged a stovepipe shoulder.   90
"It's good luck when you move in to begin
With good luck with your stovepipe. Never mind,
It's not so bad in the country, settled down,
When people're getting on in life. You'll like it."

Joe said: "You big boys ought to find a farm,   95

113

And make good farmers, and leave other fellows
The city work to do. There's not enough
For everybody as it is in there."

"God!" one said wildly, and, when no one spoke:
"Say that to Jimmy here. He needs a farm."   100
But Jimmy only made his jaw recede
Fool-like, and rolled his eyes as if to say
He saw himself a farmer. Then there was a French boy
Who said with seriousness that made them laugh,
"Ma friend, you ain't know what it is you're ask."   105
He doffed his cap and held it with both hands
Across his chest to make as 'twere a bow:
"We're giving you our chances on de farm."
And then they all turned to with deafening boots
And put each other bodily out of the house.   110

"Good-by to them! We puzzle them. They think—
I don't know what they think we see in what
They leave us to: that pasture slope that seems
The back some farm presents us; and your woods
To northward from your window at the sink,   115
Waiting to steal a step on us whenever
We drop our eyes or turn to other things,
As in the game 'ten-step' the children play."

"Good boys they seemed, and let them love the city.
All they could say was 'God!' when you proposed   120
Their coming out and making useful farmers."

"Did they make something lonesome go through you?
It would take more than them to sicken you—
Us of our bargain. But they left us so
As to our fate, like fools past reasoning with.   125
They almost shook *me*."

114

                    "It's all so much
What we have always wanted, I confess
Its seeming bad for a moment makes it seem
Even worse still, and so on down, down, down.
It's nothing; it's their leaving us at dusk.   130
I never bore it well when people went.
The first night after guests have gone, the house
Seems haunted or exposed. I always take
A personal interest in the locking up
At bedtime; but the strangeness soon wears off."   135
He fetched a dingy lantern from behind
A door. "There's that we didn't lose! And these!"—
Some matches he unpocketed. "For food—
The meals we've had no one can take from us.
I wish that everything on earth were just   140
As certain as the meals we've had. I wish
The meals we haven't had were, anyway.
What have you you know where to lay your hands on?"

"The bread we bought in passing at the store.
There's butter somewhere, too."

                    "Let's rend the bread.   145
I'll light the fire for company for you;
You'll not have any other company
Till Ed begins to get out on a Sunday
To look us over and give us his idea
Of what wants pruning, shingling, breaking up.   150
He'll know what he would do if he were we,
And all at once. He'll plan for us and plan
To help us, but he'll take it out in planning.
Well, you can set the table with the loaf.
Let's see you find your loaf. I'll light the fire.   155
I like chairs occupying other chairs

Not offering a lady——"

                 "There again, Joe!
You're tired."

                 "I'm drunk-nonsensical tired out;
Don't mind a word I say. It's a day's work
To empty one house of all household goods   160
And fill another with 'em fifteen miles away,
Although you do no more than dump them down."

"Dumped down in paradise we are and happy."

"It's all so much what I have always wanted,
I can't believe it's what you wanted, too."   165

"Shouldn't you like to know?"

                 "I'd like to know
If it is what you wanted, then how much
You wanted it for me."

                 "A troubled conscience!
You don't want me to tell if *I* don't know."

"I don't want to find out what can't be known.   170
But who first said the word to come?"

                 "My dear,
It's who first thought the thought. You're searching, Joe,
For things that don't exist; I mean beginnings.
Ends and beginnings—there are no such things.
There are only middles."

               "What is this?"

                 "This life?   175
Our sitting here by lantern-light together
Amid the wreckage of a former home?
You won't deny the lantern isn't new.

116

The stove is not, and you are not to me,
Nor I to you."

                    "Perhaps you never were?"   180

"It would take me forever to recite
All that's not new in where we find ourselves.
New is a word for fools in towns who think
Style upon style in dress and thought at last
Must get somewhere. I've heard you say as much.   185
No, this is no beginning."

                    "Then an end?"

"End is a gloomy word."

                    "Is it too late
To drag you out for just a good-night call
On the old peach trees on the knoll, to grope
By starlight in the grass for a last peach   190
The neighbors may not have taken as their right
When the house wasn't lived in? I've been looking:
I doubt if they have left us many grapes.
Before we set ourselves to right the house,
The first thing in the morning, out we go   195
To go the round of apple, cherry, peach,
Pine, alder, pasture, mowing, well, and brook.
All of a farm it is."

                    "I know this much:
I'm going to put you in your bed, if first
I have to make you build it. Come, the light."   200

When there was no more lantern in the kitchen,
The fire got out through crannies in the stove
And danced in yellow wrigglers on the ceiling,
As much at home as if they'd always danced there.

THE TELEPHONE

"When I was just as far as I could walk
From here today,
There was an hour
All still
When leaning with my head against a flower   5
I heard you talk.
Don't say I didn't, for I heard you say—
You spoke from that flower on the windowsill—
Do you remember what it was you said?"

"First tell me what it was you thought you heard."   10

"Having found the flower and driven a bee away,
I leaned my head,
And holding by the stalk,
I listened and I thought I caught the word—
What was it? Did you call me by my name?   15
Or did you say—
Someone said 'Come'—I heard it as I bowed."

"I may have thought as much, but not aloud."

"Well, so I came."

MEETING AND PASSING

As I went down the hill along the wall
There was a gate I had leaned at for the view
And had just turned from when I first saw you
As you came up the hill. We met. But all
We did that day was mingle great and small   5
Footprints in summer dust as if we drew
The figure of our being less than two

But more than one as yet. Your parasol
Pointed the decimal off with one deep thrust.
And all the time we talked you seemed to see   10
Something down there to smile at in the dust.
(Oh, it was without prejudice to me!)
Afterward I went past what you had passed
Before we met, and you what I had passed.

HYLA BROOK

By June our brook's run out of song and speed.
Sought for much after that, it will be found
Either to have gone groping underground
(And taken with it all the Hyla breed
That shouted in the mist a month ago,   5
Like ghost of sleigh bells in a ghost of snow)—
Or flourished and come up in jewelweed,
Weak foliage that is blown upon and bent,
Even against the way its waters went.
Its bed is left a faded paper sheet   10
Of dead leaves stuck together by the heat—
A brook to none but who remember long.
This as it will be seen is other far
Than with brooks taken otherwhere in song.
We love the things we love for what they are.   15

THE OVEN BIRD

There is a singer everyone has heard,
Loud, a mid-summer and a mid-wood bird,
Who makes the solid tree trunks sound again.
He says that leaves are old and that for flowers

Mid-summer is to spring as one to ten.   5
He says the early petal-fall is past,
When pear and cherry bloom went down in showers
On sunny days a moment overcast;
And comes that other fall we name the fall.
He says the highway dust is over all.   10
The bird would cease and be as other birds
But that he knows in singing not to sing.
The question that he frames in all but words
Is what to make of a diminished thing.

BOND AND FREE

Love has earth to which she clings
With hills and circling arms about—
Wall within wall to shut fear out.
But Thought has need of no such things,
For Thought has a pair of dauntless wings.   5

On snow and sand and turf, I see
Where Love has left a printed trace
With straining in the world's embrace.
And such is Love and glad to be.
But Thought has shaken his ankles free.   10

Thought cleaves the interstellar gloom
And sits in Sirius' disc all night,
Till day makes him retrace his flight,
With smell of burning on every plume,
Back past the sun to an earthly room.   15

His gains in heaven are what they are.
Yet some say Love by being thrall
And simply staying possesses all

In several beauty that Thought fares far
To find fused in another star.   20

BIRCHES

When I see birches bend to left and right
Across the lines of straighter darker trees,
I like to think some boy's been swinging them.
But swinging doesn't bend them down to stay
As ice storms do. Often you must have seen them   5
Loaded with ice a sunny winter morning
After a rain. They click upon themselves
As the breeze rises, and turn many-colored
As the stir cracks and crazes their enamel.
Soon the sun's warmth makes them shed crystal shells   10
Shattering and avalanching on the snow crust—
Such heaps of broken glass to sweep away
You'd think the inner dome of heaven had fallen.
They are dragged to the withered bracken by the load,
And they seem not to break; though once they are bowed
So low for long, they never right themselves:
You may see their trunks arching in the woods
Years afterwards, trailing their leaves on the ground
Like girls on hands and knees that throw their hair
Before them over their heads to dry in the sun.   20
But I was going to say when Truth broke in
With all her matter of fact about the ice storm,
I should prefer to have some boy bend them
As he went out and in to fetch the cows—
Some boy too far from town to learn baseball,   25
Whose only play was what he found himself,
Summer or winter, and could play alone.

121

One by one he subdued his father's trees
By riding them down over and over again
Until he took the stiffness out of them,   30
And not one but hung limp, not one was left
For him to conquer. He learned all there was
To learn about not launching out too soon
And so not carrying the tree away
Clear to the ground. He always kept his poise   35
To the top branches, climbing carefully
With the same pains you use to fill a cup
Up to the brim, and even above the brim.
Then he flung outward, feet first, with a swish,
Kicking his way down through the air to the ground.   40
So was I once myself a swinger of birches.
And so I dream of going back to be.
It's when I'm weary of considerations,
And life is too much like a pathless wood
Where your face burns and tickles with the cobwebs   45
Broken across it, and one eye is weeping
From a twig's having lashed across it open.
I'd like to get away from earth awhile
And then come back to it and begin over.
May no fate willfully misunderstand me   50
And half grant what I wish and snatch me away
Not to return. Earth's the right place for love:
I don't know where it's likely to go better.
I'd like to go by climbing a birch tree,
And climb black branches up a snow-white trunk   55
Toward heaven, till the tree could bear no more,
But dipped its top and set me down again.
That would be good both going and coming back.
One could do worse than be a swinger of birches.

PEA BRUSH

I walked down alone Sunday after church
  To the place where John has been cutting trees,
To see for myself about the birch
  He said I could have to bush my peas.

The sun in the new-cut narrow gap   5
  Was hot enough for the first of May,
And stifling hot with the odor of sap
  From stumps still bleeding their life away.

The frogs that were peeping a thousand shrill
  Wherever the ground was low and wet,   10
The minute they heard my step went still
  To watch me and see what I came to get.

Birch boughs enough piled everywhere!—
  All fresh and sound from the recent ax.
Time someone came with cart and pair   15
  And got them off the wild flowers' backs.

They might be good for garden things
  To curl a little finger round,
The same as you seize cat's-cradle strings,
  And lift themselves up off the ground.   20

Small good to anything growing wild,
  They were crooking many a trillium
That had budded before the boughs were piled
  And since it was coming up had to come.

PUTTING IN THE SEED

You come to fetch me from my work tonight
When supper's on the table, and we'll see

If I can leave off burying the white
Soft petals fallen from the apple tree
(Soft petals, yes, but not so barren quite,   5
Mingled with these, smooth bean and wrinkled pea),
And go along with you ere you lose sight
Of what you came for and become like me,
Slave to a springtime passion for the earth.
How Love burns through the Putting in the Seed   10
On through the watching for that early birth
When, just as the soil tarnishes with weed,
The sturdy seedling with arched body comes
Shouldering its way and shedding the earth crumbs.

A TIME TO TALK

When a friend calls to me from the road
And slows his horse to a meaning walk,
I don't stand still and look around
On all the hills I haven't hoed,
And shout from where I am, "What is it?"   5
No, not as there is a time to talk.
I thrust my hoe in the mellow ground,
Blade-end up and five feet tall,
And plod: I go up to the stone wall
For a friendly visit.   10

THE COW IN APPLE TIME

Something inspires the only cow of late
To make no more of a wall than an open gate,
And think no more of wall-builders than fools.
Her face is flecked with pomace and she drools
A cider syrup. Having tasted fruit,   5

124

She scorns a pasture withering to the root.
She runs from tree to tree where lie and sweeten
The windfalls spiked with stubble and worm-eaten.
She leaves them bitten when she has to fly.
She bellows on a knoll against the sky.　　10
Her udder shrivels and the milk goes dry.

AN ENCOUNTER

Once on the kind of day called "weather breeder,"
When the heat slowly hazes and the sun
By its own power seems to be undone,
I was half boring through, half climbing through
A swamp of cedar. Choked with oil of cedar　　5
And scurf of plants, and weary and overheated,
And sorry I ever left the road I knew,
I paused and rested on a sort of hook
That had me by the coat as good as seated,
And since there was no other way to look,　　10
Looked up toward heaven, and there against the blue,
Stood over me a resurrected tree,
A tree that had been down and raised again—
A barkless specter. He had halted too,
As if for fear of treading upon me.　　15
I saw the strange position of his hands—
Up at his shoulders, dragging yellow strands
Of wire with something in it from men to men.
"You here?" I said. "Where aren't you nowadays?
And what's the news you carry—if you know?　　20
And tell me where you're off for—Montreal?
Me? I'm not off for anywhere at all.
Sometimes I wander out of beaten ways
Half looking for the orchid Calypso."

RANGE-FINDING

The battle rent a cobweb diamond-strung
And cut a flower beside a groundbird's nest
Before it stained a single human breast.
The stricken flower bent double and so hung.
And still the bird revisited her young. 5
A butterfly its fall had dispossessed,
A moment sought in air his flower of rest,
Then lightly stooped to it and fluttering clung.
On the bare upland pasture there had spread
O'ernight 'twixt mullein stalks a wheel of thread 10
And straining cables wet with silver dew.
A sudden passing bullet shook it dry.
The indwelling spider ran to greet the fly,
But finding nothing, sullenly withdrew.

THE HILL WIFE

I. LONELINESS

Her Word

One ought not to have to care
  So much as you and I
Care when the birds come round the house
  To seem to say good-by;

Or care so much when they come back 5
  With whatever it is they sing;
The truth being we are as much
  Too glad for the one thing

As we are too sad for the other here—
  With birds that fill their breasts 10

But with each other and themselves
And their built or driven nests.

II. HOUSE FEAR

Always—I tell you this they learned—
Always at night when they returned
To the lonely house from far away,
To lamps unlighted and fire gone gray,
They learned to rattle the lock and key   5
To give whatever might chance to be,
Warning and time to be off in flight:
And preferring the out- to the indoor night,
They learned to leave the house door wide
Until they had lit the lamp inside.   10

III. THE SMILE

Her Word

I didn't like the way he went away.
That smile! It never came of being gay.
Still he smiled—did you see him?—I was sure!
Perhaps because we gave him only bread
And the wretch knew from that that we were poor.   5
Perhaps because he let us give instead
Of seizing from us as he might have seized.
Perhaps he mocked at us for being wed,
Or being very young (and he was pleased
To have a vision of us old and dead).   10
I wonder how far down the road he's got.
He's watching from the woods as like as not.

IV. THE OFT-REPEATED DREAM

She had no saying dark enough
   For the dark pine that kept
Forever trying the window latch
   Of the room where they slept.

The tireless but ineffectual hands   5
   That with every futile pass
Made the great tree seem as a little bird
   Before the mystery of glass!

It never had been inside the room,
   And only one of the two   10
Was afraid in an oft-repeated dream
   Of what the tree might do.

V. THE IMPULSE

It was too lonely for her there,
   And too wild,
And since there were but two of them,
   And no child,

And work was little in the house,   5
   She was free,
And followed where he furrowed field,
   Or felled tree.

She rested on a log and tossed
   The fresh chips,   10
With a song only to herself
   On her lips.

And once she went to break a bough
    Of black alder.
She strayed so far she scarcely heard   15
    When he called her—

And didn't answer—didn't speak—
    Or return.
She stood, and then she ran and hid
    In the fern.   20

He never found her, though he looked
    Everywhere,
And he asked at her mother's house
    Was she there.

Sudden and swift and light as that   25
    The ties gave,
And he learned of finalities
    Besides the grave.

THE BONFIRE

"Oh, let's go up the hill and scare ourselves,
As reckless as the best of them tonight,
By setting fire to all the brush we piled
With pitchy hands to wait for rain or snow.
Oh, let's not wait for rain to make it safe.   5
The pile is ours: we dragged it bough on bough
Down dark converging paths between the pines.
Let's not care what we do with it tonight.
Divide it? No! But burn it as one pile
The way we piled it. And let's be the talk   10
Of people brought to windows by a light
Thrown from somewhere against their wallpaper.

Rouse them all, both the free and not so free
With saying what they'd like to do to us
For what they'd better wait till we have done.   15
Let's all but bring to life this old volcano,
If that is what the mountain ever was—
And scare ourselves. Let wild fire loose we will——"

"And scare you too?" the children said together.

"Why wouldn't it scare me to have a fire   20
Begin in smudge with ropy smoke, and know
That still, if I repent, I may recall it,
But in a moment not: a little spurt
Of burning fatness, and then nothing but
The fire itself can put it out, and that   25
By burning out, and before it burns out
It will have roared first and mixed sparks with stars,
And sweeping round it with a flaming sword,
Made the dim trees stand back in wider circle—
Done so much and I know not how much more   30
I mean it shall not do if I can bind it.
Well if it doesn't with its draft bring on
A wind to blow in earnest from some quarter,
As once it did with me upon an April.
The breezes were so spent with winter blowing   35
They seemed to fail the bluebirds under them
Short of the perch their languid flight was toward;
And my flame made a pinnacle to heaven
As I walked once around it in possession.
But the wind out-of-doors—you know the saying.   40
There came a gust. (You used to think the trees
Made wind by fanning, since you never knew
It blow but that you saw the trees in motion.)
Something or someone watching made that gust.

It put the flame tip-down and dabbed the grass   45
Of over-winter with the least tip-touch
Your tongue gives salt or sugar in your hand.
The place it reached to blackened instantly.
The black was almost all there was by daylight,
That and the merest curl of cigarette smoke—   50
And a flame slender as the hepaticas,
Bloodroot, and violets so soon to be now.
But the black spread like black death on the ground,
And I think the sky darkened with a cloud
Like winter and evening coming on together.   55
There were enough things to be thought of then.
Where the field stretches toward the north
And setting sun to Hyla brook, I gave it
To flames without twice thinking, where it verges
Upon the road, to flames too, though in fear   60
They might find fuel there, in withered brake,
Grass its full length, old silver goldenrod,
And alder and grape vine entanglement,
To leap the dusty deadline. For my own
I took what front there was beside. I knelt   65
And thrust hands in and held my face away.
Fight such a fire by rubbing not by beating.
A board is the best weapon if you have it.
I had my coat. And oh, I knew, I knew,
And said out loud, I couldn't bide the smother   70
And heat so close in; but the thought of all
The woods and town on fire by me, and all
The town turned out to fight for me—that held me.
I trusted the brook barrier, but feared
The road would fail; and on that side the fire   75
Died not without a noise of crackling wood—
Of something more than tinder-grass and weed—

131

That brought me to my feet to hold it back
By leaning back myself, as if the reins
Were round my neck and I was at the plow.   80
I won! But I'm sure no one ever spread
Another color over a tenth the space
That I spread coal-black over in the time
It took me. Neighbors coming home from town
Couldn't believe that so much black had come there   85
While they had backs turned, that it hadn't been there
When they had passed an hour or so before
Going the other way and they not seen it.
They looked about for someone to have done it.
But there was no one. I was somewhere wondering   90
Where all my weariness had gone and why
I walked so light on air in heavy shoes
In spite of a scorched Fourth-of-July feeling.
Why wouldn't I be scared remembering that?"

"If it scares you, what will it do to us?"   95

"Scare you. But if you shrink from being scared,
What would you say to war if it should come?
That's what for reasons I should like to know—
If you can comfort me by any answer."

"Oh, but war's not for children—it's for men."   100

"Now we are digging almost down to China.
My dears, my dears, you thought that—we all thought it.
So your mistake was ours. Haven't you heard, though,
About the ships where war has found them out
At sea, about the towns where war has come   105
Through opening clouds at night with droning speed
Further o'erhead than all but stars and angels—
And children in the ships and in the towns?

132

Haven't you heard what we have lived to learn?
Nothing so new—something we had forgotten: 110
War is for everyone, for children too.
I wasn't going to tell you and I mustn't.
The best way is to come uphill with me
And have our fire and laugh and be afraid."

A GIRL'S GARDEN

A neighbor of mine in the village
    Likes to tell how one spring
When she was a girl on the farm, she did
    A childlike thing.

One day she asked her father 5
    To give her a garden plot
To plant and tend and reap herself,
    And he said, "Why not?"

In casting about for a corner
    He thought of an idle bit 10
Of walled-off ground where a shop had stood,
    And he said, "Just it."

And he said, "That ought to make you
    An ideal one-girl farm,
And give you a chance to put some strength 15
    On your slim-jim arm."

It was not enough of a garden,
    Her father said, to plow;
So she had to work it all by hand,
    But she don't mind now. 20

She wheeled the dung in the wheelbarrow
    Along a stretch of road;
But she always ran away and left
    Her not-nice load,

And hid from anyone passing.   25
    And then she begged the seed.
She says she thinks she planted one
    Of all things but weed.

A hill each of potatoes,
    Radishes, lettuce, peas,   30
Tomatoes, beets, beans, pumpkins, corn,
    And even fruit trees.

And yes, she has long mistrusted
    That a cider-apple tree
In bearing there today is hers,   35
    Or at least may be.

Her crop was a miscellany
    When all was said and done,
A little bit of everything,
    A great deal of none.   40

Now when she sees in the village
    How village things go,
Just when it seems to come in right,
    She says, "*I* know!

"It's as when I was a farmer. . . ."   45
    Oh, never by way of advice!
And she never sins by telling the tale
    To the same person twice.

LOCKED OUT

As told to a child

When we locked up the house at night,
We always locked the flowers outside
And cut them off from window light.
The time I dreamed the door was tried
And brushed with buttons upon sleeves,   5
The flowers were out there with the thieves.
Yet nobody molested them!
We did find one nasturtium
Upon the steps with bitten stem.
I may have been to blame for that: 10
I always thought it must have been
Some flower I played with as I sat
At dusk to watch the moon down early.

THE LAST WORD OF A BLUEBIRD

As told to a child

As I went out a Crow
In a low voice said, "Oh,
I was looking for you.
How do you do?
I just came to tell you   5
To tell Lesley (will you?)
That her little Bluebird
Wanted me to bring word
That the north wind last night
That made the stars bright   10
And made ice on the trough
Almost made him cough
His tail feathers off.

135

He just had to fly!
But he sent her Good-by, 15
And said to be good,
And wear her red hood,
And look for skunk tracks
In the snow with an ax—
And do everything! 20
And perhaps in the spring
He would come back and sing."

"OUT, OUT—"

The buzz saw snarled and rattled in the yard
And made dust and dropped stove-length sticks of wood,
Sweet-scented stuff when the breeze drew across it.
And from there those that lifted eyes could count
Five mountain ranges one behind the other 5
Under the sunset far into Vermont.
And the saw snarled and rattled, snarled and rattled,
As it ran light, or had to bear a load.
And nothing happened: day was all but done.
Call it a day, I wish they might have said 10
To please the boy by giving him the half hour
That a boy counts so much when saved from work.
His sister stood beside them in her apron
To tell them "Supper." At the word, the saw,
As if to prove saws knew what supper meant, 15
Leaped out at the boy's hand, or seemed to leap—
He must have given the hand. However it was,
Neither refused the meeting. But the hand!
The boy's first outcry was a rueful laugh,
As he swung toward them holding up the hand, 20

Half in appeal, but half as if to keep
The life from spilling. Then the boy saw all—
Since he was old enough to know, big boy
Doing a man's work, though a child at heart—
He saw all spoiled. "Don't let him cut my hand off— 25
The doctor, when he comes. Don't let him, sister!"
So. But the hand was gone already.
The doctor put him in the dark of ether.
He lay and puffed his lips out with his breath.
And then—the watcher at his pulse took fright. 30
No one believed. They listened at his heart.
Little—less—nothing!—and that ended it.
No more to build on there. And they, since they
Were not the one dead, turned to their affairs.

BROWN'S DESCENT

Brown lived at such a lofty farm
    That everyone for miles could see
His lantern when he did his chores
    In winter after half-past three.

And many must have seen him make 5
    His wild descent from there one night,
'Cross lots, 'cross walls, 'cross everything,
    Describing rings of lantern-light.

Between the house and barn the gale
    Got him by something he had on 10
And blew him out on the icy crust
    That cased the world, and he was gone!

Walls were all buried, trees were few:
    He saw no stay unless he stove

A hole in somewhere with his heel.   15
    But though repeatedly he strove

And stamped and said things to himself,
    And sometimes something seemed to yield,
He gained no foothold, but pursued
    His journey down from field to field.   20

Sometimes he came with arms outspread
    Like wings, revolving in the scene
Upon his longer axis, and
    With no small dignity of mien.

Faster or slower as he chanced,   25
    Sitting or standing as he chose,
According as he feared to risk
    His neck, or thought to spare his clothes.

He never let the lantern drop.
    And some exclaimed who saw afar   30
The figures he described with it,
    "I wonder what those signals are

"Brown makes at such an hour of night!
    He's celebrating something strange.
I wonder if he's sold his farm,   35
    Or been made Master of the Grange."

He reeled, he lurched, he bobbed, he checked;
    He fell and made the lantern rattle
(But saved the light from going out).
    So halfway down he fought the battle,   40

Incredulous of his own bad luck.
    And then becoming reconciled

To everything, he gave it up
    And came down like a coasting child.

"Well—I—be—" that was all he said,   45
    As standing in the river road
He looked back up the slippery slope
    (Two miles it was) to his abode.

Sometimes as an authority
    On motorcars, I'm asked if I   50
Should say our stock was petered out,
    And this is my sincere reply:

Yankees are what they always were.
    Don't think Brown ever gave up hope
Of getting home again because   55
    He couldn't climb that slippery slope;

Or even thought of standing there
    Until the January thaw
Should take the polish off the crust.
    He bowed with grace to natural law,   60

And then went round it on his feet,
    After the manner of our stock;
Not much concerned for those to whom,
    At that particular time o'clock,

It must have looked as if the course   65
    He steered was really straight away
From that which he was headed for—
    Not much concerned for them, I say;

No more so than became a man—
    And politician at odd seasons.   70

I've kept Brown standing in the cold
   While I invested him with reasons;

But now he snapped his eyes three times;
   Then shook his lantern, saying, "Ile's
'Bout out!" and took the long way home   75
   By road, a matter of several miles.

THE GUM-GATHERER

There overtook me and drew me in
To his downhill, early-morning stride,
And set me five miles on my road
Better than if he had had me ride,
A man with a swinging bag for load   5
And half the bag wound round his hand.
We talked like barking above the din
Of water we walked along beside.
And for my telling him where I'd been
And where I lived in mountain land   10
To be coming home the way I was,
He told me a little about himself.
He came from higher up in the pass
Where the grist of the new-beginning brooks
Is blocks split off the mountain mass—   15
And hopeless grist enough it looks
Ever to grind to soil for grass.
(The way it is will do for moss.)
There he had built his stolen shack.
It had to be a stolen shack   20
Because of the fears of fire and loss
That trouble the sleep of lumber folk:
Visions of half the world burned black

And the sun shrunken yellow in smoke.
We know who when they come to town   25
Bring berries under the wagon seat,
Or a basket of eggs between their feet;
What this man brought in a cotton sack
Was gum, the gum of the mountain spruce.
He showed me lumps of the scented stuff   30
Like uncut jewels, dull and rough.
It comes to market golden brown;
But turns to pink between the teeth.

I told him this is a pleasant life,
To set your breast to the bark of trees   35
That all your days are dim beneath,
And reaching up with a little knife,
To loose the resin and take it down
And bring it to market when you please.

THE LINE-GANG

Here come the line-gang pioneering by.
They throw a forest down less cut than broken.
They plant dead trees for living, and the dead
They string together with a living thread.
They string an instrument against the sky   5
Wherein words whether beaten out or spoken
Will run as hushed as when they were a thought.
But in no hush they string it: they go past
With shouts afar to pull the cable taut,
To hold it hard until they make it fast,   10
To ease away—they have it. With a laugh,
An oath of towns that set the wild at naught,
They bring the telephone and telegraph.

THE VANISHING RED

He is said to have been the last Red Man
In Acton. And the Miller is said to have laughed—
If you like to call such a sound a laugh.
But he gave no one else a laugher's license.
For he turned suddenly grave as if to say,   5
"Whose business—if I take it on myself,
Whose business—but why talk round the barn?—
When it's just that I hold with getting a thing done with."

You can't get back and see it as he saw it.
It's too long a story to go into now.   10
You'd have to have been there and lived it.
Then you wouldn't have looked on it as just a matter
Of who began it between the two races.

Some guttural exclamation of surprise
The Red Man gave in poking about the mill,   15
Over the great big thumping, shuffling millstone,
Disgusted the Miller physically as coming
From one who had no right to be heard from.

"Come, John," he said, "you want to see the wheel pit?"

He took him down below a cramping rafter,   20
And showed him, through a manhole in the floor,
The water in desperate straits like frantic fish,
Salmon and sturgeon, lashing with their tails.
Then he shut down the trap door with a ring in it
That jangled even above the general noise,   25
And came upstairs alone—and gave that laugh,
And said something to a man with a meal sack
That the man with the meal sack didn't catch—then.
Oh, yes, he showed John the wheel pit all right.

SNOW

The three stood listening to a fresh access
Of wind that caught against the house a moment,
Gulped snow, and then blew free again—the Coles,
Dressed, but disheveled from some hours of sleep;
Meserve, belittled in the great skin coat he wore.   5

Meserve was first to speak. He pointed backward
Over his shoulder with his pipestem, saying,
"You can just see it glancing off the roof
Making a great scroll upward toward the sky,
Long enough for recording all our names on.—   10
I think I'll just call up my wife and tell her
I'm here—so far—and starting on again.
I'll call her softly so that if she's wise
And gone to sleep, she needn't wake to answer."
Three times he barely stirred the bell, then listened.   15
"Why, Lett, still up? Lett, I'm at Cole's. I'm late.
I called you up to say Good-night from here
Before I went to say Good-morning there.—
I thought I would.—I know, but, Lett—I know—
I could, but what's the sense? The rest won't be   20
So bad.—Give me an hour for it.— Ho, ho,
Three hours to here! But that was all uphill;
The rest is down.—Why no, no, not a wallow:
They kept their heads and took their time to it
Like darlings, both of them. They're in the barn.—   25
My dear, I'm coming just the same. I didn't
Call you to ask you to invite me home.—"
He lingered for some word she wouldn't say,
Said it at last himself, "Good-night," and then,
Getting no answer, closed the telephone.   30

143

The three stood in the lamplight round the table
With lowered eyes a moment till he said,
"I'll just see how the horses are."

                        "Yes, do,"
Both the Coles said together. Mrs. Cole
Added: "You can judge better after seeing.—   35
I want you here with me, Fred.—Leave him here,
Brother Meserve. You know to find your way
Out through the shed."

                           "I guess I know my way.
I guess I know where I can find my name
Carved in the shed to tell me who I am   40
If it don't tell me where I am. I used
To play——"

                  "You tend your horses and come back.—
Fred Cole, you're going to let him!"

                               "Well, aren't you?
How can you help yourself?"

                         "I called him Brother.
Why did I call him that?"

                       "It's right enough.   45
That's all you ever heard him called round here.
He seems to have lost off his Christian name."

"Christian enough I should call that myself.
He took no notice, did he? Well, at least
I didn't use it out of love of him,   50
The dear knows. I detest the thought of him—
With his ten children under ten years old.
I hate his wretched little Racker Sect,
All's ever I heard of it, which isn't much.
But that's not saying—look, Fred Cole, it's twelve,   55

144

Isn't it, now? He's been here half an hour.
He says he left the village store at nine:
Three hours to do four miles—a mile an hour
Or not much better. Why, it doesn't seem
As if a man could move that slow and move.   60
Try to think what he did with all that time.
And three miles more to go!"

                    "Don't let him go.
Stick to him, Helen. Make him answer you.
That sort of man talks straight-on all his life
From the last thing he said himself, stone deaf   65
To anything anyone else may say.
I should have thought, though, you could make him hear you."

"What is he doing out a night like this?
Why can't he stay at home?"

                    "He had to preach."

"It's no night to be out."

                    "He may be small,   70
He may be good, but one thing's sure, he's tough."

"And strong of stale tobacco."

                    "He'll pull through."

"You only say so. Not another house
Or shelter to put into from this place
To theirs. I'm going to call his wife again."   75

"Wait and he may. Let's see what he will do.
Let's see if he will think of her again.
But then, I doubt he's thinking of himself.
He doesn't look on it as anything."

"He shan't go—there!"

145

"It *is* a night, my dear."   80

"One thing: he didn't drag God into it."

"He don't consider it a case for God."

"You think so, do you? You don't know the kind.
He's getting up a miracle this minute.
Privately—to himself, right now, he's thinking   85
He'll make a case of it if he succeeds,
But keep still if he fails."

               "Keep still all over.
He'll be dead—dead and buried."

                      "Such a trouble!
Not but I've every reason not to care
What happens to him if it only takes   90
Some of the sanctimonious conceit
Out of one of those pious scalawags."

"Nonsense to that! You want to see him safe."

"You like the runt."

               "Don't you a little?"

                        "Well,
I don't like what he's doing, which is what   95
You like, and like him for."

                 "Oh, yes you do.
You like your fun as well as anyone;
Only you women have to put these airs on
To impress men. You've got us so ashamed
Of being men we can't look at a good fight   100
Between two boys and not feel bound to stop it.
Let the man freeze an ear or two, I say.—
He's here. I leave him all to you. Go in

146

And save his life.—All right, come in, Meserve.
Sit down, sit down. How did you find the horses?"   105

"Fine, fine."

        "And ready for some more? My wife here
Says it won't do. You've got to give it up."

"Won't you to please me? Please! If I say Please?
Mr. Meserve, I'll leave it to *your* wife.
What *did* your wife say on the telephone?"   110

Meserve seemed to heed nothing but the lamp
Or something not far from it on the table.
By straightening out and lifting a forefinger,
He pointed with his hand from where it lay
Like a white crumpled spider on his knee: 115
"That leaf there in your open book! It moved
Just then, I thought. It's stood erect like that,
There on the table, ever since I came,
Trying to turn itself backward or forward,
I've had my eye on it to make out which: 120
If forward, then it's with a friend's impatience—
You see I know—to get you on to things
It wants to see how you will take; if backward,
It's from regret for something you have passed
And failed to see the good of. Never mind,   125
Things must expect to come in front of us
A many times—I don't say just how many—
That varies with the things—before we see them.
One of the lies would make it out that nothing
Ever presents itself before us twice.   130
Where would we be at last if that were so?
Our very life depends on everything's
Recurring till we answer from within.

147

The thousandth time may prove the charm.—That leaf!
It can't turn either way. It needs the wind's help.   135
But the wind didn't move it if it moved.
It moved itself. The wind's at naught in here.
It couldn't stir so sensitively poised
A thing as that. It couldn't reach the lamp
To get a puff of black smoke from the flame,   140
Or blow a rumple in the collie's coat.
You make a little foursquare block of air,
Quiet and light and warm, in spite of all
The illimitable dark and cold and storm,
And by so doing give these three, lamp, dog,   145
And book-leaf, that keep near you, their repose;
Though for all anyone can tell, repose
May be the thing you haven't, yet you give it.
So false it is that what we haven't we can't give;
So false, that what we always say is true.   150
I'll have to turn the leaf if no one else will.
It won't lie down. Then let it stand. Who cares?"

"I shouldn't want to hurry you, Meserve,
But if you're going—say you'll stay, you know.
But let me raise this curtain on a scene,   155
And show you how it's piling up against you.
You see the snow-white through the white of frost?
Ask Helen how far up the sash it's climbed
Since last we read the gauge."

                              "It looks as if
Some pallid thing had squashed its features flat   160
And its eyes shut with overeagerness
To see what people found so interesting
In one another, and had gone to sleep
Of its own stupid lack of understanding,

148

Or broke its white neck of mushroom stuff   165
Short off, and died against the windowpane."

"Brother Meserve, take care, you'll scare yourself
More than you will us with such nightmare talk.
It's you it matters to, because it's you
Who have to go out into it alone."   170

"Let him talk, Helen, and perhaps he'll stay."

"Before you drop the curtain—I'm reminded:
You recollect the boy who came out here
To breathe the air one winter—had a room
Down at the Averys'? Well, one sunny morning   175
After a downy storm, he passed our place
And found me banking up the house with snow.
And I was burrowing in deep for warmth,
Piling it well above the windowsills.
The snow against the window caught his eye.   180
'Hey, that's a pretty thought'—those were his words—
'So you can think it's six feet deep outside,
While you sit warm and read up balanced rations.
You can't get too much winter in the winter.'
Those were his words. And he went home and all   185
But banked the daylight out of Avery's windows.
Now you and I would go to no such length.
At the same time you can't deny it makes
It not a mite worse, sitting here, we three,
Playing our fancy, to have the snow-line run   190
So high across the pane outside. There where
There is a sort of tunnel in the frost—
More like a tunnel than a hole—way down
At the far end of it you see a stir
And quiver like the frayed edge of the drift   195

149

Blown in the wind. I *like* that—I like *that.*
Well, now I leave you, people."

                    "Come, Meserve,
We thought you were deciding not to go—
The ways you found to say the praise of comfort
And being where you are. You want to stay."   200

"I'll own it's cold for such a fall of snow.
This house is frozen brittle, all except
This room you sit in. If you think the wind
Sounds further off, it's not because it's dying;
You're further under in the snow—that's all—   205
And feel it less. Hear the soft bombs of dust
It bursts against us at the chimney mouth,
And at the eaves. I like it from inside
More than I shall out in it. But the horses
Are rested and it's time to say Good-night,   210
And let you get to bed again. Good-night,
Sorry I had to break in on your sleep."

"Lucky for you you did. Lucky for you
You had us for a halfway station
To stop at. If you were the kind of man   215
Paid heed to women, you'd take my advice
And for your family's sake stay where you are.
But what good is my saying it over and over?
You've done more than you had a right to think
You could do—*now.* You know the risk you take   220
In going on."

                    "Our snowstorms as a rule
Aren't looked on as man-killers, and although
I'd rather be the beast that sleeps the sleep
Under it all, his door sealed up and lost,

Than the man fighting it to keep above it,   225
Yet think of the small birds at roost and not
In nests. Shall I be counted less than they are?
Their bulk in water would be frozen rock
In no time out tonight. And yet tomorrow
They will come budding boughs from tree to tree,   230
Flirting their wings and saying Chickadee,
As if not knowing what you meant by the word storm."

"But why, when no one wants you to, go on?
Your wife—she doesn't want you to. We don't,
And you yourself don't want to. Who else is there?"   235

"Save us from being cornered by a woman.
Well, there's—" She told Fred afterward that in
The pause right there, she thought the dreaded word
Was coming, "God." But no, he only said,
"Well, there's—the storm. That says I must go on.   240
That wants me as a war might if it came.
Ask any man."

                        He threw her that as something
To last her till he got outside the door.
He had Cole with him to the barn to see him off.
When Cole returned he found his wife still standing   245
Beside the table, near the open book,
Not reading it.

                        "Well, what kind of a man
Do you call that?" she said.

                        "He had the gift
Of words, or is it tongues I ought to say?"

"Was ever such a man for seeing likeness?"   250

"Or disregarding people's civil questions—

151

What? We've found out in one hour more about him
Than we had seeing him pass by in the road
A thousand times. If that's the way he preaches!
You didn't think you'd keep him after all.   255
Oh, I'm not blaming you. He didn't leave you
Much say in the matter, and I'm just as glad
We're not in for a night of him. No sleep
If he had stayed. The least thing set him going.
It's quiet as an empty church without him."   260

"But how much better off are we as it is?
We'll have to sit here till we know he's safe."

"Yes, I suppose you'll want to, but I shouldn't.
He knows what he can do, or he wouldn't try.
Get into bed I say, and get some rest.   265
He won't come back, and if he telephones,
It won't be for an hour or two."

                              "Well then—
We can't be any help by sitting here
And living his fight through with him, I suppose."

                    *   *   *

Cole had been telephoning in the dark.   270
Mrs. Cole's voice came from an inner room:
"Did she call you or you call her?"

                              "She me.
You'd better dress: you won't go back to bed.
We must have been asleep: it's three and after."

"Had she been ringing long? I'll get my wrapper.   275
I want to speak to her."

                    "All she said was,
He hadn't come and had he really started."

"She knew he had, poor thing, two hours ago."

"He had the shovel. He'll have made a fight."

"Why did I ever let him leave this house!"   280

"Don't begin that. You did the best you could
To keep him—though perhaps you didn't quite
Conceal a wish to see him show the spunk
To disobey you. Much his wife'll thank you."

"Fred, after all I said! You shan't make out   285
That it was any way but what it was.
Did she let on by any word she said
She didn't thank me?"

             "When I told her 'Gone,'
'Well then,' she said, and 'Well then'—like a threat.
And then her voice came scraping slow: 'Oh, you,   290
Why did you let him go?' "

                "Asked why we let him?
You let me there. I'll ask her why she let him.
She didn't dare to speak when he was here.
Their number's—twenty-one?—The thing won't work.
Someone's receiver's down. The handle stumbles.   295
The stubborn thing, the way it jars your arm!—
It's theirs. She's dropped it from her hand and gone."

"Try speaking. Say 'Hello!' "

              "Hello. Hello."

"What do you hear?"

           "I hear an empty room—
You know—it sounds that way. And yes, I hear—   300
I think I hear a clock—and windows rattling.
No step, though. If she's there she's sitting down."

"Shout, she may hear you."

"Shouting is no good."

"Keep speaking, then."

"Hello. Hello. Hello.—
You don't suppose?—she wouldn't go outdoors?"   305

"I'm half afraid that's just what she might do."

"And leave the children?"

"Wait and call again.
You can't hear whether she has left the door
Wide open and the wind's blown out the lamp
And the fire's died and the room's dark and cold?"   310

"One of two things, either she's gone to bed
Or gone outdoors."

"In which case both are lost.
Do you know what she's like? Have you ever met her?
It's strange she doesn't want to speak to us."

"Fred, see if you can hear what I hear. Come."   315

"A clock maybe."

"Don't you hear something else?"

"Not talking."

"No."

"Why, yes, I hear—what is it?"

"What do you say it is?"

"A baby's crying!
Frantic it sounds, though muffled and far off.
Its mother wouldn't let it cry like that,   320
Not if she's there."

154

"What do you make of it?"

"There's only one thing possible to make,
That is, assuming—that she has gone out.
Of course she hasn't, though." They both sat down
Helpless. "There's nothing we can do till morning."   325

"Fred, I shan't let you think of going out."

"Hold on." The double bell began to chirp.
They started up. Fred took the telephone.
"Hello, Meserve. You're there, then!—and your wife?
Good! Why I asked—she didn't seem to answer.—   330
He says she went to let him in the barn.—
We're glad. Oh, say no more about it, man.
Drop in and see us when you're passing."

                                        "Well,
She has him, then, though what she wants him for
I *don't* see."

                        "Possibly not for herself.   335
Maybe she only wants him for the children."

"The whole to-do seems to have been for nothing.
What spoiled our night was to him just his fun.
What did he come in for?—to talk and visit?
Thought he'd just call to tell us it was snowing.   340
If he thinks he is going to make our house
A halfway coffee house 'twixt town and nowhere——"

"I thought you'd feel you'd been too much concerned."

"You think you haven't been concerned yourself."

"If you mean he was inconsiderate   345
To rout us out to think for him at midnight
And then take our advice no more than nothing,

155

Why, I agree with you. But let's forgive him.
We've had a share in one night of his life.
What'll you bet he ever calls again?"

THE SOUND OF TREES

I wonder about the trees.
Why do we wish to bear
Forever the noise of these
More than another noise
So close to our dwelling place?   5
We suffer them by the day
Till we lose all measure of pace,
And fixity in our joys,
And acquire a listening air.
They are that that talks of going   10
But never gets away;
And that talks no less for knowing,
As it grows wiser and older,
That now it means to stay.
My feet tug at the floor   15
And my head sways to my shoulder
Sometimes when I watch trees sway,
From the window or the door.
I shall set forth for somewhere,
I shall make the reckless choice   20
Some day when they are in voice
And tossing so as to scare
The white clouds over them on.
I shall have less to say,
But I shall be gone.   25

New Hampshire

: 1923 :

NEW HAMPSHIRE

I met a lady from the South who said
(You won't believe she said it, but she said it):
"None of my family ever worked, or had
A thing to sell." I don't suppose the work
Much matters. You may work for all of me.   5
I've seen the time I've had to work myself.
The having anything to sell is what
Is the disgrace in man or state or nation.

I met a traveler from Arkansas
Who boasted of his state as beautiful   10
For diamonds and apples. "Diamonds
And apples in commercial quantities?"
I asked him, on my guard. "Oh, yes," he answered,
Off his. The time was evening in the Pullman.
"I see the porter's made your bed," I told him.   15

I met a Californian who would
Talk California—a state so blessed,
He said, in climate, none had ever died there
A natural death, and Vigilance Committees
Had had to organize to stock the graveyards   20
And vindicate the state's humanity.
"Just the way Stefansson runs on," I murmured,
"About the British Arctic. That's what comes
Of being in the market with a climate."

I met a poet from another state,   25
A zealot full of fluid inspiration,
Who in the name of fluid inspiration,

159

But in the best style of bad salesmanship,
Angrily tried to make me write a protest
(In verse I think) against the Volstead Act.   30
He didn't even offer me a drink
Until I asked for one to steady *him*.
This is called having an idea to sell.

It never could have happened in New Hampshire.

The only person really soiled with trade   35
I ever stumbled on in old New Hampshire
Was someone who had just come back ashamed
From selling things in California.
He'd built a noble mansard roof with balls
On turrets, like Constantinople, deep   40
In woods some ten miles from a railroad station,
As if to put forever out of mind
The hope of being, as we say, received.
I found him standing at the close of day
Inside the threshold of his open barn,   45
Like a lone actor on a gloomy stage—
And recognized him, through the iron gray
In which his face was muffled to the eyes,
As an old boyhood friend, and once indeed
A drover with me on the road to Brighton.   50
His farm was "grounds," and not a farm at all;
His house among the local sheds and shanties
Rose like a factor's at a trading station.
And he was rich, and I was still a rascal.
I couldn't keep from asking impolitely,   55
Where had he been and what had he been doing?
How did he get so? (Rich was understood.)
In dealing in "old rags" in San Francisco.
Oh, it was terrible as well could be.

We both of us turned over in our graves.   60

Just specimens is all New Hampshire has,
One each of everything as in a showcase,
Which naturally she doesn't care to sell.

She had one President. (Pronounce him Purse,
And make the most of it for better or worse.   65
He's your one chance to score against the state.)
She had one Daniel Webster. He was all
The Daniel Webster ever was or shall be.
She had the Dartmouth needed to produce him.

I call her old. She has one family   70
Whose claim is good to being settled here
Before the era of colonization,
And before that of exploration even.
John Smith remarked them as he coasted by,
Dangling their legs and fishing off a wharf   75
At the Isles of Shoals, and satisfied himself
They weren't Red Indians but veritable
Pre-primitives of the white race, dawn people,
Like those who furnished Adam's sons with wives;
However uninnocent they may have been   80
In being there so early in our history.
They'd been there then a hundred years or more.
Pity he didn't ask what they were up to
At that date with a wharf already built,
And take their name. They've since told me their name—
Today an honored one in Nottingham.
As for what they were up to more than fishing—
Suppose they weren't behaving Puritanly,
The hour had not yet struck for being good,
Mankind had not yet gone on the Sabbatical.   90

161

It became an explorer of the deep
Not to explore too deep in others' business.

Did you but know of him, New Hampshire has
One real reformer who would change the world
So it would be accepted by two classes,   95
Artists the minute they set up as artists,
Before, that is, they are themselves accepted,
And boys the minute they get out of college.
I can't help thinking those are tests to go by.

And she has one I don't know what to call him,   100
Who comes from Philadelphia every year
With a great flock of chickens of rare breeds
He wants to give the educational
Advantages of growing almost wild
Under the watchful eye of hawk and eagle—   105
Dorkings because they're spoken of by Chaucer,
Sussex because they're spoken of by Herrick.

She has a touch of gold. New Hampshire gold—
You may have heard of it. I had a farm
Offered me not long since up Berlin way   110
With a mine on it that was worked for gold;
But not gold in commercial quantities,
Just enough gold to make the engagement rings
And marriage rings of those who owned the farm.
What gold more innocent could one have asked for?   115
One of my children ranging after rocks
Lately brought home from Andover or Canaan
A specimen of beryl with a trace
Of radium. I know with radium
The trace would have to be the merest trace   120
To be below the threshold of commercial;

162

But trust New Hampshire not to have enough
Of radium or anything to sell.

A specimen of everything, I said.
She has one witch—old style. She lives in Colebrook.   125
(The only other witch I ever met
Was lately at a cut-glass dinner in Boston.
There were four candles and four people present.
The witch was young, and beautiful (new style),
And open-minded. She was free to question   130
Her gift for reading letters locked in boxes.
Why was it so much greater when the boxes
Were metal than it was when they were wooden?
It made the world seem so mysterious.
The S'ciety for Psychical Research   135
Was cognizant. Her husband was worth millions.
I think he owned some shares in Harvard College.)

New Hampshire *used* to have at Salem
A company we called the White Corpuscles,
Whose duty was at any hour of night   140
To rush in sheets and fool's caps where they smelled
A thing the least bit doubtfully perscented
And give someone the Skipper Ireson's Ride.

One each of everything as in a showcase.

More than enough land for a specimen   145
You'll say she has, but there there enters in
Something else to protect her from herself.
There quality makes up for quantity.
Not even New Hampshire farms are much for sale.
The farm I made my home on in the mountains   150
I had to take by force rather than buy.

163

I caught the owner outdoors by himself
Raking up after winter, and I said,
"I'm going to put you off this farm: I want it."
"Where are you going to put me? In the road?"   155
"I'm going to put you on the farm next to it."
"Why won't the farm next to it do for you?"
"I like this better." It was really better.

Apples? New Hampshire has them, but unsprayed,
With no suspicion in stem end or blossom end   160
Of vitriol or arsenate of lead,
And so not good for anything but cider.
Her unpruned grapes are flung like lariats
Far up the birches out of reach of man.

A state producing precious metals, stones,   165
And—writing; none of these except perhaps
The precious literature in quantity
Or quality to worry the producer
About disposing of it. Do you know,
Considering the market, there are more   170
Poems produced than any other thing?
No wonder poets sometimes have to *seem*
So much more businesslike than businessmen.
Their wares are so much harder to get rid of.

She's one of the two best states in the Union.   175
Vermont's the other. And the two have been
Yokefellows in the sap yoke from of old
In many Marches. And they lie like wedges,
Thick end to thin end and thin end to thick end,
And are a figure of the way the strong   180
Of mind and strong of arm should fit together,
One thick where one is thin and vice versa.

New Hampshire raises the Connecticut
In a trout hatchery near Canada,
But soon divides the river with Vermont.   185
Both are delightful states for their absurdly
Small towns—Lost Nation, Bungey, Muddy Boo,
Poplin, Still Corners (so called not because
The place is silent all day long, nor yet
Because it boasts a whisky still—because   190
It set out once to be a city and still
Is only corners, crossroads in a wood).
And I remember one whose name appeared
Between the pictures on a movie screen
Election night once in Franconia,   195
When everything had gone Republican
And Democrats were sore in need of comfort:
Easton goes Democratic, Wilson 4
Hughes 2. And everybody to the saddest
Laughed the loud laugh the big laugh at the little.   200
New York (five million) laughs at Manchester,
Manchester (sixty or seventy thousand) laughs
At Littleton (four thousand), Littleton
Laughs at Franconia (seven hundred), and
Franconia laughs, I fear—did laugh that night—   205
At Easton. What has Easton left to laugh at,
And like the actress exclaim "Oh, my God" at?
There's Bungey; and for Bungey there are towns,
Whole townships named but without population.

Anything I can say about New Hampshire   210
Will serve almost as well about Vermont,
Excepting that they differ in their mountains.
The Vermont mountains stretch extended straight;
New Hampshire mountains curl up in a coil.

I had been coming to New Hampshire mountains.   215
And here I am and what am I to say?
Here first my theme becomes embarrassing.
Emerson said, "The God who made New Hampshire
Taunted the lofty land with little men."
Another Massachusetts poet said,   220
"I go no more to summer in New Hampshire.
I've given up my summer place in Dublin."
But when I asked to know what ailed New Hampshire,
She said she couldn't stand the people in it,
The little men (it's Massachusetts speaking).   225
And when I asked to know what ailed the people,
She said, "Go read your own books and find out."
I may as well confess myself the author
Of several books against the world in general.
To take them as against a special state   230
Or even nation's to restrict my meaning.
I'm what is called a sensibilitist,
Or otherwise an environmentalist.
I refuse to adapt myself a mite
To any change from hot to cold, from wet   235
To dry, from poor to rich, or back again.
I make a virtue of my suffering
From nearly everything that goes on round me.
In other words, I know wherever I am,
Being the creature of literature I am,   240
I shall not lack for pain to keep me awake.
Kit Marlowe taught me how to say my prayers:
"Why, this is Hell, nor am I out of it."
Samoa, Russia, Ireland I complain of,
No less than England, France, and Italy.   245
Because I wrote my novels in New Hampshire
Is no proof that I aimed them at New Hampshire.

When I left Massachusetts years ago
Between two days, the reason why I sought
New Hampshire, not Connecticut,   250
Rhode Island, New York, or Vermont was this:
Where I was living then, New Hampshire offered
The nearest boundary to escape across.
I hadn't an illusion in my handbag
About the people being better there   255
Than those I left behind. I thought they weren't.
I thought they couldn't be. And yet they were.
I'd sure had no such friends in Massachusetts
As Hall of Windham, Gay of Atkinson,
Bartlett of Raymond (now of Colorado),   260
Harris of Derry, and Lynch of Bethlehem.

The glorious bards of Massachusetts seem
To want to make New Hampshire people over.
They taunt the lofty land with little men.
I don't know what to say about the people.   265
For art's sake one could almost wish them worse
Rather than better. How are we to write
The Russian novel in America
As long as life goes so unterribly?
There is the pinch from which our only outcry   270
In literature to date is heard to come.
We get what little misery we can
Out of not having cause for misery.
It makes the guild of novel writers sick
To be expected to be Dostoievskis   275
On nothing worse than too much luck and comfort.
This is not sorrow, though; it's just the vapors,
And recognized as such in Russia itself
Under the new regime, and so forbidden.

167

If well it is with Russia, then feel free   280
To say so or be stood against the wall
And shot. It's Pollyanna now or death.
This, then, is the new freedom we hear tell of;
And very sensible. No state can build
A literature that shall at once be sound   285
And sad on a foundation of well-being.

To show the level of intelligence
Among us: it was just a Warren farmer
Whose horse had pulled him short up in the road
By me, a stranger. This is what he said,   290
From nothing but embarrassment and want
Of anything more sociable to say:
"You hear those hound dogs sing on Moosilauke?
Well, they remind me of the hue and cry
We've heard against the Mid-Victorians   295
And never rightly understood till Bryan
Retired from politics and joined the chorus.
The matter with the Mid-Victorians
Seems to have been a man named John L. Darwin."
"Go 'long," I said to him, he to his horse.   300

I knew a man who failing as a farmer
Burned down his farmhouse for the fire insurance,
And spent the proceeds on a telescope
To satisfy a lifelong curiosity
About our place among the infinities.   305
And how was that for otherworldliness?

If I must choose which I would elevate—
The people or the already lofty mountains,
I'd elevate the already lofty mountains.
The only fault I find with old New Hampshire   310

Is that her mountains aren't quite high enough.
I was not always so; I've come to be so.
How, to my sorrow, how have I attained
A height from which to look down critical
On mountains? What has given me assurance   315
To say what height becomes New Hampshire mountains,
Or any mountains? Can it be some strength
I feel, as of an earthquake in my back,
To heave them higher to the morning star?
Can it be foreign travel in the Alps?   320
Or having seen and credited a moment
The solid molding of vast peaks of cloud
Behind the pitiful reality
Of Lincoln, Lafayette, and Liberty?
Or some such sense as says how high shall jet   325
The fountain in proportion to the basin?
No, none of these has raised me to my throne
Of intellectual dissatisfaction,
But the sad accident of having seen
Our actual mountains given in a map   330
Of early times as twice the height they are—
Ten thousand feet instead of only five—
Which shows how sad an accident may be.
Five thousand is no longer high enough.
Whereas I never had a good idea   335
About improving people in the world,
Here I am overfertile in suggestion,
And cannot rest from planning day or night
How high I'd thrust the peaks in summer snow
To tap the upper sky and draw a flow   340
Of frosty night air on the vale below
Down from the stars to freeze the dew as starry.

The more the sensibilitist I am
The more I seem to want my mountains wild;
The way the wiry gang-boss liked the logjam.   345
After he'd picked the lock and got it started,
He dodged a log that lifted like an arm
Against the sky to break his back for him,
Then came in dancing, skipping with his life
Across the roar and chaos, and the words   350
We saw him say along the zigzag journey
Were doubtless as the words we heard him say
On coming nearer: "Wasn't she an *i*-deal
Son-of-a-bitch? You bet she was an *i*-deal."

For all her mountains fall a little short,   355
Her people not quite short enough for Art,
She's still New Hampshire, a most restful state.

Lately in converse with a New York alec
About the new school of the pseudo-phallic,
I found myself in a close corner where   360
I had to make an almost funny choice.
"Choose you which you will be—a prude, or puke,
Mewling and puking in the public arms."
"Me for the hills where I don't have to choose."
"But if you had to choose, which would you be?"   365
I wouldn't be a prude afraid of nature.
I know a man who took a double ax
And went alone against a grove of trees;
But his heart failing him, he dropped the ax
And ran for shelter quoting Matthew Arnold: 370
" 'Nature is cruel, man is sick of blood';
There's been enough shed without shedding mine.
Remember Birnam Wood! The wood's in flux!"

He had a special terror of the flux
That showed itself in dendrophobia.   375
The only decent tree had been to mill
And educated into boards, he said.
He knew too well for any earthly use
The line where man leaves off and nature starts,
And never overstepped it save in dreams.   380
He stood on the safe side of the line talking—
Which is sheer Matthew Arnoldism,
The cult of one who owned himself "a foiled
Circuitous wanderer," and "took dejectedly
His seat upon the intellectual throne"—   385
Agreed in frowning on these improvised
Altars the woods are full of nowadays,
Again as in the days when Ahaz sinned
By worship under green trees in the open.
Scarcely a mile but that I come on one,   390
A black-cheeked stone and stick of rain-washed charcoal.
Even to say the groves were God's first temples
Comes too near to Ahaz' sin for safety.
Nothing not built with hands of course is sacred.
But here is not a question of what's sacred;   395
Rather of what to face or run away from.
I'd hate to be a runaway from nature.
And neither would I choose to be a puke
Who cares not what he does in company,
And when he can't do anything, falls back   400
On words, and tries his worst to make words speak
Louder than actions, and sometimes achieves it.
It seems a narrow choice the age insists on.
How about being a good Greek, for instance?
That course, they tell me, isn't offered this year.   405
"Come, but this isn't choosing—puke or prude?"

171

Well, if I have to choose one or the other,
I choose to be a plain New Hampshire farmer
With an income in cash of, say, a thousand
(From, say, a publisher in New York City).   410
It's restful to arrive at a decision,
And restful just to think about New Hampshire.
At present I am living in Vermont.

A STAR IN A STONEBOAT

For Lincoln MacVeagh

Never tell me that not one star of all
That slip from heaven at night and softly fall
Has been picked up with stones to build a wall.

Some laborer found one faded and stone-cold,
And saving that its weight suggested gold   5
And tugged it from his first too certain hold,

He noticed nothing in it to remark.
He was not used to handling stars thrown dark
And lifeless from an interrupted arc.

He did not recognize in that smooth coal   10
The one thing palpable besides the soul
To penetrate the air in which we roll.

He did not see how like a flying thing
It brooded ant eggs, and had one large wing,
One not so large for flying in a ring,   15

And a long Bird of Paradise's tail
(Though these when not in use to fly and trail
It drew back in its body like a snail);

172

Nor know that he might move it from the spot—
The harm was done: from having been star-shot   20
The very nature of the soil was hot

And burning to yield flowers instead of grain,
Flowers fanned and not put out by all the rain
Poured on them by his prayers prayed in vain.

He moved it roughly with an iron bar,   25
He loaded an old stoneboat with the star
And not, as you might think, a flying car,

Such as even poets would admit perforce
More practical than Pegasus the horse
If it could put a star back in its course.   30

He dragged it through the plowed ground at a pace
But faintly reminiscent of the race
Of jostling rock in interstellar space.

It went for building stone, and I, as though
Commanded in a dream, forever go   35
To right the wrong that this should have been so.

Yet ask where else it could have gone as well,
I do not know—I cannot stop to tell:
He might have left it lying where it fell.

From following walls I never lift my eye,   40
Except at night to places in the sky
Where showers of charted meteors let fly.

Some may know what they seek in school and church,
And why they seek it there; for what I search
I must go measuring stone walls, perch on perch;   45

173

Sure that though not a star of death and birth,
So not to be compared, perhaps, in worth
To such resorts of life as Mars and Earth—

Though not, I say, a star of death and sin,
It yet has poles, and only needs a spin   50
To show its worldly nature and begin

To chafe and shuffle in my calloused palm
And run off in strange tangents with my arm,
As fish do with the line in first alarm.

Such as it is, it promises the prize   55
Of the one world complete in any size
That I am like to compass, fool or wise.

THE CENSUS-TAKER

I came an errand one cloud-blowing evening
To a slab-built, black-paper-covered house
Of one room and one window and one door,
The only dwelling in a waste cut over
A hundred square miles round it in the mountains: 5
And that not dwelt in now by men or women.
(It never had been dwelt in, though, by women,
So what is this I make a sorrow of?)
I came as census-taker to the waste
To count the people in it and found none,   10
None in the hundred miles, none in the house,
Where I came last with some hope, but not much,
After hours' overlooking from the cliffs
An emptiness flayed to the very stone.
I found no people that dared show themselves,   15
None not in hiding from the outward eye.

174

The time was autumn, but how anyone
Could tell the time of year when every tree
That could have dropped a leaf was down itself
And nothing but the stump of it was left   20
Now bringing out its rings in sugar of pitch;
And every tree up stood a rotting trunk
Without a single leaf to spend on autumn,
Or branch to whistle after what was spent.
Perhaps the wind the more without the help   25
Of breathing trees said something of the time
Of year or day the way it swung a door
Forever off the latch, as if rude men
Passed in and slammed it shut each one behind him
For the next one to open for himself.   30
I counted nine I had no right to count
(But this was dreamy unofficial counting)
Before I made the tenth across the threshold.
Where was my supper? Where was anyone's?
No lamp was lit. Nothing was on the table.   35
The stove was cold—the stove was off the chimney—
And down by one side where it lacked a leg.
The people that had loudly passed the door
Were people to the ear but not the eye.
They were not on the table with their elbows.   40
They were not sleeping in the shelves of bunks.
I saw no men there and no bones of men there.
I armed myself against such bones as might be
With the pitch-blackened stub of an ax-handle
I picked up off the straw-dust-covered floor.   45
Not bones, but the ill-fitted window rattled.
The door was still because I held it shut
While I thought what to do that could be done—
About the house—about the people not there.

This house in one year fallen to decay   50
Filled me with no less sorrow than the houses
Fallen to ruin in ten thousand years
Where Asia wedges Africa from Europe.
Nothing was left to do that I could see
Unless to find that there was no one there   55
And declare to the cliffs too far for echo,
"The place is desert, and let whoso lurks
In silence, if in this he is aggrieved,
Break silence now or be forever silent.
Let him say why it should not be declared so."   60
The melancholy of having to count souls
Where they grow fewer and fewer every year
Is extreme where they shrink to none at all.
It must be I want life to go on living.

THE STAR-SPLITTER

"You know Orion always comes up sideways.
Throwing a leg up over our fence of mountains,
And rising on his hands, he looks in on me
Busy outdoors by lantern-light with something
I should have done by daylight, and indeed,   5
After the ground is frozen, I should have done
Before it froze, and a gust flings a handful
Of waste leaves at my smoky lantern chimney
To make fun of my way of doing things,
Or else fun of Orion's having caught me.   10
Has a man, I should like to ask, no rights
These forces are obliged to pay respect to?"
So Brad McLaughlin mingled reckless talk
Of heavenly stars with hugger-mugger farming,

Till having failed at hugger-mugger farming   15
He burned his house down for the fire insurance
And spent the proceeds on a telescope
To satisfy a lifelong curiosity
About our place among the infinities.

"What do you want with one of those blame things?"   20
I asked him well beforehand. "Don't you get one!"

"Don't call it blamed; there isn't anything
More blameless in the sense of being less
A weapon in our human fight," he said.
"I'll have one if I sell my farm to buy it."   25
There where he moved the rocks to plow the ground
And plowed between the rocks he couldn't move,
Few farms changed hands; so rather than spend years
Trying to sell his farm and then not selling,
He burned his house down for the fire insurance   30
And bought the telescope with what it came to.
He had been heard to say by several:
"The best thing that we're put here for's to see;
The strongest thing that's given us to see with's
A telescope. Someone in every town   35
Seems to me owes it to the town to keep one.
In Littleton it may as well be me."
After such loose talk it was no surprise
When he did what he did and burned his house down.

Mean laughter went about the town that day   40
To let him know we weren't the least imposed on,
And he could wait—we'd see to him tomorrow.
But the first thing next morning we reflected
If one by one we counted people out
For the least sin, it wouldn't take us long   45

177

To get so we had no one left to live with.
For to be social is to be forgiving.
Our thief, the one who does our stealing from us,
We don't cut off from coming to church suppers,
But what we miss we go to him and ask for.   50
He promptly gives it back, that is if still
Uneaten, unworn out, or undisposed of.
It wouldn't do to be too hard on Brad
About his telescope. Beyond the age
Of being given one for Christmas gift,   55
He had to take the best way he knew how
To find himself in one. Well, all we said was
He took a strange thing to be roguish over.
Some sympathy was wasted on the house,
A good old-timer dating back along;   60
But a house isn't sentient; the house
Didn't feel anything. And if it did,
Why not regard it as a sacrifice,
And an old-fashioned sacrifice by fire,
Instead of a new-fashioned one at auction?   65

Out of a house and so out of a farm
At one stroke (of a match), Brad had to turn
To earn a living on the Concord railroad,
As under-ticket-agent at a station
Where his job, when he wasn't selling tickets,   70
Was setting out, up track and down, not plants
As on a farm, but planets, evening stars
That varied in their hue from red to green.

He got a good glass for six hundred dollars.
His new job gave him leisure for stargazing.   75
Often he bid me come and have a look

Up the brass barrel, velvet black inside,
At a star quaking in the other end.
I recollect a night of broken clouds
And underfoot snow melted down to ice,   80
And melting further in the wind to mud.
Bradford and I had out the telescope.
We spread our two legs as we spread its three,
Pointed our thoughts the way we pointed it,
And standing at our leisure till the day broke,   85
Said some of the best things we ever said.
That telescope was christened the Star-Splitter,
Because it didn't do a thing but split
A star in two or three, the way you split
A globule of quicksilver in your hand   90
With one stroke of your finger in the middle.
It's a star-splitter if there ever was one,
And ought to do some good if splitting stars
'Sa thing to be compared with splitting wood.

We've looked and looked, but after all where are we?   95
Do we know any better where we are,
And how it stands between the night tonight
And a man with a smoky lantern chimney?
How different from the way it ever stood?

MAPLE

Her teacher's certainty it must be Mabel
Made Maple first take notice of her name.
She asked her father and he told her, "Maple—
Maple is right."

        "But teacher told the school
There's no such name."

As fathers about children, you tell teacher.
You tell her that it's M–A–P–L–E.
You ask her if she knows a maple tree.
Well, you were named after a maple tree.
Your mother named you. You and she just saw   10
Each other in passing in the room upstairs,
One coming this way into life, and one
Going the other out of life—you know?
So you can't have much recollection of her.
She had been having a long look at you.   15
She put her finger in your cheek so hard
It must have made your dimple there, and said,
'Maple.' I said it too: 'Yes, for her name.'
She nodded. So we're sure there's no mistake.
I don't know what she wanted it to mean,   20
But it seems like some word she left to bid you
Be a good girl—be like a maple tree.
How like a maple tree's for us to guess.
Or for a little girl to guess sometime.
Not now—at least I shouldn't try too hard now.   25
By and by I will tell you all I know
About the different trees, and something, too,
About your mother that perhaps may help."
Dangerous self-arousing words to sow.
Luckily all she wanted of her name then   30
Was to rebuke her teacher with it next day,
And give the teacher a scare as from her father.
Anything further had been wasted on her,
Or so he tried to think to avoid blame.
She would forget it. She all but forgot it.   35
What he sowed with her slept so long a sleep,
And came so near death in the dark of years,

180

That when it woke and came to life again
The flower was different from the parent seed.
It came back vaguely at the glass one day,   40
As she stood saying her name over aloud,
Striking it gently across her lowered eyes
To make it go well with the way she looked.
What was it about her name? Its strangeness lay
In having too much meaning. Other names,   45
As Lesley, Carol, Irma, Marjorie,
Signified nothing. Rose could have a meaning,
But hadn't as it went. (She knew a Rose.)
This difference from other names it was
Made people notice it—and notice her.   50
(They either noticed it, or got it wrong.)
Her problem was to find out what it asked
In dress or manner of the girl who bore it.
If she could form some notion of her mother—
What she had thought was lovely, and what good.   55
This was her mother's childhood home;
The house one story high in front, three stories
On the end it presented to the road.
(The arrangement made a pleasant sunny cellar.)
Her mother's bedroom was her father's still,   60
Where she could watch her mother's picture fading.
Once she found for a bookmark in the Bible
A maple leaf she thought must have been laid
In wait for her there. She read every word
Of the two pages it was pressed between,   65
As if it was her mother speaking to her.
But forgot to put the leaf back in closing
And lost the place never to read again.
She was sure, though, there had been nothing in it.

So she looked for herself, as everyone 70
Looks for himself, more or less outwardly.
And her self-seeking, fitful though it was,
May still have been what led her on to read,
And think a little, and get some city schooling.
She learned shorthand, whatever shorthand may 75
Have had to do with it—she sometimes wondered.
So, till she found herself in a strange place
For the name Maple to have brought her to,
Taking dictation on a paper pad
And, in the pauses when she raised her eyes, 80
Watching out of a nineteenth story window
An airship laboring with unshiplike motion
And a vague all-disturbing roar above the river
Beyond the highest city built with hands.
Someone was saying in such natural tones 85
She almost wrote the words down on her knee,
"Do you know you remind me of a tree—
A maple tree?"

                    "Because my name is Maple?"

"Isn't it Mabel? I thought it was Mabel."

"No doubt you've heard the office call me Mabel. 90
I have to let them call me what they like."

They were both stirred that he should have divined
Without the name her personal mystery.
It made it seem as if there must be something
She must have missed herself. So they were married, 95
And took the fancy home with them to live by.

They went on pilgrimage once to her father's
(The house one story high in front, three stories
On the side it presented to the road)

To see if there was not some special tree   100
She might have overlooked. They could find none,
Not so much as a single tree for shade,
Let alone grove of trees for sugar orchard.
She told him of the bookmark maple leaf
In the big Bible, and all she remembered   105
Of the place marked with it—"Wave offering,
Something about wave offering, it said."

"You've never asked your father outright, have you?"

"I have, and been put off sometime, I think."
(This was her faded memory of the way   110
Once long ago her father had put himself off.)

"Because no telling but it may have been
Something between your father and your mother
Not meant for us at all."
                    "Not meant for me?
Where would the fairness be in giving me   115
A name to carry for life and never know
The secret of?"
                    "And then it may have been
Something a father couldn't tell a daughter
As well as could a mother. And again
It may have been their one lapse into fancy   120
'Twould be too bad to make him sorry for
By bringing it up to him when he was too old.
Your father feels us round him with our questing,
And holds us off unnecessarily,
As if he didn't know what little thing   125
Might lead us on to a discovery.
It was as personal as he could be
About the way he saw it was with you

To say your mother, had she lived, would be
As far again as from being born to bearing."   130

"Just one look more with what you say in mind,
And I give up"; which last look came to nothing.
But though they now gave up the search forever,
They clung to what one had seen in the other
By inspiration. It proved there was something.   135
They kept their thoughts away from when the maples
Stood uniform in buckets, and the steam
Of sap and snow rolled off the sugarhouse.
When they made her related to the maples,
It was the tree the autumn fire ran through   140
And swept of leathern leaves, but left the bark
Unscorched, unblackened, even, by any smoke.
They always took their holidays in autumn.
Once they came on a maple in a glade,
Standing alone with smooth arms lifted up,   145
And every leaf of foliage she'd worn
Laid scarlet and pale pink about her feet.
But its age kept them from considering this one.
Twenty-five years ago at Maple's naming
It hardly could have been a two-leaved seedling   150
The next cow might have licked up out at pasture.
Could it have been another maple like it?
They hovered for a moment near discovery,
Figurative enough to see the symbol,
But lacking faith in anything to mean   155
The same at different times to different people.
Perhaps a filial diffidence partly kept them
From thinking it could be a thing so bridal.
And anyway it came too late for Maple.
She used her hands to cover up her eyes.   160

"We would not see the secret if we could now:
We are not looking for it any more."

Thus had a name with meaning, given in death,
Made a girl's marriage, and ruled in her life.
No matter that the meaning was not clear.   165
A name with meaning could bring up a child,
Taking the child out of the parents' hands.
Better a meaningless name, I should say,
As leaving more to nature and happy chance.
Name children some names and see what you do.   170

THE AX-HELVE

I've known ere now an interfering branch
Of alder catch my lifted ax behind me.
But that was in the woods, to hold my hand
From striking at another alder's roots,
And that was, as I say, an alder branch.   5
This was a man, Baptiste, who stole one day
Behind me on the snow in my own yard
Where I was working at the chopping block,
And cutting nothing not cut down already.
He caught my ax expertly on the rise,   10
When all my strength put forth was in his favor,
Held it a moment where it was, to calm me,
Then took it from me—and I let him take it.
I didn't know him well enough to know
What it was all about. There might be something   15
He had in mind to say to a bad neighbor
He might prefer to say to him disarmed.
But all he had to tell me in French-English
Was what he thought of—not me, but my ax,

185

Me only as I took my ax to heart.   20
It was the bad ax-helve someone had sold me—
"Made on machine," he said, plowing the grain
With a thick thumbnail to show how it ran
Across the handle's long-drawn serpentine,
Like the two strokes across a dollar sign.   25
"You give her one good crack, she's snap raght off.
Den where's your hax-ead flying t'rough de hair?"
Admitted; and yet, what was that to him?

"Come on my house and I put you one in
What's las' awhile—good hick'ry what's grow crooked,   30
De second growt' I cut myself—tough, tough!"

Something to sell? That wasn't how it sounded.

"Den when you say you come? It's cost you nothing.
Tonaght?"

       As well tonight as any night.

Beyond an over-warmth of kitchen stove   35
My welcome differed from no other welcome.
Baptiste knew best why I was where I was.
So long as he would leave enough unsaid,
I shouldn't mind his being overjoyed
(If overjoyed he was) at having got me   40
Where I must judge if what he knew about an ax
That not everybody else knew was to count
For nothing in the measure of a neighbor.
Hard if, though cast away for life with Yankees,
A Frenchman couldn't get his human rating!   45

Mrs. Baptiste came in and rocked a chair
That had as many motions as the world:
One back and forward, in and out of shadow,

That got her nowhere; one more gradual,
Sideways, that would have run her on the stove   50
In time, had she not realized her danger
And caught herself up bodily, chair and all,
And set herself back where she started from.
"She ain't spick too much Henglish—dat's too bad."
I was afraid, in brightening first on me,   55
Then on Baptiste, as if she understood
What passed between us, she was only feigning.
Baptiste was anxious for her; but no more
Than for himself, so placed he couldn't hope
To keep his bargain of the morning with me   60
In time to keep me from suspecting him
Of really never having meant to keep it.

Needlessly soon he had his ax-helves out,
A quiverful to choose from, since he wished me
To have the best he had, or had to spare—   65
Not for me to ask which, when what he took
Had beauties he had to point me out at length
To insure their not being wasted on me.
He liked to have it slender as a whipstock,
Free from the least knot, equal to the strain   70
Of bending like a sword across the knee.
He showed me that the lines of a good helve
Were native to the grain before the knife
Expressed them, and its curves were no false curves
Put on it from without. And there its strength lay   75
For the hard work. He chafed its long white body
From end to end with his rough hand shut round it.
He tried it at the eyehole in the ax-head.
"Hahn, hahn," he mused, "don't need much taking down."
Baptiste knew how to make a short job long   80

187

For love of it, and yet not waste time either.

Do you know, what we talked about was knowledge?
Baptiste on his defense about the children
He kept from school, or did his best to keep—
Whatever school and children and our doubts   85
Of laid-on education had to do
With the curves of his ax-helves and his having
Used these unscrupulously to bring me
To see for once the inside of his house.
Was I desired in friendship, partly as someone   90
To leave it to, whether the right to hold
Such doubts of education should depend
Upon the education of those who held them?

But now he brushed the shavings from his knee
And stood the ax there on its horse's hoof,   95
Erect, but not without its waves, as when
The snake stood up for evil in the Garden—
Top-heavy with a heaviness his short,
Thick hand made light of, steel-blue chin drawn down
And in a little—a French touch in that.   100
Baptiste drew back and squinted at it, pleased:
"See how she's cock her head!"

THE GRINDSTONE

Having a wheel and four legs of its own
Has never availed the cumbersome grindstone
To get it anywhere that I can see.
These hands have helped it go, and even race;
Not all the motion, though, they ever lent,   5
Not all the miles it may have thought it went,

Have got it one step from the starting place.
It stands beside the same old apple tree.
The shadow of the apple tree is thin
Upon it now; its feet are fast in snow.   10
All other farm machinery's gone in,
And some of it on no more legs and wheel
Than the grindstone can boast to stand or go.
(I'm thinking chiefly of the wheelbarrow.)
For months it hasn't known the taste of steel   15
Washed down with rusty water in a tin.
But standing outdoors hungry, in the cold,
Except in towns at night, is not a sin.
And, anyway, its standing in the yard
Under a ruinous live apple tree   20
Has nothing any more to do with me,
Except that I remember how of old
One summer day, all day I drove it hard,
And someone mounted on it rode it hard,
And he and I between us ground a blade.   25

I gave it the preliminary spin,
And poured on water (tears it might have been);
And when it almost gaily jumped and flowed,
A Father-Time-like man got on and rode,
Armed with a scythe and spectacles that glowed.   30
He turned on willpower to increase the load
And slow me down—and I abruptly slowed,
Like coming to a sudden railroad station.
I changed from hand to hand in desperation.
I wondered what machine of ages gone   35
This represented an improvement on.
For all I knew it may have sharpened spears
And arrowheads itself. Much use for years

189

Had gradually worn it an oblate
Spheroid that kicked and struggled in its gait, 40
Appearing to return me hate for hate
(But I forgive it now as easily
As any other boyhood enemy
Whose pride has failed to get him anywhere).
I wondered who it was the man thought ground— 45
The one who held the wheel back or the one
Who gave his life to keep it going round?
I wondered if he really thought it fair
For him to have the say when we were done.
Such were the bitter thoughts to which I turned. 50

Not for myself was I so much concerned.
Oh no!—although, of course, I could have found
A better way to pass the afternoon
Than grinding discord out of a grindstone,
And beating insects at their gritty tune. 55
Nor was I for the man so much concerned.
Once when the grindstone almost jumped its bearing
It looked as if he might be badly thrown
And wounded on his blade. So far from caring,
I laughed inside, and only cranked the faster 60
(It ran as if it wasn't greased but glued);
I'd welcome any moderate disaster
That might be calculated to postpone
What evidently nothing could conclude.
The thing that made me more and more afraid 65
Was that we'd ground it sharp and hadn't known,
And now were only wasting precious blade.
And when he raised it dripping once and tried
The creepy edge of it with wary touch,
And viewed it over his glasses funny-eyed, 70

190

Only disinterestedly to decide
It needed a turn more, I could have cried
Wasn't there danger of a turn too much?
Mightn't we make it worse instead of better?
I was for leaving something to the whetter.   75
What if it wasn't all it should be? I'd
Be satisfied if he'd be satisfied.

PAUL'S WIFE

To drive Paul out of any lumber camp
All that was needed was to say to him,
"How is the wife, Paul?"—and he'd disappear.
Some said it was because he had no wife,
And hated to be twitted on the subject;   5
Others because he'd come within a day
Or so of having one, and then been jilted;
Others because he'd had one once, a good one,
Who'd run away with someone else and left him;
And others still because he had one now   10
He only had to be reminded of—
He was all duty to her in a minute:
He had to run right off to look her up,
As if to say, "That's so, how is my wife?
I hope she isn't getting into mischief."   15
No one was anxious to get rid of Paul.
He'd been the hero of the mountain camps
Ever since, just to show them, he had slipped
The bark of a whole tamarack off whole,
As clean as boys do off a willow twig   20
To make a willow whistle on a Sunday
In April by subsiding meadow brooks.
They seemed to ask him just to see him go,

"How is the wife, Paul?" and he always went.
He never stopped to murder anyone   25
Who asked the question. He just disappeared—
Nobody knew in what direction,
Although it wasn't usually long
Before they heard of him in some new camp,
The same Paul at the same old feats of logging.   30
The question everywhere was why should Paul
Object to being asked a civil question—
A man you could say almost anything to
Short of a fighting word. You have the answers.
And there was one more not so fair to Paul: 35
That Paul had married a wife not his equal.
Paul was ashamed of her. To match a hero
She would have had to be a heroine;
Instead of which she was some half-breed squaw.
But if the story Murphy told was true,   40
She wasn't anything to be ashamed of.

You know Paul could do wonders. Everyone's
Heard how he thrashed the horses on a load
That wouldn't budge, until they simply stretched
Their rawhide harness from the load to camp.   45
Paul told the boss the load would be all right,
"The sun will bring your load in"—and it did—
By shrinking the rawhide to natural length.
That's what is called a stretcher. But I guess
The one about his jumping so's to land   50
With both his feet at once against the ceiling,
And then land safely right side up again,
Back on the floor, is fact or pretty near fact.
Well, this is such a yarn. Paul sawed his wife
Out of a white-pine log. Murphy was there   55

And, as you might say, saw the lady born.
Paul worked at anything in lumbering.
He'd been hard at it taking boards away
For—I forget—the last ambitious sawyer
To want to find out if he couldn't pile   60
The lumber on Paul till Paul begged for mercy.
They'd sliced the first slab off a big butt log,
And the sawyer had slammed the carriage back
To slam end-on again against the saw teeth.
To judge them by the way they caught themselves   65
When they saw what had happened to the log,
They must have had a guilty expectation
Something was going to go with their slambanging.
Something had left a broad black streak of grease
On the new wood the whole length of the log   70
Except, perhaps, a foot at either end.
But when Paul put his finger in the grease,
It wasn't grease at all, but a long slot.
The log was hollow. They were sawing pine.
"First time I ever saw a hollow pine.   75
That comes of having Paul around the place.
Take it to hell for me," the sawyer said.
Everyone had to have a look at it,
And tell Paul what he ought to do about it.
(They treated it as his.) "You take a jackknife, 80
And spread the opening, and you've got a dugout
All dug to go a-fishing in." To Paul
The hollow looked too sound and clean and empty
Ever to have housed birds or beasts or bees.
There was no entrance for them to get in by.   85
It looked to him like some new kind of hollow
He thought he'd *better* take his jackknife to.

So after work that evening he came back
And let enough light into it by cutting
To see if it was empty. He made out in there   90
A slender length of pith, or was it pith?
It might have been the skin a snake had cast
And left stood up on end inside the tree
The hundred years the tree must have been growing.
More cutting and he had this in both hands,   95
And looking from it to the pond nearby,
Paul wondered how it would respond to water.
Not a breeze stirred, but just the breath of air
He made in walking slowly to the beach
Blew it once off his hands and almost broke it.   100
He laid it at the edge, where it could drink.
At the first drink it rustled and grew limp.
At the next drink it grew invisible.
Paul dragged the shallows for it with his fingers,
And thought it must have melted. It was gone.   105
And then beyond the open water, dim with midges,
Where the log drive lay pressed against the boom,
It slowly rose a person, rose a girl,
Her wet hair heavy on her like a helmet,
Who, leaning on a log, looked back at Paul.   110
And that made Paul in turn look back
To see if it was anyone behind him
That she was looking at instead of him.
(Murphy had been there watching all the time,
But from a shed where neither of them could see him.) 115
There was a moment of suspense in birth
When the girl seemed too waterlogged to live,
Before she caught her first breath with a gasp
And laughed. Then she climbed slowly to her feet,

And walked off, talking to herself or Paul,   120
Across the logs like backs of alligators,
Paul taking after her around the pond.

Next evening Murphy and some other fellows
Got drunk, and tracked the pair up Catamount,
From the bare top of which there is a view   125
To other hills across a kettle valley.
And there, well after dark, let Murphy tell it,
They saw Paul and his creature keeping house.
It was the only glimpse that anyone
Has had of Paul and her since Murphy saw them   130
Falling in love across the twilight millpond.
More than a mile across the wilderness
They sat together halfway up a cliff
In a small niche let into it, the girl
Brightly, as if a star played on the place,   135
Paul darkly, like her shadow. All the light
Was from the girl herself, though, not from a star,
As was apparent from what happened next.
All those great ruffians put their throats together,
And let out a loud yell, and threw a bottle,   140
As a brute tribute of respect to beauty.
Of course the bottle fell short by a mile,
But the shout reached the girl and put her light out.
She went out like a firefly, and that was all.

So there were witnesses that Paul was married,   145
And not to anyone to be ashamed of.
Everyone had been wrong in judging Paul.
Murphy told me Paul put on all those airs
About his wife to keep her to himself.
Paul was what's called a terrible possessor.   150

Owning a wife with him meant owning her.
She wasn't anybody else's business,
Either to praise her or so much as name her,
And he'd thank people not to think of her.
Murphy's idea was that a man like Paul   155
Wouldn't be spoken to about a wife
In any way the world knew how to speak.

WILD GRAPES

What tree may not the fig be gathered from?
The grape may not be gathered from the birch?
It's all you know the grape, or know the birch.
As a girl gathered from the birch myself
Equally with my weight in grapes, one autumn,   5
I ought to know what tree the grape is fruit of.
I was born, I suppose, like anyone,
And grew to be a little boyish girl
My brother could not always leave at home.
But that beginning was wiped out in fear   10
The day I swung suspended with the grapes,
And was come after like Eurydice
And brought down safely from the upper regions;
And the life I live now's an extra life
I can waste as I please on whom I please.   15
So if you see me celebrate two birthdays,
And give myself out as two different ages,
One of them five years younger than I look—

One day my brother led me to a glade
Where a white birch he knew of stood alone,   20
Wearing a thin headdress of pointed leaves,
And heavy on her heavy hair behind,

Against her neck, an ornament of grapes.
Grapes, I knew grapes from having seen them last year.
One bunch of them, and there began to be   25
Bunches all round me growing in white birches,
The way they grew round Leif the Lucky's German;
Mostly as much beyond my lifted hands, though,
As the moon used to seem when I was younger,
And only freely to be had for climbing.   30
My brother did the climbing; and at first
Threw me down grapes to miss and scatter
And have to hunt for in sweet fern and hardhack;
Which gave him some time to himself to eat,
But not so much, perhaps, as a boy needed.   35
So then, to make me wholly self-supporting,
He climbed still higher and bent the tree to earth
And put it in my hands to pick my own grapes.
"Here, take a treetop, I'll get down another.
Hold on with all your might when I let go."   40
I said I had the tree. It wasn't true.
The opposite was true. The tree had me.
The minute it was left with me alone,
It caught me up as if I were the fish
And it the fishpole. So I was translated,   45
To loud cries from my brother of "Let go!
Don't you know anything, you girl? Let go!"
But I, with something of the baby grip
Acquired ancestrally in just such trees
When wilder mothers than our wildest now   50
Hung babies out on branches by the hands
To dry or wash or tan, I don't know which
(You'll have to ask an evolutionist)—
I held on uncomplainingly for life.
My brother tried to make me laugh to help me.   55

197

"What are you doing up there in those grapes?
Don't be afraid. A few of them won't hurt you.
I mean, they won't pick you if you don't them."
Much danger of my picking anything!
By that time I was pretty well reduced   60
To a philosophy of hang-and-let-hang.
"Now you know how it feels," my brother said,
"To be a bunch of fox grapes, as they call them,
That when it thinks it has escaped the fox
By growing where it shouldn't—on a birch,   65
Where a fox wouldn't think to look for it—
And if he looked and found it, couldn't reach it—
Just then come you and I to gather it.
Only you have the advantage of the grapes
In one way: you have one more stem to cling by,   70
And promise more resistance to the picker."

One by one I lost off my hat and shoes,
And still I clung. I let my head fall back,
And shut my eyes against the sun, my ears
Against my brother's nonsense. "Drop," he said,   75
"I'll catch you in my arms. It isn't far."
(Stated in lengths of him it might not be.)
"Drop or I'll shake the tree and shake you down."
Grim silence on my part as I sank lower,
My small wrists stretching till they showed the banjo strings.
"Why, if she isn't serious about it!
Hold tight awhile till I think what to do.
I'll bend the tree down and let you down by it."
I don't know much about the letting down;
But once I felt ground with my stocking feet   85
And the world came revolving back to me,
I know I looked long at my curled-up fingers,

Before I straightened them and brushed the bark off.
My brother said: "Don't you weigh anything?
Try to weigh something next time, so you won't   90
Be run off with by birch trees into space."

It wasn't my not weighing anything
So much as my not knowing anything—
My brother had been nearer right before.
I had not taken the first step in knowledge;   95
I had not learned to let go with the hands,
As still I have not learned to with the heart,
And have no wish to with the heart—nor need,
That I can see. The mind—is not the heart.
I may yet live, as I know others live,   100
To wish in vain to let go with the mind—
Of cares, at night, to sleep; but nothing tells me
That I need learn to let go with the heart.

PLACE FOR A THIRD

Nothing to say to all those marriages!
She had made three herself to three of his.
The score was even for them, three to three.
But come to die she found she cared so much:
She thought of children in a burial row;   5
Three children in a burial row were sad.
One man's three women in a burial row
Somehow made her impatient with the man.
And so she said to Laban, "You have done
A good deal right; don't do the last thing wrong.   10
Don't make me lie with those two other women."

Laban said, No, he would not make her lie

199

With anyone but that she had a mind to,
If that was how she felt, of course, he said.
She went her way. But Laban having caught   15
This glimpse of lingering person in Eliza,
And anxious to make all he could of it
With something he remembered in himself,
Tried to think how he could exceed his promise,
And give good measure to the dead, though thankless.   20
If that was how she felt, he kept repeating.
His first thought under pressure was a grave
In a new-boughten grave plot by herself,
Under he didn't care how great a stone:
He'd sell a yoke of steers to pay for it.   25
And weren't there special cemetery flowers,
That, once grief sets to growing, grief may rest:
The flowers will go on with grief awhile,
And no one seem neglecting or neglected?
A prudent grief will not despise such aids.   30
He thought of evergreen and everlasting.
And then he had a thought worth many of these.
Somewhere must be the grave of the young boy
Who married her for playmate more than helpmate,
And sometimes laughed at what it was between them.   35
How would she like to sleep her last with him?
Where was his grave? Did Laban know his name?

He found the grave a town or two away,
The headstone cut with *John, Beloved Husband*,
Beside it room reserved; the say a sister's,   40
A never-married sister's of that husband,
Whether Eliza would be welcome there.
The dead was bound to silence: ask the sister.
So Laban saw the sister, and, saying nothing

Of where Eliza wanted *not* to lie,   45
And who had thought to lay her with her first love,
Begged simply for the grave. The sister's face
Fell all in wrinkles of responsibility.
She wanted to do right. She'd have to think.
Laban was old and poor, yet seemed to care;   50
And she was old and poor—but she cared, too.
They sat. She cast one dull, old look at him,
Then turned him out to go on other errands
She said he might attend to in the village,
While she made up her mind how much she cared—   55
And how much Laban cared—and why he cared.
(She made shrewd eyes to see where he came in.)

She'd looked Eliza up her second time,
A widow at her second husband's grave,
And offered her a home to rest awhile   60
Before she went the poor man's widow's way,
Housekeeping for the next man out of wedlock.
She and Eliza had been friends through all.
Who was she to judge marriage in a world
Whose Bible's so confused in marriage counsel?   65
The sister had not come across this Laban;
A decent product of life's ironing-out;
She must not keep him waiting. Time would press
Between the death day and the funeral day.
So when she saw him coming in the street   70
She hurried her decision to be ready
To meet him with his answer at the door.
Laban had known about what it would be
From the way she had set her poor old mouth,
To do, as she had put it, what was right.   75

She gave it through the screen door closed between them:

"No, not with John. There wouldn't be no sense.
Eliza's had too many other men."

Laban was forced to fall back on his plan
To buy Eliza a plot to lie alone in: 80
Which gives him for himself a choice of lots
When his time comes to die and settle down.

TWO WITCHES

I. THE WITCH OF COÖS

I stayed the night for shelter at a farm
Behind the mountain, with a mother and son,
Two old-believers. They did all the talking.

MOTHER.   Folks think a witch who has familiar spirits
She could call up to pass a winter evening,   5
But won't, should be burned at the stake or something.
Summoning spirits isn't "Button, button,
Who's got the button," I would have them know.

SON.   Mother can make a common table rear
And kick with two legs like an army mule.   10

MOTHER.   And when I've done it, what good have I done?
Rather than tip a table for you, let me
Tell you what Ralle the Sioux Control once told me.
He said the dead had souls, but when I asked him
How could that be—I thought the dead were souls—   15
He broke my trance. Don't that make you suspicious
That there's something the dead are keeping back?
Yes, there's something the dead are keeping back.

SON.   You wouldn't want to tell him what we have
Up attic, mother?

MOTHER.   Bones—a skeleton.   20

SON.   But the headboard of mother's bed is pushed
Against the attic door: the door is nailed.
It's harmless. Mother hears it in the night,
Halting perplexed behind the barrier
Of door and headboard. Where it wants to get   25
Is back into the cellar where it came from.

MOTHER.   We'll never let them, will we, son? We'll never!

SON.   It left the cellar forty years ago
And carried itself like a pile of dishes
Up one flight from the cellar to the kitchen,   30
Another from the kitchen to the bedroom,
Another from the bedroom to the attic,
Right past both father and mother, and neither stopped it.
Father had gone upstairs; mother was downstairs.
I was a baby: I don't know where I was.   35

MOTHER.   The only fault my husband found with me—
I went to sleep before I went to bed,
Especially in winter when the bed
Might just as well be ice and the clothes snow.
The night the bones came up the cellar stairs   40
Toffile had gone to bed alone and left me,
But left an open door to cool the room off
So as to sort of turn me out of it.
I was just coming to myself enough
To wonder where the cold was coming from,   45
When I heard Toffile upstairs in the bedroom
And thought I heard him downstairs in the cellar.

The board we had laid down to walk dry-shod on
When there was water in the cellar in spring
Struck the hard cellar bottom. And then someone   50
Began the stairs, two footsteps for each step,
The way a man with one leg and a crutch,
Or a little child, comes up. It wasn't Toffile:
It wasn't anyone who could be there.
The bulkhead double doors were double-locked   55
And swollen tight and buried under snow.
The cellar windows were banked up with sawdust
And swollen tight and buried under snow.
It was the bones. I knew them—and good reason.
My first impulse was to get to the knob   60
And hold the door. But the bones didn't try
The door; they halted helpless on the landing,
Waiting for things to happen in their favor.
The faintest restless rustling ran all through them.
I never could have done the thing I did   65
If the wish hadn't been too strong in me
To see how they were mounted for this walk.
I had a vision of them put together
Not like a man, but like a chandelier.
So suddenly I flung the door wide on him.   70
A moment he stood balancing with emotion,
And all but lost himself. (A tongue of fire
Flashed out and licked along his upper teeth.
Smoke rolled inside the sockets of his eyes.)
Then he came at me with one hand outstretched,   75
The way he did in life once; but this time
I struck the hand off brittle on the floor,
And fell back from him on the floor myself.
The finger-pieces slid in all directions.

(Where did I see one of those pieces lately?   80
Hand me my button box—it must be there.)
I sat up on the floor and shouted, "Toffile,
It's coming up to you." It had its choice
Of the door to the cellar or the hall.
It took the hall door for the novelty,   85
And set off briskly for so slow a thing,
Still going every which way in the joints, though,
So that it looked like lightning or a scribble,
From the slap I had just now given its hand.
I listened till it almost climbed the stairs   90
From the hall to the only finished bedroom,
Before I got up to do anything;
Then ran and shouted, "Shut the bedroom door,
Toffile, for my sake!" "Company?" he said,
"Don't make me get up; I'm too warm in bed."   95
So lying forward weakly on the handrail
I pushed myself upstairs, and in the light
(The kitchen had been dark) I had to own
I could see nothing. "Toffile, I don't see it.
It's with us in the room, though. It's the bones."   100
"What bones?" "The cellar bones—out of the grave."
That made him throw his bare legs out of bed
And sit up by me and take hold of me.
I wanted to put out the light and see
If I could see it, or else mow the room,   105
With our arms at the level of our knees,
And bring the chalk-pile down. "I'll tell you what—
It's looking for another door to try.
The uncommonly deep snow has made him think
Of his old song, 'The Wild Colonial Boy,'   110
He always used to sing along the tote road.
He's after an open door to get outdoors.

205

Let's trap him with an open door up attic."
Toffile agreed to that, and sure enough,
Almost the moment he was given an opening,   115
The steps began to climb the attic stairs.
I heard them. Toffile didn't seem to hear them.
"Quick!" I slammed to the door and held the knob.
"Toffile, get nails." I made him nail the door shut
And push the headboard of the bed against it.   120
Then we asked was there anything
Up attic that we'd ever want again.
The attic was less to us than the cellar.
If the bones liked the attic, let them have it.
Let them stay in the attic. When they sometimes   125
Come down the stairs at night and stand perplexed
Behind the door and headboard of the bed,
Brushing their chalky skull with chalky fingers,
With sounds like the dry rattling of a shutter,
That's what I sit up in the dark to say—   130
To no one anymore since Toffile died.
Let them stay in the attic since they went there.
I promised Toffile to be cruel to them
For helping them be cruel once to him.

SON.   We think they had a grave down in the cellar.   135

MOTHER.   We know they had a grave down in the cellar.

SON.   We never could find out whose bones they were.

MOTHER.   Yes, we could too, son. Tell the truth for once.
They were a man's his father killed for me.
I mean a man he killed instead of me.   140
The least I could do was help dig their grave.
We were about it one night in the cellar.
Son knows the story: but 'twas not for him

206

To tell the truth, suppose the time had come.
Son looks surprised to see me end a lie   145
We'd kept up all these years between ourselves
So as to have it ready for outsiders.
But tonight I don't care enough to lie—
I don't remember why I ever cared.
Toffile, if he were here, I don't believe   150
Could tell you why he ever cared himself. . . .

She hadn't found the finger-bone she wanted
Among the buttons poured out in her lap.
I verified the name next morning: Toffile.
The rural letter box said Toffile Lajway.   155

II.   THE PAUPER WITCH OF GRAFTON

Now that they've got it settled whose I be,
I'm going to tell them something they won't like:
They've got it settled wrong, and I can prove it.
Flattered I must be to have two towns fighting
To make a present of me to each other.   5
They don't dispose me, either one of them,
To spare them any trouble. Double trouble's
Always the witch's motto anyway.
I'll double theirs for both of them—you watch me.
They'll find they've got the whole thing to do over,   10
That is, if facts is what they want to go by.
They set a lot (now don't they?) by a record
Of Arthur Amy's having once been up
For Hog Reeve in March Meeting here in Warren.
I could have told them any time this twelvemonth   15
The Arthur Amy I was married to
Couldn't have been the one they say was up

207

In Warren at March Meeting, for the reason
He wa'n't but fifteen at the time they say.
The Arthur Amy I was married to   20
Voted the only times he ever voted,
Which wasn't many, in the town of Wentworth.
One of the times was when 'twas in the warrant
To see if the town wanted to take over
The tote road to our clearing where we lived.   25
I'll tell you who'd remember—Heman Lapish.
Their Arthur Amy was the father of mine.
So now they've dragged it through the law courts once,
I guess they'd better drag it through again.
Wentworth and Warren's both good towns to live in,   30
Only I happen to prefer to live
In Wentworth from now on; and when all's said,
Right's right, and the temptation to do right
When I can hurt someone by doing it
Has always been too much for me, it has.   35
I know of some folks that'd be set up
At having in their town a noted witch:
But most would have to think of the expense
That even I would be. They ought to know
That as a witch I'd often milk a bat   40
And that'd be enough to last for days.
It'd make my position stronger, think,
If I was to consent to give some sign
To make it surer that I was a witch?
It wa'n't no sign, I s'pose, when Mallice Huse   45
Said that I took him out in his old age
And rode all over everything on him
Until I'd had him worn to skin and bones,
And if I'd left him hitched unblanketed
In front of one Town Hall, I'd left him hitched   50

208

In front of every one in Grafton County.
Some cried shame on me not to blanket him,
The poor old man. It would have been all right
If someone hadn't said to gnaw the posts
He stood beside and leave his trademark on them,   55
So they could recognize them. Not a post
That they could hear tell of was scarified.
They made him keep on gnawing till he whined.
Then that same smarty someone said to look—
He'd bet Huse was a cribber and had gnawed   60
The crib he slept in—and as sure's you're born
They found he'd gnawed the four posts of his bed,
All four of them to splinters. What did that prove?
Not that he hadn't gnawed the hitching posts
He said he had, besides. Because a horse   65
Gnaws in the stable ain't no proof to me
He don't gnaw trees and posts and fences too.
But everybody took it for a proof.
I was a strapping girl of twenty then.
The smarty someone who spoiled everything   70
Was Arthur Amy. You know who he was.
That was the way he started courting me.
He never said much after we were married,
But I mistrusted he was none too proud
Of having interfered in the Huse business.   75
I guess he found he got more out of me
By having me a witch. Or something happened
To turn him round. He got to saying things
To undo what he'd done and make it right,
Like, "No, she ain't come back from kiting yet.   80
Last night was one of her nights out. She's kiting.
She thinks when the wind makes a night of it
She might as well herself." But he liked best

To let on he was plagued to death with me:
If anyone had seen me coming home   85
Over the ridgepole, 'stride of a broomstick,
As often as he had in the tail of the night,
He guessed they'd know what he had to put up with.
Well, I showed Arthur Amy signs enough
Off from the house as far as we could keep   90
And from barn smells you can't wash out of plowed ground
With all the rain and snow of seven years;
And I don't mean just skulls of Rogers' Rangers
On Moosilauke, but woman signs to man,
Only bewitched so I would last him longer.   95
Up where the trees grow short, the mosses tall,
I made him gather me wet snowberries
On slippery rocks beside a waterfall.
I made him do it for me in the dark.
And he liked everything I made him do.   100
I hope if he is where he sees me now
He's so far off he can't see what I've come to.
You *can* come down from everything to nothing.
All is, if I'd a-known when I was young
And full of it, that this would be the end,   105
It doesn't seem as if I'd had the courage
To make so free and kick up in folks' faces.
I might have, but it doesn't seem as if.

AN EMPTY THREAT

I stay;
But it isn't as if
There wasn't always Hudson's Bay
And the fur trade,

210

A small skiff   5
And a paddle blade.

I can just see my tent pegged,
And me on the floor,
Cross-legged,
And a trapper looking in at the door   10
With furs to sell.

His name's Joe,
Alias John,
And between what he doesn't know
And won't tell   15
About where Henry Hudson's gone,
I can't say he's much help;
But we get on.

The seal yelp
On an ice cake.   20
It's not men by some mistake?

No,
There's not a soul
For a windbreak
Between me and the North Pole—   25

Except always John-Joe,
My French Indian Esquimaux,
And he's off setting traps—
In one himself perhaps.

Give a headshake   30
Over so much bay
Thrown away
In snow and mist
That doesn't exist,

211

I was going to say,   35
For God, man, or beast's sake,
Yet does perhaps for all three.

Don't ask Joe
What it is to him.
It's sometimes dim   40
What it is to me,
Unless it be
It's the old captain's dark fate
Who failed to find or force a strait
In its two-thousand-mile coast;   45
And his crew left him where he failed,
And nothing came of all he sailed.

It's to say, "You and I—"
To such a ghost—
"You and I   50
Off here
With the dead race of the Great Auk!"
And, "Better defeat almost,
If seen clear,
Than life's victories of doubt   55
That need endless talk-talk
To make them out."

A FOUNTAIN, A BOTTLE,
A DONKEY'S EARS, AND SOME BOOKS

Old Davis owned a solid mica mountain
In Dalton that would someday make his fortune.
There'd been some Boston people out to see it:
And experts said that deep down in the mountain

212

The mica sheets were big as plate-glass windows.   5
He'd like to take me there and show it to me.

"I'll tell you what you show me. You remember
You said you knew the place where once, on Kinsman,
The early Mormons made a settlement
And built a stone baptismal font outdoors—   10
But Smith, or someone, called them off the mountain
To go West to a worse fight with the desert.
You said you'd seen the stone baptismal font.
Well, take me there."
                              "Someday I will."
                                        "Today."

"Huh, that old bathtub, what is that to see?   15
Let's talk about it."
                         "Let's go see the place."

"To shut you up I'll tell you what I'll do:
I'll find that fountain if it takes all summer,
And both of our united strengths, to do it."

"You've lost it, then?"
                              "Not so but I can find it.   20
No doubt it's grown up some to woods around it.
The mountain may have shifted since I saw it
In eighty-five."
                     "As long ago as that?"

"If I remember rightly, it had sprung
A leak and emptied then. And forty years   25
Can do a good deal to bad masonry.
You won't see any Mormon swimming in it.
But you have said it, and we're off to find it.

Old as I am, I'm going to let myself
Be dragged by you all over everywhere———" 30

"I thought you were a guide."

       "I *am* a guide,
And that's why I can't decently refuse you."

We made a day of it out of the world,
Ascending to descend to reascend.
The old man seriously took his bearings, 35
And spoke his doubts in every open place.

We came out on a look-off where we faced
A cliff, and on the cliff a bottle painted,
Or stained by vegetation from above,
A likeness to surprise the thrilly tourist. 40

"Well, if I haven't brought you to the fountain,
At least I've brought you to the famous Bottle."

"I won't accept the substitute. It's empty."

"So's everything."

      "I want my fountain."

"I guess you'd find the fountain just as empty. 45
And anyway this tells me where I am."

"Hadn't you long suspected where you were?"

"You mean miles from that Mormon settlement?
Look here, you treat your guide with due respect
If you don't want to spend the night outdoors. 50
I vow we must be near the place from where
The two converging slides, the avalanches,
On Marshall, look like donkey's ears.
We may as well see that and save the day."

214

"Don't donkey's ears suggest we shake our own?"   55

"For God's sake, aren't you fond of viewing nature?
You don't like nature. All you like is books.
What signify a donkey's ears and bottle,
However natural? Give you your books!
Well then, right here is where I show you books.   60
Come straight down off this mountain just as fast
As we can fall and keep a-bouncing on our feet.
It's hell for knees unless done hell-for-leather."

Be ready, I thought, for almost anything.

We struck a road I didn't recognize,   65
But welcomed for the chance to lave my shoes
In dust once more. We followed this a mile,
Perhaps, to where it ended at a house
I didn't know was there. It was the kind
To bring me to for broad-board paneling.   70
I never saw so good a house deserted.

"Excuse me if I ask you in a window
That happens to be broken," Davis said.
"The outside doors as yet have held against us.
I want to introduce you to the people   75
Who used to live here. They were Robinsons.
You must have heard of Clara Robinson,
The poetess who wrote the book of verses
And had it published. It was all about
The posies on her inner windowsill,   80
And the birds on her outer windowsill,
And how she tended both, or had them tended:
She never tended anything herself.
She was 'shut in' for life. She lived her whole
Life long in bed, and wrote her things in bed.   85

215

I'll show you how she had her sills extended
To entertain the birds and hold the flowers.
Our business first's up attic with her books."

We trod uncomfortably on crunching glass
Through a house stripped of everything   90
Except, it seemed, the poetess's poems.
Books, I should say!—if books are what is needed.
A whole edition in a packing case
That, overflowing like a horn of plenty,
Or like the poetess's heart of love,   95
Had spilled them near the window, toward the light,
Where driven rain had wet and swollen them.
Enough to stock a village library—
Unfortunately all of one kind, though.
They had been brought home from some publisher   100
And taken thus into the family.
Boys and bad hunters had known what to do
With stone and lead to unprotected glass:
Shatter it inward on the unswept floors.
How had the tender verse escaped their outrage?   105
By being invisible for what it was,
Or else by some remoteness that defied them
To find out what to do to hurt a poem.
Yet oh! the tempting flatness of a book,
To send it sailing out the attic window   110
Till it caught wind and, opening out its covers,
Tried to improve on sailing like a tile
By flying like a bird (silent in flight,
But all the burden of its body song),
Only to tumble like a stricken bird,   115
And lie in stones and bushes unretrieved.
Books were not thrown irreverently about.

216

They simply lay where someone now and then,
Having tried one, had dropped it at his feet
And left it lying where it fell rejected.   120
Here were all those the poetess's life
Had been too short to sell or give away.

"Take one," Old Davis bade me graciously.

"Why not take two or three?"

                              "Take all you want.
Good-looking books like that." He picked one fresh   125
In virgin wrapper from deep in the box,
And stroked it with a horny-handed kindness.
He read in one and I read in another,
Both either looking for or finding something.

The attic wasps went missing by like bullets.   130

I was soon satisfied for the time being.

All the way home I kept remembering
The small book in my pocket. It was there.
The poetess had sighed, I knew, in heaven
At having eased her heart of one more copy—   135
Legitimately. My demand upon her,
Though slight, was a demand. She felt the tug.
In time she would be rid of all her books.

I WILL SING YOU ONE-O

It was long I lay
Awake that night
Wishing the tower
Would name the hour
And tell me whether   5

To call it day
(Though not yet light)
And give up sleep.
The snow fell deep
With the hiss of spray;   10
Two winds would meet,
One down one street,
One down another,
And fight in a smother
Of dust and feather.   15
I could not say,
But feared the cold
Had checked the pace
Of the tower clock
By tying together   20
Its hands of gold
Before its face.

Then came one knock!
A note unruffled
Of earthly weather,   25
Though strange and muffled.
The tower said, "One!"
And then a steeple.
They spoke to themselves
And such few people   30
As winds might rouse
From sleeping warm
(But not unhouse).
They left the storm
That struck en masse   35
My window glass
Like a beaded fur.

In that grave One
They spoke of the sun
And moon and stars,   40
Saturn and Mars
And Jupiter.
Still more unfettered,
They left the named
And spoke of the lettered,   45
The sigmas and taus
Of constellations.
They filled their throats
With the furthest bodies
To which man sends his   50
Speculation,
Beyond which God is;
The cosmic motes
Of yawning lenses.
Their solemn peals   55
Were not their own:
They spoke for the clock
With whose vast wheels
Theirs interlock.
In that grave word   60
Uttered alone
The utmost star
Trembled and stirred,
Though set so far
Its whirling frenzies   65
Appear like standing
In one self station.
It has not ranged,
And save for the wonder
Of once expanding   70

To be a nova,
It has not changed
To the eye of man
On planets over,
Around, and under
It in creation
Since man began
To drag down man
And nation nation.

FRAGMENTARY BLUE

Why make so much of fragmentary blue
In here and there a bird, or butterfly,
Or flower, or wearing-stone, or open eye,
When heaven presents in sheets the solid hue?

Since earth is earth, perhaps, not heaven (as yet)— 5
Though some savants make earth include the sky;
And blue so far above us comes so high,
It only gives our wish for blue a whet.

FIRE AND ICE

Some say the world will end in fire,
Some say in ice.
From what I've tasted of desire
I hold with those who favor fire.
But if it had to perish twice, 5
I think I know enough of hate
To say that for destruction ice
Is also great
And would suffice.

IN A DISUSED GRAVEYARD

The living come with grassy tread
To read the gravestones on the hill;
The graveyard draws the living still,
But never anymore the dead.

The verses in it say and say: 5
"The ones who living come today
To read the stones and go away
Tomorrow dead will come to stay."

So sure of death the marbles rhyme,
Yet can't help marking all the time   10
How no one dead will seem to come.
What is it men are shrinking from?

It would be easy to be clever
And tell the stones: Men hate to die
And have stopped dying now forever.   15
I think they would believe the lie.

DUST OF SNOW

The way a crow
Shook down on me
The dust of snow
From a hemlock tree

Has given my heart   5
A change of mood
And saved some part
Of a day I had rued.

TO E.T.

I slumbered with your poems on my breast,
Spread open as I dropped them half-read through
Like dove wings on a figure on a tomb,
To see if in a dream they brought of you

I might not have the chance I missed in life   5
Through some delay, and call you to your face
First soldier, and then poet, and then both,
Who died a soldier-poet of your race.

I meant, you meant, that nothing should remain
Unsaid between us, brother, and this remained—   10
And one thing more that was not then to say:
The Victory for what it lost and gained.

You went to meet the shell's embrace of fire
On Vimy Ridge; and when you fell that day
The war seemed over more for you than me,   15
But now for me than you—the other way.

How over, though, for even me who knew
The foe thrust back unsafe beyond the Rhine,
If I was not to speak of it to you
And see you pleased once more with words of mine?   20

NOTHING GOLD CAN STAY

Nature's first green is gold,
Her hardest hue to hold.
Her early leaf's a flower;
But only so an hour.
Then leaf subsides to leaf.   5
So Eden sank to grief,

So dawn goes down to day.
Nothing gold can stay.

THE RUNAWAY

Once when the snow of the year was beginning to fall,
We stopped by a mountain pasture to say, "Whose colt?"
A little Morgan had one forefoot on the wall,
The other curled at his breast. He dipped his head
And snorted at us. And then he had to bolt.   5
We heard the miniature thunder where he fled,
And we saw him, or thought we saw him, dim and gray,
Like a shadow against the curtain of falling flakes.
"I think the little fellow's afraid of the snow.
He isn't winter-broken. It isn't play   10
With the little fellow at all. He's running away.
I doubt if even his mother could tell him, 'Sakes,
It's only weather.' He'd think she didn't know!
Where is his mother? He can't be out alone."
And now he comes again with clatter of stone,   15
And mounts the wall again with whited eyes
And all his tail that isn't hair up straight.
He shudders his coat as if to throw off flies.
"Whoever it is that leaves him out so late,
When other creatures have gone to stall and bin,   20
Ought to be told to come and take him in."

THE AIM WAS SONG

Before man came to blow it right
    The wind once blew itself untaught,
And did its loudest day and night
    In any rough place where it caught.

Man came to tell it what was wrong: 5
  It hadn't found the place to blow;
It blew too hard—the aim was song.
  And listen—how it ought to go!

He took a little in his mouth,
  And held it long enough for north   10
To be converted into south,
  And then by measure blew it forth.

By measure. It was word and note,
  The wind the wind had meant to be—
A little through the lips and throat.   15
  The aim was song—the wind could see.

STOPPING BY WOODS
ON A SNOWY EVENING

Whose woods these are I think I know.
His house is in the village, though;
He will not see me stopping here
To watch his woods fill up with snow.

My little horse must think it queer   5
To stop without a farmhouse near
Between the woods and frozen lake
The darkest evening of the year.

He gives his harness bells a shake
To ask if there is some mistake.   10
The only other sound's the sweep
Of easy wind and downy flake.

The woods are lovely, dark, and deep,

But I have promises to keep,
And miles to go before I sleep,   15
And miles to go before I sleep.

FOR ONCE, THEN, SOMETHING

Others taunt me with having knelt at well-curbs
Always wrong to the light, so never seeing
Deeper down in the well than where the water
Gives me back in a shining surface picture
Me myself in the summer heaven, godlike,   5
Looking out of a wreath of fern and cloud puffs.
Once, when trying with chin against a well-curb,
I discerned, as I thought, beyond the picture,
Through the picture, a something white, uncertain,
Something more of the depths—and then I lost it.   10
Water came to rebuke the too clear water.
One drop fell from a fern, and lo, a ripple
Shook whatever it was lay there at bottom,
Blurred it, blotted it out. What was that whiteness?
Truth? A pebble of quartz? For once, then, something.   15

BLUE-BUTTERFLY DAY

It is blue-butterfly day here in spring,
And with these sky-flakes down in flurry on flurry
There is more unmixed color on the wing
Than flowers will show for days unless they hurry.

But these are flowers that fly and all but sing: 5
And now from having ridden out desire
They lie closed over in the wind and cling
Where wheels have freshly sliced the April mire.

225

THE ONSET

Always the same, when on a fated night
At last the gathered snow lets down as white
As may be in dark woods, and with a song
It shall not make again all winter long
Of hissing on the yet uncovered ground,   5
I almost stumble looking up and round,
As one who overtaken by the end
Gives up his errand, and lets death descend
Upon him where he is, with nothing done
To evil, no important triumph won,   10
More than if life had never been begun.

Yet all the precedent is on my side:
I know that winter death has never tried
The earth but it has failed: the snow may heap
In long storms an undrifted four feet deep   15
As measured against maple, birch, and oak,
It cannot check the peeper's silver croak;
And I shall see the snow all go downhill
In water of a slender April rill
That flashes tail through last year's withered brake   20
And dead weeds, like a disappearing snake.
Nothing will be left white but here a birch,
And there a clump of houses with a church.

TO EARTHWARD

Love at the lips was touch
As sweet as I could bear;
And once that seemed too much;
I lived on air

226

That crossed me from sweet things,   5
The flow of—was it musk
From hidden grapevine springs
Downhill at dusk?

I had the swirl and ache
From sprays of honeysuckle   10
That when they're gathered shake
Dew on the knuckle.

I craved strong sweets, but those
Seemed strong when I was young;
The petal of the rose   15
It was that stung.

Now no joy but lacks salt,
That is not dashed with pain
And weariness and fault;
I crave the stain   20

Of tears, the aftermark
Of almost too much love,
The sweet of bitter bark
And burning clove.

When stiff and sore and scarred   25
I take away my hand
From leaning on it hard
In grass and sand,

The hurt is not enough:
I long for weight and strength   30
To feel the earth as rough
To all my length.

GOOD-BY AND KEEP COLD

This saying good-by on the edge of the dark
And the cold to an orchard so young in the bark
Reminds me of all that can happen to harm
An orchard away at the end of the farm
All winter, cut off by a hill from the house.   5
I don't want it girdled by rabbit and mouse,
I don't want it dreamily nibbled for browse
By deer, and I don't want it budded by grouse.
(If certain it wouldn't be idle to call
I'd summon grouse, rabbit, and deer to the wall   10
And warn them away with a stick for a gun.)
I don't want it stirred by the heat of the sun.
(We made it secure against being, I hope,
By setting it out on a northerly slope.)
No orchard's the worse for the wintriest storm;   15
But one thing about it, it mustn't get warm.
"How often already you've had to be told,
Keep cold, young orchard. Good-by and keep cold.
Dread fifty above more than fifty below."
I have to be gone for a season or so.   20
My business awhile is with different trees,
Less carefully nurtured, less fruitful than these,
And such as is done to their wood with an ax—
Maples and birches and tamaracks.
I wish I could promise to lie in the night   25
And think of an orchard's arboreal plight
When slowly (and nobody comes with a light)
Its heart sinks lower under the sod.
But something has to be left to God.

TWO LOOK AT TWO

Love and forgetting might have carried them
A little further up the mountainside
With night so near, but not much further up.
They must have halted soon in any case
With thoughts of the path back, how rough it was   5
With rock and washout, and unsafe in darkness;
When they were halted by a tumbled wall
With barbed-wire binding. They stood facing this,
Spending what onward impulse they still had
In one last look the way they must not go,   10
On up the failing path, where, if a stone
Or earthslide moved at night, it moved itself;
No footstep moved it. "This is all," they sighed,
"Good-night to woods." But not so; there was more.
A doe from round a spruce stood looking at them   15
Across the wall, as near the wall as they.
She saw them in their field, they her in hers.
The difficulty of seeing what stood still,
Like some up-ended boulder split in two,
Was in her clouded eyes: they saw no fear there.   20
She seemed to think that, two thus, they were safe.
Then, as if they were something that, though strange,
She could not trouble her mind with too long,
She sighed and passed unscared along the wall.
"*This,* then, is all. What more is there to ask?"   25
But no, not yet. A snort to bid them wait.
A buck from round the spruce stood looking at them
Across the wall, as near the wall as they.
This was an antlered buck of lusty nostril,
Not the same doe come back into her place.   30
He viewed them quizzically with jerks of head,

229

As if to ask, "Why don't you make some motion?
Or give some sign of life? Because you can't.
I doubt if you're as living as you look."
Thus till he had them almost feeling dared   35
To stretch a proffering hand—and a spell-breaking.
Then he too passed unscared along the wall.
Two had seen two, whichever side you spoke from.
"This *must* be all." It was all. Still they stood,
A great wave from it going over them,   40
As if the earth in one unlooked-for favor
Had made them certain earth returned their love.

NOT TO KEEP

They sent him back to her. The letter came
Saying. . . . And she could have him. And before
She could be sure there was no hidden ill
Under the formal writing, he was there,
Living. They gave him back to her alive—   5
How else? They are not known to send the dead.—
And not disfigured visibly. His face?
His hands? She had to look, to look and ask,
"What is it, dear?" And she had given all
And still she had all—*they* had—they the lucky!   10
Wasn't she glad now? Everything seemed won,
And all the rest for them permissible ease.
She had to ask, "What was it, dear?"

                                        "Enough,
Yet not enough. A bullet through and through,
High in the breast. Nothing but what good care   15
And medicine and rest, and you a week,
Can cure me of to go again." The same

230

Grim giving to do over for them both.
She dared no more than ask him with her eyes
How was it with him for a second trial.   20
And with his eyes he asked her not to ask.
They had given him back to her, but not to keep.

A BROOK IN THE CITY

The farmhouse lingers, though averse to square
With the new city street it has to wear
A number in. But what about the brook
That held the house as in an elbow-crook?
I ask as one who knew the brook, its strength   5
And impulse, having dipped a finger length
And made it leap my knuckle, having tossed
A flower to try its currents where they crossed.
The meadow grass could be cemented down
From growing under pavements of a town;   10
The apple trees be sent to hearthstone flame.
Is water wood to serve a brook the same?
How else dispose of an immortal force
No longer needed? Staunch it at its source
With cinder loads dumped down? The brook was thrown
Deep in a sewer dungeon under stone
In fetid darkness still to live and run—
And all for nothing it had ever done,
Except forget to go in fear perhaps.
No one would know except for ancient maps   20
That such a brook ran water. But I wonder
If from its being kept forever under,
The thoughts may not have risen that so keep
This new-built city from both work and sleep.

231

THE KITCHEN CHIMNEY

Builder, in building the little house,
In every way you may please yourself;
But please please me in the kitchen chimney:
Don't build me a chimney upon a shelf.

However far you must go for bricks,   5
Whatever they cost apiece or a pound,
Buy me enough for a full-length chimney,
And build the chimney clear from the ground.

It's not that I'm greatly afraid of fire,
But I never heard of a house that throve   10
(And I know of one that didn't thrive)
Where the chimney started above the stove.

And I dread the ominous stain of tar
That there always is on the papered walls,
And the smell of fire drowned in rain   15
That there always is when the chimney's false.

A shelf's for a clock or vase or picture,
But I don't see why it should have to bear
A chimney that only would serve to remind me
Of castles I used to build in air.   20

LOOKING FOR A SUNSET BIRD
IN WINTER

The west was getting out of gold,
The breath of air had died of cold,
When shoeing home across the white,
I thought I saw a bird alight.

In summer when I passed the place,   5
I had to stop and lift my face;
A bird with an angelic gift
Was singing in it sweet and swift.

No bird was singing in it now.
A single leaf was on a bough,   10
And that was all there was to see
In going twice around the tree.

From my advantage on a hill
I judged that such a crystal chill
Was only adding frost to snow   15
As gilt to gold that wouldn't show.

A brush had left a crooked stroke
Of what was either cloud or smoke
From north to south across the blue;
A piercing little star was through.   20

A BOUNDLESS MOMENT

He halted in the wind, and—what was that
Far in the maples, pale, but not a ghost?
He stood there bringing March against his thought,
And yet too ready to believe the most.

"Oh, that's the Paradise-in-Bloom," I said;   5
And truly it was fair enough for flowers
Had we but in us to assume in March
Such white luxuriance of May for ours.

We stood a moment so, in a strange world,
Myself as one his own pretense deceives;   10

And then I said the truth (and we moved on).
A young beech clinging to its last year's leaves.

EVENING IN A SUGAR ORCHARD

From where I lingered in a lull in March
Outside the sugarhouse one night for choice,
I called the fireman with a careful voice
And bade him leave the pan and stoke the arch:
"O fireman, give the fire another stoke,   5
And send more sparks up chimney with the smoke."
I thought a few might tangle, as they did,
Among bare maple boughs, and in the rare
Hill atmosphere not cease to glow,
And so be added to the moon up there.   10
The moon, though slight, was moon enough to show
On every tree a bucket with a lid,
And on black ground a bear-skin rug of snow.
The sparks made no attempt to be the moon.
They were content to figure in the trees   15
As Leo, Orion, and the Pleiades.
And that was what the boughs were full of soon.

GATHERING LEAVES

Spades take up leaves
No better than spoons,
And bags full of leaves
Are light as balloons.

I make a great noise   5
Of rustling all day

234

Like rabbit and deer
Running away.

But the mountains I raise
Elude my embrace,   10
Flowing over my arms
And into my face.

I may load and unload
Again and again
Till I fill the whole shed,   15
And what have I then?

Next to nothing for weight;
And since they grew duller
From contact with earth,
Next to nothing for color.   20

Next to nothing for use.
But a crop is a crop,
And who's to say where
The harvest shall stop?

THE VALLEY'S SINGING DAY

The sound of the closing outside door was all.
You made no sound in the grass with your footfall,
As far as you went from the door, which was not far;
But you had awakened under the morning star
The first songbird that awakened all the rest.   5
He could have slept but a moment more at best.
Already determined dawn began to lay
In place across a cloud the slender ray
For prying beneath and forcing the lids of sight,

And loosing the pent-up music of overnight.   10
But dawn was not to begin their "pearly-pearly"
(By which they mean the rain is pearls so early,
Before it changes to diamonds in the sun),
Neither was song that day to be self-begun.
You had begun it, and if there needed proof—   15
I was asleep still under the dripping roof,
My window curtain hung over the sill to wet;
But I should awake to confirm your story yet;
I should be willing to say and help you say
That once you had opened the valley's singing day.   20

MISGIVING

All crying, "We will go with you, O Wind!"
The foliage follow him, leaf and stem;
But a sleep oppresses them as they go,
And they end by bidding him stay with them.

Since ever they flung abroad in spring   5
The leaves had promised themselves this flight,
Who now would fain seek sheltering wall,
Or thicket, or hollow place for the night.

And now they answer his summoning blast
With an ever vaguer and vaguer stir,   10
Or at utmost a little reluctant whirl
That drops them no further than where they were.

I only hope that when I am free,
As they are free, to go in quest
Of the knowledge beyond the bounds of life   15
It may not seem better to me to rest.

A HILLSIDE THAW

To think to know the country and not know
The hillside on the day the sun lets go
Ten million silver lizards out of snow!
As often as I've seen it done before
I can't pretend to tell the way it's done.   5
It looks as if some magic of the sun
Lifted the rug that bred them on the floor
And the light breaking on them made them run.
But if I thought to stop the wet stampede,
And caught one silver lizard by the tail,   10
And put my foot on one without avail,
And threw myself wet-elbowed and wet-kneed
In front of twenty others' wriggling speed—
In the confusion of them all aglitter,
And birds that joined in the excited fun   15
By doubling and redoubling song and twitter—
I have no doubt I'd end by holding none.

It takes the moon for this. The sun's a wizard
By all I tell; but so's the moon a witch.
From the high west she makes a gentle cast   20
And suddenly, without a jerk or twitch,
She has her spell on every single lizard.
I fancied when I looked at six o'clock
The swarm still ran and scuttled just as fast.
The moon was waiting for her chill effect.   25
I looked at nine: the swarm was turned to rock
In every lifelike posture of the swarm,
Transfixed on mountain slopes almost erect.
Across each other and side by side they lay.
The spell that so could hold them as they were   30

237

Was wrought through trees without a breath of storm
To make a leaf, if there had been one, stir.
It was the moon's: she held them until day,
One lizard at the end of every ray.
The thought of my attempting such a stay! 35

PLOWMEN

A plow, they say, to plow the snow.
They cannot mean to plant it, no—
Unless in bitterness to mock
At having cultivated rock.

ON A TREE FALLEN ACROSS THE ROAD

(To hear us talk)

The tree the tempest with a crash of wood
Throws down in front of us is not to bar
Our passage to our journey's end for good,
But just to ask us who we think we are

Insisting always on our own way so. 5
She likes to halt us in our runner tracks,
And make us get down in a foot of snow
Debating what to do without an ax.

And yet she knows obstruction is in vain:
We will not be put off the final goal 10
We have it hidden in us to attain,
Not though we have to seize earth by the pole

And, tired of aimless circling in one place,
Steer straight off after something into space.

OUR SINGING STRENGTH

It snowed in spring on earth so dry and warm
The flakes could find no landing place to form.
Hordes spent themselves to make it wet and cold,
And still they failed of any lasting hold.
They made no white impression on the black.   5
They disappeared as if earth sent them back.
Not till from separate flakes they changed at night
To almost strips and tapes of ragged white
Did grass and garden ground confess it snowed,
And all go back to winter but the road.   10
Next day the scene was piled and puffed and dead.
The grass lay flattened under one great tread.
Borne down until the end almost took root,
The rangey bough anticipated fruit
With snowballs cupped in every opening bud.   15
The road alone maintained itself in mud,
Whatever its secret was of greater heat
From inward fires or brush of passing feet.

In spring more mortal singers than belong
To any one place cover us with song.   20
Thrush, bluebird, blackbird, sparrow, and robin throng;
Some to go further north to Hudson's Bay,
Some that have come too far north back away,
Really a very few to build and stay.
Now was seen how these liked belated snow.   25
The fields had nowhere left for them to go;
They'd soon exhausted all there was in flying;
The trees they'd had enough of with once trying
And setting off their heavy powder load.
They could find nothing open but the road.   30

239

So there they let their lives be narrowed in
By thousands the bad weather made akin.
The road became a channel running flocks
Of glossy birds like ripples over rocks.
I drove them underfoot in bits of flight   35
That kept the ground, almost disputing right
Of way with me from apathy of wing,
A talking twitter all they had to sing.
A few I must have driven to despair
Made quick asides, but having done in air   40
A whir among white branches great and small,
As in some too much carven marble hall
Where one false wing beat would have brought down all,
Came tamely back in front of me, the Drover,
To suffer the same driven nightmare over.   45
One such storm in a lifetime couldn't teach them
That back behind pursuit it couldn't reach them;
None flew behind me to be left alone.

Well, something for a snowstorm to have shown
The country's singing strength thus brought together,   50
That though repressed and moody with the weather
Was nonetheless there ready to be freed
And sing the wild flowers up from root and seed.

THE LOCKLESS DOOR

It went many years,
But at last came a knock,
And I thought of the door
With no lock to lock.

I blew out the light,   5
I tiptoed the floor,

240

And raised both hands
In prayer to the door.

But the knock came again.
My window was wide;   10
I climbed on the sill
And descended outside.

Back over the sill
I bade a "Come in"
To whatever the knock   15
At the door may have been.

So at a knock
I emptied my cage
To hide in the world
And alter with age.   20

THE NEED OF BEING VERSED
IN COUNTRY THINGS

The house had gone to bring again
To the midnight sky a sunset glow.
Now the chimney was all of the house that stood,
Like a pistil after the petals go.

The barn opposed across the way,   5
That would have joined the house in flame
Had it been the will of the wind, was left
To bear forsaken the place's name.

No more it opened with all one end
For teams that came by the stony road   10
To drum on the floor with scurrying hoofs

241

And brush the mow with the summer load.

The birds that came to it through the air
At broken windows flew out and in,
Their murmur more like the sigh we sigh   15
From too much dwelling on what has been.

Yet for them the lilac renewed its leaf,
And the aged elm, though touched with fire;
And the dry pump flung up an awkward arm;
And the fence post carried a strand of wire.   20

For them there was really nothing sad.
But though they rejoiced in the nest they kept,
One had to be versed in country things
Not to believe the phoebes wept.

West-Running Brook

: 1928 :

SPRING POOLS

These pools that, though in forests, still reflect
The total sky almost without defect,
And like the flowers beside them, chill and shiver,
Will like the flowers beside them soon be gone,
And yet not out by any brook or river,   5
But up by roots to bring dark foliage on.

The trees that have it in their pent-up buds
To darken nature and be summer woods—
Let them think twice before they use their powers
To blot out and drink up and sweep away   10
These flowery waters and these watery flowers
From snow that melted only yesterday.

THE FREEDOM OF THE MOON

I've tried the new moon tilted in the air
Above a hazy tree-and-farmhouse cluster
As you might try a jewel in your hair.
I've tried it fine with little breadth of luster,
Alone, or in one ornament combining   5
With one first-water star almost as shining.

I put it shining anywhere I please.
By walking slowly on some evening later
I've pulled it from a crate of crooked trees,
And brought it over glossy water, greater,   10
And dropped it in, and seen the image wallow,
The color run, all sorts of wonder follow.

THE ROSE FAMILY

The rose is a rose,
And was always a rose.
But the theory now goes
That the apple's a rose,
And the pear is, and so's 5
The plum, I suppose.
The dear only knows
What will next prove a rose.
You, of course, are a rose—
But were always a rose. 10

FIREFLIES IN THE GARDEN

Here come real stars to fill the upper skies,
And here on earth come emulating flies
That, though they never equal stars in size
(And they were never really stars at heart),
Achieve at times a very starlike start. 5
Only, of course, they can't sustain the part.

ATMOSPHERE

Inscription for a garden wall

Winds blow the open grassy places bleak;
But where this old wall burns a sunny cheek,
They eddy over it too toppling weak
To blow the earth or anything self-clear;
Moisture and color and odor thicken here. 5
The hours of daylight gather atmosphere.

DEVOTION

The heart can think of no devotion
Greater than being shore to the ocean—
Holding the curve of one position,
Counting an endless repetition.

ON GOING UNNOTICED

As vain to raise a voice as a sigh
In the tumult of free leaves on high.
What are you, in the shadow of trees
Engaged up there with the light and breeze?

Less than the coralroot, you know,   5
That is content with the daylight low,
And has no leaves at all of its own;
Whose spotted flowers hang meanly down.

You grasp the bark by a rugged pleat,
And look up small from the forest's feet.   10
The only leaf it drops goes wide,
Your name not written on either side.

You linger your little hour and are gone,
And still the woods sweep leafily on,
Not even missing the coralroot flower   15
You took as a trophy of the hour.

THE COCOON

As far as I can see, this autumn haze
That spreading in the evening air both ways
Makes the new moon look anything but new

And pours the elm-tree meadow full of blue,
Is all the smoke from one poor house alone,   5
With but one chimney it can call its own;
So close it will not light an early light,
Keeping its life so close and out of sight
No one for hours has set a foot outdoors
So much as to take care of evening chores.   10
The inmates may be lonely womenfolk.
I want to tell them that with all this smoke
They prudently are spinning their cocoon
And anchoring it to an earth and moon
From which no winter gale can hope to blow it—   15
Spinning their own cocoon did they but know it.

A PASSING GLIMPSE

*To Ridgely Torrence
on last looking into his "Hesperides"*

I often see flowers from a passing car
That are gone before I can tell what they are.

I want to get out of the train and go back
To see what they were beside the track.

I name all the flowers I am sure they weren't: 5
Not fireweed loving where woods have burnt—

Not bluebells gracing a tunnel mouth—
Not lupine living on sand and drouth.

Was something brushed across my mind
That no one on earth will ever find?   10

Heaven gives its glimpses only to those
Not in position to look too close.

A PECK OF GOLD

Dust always blowing about the town,
Except when sea fog laid it down,
And I was one of the children told
Some of the blowing dust was gold.

All the dust the wind blew high   5
Appeared like gold in the sunset sky,
But I was one of the children told
Some of the dust was really gold.

Such was life in the Golden Gate:
Gold dusted all we drank and ate,   10
And I was one of the children told,
"We all must eat our peck of gold."

ACCEPTANCE

When the spent sun throws up its rays on cloud
And goes down burning into the gulf below,
No voice in nature is heard to cry aloud
At what has happened. Birds, at least, must know
It is the change to darkness in the sky.   5
Murmuring something quiet in her breast,
One bird begins to close a faded eye;
Or overtaken too far from his nest,
Hurrying low above the grove, some waif
Swoops just in time to his remembered tree.   10
At most he thinks or twitters softly, "Safe!
Now let the night be dark for all of me.
Let the night be too dark for me to see
Into the future. Let what will be, be."

ONCE BY THE PACIFIC

The shattered water made a misty din.
Great waves looked over others coming in,
And thought of doing something to the shore
That water never did to land before.
The clouds were low and hairy in the skies,   5
Like locks blown forward in the gleam of eyes.
You could not tell, and yet it looked as if
The shore was lucky in being backed by cliff,
The cliff in being backed by continent;
It looked as if a night of dark intent   10
Was coming, and not only a night, an age.
Someone had better be prepared for rage.
There would be more than ocean-water broken
Before God's last *Put out the Light* was spoken.

LODGED

The rain to the wind said,
"You push and I'll pelt."
They so smote the garden bed
That the flowers actually knelt,
And lay lodged—though not dead.   5
I know how the flowers felt.

A MINOR BIRD

I have wished a bird would fly away,
And not sing by my house all day;

Have clapped my hands at him from the door
When it seemed as if I could bear no more.

250

The fault must partly have been in me.   5
The bird was not to blame for his key.

And of course there must be something wrong
In wanting to silence any song.

BEREFT

Where had I heard this wind before
Change like this to a deeper roar?
What would it take my standing there for,
Holding open a restive door,
Looking downhill to a frothy shore?   5
Summer was past and day was past.
Somber clouds in the west were massed.
Out in the porch's sagging floor
Leaves got up in a coil and hissed,
Blindly struck at my knee and missed.   10
Something sinister in the tone
Told me my secret must be known:
Word I was in the house alone
Somehow must have gotten abroad,
Word I was in my life alone,   15
Word I had no one left but God.

TREE AT MY WINDOW

Tree at my window, window tree,
My sash is lowered when night comes on;
But let there never be curtain drawn
Between you and me.

Vague dream-head lifted out of the ground,   5
And thing next most diffuse to cloud,

Not all your light tongues talking aloud
Could be profound.

But, tree, I have seen you taken and tossed,
And if you have seen me when I slept,   10
You have seen me when I was taken and swept
And all but lost.

That day she put our heads together,
Fate had her imagination about her,
Your head so much concerned with outer,   15
Mine with inner, weather.

THE PEACEFUL SHEPHERD

If heaven were to do again,
And on the pasture bars
I leaned to line the figures in
Between the dotted stars,

I should be tempted to forget,   5
I fear, the Crown of Rule,
The Scales of Trade, the Cross of Faith,
As hardly worth renewal.

For these have governed in our lives,
And see how men have warred.   10
The Cross, the Crown, the Scales may all
As well have been the Sword.

THE THATCH

Out alone in the winter rain,
Intent on giving and taking pain.

But never was I far out of sight
Of a certain upper-window light.
The light was what it was all about: 5
I would not go in till the light went out;
It would not go out till I came in.
Well, we should see which one would win,
We should see which one would be first to yield.
The world was a black invisible field. 10
The rain by rights was snow for cold.
The wind was another layer of mold.
But the strangest thing: in the thick old thatch,
Where summer birds had been given hatch,
Had fed in chorus, and lived to fledge, 15
Some still were living in hermitage.
And as I passed along the eaves
So low I brushed the straw with my sleeves,
I flushed birds out of hole after hole,
Into the darkness. It grieved my soul, 20
It started a grief within a grief,
To think their case was beyond relief—
They could not go flying about in search
Of their nest again, nor find a perch.
They must brood where they fell in mulch and mire, 25
Trusting feathers and inward fire
Till daylight made it safe for a flyer.
My greater grief was by so much reduced
As I thought of them without nest or roost.
That was how that grief started to melt. 30
They tell me the cottage where we dwelt,
Its wind-torn thatch goes now unmended;
Its life of hundreds of years has ended
By letting the rain I knew outdoors
In onto the upper chamber floors. 35

253

A WINTER EDEN

A winter garden in an alder swamp,
Where conies now come out to sun and romp,
As near a paradise as it can be
And not melt snow or start a dormant tree.

It lifts existence on a plane of snow   5
One level higher than the earth below,
One level nearer heaven overhead,
And last year's berries shining scarlet red.

It lifts a gaunt luxuriating beast
Where he can stretch and hold his highest feast   10
On some wild apple-tree's young tender bark,
What well may prove the year's high girdle mark.

So near to paradise all pairing ends:
Here loveless birds now flock as winter friends,
Content with bud-inspecting. They presume   15
To say which buds are leaf and which are bloom.

A feather-hammer gives a double knock.
This Eden day is done at two o'clock.
An hour of winter day might seem too short
To make it worth life's while to wake and sport.   20

THE FLOOD

Blood has been harder to dam back than water.
Just when we think we have it impounded safe
Behind new barrier walls (and let it chafe!),
It breaks away in some new kind of slaughter.
We choose to say it is let loose by the devil;   5
But power of blood itself releases blood.

254

It goes by might of being such a flood
Held high at so unnatural a level.
It will have outlet, brave and not so brave.
Weapons of war and implements of peace   10
Are but the points at which it finds release.
And now it is once more the tidal wave
That when it has swept by, leaves summits stained.
Oh, blood will out. It cannot be contained.

ACQUAINTED WITH THE NIGHT

I have been one acquainted with the night.
I have walked out in rain—and back in rain.
I have outwalked the furthest city light.

I have looked down the saddest city lane.
I have passed by the watchman on his beat   5
And dropped my eyes, unwilling to explain.

I have stood still and stopped the sound of feet
When far away an interrupted cry
Came over houses from another street,

But not to call me back or say good-by;   10
And further still at an unearthly height
One luminary clock against the sky

Proclaimed the time was neither wrong nor right.
I have been one acquainted with the night.

THE LOVELY SHALL BE CHOOSERS

The Voice said, "Hurl her down!"

The Voices, "How far down?"

"Seven levels of the world."

"How much time have we?"

"Take twenty years.   5
She *would* refuse love safe with wealth and honor!
The lovely shall be choosers, shall they?
Then let them choose!"

"Then we shall let her choose?"

"Yes, let her choose.   10
Take up the task beyond her choosing."

Invisible hands crowded on her shoulder
In readiness to weigh upon her.
But she stood straight still,
In broad round earrings, gold and jet with pearls,   15
And broad round suchlike brooch,
Her cheeks high-colored,
Proud and the pride of friends.

The Voice asked, "You can let her choose?"

"Yes, we can let her and still triumph."   20

"Do it by joys, and leave her always blameless.
Be her first joy her wedding,
That though a wedding,
Is yet—well, something they know, he and she.
And after that her next joy   25
That though she grieves, her grief is secret:
Those friends know nothing of her grief to make it shameful.
Her third joy that though now they cannot help but know,
They move in pleasure too far off
To think much or much care.   30
Give her a child at either knee for fourth joy

256

To tell once and once only, for them never to forget,
How once she walked in brightness,
And make them see it in the winter firelight.
But give her friends, for then she dare not tell   35
For their foregone incredulousness.
And be her next joy this:
Her never having deigned to tell them.
Make her among the humblest even
Seem to them less than they are.   40
Hopeless of being known for what she has been,
Failing of being loved for what she is,
Give her the comfort for her sixth of knowing
She fails from strangeness to a way of life
She came to from too high too late to learn.   45
Then send some *one* with eyes to see
And wonder at her where she is,
And words to wonder in her hearing how she came there,
But without time to linger for her story.
Be her last joy her heart's going out to this one   50
So that she almost speaks.
You know them—seven in all."

"Trust us," the Voices said.

WEST-RUNNING BROOK

"Fred, where is north?"

              "North? North is there, my love.
The brook runs west."

              "West-Running Brook then call it."
(West-Running Brook men call it to this day.)
"What does it think it's doing running west

When all the other country brooks flow east   5
To reach the ocean? It must be the brook
Can trust itself to go by contraries
The way I can with you—and you with me—
Because we're—we're—I don't know what we are.   9
What are we?"

        "Young or new?"

                        "We must be something.
We've said we two. Let's change that to we three.
As you and I are married to each other,
We'll both be married to the brook. We'll build
Our bridge across it, and the bridge shall be
Our arm thrown over it asleep beside it.   15
Look, look, it's waving to us with a wave
To let us know it hears me."

                  "Why, my dear,
That wave's been standing off this jut of shore—"
(The black stream, catching on a sunken rock,
Flung backward on itself in one white wave,   20
And the white water rode the black forever,
Not gaining but not losing, like a bird
White feathers from the struggle of whose breast
Flecked the dark stream and flecked the darker pool
Below the point, and were at last driven wrinkled   25
In a white scarf against the far-shore alders.)
"That wave's been standing off this jut of shore
Ever since rivers, I was going to say,
Were made in heaven. It wasn't waved to us."

"It wasn't, yet it was. If not to you,   30
It was to me—in an annunciation."

"Oh, if you take it off to lady-land,

As't were the country of the Amazons
We men must see you to the confines of
And leave you there, ourselves forbid to enter—   35
It is your brook! I have no more to say."

"Yes, you have, too. Go on. You thought of something."

"Speaking of contraries, see how the brook
In that white wave runs counter to itself.
It is from that in water we were from   40
Long, long before we were from any creature.
Here we, in our impatience of the steps,
Get back to the beginning of beginnings,
The stream of everything that runs away.
Some say existence like a Pirouot   45
And Pirouette, forever in one place,
Stands still and dances, but it runs away;
It seriously, sadly, runs away
To fill the abyss's void with emptiness.
It flows beside us in this water brook,   50
But it flows over us. It flows between us
To separate us for a panic moment.
It flows between us, over us, and *with* us.
And it is time, strength, tone, light, life, and love—
And even substance lapsing unsubstantial;   55
The universal cataract of death
That spends to nothingness—and unresisted,
Save by some strange resistance in itself,
Not just a swerving, but a throwing back,
As if regret were in it and were sacred.   60
It has this throwing backward on itself
So that the fall of most of it is always
Raising a little, sending up a little.
Our life runs down in sending up the clock.

The brook runs down in sending up our life.   65
The sun runs down in sending up the brook.
And there is something sending up the sun.
It is this backward motion toward the source,
Against the stream, that most we see ourselves in,
The tribute of the current to the source.   70
It is from this in nature we are from.
It is most us."

                "Today will be the day
You said so."

                 "No, today will be the day
You said the brook was called West-Running Brook."

"Today will be the day of what we both said."   75

SAND DUNES

Sea waves are green and wet,
But up from where they die
Rise others vaster yet,
And those are brown and dry.

They are the sea made land   5
To come at the fisher town
And bury in solid sand
The men she could not drown.

She may know cove and cape,
But she does not know mankind   10
If by any change of shape
She hopes to cut off mind.

Men left her a ship to sink:
They can leave her a hut as well;

260

And be but more free to think 15
For the one more cast-off shell.

CANIS MAJOR

The great Overdog,
That heavenly beast
With a star in one eye,
Gives a leap in the east.

He dances upright 5
All the way to the west
And never once drops
On his forefeet to rest.

I'm a poor underdog,
But tonight I will bark 10
With the great Overdog
That romps through the dark.

A SOLDIER

He is that fallen lance that lies as hurled,
That lies unlifted now, come dew, come rust,
But still lies pointed as it plowed the dust.
If we who sight along it round the world,
See nothing worthy to have been its mark, 5
It is because like men we look too near,
Forgetting that as fitted to the sphere,
Our missiles always make too short an arc.
They fall, they rip the grass, they intersect
The curve of earth, and striking, break their own; 10
They make us cringe for metal-point on stone.
But this we know, the obstacle that checked

261

And tripped the body, shot the spirit on
Further than target ever showed or shone.

IMMIGRANTS

No ship of all that under sail or steam
Have gathered people to us more and more
But, Pilgrim-manned, the *Mayflower* in a dream
Has been her anxious convoy in to shore.

HANNIBAL

Was there ever a cause too lost,
Ever a cause that was lost too long,
Or that showed with the lapse of time too vain
For the generous tears of youth and song?

THE FLOWER BOAT

The fisherman's swapping a yarn for a yarn
Under the hand of the village barber,
And here in the angle of house and barn
His deep-sea dory has found a harbor.

At anchor she rides the sunny sod,   5
As full to the gunnel of flowers growing
As ever she turned her home with cod
From Georges Bank when winds were blowing.

And I judge from that Elysian freight
That all they ask is rougher weather,   10
And dory and master will sail by fate
To seek for the Happy Isles together.

262

THE TIMES TABLE

More than halfway up the pass
Was a spring with a broken drinking glass,
And whether the farmer drank or not
His mare was sure to observe the spot
By cramping the wheel on a water bar,   5
Turning her forehead with a star,
And straining her ribs for a monster sigh;
To which the farmer would make reply,
"A sigh for every so many breath,
And for every so many sigh a death.   10
That's what I always tell my wife
Is the multiplication table of life."
The saying may be ever so true;
But it's just the kind of a thing that you
Nor I nor nobody else may say,   15
Unless our purpose is doing harm,
And then I know of no better way
To close a road, abandon a farm,
Reduce the births of the human race,
And bring back nature in people's place.   20

THE INVESTMENT

Over back where they speak of life as staying
("You couldn't call it living, for it ain't"),
There was an old, old house renewed with paint,
And in it a piano loudly playing.

Out in the plowed ground in the cold a digger,   5
Among unearthed potatoes standing still,
Was counting winter dinners, one a hill,
With half an ear to the piano's vigor.

263

All that piano and new paint back there,
Was it some money suddenly come into?　　　10
Or some extravagance young love had been to?
Or old love on an impulse not to care—

Not to sink under being man and wife,
But get some color and music out of life?

THE LAST MOWING

There's a place called Faraway Meadow
We never shall mow in again,
Or such is the talk at the farmhouse:
The meadow is finished with men.
Then now is the chance for the flowers　　　5
That can't stand mowers and plowers.
It must be now, though, in season
Before the not mowing brings trees on,
Before trees, seeing the opening,
March into a shadowy claim.　　　10
The trees are all I'm afraid of,
That flowers can't bloom in the shade of;
It's no more men I'm afraid of;
The meadow is done with the tame.
The place for the moment is ours　　　15
For you, O tumultuous flowers,
To go to waste and go wild in,
All shapes and colors of flowers,
I needn't call you by name.

THE BIRTHPLACE

Here further up the mountain slope
Than there was ever any hope,

264

My father built, enclosed a spring,
Strung chains of wall round everything,
Subdued the growth of earth to grass,   5
And brought our various lives to pass.
A dozen girls and boys we were.
The mountain seemed to like the stir,
And made of us a little while—
With always something in her smile.   10
Today she wouldn't know our name.
(No girl's, of course, has stayed the same.)
The mountain pushed us off her knees.
And now her lap is full of trees.

THE DOOR IN THE DARK

In going from room to room in the dark
I reached out blindly to save my face,
But neglected, however lightly, to lace
My fingers and close my arms in an arc.
A slim door got in past my guard,   5
And hit me a blow in the head so hard
I had my native simile jarred.
So people and things don't pair anymore
With what they used to pair with before.

DUST IN THE EYES

If, as they say, some dust thrown in my eyes
Will keep my talk from getting overwise,
I'm not the one for putting off the proof.
Let it be overwhelming, off a roof
And round a corner, blizzard snow for dust,   5
And blind me to a standstill if it must.

265

SITTING BY A BUSH IN BROAD SUNLIGHT

When I spread out my hand here today,
I catch no more than a ray
To feel of between thumb and fingers;
No lasting effect of it lingers.

There was one time and only the one   5
When dust really took in the sun;
And from that one intake of fire
All creatures still warmly suspire.

And if men have watched a long time
And never seen sun-smitten slime   10
Again come to life and crawl off,
We must not be too ready to scoff.

God once declared He was true
And then took the veil and withdrew,
And remember how final a hush   15
Then descended of old on the bush.

God once spoke to people by name.
The sun once imparted its flame.
One impulse persists as our breath;
The other persists as our faith.   20

THE ARMFUL

For every parcel I stoop down to seize
I lose some other off my arms and knees,
And the whole pile is slipping, bottles, buns—
Extremes too hard to comprehend at once,
Yet nothing I should care to leave behind.   5

With all I have to hold with, hand and mind
And heart, if need be, I will do my best
To keep their building balanced at my breast.
I crouch down to prevent them as they fall;
Then sit down in the middle of them all.   10
I had to drop the armful in the road
And try to stack them in a better load.

WHAT FIFTY SAID

When I was young my teachers were the old.
I gave up fire for form till I was cold.
I suffered like a metal being cast.
I went to school to age to learn the past.

Now I am old my teachers are the young.   5
What can't be molded must be cracked and sprung.
I strain at lessons fit to start a suture.
I go to school to youth to learn the future.

RIDERS

The surest thing there is is we are riders,
And though none too successful at it, guiders,
Through everything presented, land and tide
And now the very air, of what we ride.

What is this talked-of mystery of birth   5
But being mounted bareback on the earth?
We can just see the infant up astride,
His small fist buried in the bushy hide.

There is our wildest mount—a headless horse.

But though it runs unbridled off its course,   10
And all our blandishments would seem defied,
We have ideas yet that we haven't tried.

ON LOOKING UP BY CHANCE
AT THE CONSTELLATIONS

You'll wait a long, long time for anything much
To happen in heaven beyond the floats of cloud
And the Northern Lights that run like tingling nerves.
The sun and moon get crossed, but they never touch,
Nor strike out fire from each other, nor crash out loud.   5
The planets seem to interfere in their curves,
But nothing ever happens, no harm is done.
We may as well go patiently on with our life,
And look elsewhere than to stars and moon and sun
For the shocks and changes we need to keep us sane.   10
It is true the longest drouth will end in rain,
The longest peace in China will end in strife.
Still it wouldn't reward the watcher to stay awake
In hopes of seeing the calm of heaven break
On his particular time and personal sight.   15
That calm seems certainly safe to last tonight.

THE BEAR

The bear puts both arms around the tree above her
And draws it down as if it were a lover
And its chokecherries lips to kiss good-by,
Then lets it snap back upright in the sky.
Her next step rocks a boulder on the wall   5
(She's making her cross-country in the fall).

268

Her great weight creaks the barbed wire in its staples
As she flings over and off down through the maples,
Leaving on one wire tooth a lock of hair.
Such is the uncaged progress of the bear.   10
The world has room to make a bear feel free;
The universe seems cramped to you and me.
Man acts more like the poor bear in a cage,
That all day fights a nervous inward rage,
His mood rejecting all his mind suggests.   15
He paces back and forth and never rests
The toenail click and shuffle of his feet,
The telescope at one end of his beat,
And at the other end the microscope,
Two instruments of nearly equal hope,   20
And in conjunction giving quite a spread.
Or if he rests from scientific tread,
'Tis only to sit back and sway his head
Through ninety-odd degrees of arc, it seems,
Between two metaphysical extremes.   25
He sits back on his fundamental butt
With lifted snout and eyes (if any) shut
(He almost looks religious but he's not),
And back and forth he sways from cheek to cheek,
At one extreme agreeing with one Greek,   30
At the other agreeing with another Greek,
Which may be thought, but only so to speak.
A baggy figure, equally pathetic
When sedentary and when peripatetic.

THE EGG AND THE MACHINE

He gave the solid rail a hateful kick.
From far away there came an answering tick,

And then another tick. He knew the code:
His hate had roused an engine up the road.
He wished when he had had the track alone
He had attacked it with a club or stone
And bent some rail wide open like a switch,
So as to wreck the engine in the ditch.
Too late though, now, he had himself to thank.
Its click was rising to a nearer clank.
Here it came breasting like a horse in skirts.
(He stood well back for fear of scalding squirts.)
Then for a moment all there was was size,
Confusion, and a roar that drowned the cries
He raised against the gods in the machine.
Then once again the sandbank lay serene.
The traveler's eye picked up a turtle trail,
Between the dotted feet a streak of tail,
And followed it to where he made out vague
But certain signs of buried turtle's egg;
And probing with one finger not too rough,
He found suspicious sand, and sure enough,
The pocket of a little turtle mine.
If there was one egg in it there were nine,
Torpedo-like, with shell of gritty leather,
All packed in sand to wait the trump together.
"You'd better not disturb me anymore,"
He told the distance, "I am armed for war.
The next machine that has the power to pass
Will get this plasm in its goggle glass."

5

10

15

20

25

30

A Further Range

: 1936 :

A LONE STRIKER

The swinging mill bell changed its rate
To tolling like the count of fate,
And though at that the tardy ran,
One failed to make the closing gate.
There was a law of God or man   5
That on the one who came too late
The gate for half an hour be locked,
His time be lost, his pittance docked.
He stood rebuked and unemployed.
The straining mill began to shake.   10
The mill, though many-many-eyed,
Had eyes inscrutably opaque;
So that he couldn't look inside
To see if some forlorn machine
Was standing idle for his sake.   15
(He couldn't hope its heart would break.)

And yet he thought he saw the scene:
The air was full of dust of wool.
A thousand yarns were under pull,
But pull so slow, with such a twist,   20
All day from spool to lesser spool,
It seldom overtaxed their strength;
They safely grew in slender length.
And if one broke by any chance,
The spinner saw it at a glance.   25
The spinner still was there to spin.
That's where the human still came in.
Her deft hand showed with finger rings

273

Among the harplike spread of strings.
She caught the pieces end to end   30
And, with a touch that never missed,
Not so much tied as made them blend.
Man's ingenuity was good.
He saw it plainly where he stood,
Yet found it easy to resist.   35

He knew another place, a wood,
And in it, tall as trees, were cliffs;
And if he stood on one of these,
'Twould be among the tops of trees,
Their upper branches round him wreathing,   40
Their breathing mingled with his breathing.
If—if he stood! Enough of ifs!
He knew a path that wanted walking;
He knew a spring that wanted drinking;
A thought that wanted further thinking;   45
A love that wanted re-renewing.
Nor was this just a way of talking
To save him the expense of doing.
With him it boded action, deed.

The factory was very fine;   50
He wished it all the modern speed.
Yet, after all, 'twas not divine,
That is to say, 'twas not a church.
He never would assume that he'd
Be any institution's need.   55
But he said then and still would say,
If there should ever come a day
When industry seemed like to die
Because he left it in the lurch,

274

Or even merely seemed to pine 60
For want of his approval, why,
Come get him—they knew where to search.

TWO TRAMPS IN MUD TIME

Out of the mud two strangers came
And caught me splitting wood in the yard.
And one of them put me off my aim
By hailing cheerily "Hit them hard!"
I knew pretty well why he dropped behind 5
And let the other go on a way.
I knew pretty well what he had in mind:
He wanted to take my job for pay.

Good blocks of oak it was I split,
As large around as the chopping block; 10
And every piece I squarely hit
Fell splinterless as a cloven rock.
The blows that a life of self-control
Spares to strike for the common good,
That day, giving a loose to my soul, 15
I spent on the unimportant wood.

The sun was warm but the wind was chill.
You know how it is with an April day
When the sun is out and the wind is still,
You're one month on in the middle of May. 20
But if you so much as dare to speak,
A cloud comes over the sunlit arch,
A wind comes off a frozen peak,
And you're two months back in the middle of March.

A bluebird comes tenderly up to alight 25

275

And turns to the wind to unruffle a plume,
His song so pitched as not to excite
A single flower as yet to bloom.
It is snowing a flake: and he half knew
Winter was only playing possum.   30
Except in color he isn't blue,
But he wouldn't advise a thing to blossom.

The water for which we may have to look
In summertime with a witching wand,
In every wheelrut's now a brook,   35
In every print of a hoof a pond.
Be glad of water, but don't forget
The lurking frost in the earth beneath
That will steal forth after the sun is set
And show on the water its crystal teeth.   40

The time when most I loved my task
These two must make me love it more
By coming with what they came to ask.
You'd think I never had felt before
The weight of an ax-head poised aloft,   45
The grip on earth of outspread feet,
The life of muscles rocking soft
And smooth and moist in vernal heat.

Out of the woods two hulking tramps
(From sleeping God knows where last night,   50
But not long since in the lumber camps).
They thought all chopping was theirs of right.
Men of the woods and lumberjacks,
They judged me by their appropriate tool.
Except as a fellow handled an ax   55
They had no way of knowing a fool.

Nothing on either side was said.
They knew they had but to stay their stay
And all their logic would fill my head:
As that I had no right to play   60
With what was another man's work for gain.
My right might be love but theirs was need.
And where the two exist in twain
Theirs was the better right—agreed.

But yield who will to their separation,   65
My object in living is to unite
My avocation and my vocation
As my two eyes make one in sight.
Only where love and need are one,
And the work is play for mortal stakes,   70
Is the deed ever really done
For Heaven and the future's sakes.

THE WHITE-TAILED HORNET

The white-tailed hornet lives in a balloon
That floats against the ceiling of the woodshed.
The exit he comes out at like a bullet
Is like the pupil of a pointed gun.
And having power to change his aim in flight,   5
He comes out more unerring than a bullet.
Verse could be written on the certainty
With which he penetrates my best defense
Of whirling hands and arms about the head
To stab me in the sneeze-nerve of a nostril.   10
Such is the instinct of it I allow.
Yet how about the insect certainty
That in the neighborhood of home and children

Is such an execrable judge of motives
As not to recognize in me the exception   15
I like to think I am in everything—
One who would never hang above a bookcase
His Japanese crepe-paper globe for trophy?
He stung me first and stung me afterward.
He rolled me off the field head over heels   20
And would not listen to my explanations.

That's when I went as visitor to his house.
As visitor at my house he is better.
Hawking for flies about the kitchen door,
In at one door perhaps and out another,   25
Trust him then not to put you in the wrong.
He won't misunderstand your freest movements.
Let him light on your skin unless you mind
So many prickly grappling feet at once.
He's after the domesticated fly   30
To feed his thumping grubs as big as he is.
Here he is at his best, but even here—
I watched him where he swooped, he pounced, he struck;
But what he found he had was just a nailhead.
He struck a second time. Another nailhead.   35
"Those are just nailheads. Those are fastened down."
Then disconcerted and not unannoyed,
He stooped and struck a little huckleberry
The way a player curls around a football.
"Wrong shape, wrong color, and wrong scent," I said.   40
The huckleberry rolled him on his head.
At last it was a fly. He shot and missed;
And the fly circled round him in derision.
But for the fly he might have made me think
He had been at his poetry, comparing   45

278

Nailhead with fly and fly with huckleberry:
How like a fly, how very like a fly.
But the real fly he missed would never do;
The missed fly made me dangerously skeptic.

Won't this whole instinct matter bear revision?   50
Won't almost any theory bear revision?
To err is human, not to, animal.
Or so we pay the compliment to instinct,
Only too liberal of our compliment
That really takes away instead of gives.   55
Our worship, humor, conscientiousness
Went long since to the dogs under the table.
And served us right for having instituted
Downward comparisons. As long on earth
As our comparisons were stoutly upward   60
With gods and angels, we were men at least,
But little lower than the gods and angels.
But once comparisons were yielded downward,
Once we began to see our images
Reflected in the mud and even dust,   65
'Twas disillusion upon disillusion.
We were lost piecemeal to the animals,
Like people thrown out to delay the wolves.
Nothing but fallibility was left us,
And this day's work made even that seem doubtful.   70

A BLUE RIBBON AT AMESBURY

Such a fine pullet ought to go
All coiffured to a winter show,
And be exhibited, and win.
The answer is this one has been—

279

And come with all her honors home.   5
Her golden leg, her coral comb,
Her fluff of plumage, white as chalk,
Her style, were all the fancy's talk.

It seems as if you must have heard.
She scored an almost perfect bird.   10
In her we make ourselves acquainted
With one a Sewell might have painted.

Here common with the flock again,
At home in her abiding pen,
She lingers feeding at the trough,   15
The last to let night drive her off.

The one who gave her ankle-band,
Her keeper, empty pail in hand,
He lingers too, averse to slight
His chores for all the wintry night.   20

He leans against the dusty wall,
Immured almost beyond recall,
A depth past many swinging doors
And many litter-muffled floors.

He meditates the breeder's art.   25
He has a half a mind to start,
With her for Mother Eve, a race
That shall all living things displace.

'Tis ritual with her to lay
The full six days, then rest a day;   30
At which rate barring broodiness
She well may score an egg-success.

The gatherer can always tell

Her well-turned egg's brown sturdy shell,
As safe a vehicle of seed   35
As is vouchsafed to feathered breed.

No human specter at the feast
Can scant or hurry her the least.
She takes her time to take her fill.
She whets a sleepy sated bill.   40

She gropes across the pen alone
To peck herself a precious stone.
She waters at the patent fount.
And so to roost, the last to mount.

The roost is her extent of flight.   45
Yet once she rises to the height,
She shoulders with a wing so strong
She makes the whole flock move along.

The night is setting in to blow.
It scours the windowpane with snow,   50
But barely gets from them or her
For comment a complacent chirr.

The lowly pen is yet a hold
Against the dark and wind and cold
To give a prospect to a plan   55
And warrant prudence in a man.

A DRUMLIN WOODCHUCK

One thing has a shelving bank,
Another a rotting plank,
To give it cozier skies
And make up for its lack of size.

281

My own strategic retreat 5
Is where two rocks almost meet,
And still more secure and snug,
A two-door burrow I dug.

With those in mind at my back
I can sit forth exposed to attack, 10
As one who shrewdly pretends
That he and the world are friends.

All we who prefer to live
Have a little whistle we give,
And flash, at the least alarm 15
We dive down under the farm.

We allow some time for guile
And don't come out for a while,
Either to eat or drink.
We take occasion to think. 20

And if after the hunt goes past
And the double-barreled blast
(Like war and pestilence
And the loss of common sense),

If I can with confidence say 25
That still for another day,
Or even another year,
I will be there for you, my dear,

It will be because, though small
As measured against the All, 30
I have been so instinctively thorough
About my crevice and burrow.

THE GOLD HESPERIDEE

Square Matthew Hale's young grafted apple tree
Began to blossom at the age of five;
And after having entertained the bee,
And cast its flowers and all the stems but three,
It set itself to keep those three alive;   5
And downy wax the three began to thrive.

They had just given themselves a little twist
And turned from looking up and being kissed
To looking down and yet not being sad,
When came Square Hale with Let's see what we had;   10
And two was all he counted (one he missed);
But two for a beginning wasn't bad.

His little Matthew, also five years old,
Was led into the presence of the tree
And raised among the leaves and duly told,   15
We mustn't touch them yet, but see and see!
And what was green would by and by be gold.
Their name was called the Gold Hesperidee.

As regularly as he went to feed the pig
Or milk the cow, he visited the fruit,   20
The dew of night and morning on his boot.
Dearer to him than any barnyard brute,
Each swung in danger on its slender twig,
A bubble on a pipestem, growing big.

Long since they swung as three instead of two—   25
One more, he thought, to take him safely through.
Three made it certain nothing Fate could do
With codlin moth or rusty parasite
Would keep him now from proving with a bite

That the name Gold Hesperidee was right.   30

And so he brought them to the verge of frost.
But one day when the foliage all went swish
With autumn and the fruit was rudely tossed,
He thought no special goodness could be lost
If he fulfilled at last his summer wish,   35
And saw them picked unbruised and in a dish,

Where they could ripen safely to the eating.
But when he came to look, no apples there
Under or on the tree, or anywhere,
And the light-natured tree seemed not to care!   40
'Twas Sunday and Square Hale was dressed for meeting.
The final summons into church was beating.

Just as he was, without an uttered sound
At those who'd done him such a wrong as that,
Square Matthew Hale took off his Sunday hat   45
And ceremoniously laid it on the ground,
And leaping on it with a solemn bound,
Danced slowly on it till he trod it flat.

Then suddenly he saw the thing he did,
And looked around to see if he was seen.   50
This was the sin that Ahaz was forbid
(The meaning of the passage had been hid):
To look upon the tree when it was green
And worship apples. What else could it mean?

God saw him dancing in the orchard path,   55
But mercifully kept the passing crowd
From witnessing the fault of one so proud.
And so the story wasn't told in Gath;

In gratitude for which Square Matthew vowed
To walk a graver man restrained in wrath.   60

IN TIME OF CLOUDBURST

Let the downpour roil and toil!
The worst it can do to me
Is carry some garden soil
A little nearer the sea.

'Tis the world-old way of the rain   5
When it comes to a mountain farm
To exact for a present gain
A little of future harm.

And the harm is none too sure,
For when all that was rotted rich   10
Shall be in the end scoured poor,
When my garden has gone down ditch,

Some force has but to apply,
And summits shall be immersed,
The bottom of seas raised dry—   15
The slope of the earth reversed.

Then all I need do is run
To the other end of the slope,
And on tracts laid new to the sun,
Begin all over to hope.   20

Some worn old tool of my own
Will be turned up by the plow,
The wood of it changed to stone,
But as ready to wield as now.

May my application so close   25
To so endless a repetition
Not make me tired and morose
And resentful of man's condition.

A ROADSIDE STAND

The little old house was out with a little new shed
In front at the edge of the road where the traffic sped,
A roadside stand that too pathetically pled,
It would not be fair to say for a dole of bread,   4
But for some of the money, the cash, whose flow supports
The flower of cities from sinking and withering faint.
The polished traffic passed with a mind ahead,
Or if ever aside a moment, then out of sorts
At having the landscape marred with the artless paint
Of signs that with N turned wrong and S turned wrong 10
Offered for sale wild berries in wooden quarts,
Or crook-necked golden squash with silver warts,
Or beauty rest in a beautiful mountain scene.
You have the money, but if you want to be mean,
Why, keep your money (this crossly) and go along.   15
The hurt to the scenery wouldn't be my complaint
So much as the trusting sorrow of what is unsaid:
Here far from the city we make our roadside stand
And ask for some city money to feel in hand
To try if it will not make our being expand,   20
And give us the life of the moving-pictures' promise
That the party in power is said to be keeping from us.

It is in the news that all these pitiful kin
Are to be bought out and mercifully gathered in
To live in villages, next to the theater and store,   25

Where they won't have to think for themselves anymore;
While greedy good-doers, beneficent beasts of prey,
Swarm over their lives enforcing benefits
That are calculated to soothe them out of their wits,
And by teaching them how to sleep the sleep all day,   30
Destroy their sleeping at night the ancient way.

Sometimes I feel myself I can hardly bear
The thought of so much childish longing in vain,
The sadness that lurks near the open window there,
That waits all day in almost open prayer   35
For the squeal of brakes, the sound of a stopping car,
Of all the thousand selfish cars that pass,
Just one to inquire what a farmer's prices are.
And one did stop, but only to plow up grass
In using the yard to back and turn around;   40
And another to ask the way to where it was bound;
And another to ask could they sell it a gallon of gas
They couldn't (this crossly): they had none, didn't it see?

No, in country money, the country scale of gain,
The requisite lift of spirit has never been found,   45
Or so the voice of the country seems to complain.
I can't help owning the great relief it would be
To put these people at one stroke out of their pain.
And then next day as I come back into the sane,
I wonder how I should like you to come to me   50
And offer to put me gently out of my pain.

DEPARTMENTAL

An ant on the tablecloth
Ran into a dormant moth
Of many times his size.

287

He showed not the least surprise.
His business wasn't with such.   5
He gave it scarcely a touch,
And was off on his duty run.
Yet if he encountered one
Of the hive's enquiry squad
Whose work is to find out God   10
And the nature of time and space,
He would put him onto the case.
Ants are a curious race;
One crossing with hurried tread
The body of one of their dead   15
Isn't given a moment's arrest—
Seems not even impressed.
But he no doubt reports to any
With whom he crosses antennae,
And they no doubt report   20
To the higher-up at court.
Then word goes forth in Formic:
"Death's come to Jerry McCormic,
Our selfless forager Jerry.
Will the special Janizary   25
Whose office it is to bury
The dead of the commissary
Go bring him home to his people.
Lay him in state on a sepal.
Wrap him for shroud in a petal.   30
Embalm him with ichor of nettle.
This is the word of your Queen."
And presently on the scene
Appears a solemn mortician;
And taking formal position,   35
With feelers calmly atwiddle,

Seizes the dead by the middle,
And heaving him high in air,
Carries him out of there.
No one stands round to stare. 40
It is nobody else's affair.

It couldn't be called ungentle.
But how thoroughly departmental.

THE OLD BARN
AT THE BOTTOM OF THE FOGS

Where's this barn's house? It never had a house,
Or joined with sheds in ring-around a dooryard.
The hunter scuffling leaves goes by at dusk,
The gun reversed that he went out with shouldered.
The harvest moon and then the hunter's moon. 5
Well, the moon after that, came one at last
To close this outpost barn and close the season.
The fur-thing, muff-thing, rocking in and out
Across the threshold in the twilight fled him.
He took the props down used for propping open, 10
And set them up again for propping shut,
The widespread double doors two stories high.
The advantage-disadvantage of these doors
Was that tramp taking sanctuary there
Must leave them unlocked to betray his presence. 15
They could be locked but from the outside only.
There is a fellow on the ocean now
Or down a mine or at the mill (I met him)
Who slept there in a mow of meadow hay
One night (he told me). And the barn he meant 20
Was the one I meant. Our details agreed.

We said Well twice to what we had in common,
The old barn at the bottom of the fogs.
Its only windows were the crevices
All up and down it. So that waking there   25
Next morning to the light of day was more
Like waking in a cage of silver bars.
Its locks were props—and that reminded him.
Trust him to have his bitter politics
Against his unacquaintances the rich   30
Who sleep in houses of their own, though mortgaged.
Conservatives, they don't know what to save.
Consider what they treasure under glass,
Yet leave such lovely shafts outdoors to perish.
Would someone only act in time we yet   35
Might see them on a rack like famous oars,
Their label Prop-Locks, only specimens
In chestnut now become a precious wood
As relic of a vanished race of trees—
When these go there will be none to replace them.   40
Yes, right I was, the locks were props outside;
And it had almost given him troubled dreams
To think that though he could not lock himself in,
The cheapest tramp that came along that way
Could mischievously lock him in to stay.   45

ON THE HEART'S BEGINNING
TO CLOUD THE MIND

Something I saw or thought I saw
In the desert at midnight in Utah,
Looking out of my lower berth
At moonlit sky and moonlit earth.
The sky had here and there a star;   5

The earth had a single light afar,
A flickering, human pathetic light,
That was maintained against the night,
It seemed to me, by the people there,
With a Godforsaken brute despair.   10
It would flutter and fall in half an hour
Like the last petal off a flower.
But my heart was beginning to cloud my mind.
I knew a tale of a better kind.
That far light flickers because of trees.   15
The people can burn it as long as they please;
And when their interests in it end,
They can leave it to someone else to tend.
Come back that way a summer hence,
I should find it no more no less intense.   20
I pass, but scarcely pass no doubt,
When one will say, "Let us put it out."
The other without demur agrees.
They can keep it burning as long as they please;
They can put it out whenever they please.   25
One looks out last from the darkened room
At the shiny desert with spots of gloom
That might be people and are but cedar,
Have no purpose, have no leader,
Have never made the first move to assemble,   30
And so are nothing to make her tremble.
She can think of places that are not thus
Without indulging a "Not for us!"
Life is not so sinister-grave.
Matter of fact has made them brave.   35
He is husband, she is wife.
She fears not him, they fear not life.
They know where another light has been,

And more than one, to theirs akin,
But earlier out for bed tonight,   40
So lost on me in my surface flight.

This I saw when waking late,
Going by at a railroad rate,
Looking through wreaths of engine smoke
Far into the lives of other folk.   45

THE FIGURE IN THE DOORWAY

The grade surmounted, we were riding high
Through level mountains nothing to the eye
But scrub oak, scrub oak and the lack of earth
That kept the oaks from getting any girth.
But as through the monotony we ran,   5
We came to where there was a living man.
His great gaunt figure filled his cabin door,
And had he fallen inward on the floor,
He must have measured to the further wall.
But we who passed were not to see him fall.   10
The miles and miles he lived from anywhere
Were evidently something he could bear.
He stood unshaken, and if grim and gaunt,
It was not necessarily from want.
He had the oaks for heating and for light.   15
He had a hen, he had a pig in sight.
He had a well, he had the rain to catch.
He had a ten-by-twenty garden patch.
Nor did he lack for common entertainment.
That I assume was what our passing train meant.   20
He could look at us in our diner eating,
And if so moved uncurl a hand in greeting.

292

AT WOODWARD'S GARDENS

A boy, presuming on his intellect,
Once showed two little monkeys in a cage
A burning-glass they could not understand
And never could be made to understand.
Words are no good: to say it was a lens   5
For gathering solar rays would not have helped.
But let him show them how the weapon worked.
He made the sun a pinpoint on the nose
Of first one, then the other, till it brought
A look of puzzled dimness to their eyes   10
That blinking could not seem to blink away.
They stood arms laced together at the bars,
And exchanged troubled glances over life.
One put a thoughtful hand up to his nose
As if reminded—or as if perhaps   15
Within a million years of an idea.
He got his purple little knuckles stung.
The already known had once more been confirmed
By psychological experiment,
And that were all the finding to announce   20
Had the boy not presumed too close and long.
There was a sudden flash of arm, a snatch,
And the glass was the monkeys', not the boy's.
Precipitately they retired back-cage
And instituted an investigation   25
On their part, though without the needed insight.
They bit the glass and listened for the flavor.
They broke the handle and the binding off it.
Then none the wiser, frankly gave it up,
And having hid it in their bedding straw   30
Against the day of prisoners' ennui,

Came dryly forward to the bars again
To answer for themselves: Who said it mattered
What monkeys did or didn't understand?
They might not understand a burning-glass.   35
They might not understand the sun itself.
It's knowing what to do with things that counts.

A RECORD STRIDE

In a Vermont bedroom closet
With a door of two broad boards
And for back wall a crumbling old chimney
(And that's what their toes are towards),

I have a pair of shoes standing,   5
Old rivals of sagging leather,
Who once kept surpassing each other,
But now live even together.

They listen for me in the bedroom
To ask me a thing or two   10
About who is too old to go walking,
With too much stress on the who.

I wet one last year at Montauk
For a hat I had to save.
The other I wet at the Cliff House   15
In an extra-vagant wave.

Two entirely different grandchildren
Got me into my double adventure.
But when they grow up and can read this
I hope they won't take it for censure.   20

I touch my tongue to the shoes now,
And unless my sense is at fault,
On one I can taste Atlantic,
On the other Pacific, salt.

One foot in each great ocean   25
Is a record stride or stretch.
The authentic shoes it was made in
I should sell for what they would fetch.

But instead I proudly devote them
To my museum and muse;   30
So the thick-skins needn't act thin-skinned
About being past-active shoes.

And I ask all to try to forgive me
For being as overelated
As if I had measured the country   35
And got the United States stated.

LOST IN HEAVEN

The clouds, the source of rain, one stormy night
Offered an opening to the source of dew;
Which I accepted with impatient sight,
Looking for my old sky-marks in the blue.

But stars were scarce in that part of the sky,   5
And no two were of the same constellation—
No one was bright enough to identify;
So 'twas with not ungrateful consternation,

Seeing myself well lost once more, I sighed,
"Where, where in Heaven am I? But don't tell me!   10

O opening clouds, by opening on me wide.
Let's let my heavenly lostness overwhelm me."

DESERT PLACES

Snow falling and night falling fast, oh, fast
In a field I looked into going past,
And the ground almost covered smooth in snow,
But a few weeds and stubble showing last.

The woods around it have it—it is theirs.   5
All animals are smothered in their lairs.
I am too absent-spirited to count;
The loneliness includes me unawares.

And lonely as it is, that loneliness
Will be more lonely ere it will be less—   10
A blanker whiteness of benighted snow
With no expression, nothing to express.

They cannot scare me with their empty spaces
Between stars—on stars where no human race is.
I have it in me so much nearer home   15
To scare myself with my own desert places.

LEAVES COMPARED WITH FLOWERS

A tree's leaves may be ever so good,
So may its bark, so may its wood;
But unless you put the right thing to its root
It never will show much flower or fruit.

But I may be one who does not care   5
Ever to have tree bloom or bear.

Leaves for smooth and bark for rough,
Leaves and bark may be tree enough.

Some giant trees have bloom so small
They might as well have none at all.   10
Late in life I have come on fern.
Now lichens are due to have their turn.

I bade men tell me which in brief,
Which is fairer, flower or leaf.
They did not have the wit to say,   15
Leaves by night and flowers by day.

Leaves and bark, leaves and bark,
To lean against and hear in the dark.
Petals I may have once pursued.
Leaves are all my darker mood.   20

A LEAF-TREADER

I have been treading on leaves all day until I am autumn-
   tired.
God knows all the color and form of leaves I have trodden
   on and mired.
Perhaps I have put forth too much strength and been too
   fierce from fear.
I have safely trodden underfoot the leaves of another year.

All summer long they were overhead, more lifted up than I.   5
To come to their final place in earth they had to pass me by.
All summer long I thought I heard them threatening under
   their breath.
And when they came it seemed with a will to carry me with
   them to death.

297

They spoke to the fugitive in my heart as if it were leaf to
    leaf.
They tapped at my eyelids and touched my lips with an in-
    vitation to grief.   10
But it was no reason I had to go because they had to go.
Now up, my knee, to keep on top of another year of snow.

ON TAKING FROM THE TOP
TO BROADEN THE BASE

Roll stones down on our head!
You squat old pyramid,
Your last good avalanche
Was long since slid.

Your top has sunk too low,   5
Your base has spread too wide,
For you to roll one stone
Down if you tried.

But even at the word
A pebble hit the roof,   10
Another shot through glass,
Demanding proof.

Before their panic hands
Were fighting for the latch,
The mud came in one cold   15
Unleavened batch.

And none was left to prate
Of an old mountain's case
That still took from its top
To broaden its base.   20

THEY WERE WELCOME TO THEIR BELIEF

Grief may have thought it was grief.
Care may have thought it was care.
They were welcome to their belief,
The overimportant pair.

No, it took all the snows that clung   5
To the low roof over his bed,
Beginning when he was young,
To induce the one snow on his head.

But whenever the roof came white
The head in the dark below   10
Was a shade less the color of night,
A shade more the color of snow.

Grief may have thought it was grief.
Care may have thought it was care.
But neither one was the thief   15
Of his raven color of hair.

THE STRONG ARE SAYING NOTHING

The soil now gets a rumpling soft and damp,
And small regard to the future of any weed.
The final flat of the hoe's approval stamp
Is reserved for the bed of a few selected seed.

There is seldom more than a man to a harrowed piece.   5
Men work alone, their lots plowed far apart,
One stringing a chain of seed in an open crease,
And another stumbling after a halting cart.

To the fresh and black of the squares of early mold

299

The leafless bloom of a plum is fresh and white;   10
Though there's more than a doubt if the weather is not too cold
For the bees to come and serve its beauty aright.

Wind goes from farm to farm in wave on wave,
But carries no cry of what is hoped to be.
There may be little or much beyond the grave,   15
But the strong are saying nothing until they see.

THE MASTER SPEED

No speed of wind or water rushing by
But you have speed far greater. You can climb
Back up a stream of radiance to the sky,
And back through history up the stream of time.
And you were given this swiftness, not for haste   5
Nor chiefly that you may go where you will,
But in the rush of everything to waste,
That you may have the power of standing still—
Off any still or moving thing you say.
Two such as you with such a master speed   10
Cannot be parted nor be swept away
From one another once you are agreed
That life is only life forevermore
Together wing to wing and oar to oar.

MOON COMPASSES

I stole forth dimly in the dripping pause
Between two downpours to see what there was.
And a masked moon had spread down compass rays
To a cone mountain in the midnight haze,

As if the final estimate were hers; 5
And as it measured in her calipers,
The mountain stood exalted in its place.
So love will take between the hands a face. . . .

NEITHER OUT FAR NOR IN DEEP

The people along the sand
All turn and look one way.
They turn their back on the land.
They look at the sea all day.

As long as it takes to pass 5
A ship keeps raising its hull;
The wetter ground like glass
Reflects a standing gull.

The land may vary more;
But wherever the truth may be— 10
The water comes ashore,
And the people look at the sea.

They cannot look out far.
They cannot look in deep.
But when was that ever a bar 15
To any watch they keep?

VOICE WAYS

Some things are never clear.
But the weather is clear tonight,
Thanks to a clearing rain.
The mountains are brought up near,
The stars are brought out bright. 5

Your old sweet-cynical strain
Would come in like you here:
"So we won't say nothing is clear."

DESIGN

I found a dimpled spider, fat and white,
On a white heal-all, holding up a moth
Like a white piece of rigid satin cloth—
Assorted characters of death and blight
Mixed ready to begin the morning right,   5
Like the ingredients of a witches' broth—
A snow-drop spider, a flower like a froth,
And dead wings carried like a paper kite.

What had that flower to do with being white,
The wayside blue and innocent heal-all?   10
What brought the kindred spider to that height,
Then steered the white moth thither in the night?
What but design of darkness to appall?—
If design govern in a thing so small.

ON A BIRD SINGING IN ITS SLEEP

A bird half wakened in the lunar noon
Sang halfway through its little inborn tune.
Partly because it sang but once all night
And that from no especial bush's height,
Partly because it sang ventriloquist   5
And had the inspiration to desist
Almost before the prick of hostile ears,
It ventured less in peril than appears.
It could not have come down to us so far,

302

Through the interstices of things ajar   10
On the long bead chain of repeated birth,
To be a bird while we are men on earth,
If singing out of sleep and dream that way
Had made it much more easily a prey.

AFTERFLAKES

In the thick of a teeming snowfall
I saw my shadow on snow.
I turned and looked back up at the sky,
Where we still look to ask the why
Of everything below.   5

If I shed such a darkness,
If the reason was in me,
That shadow of mine should show in form
Against the shapeless shadow of storm,
How swarthy I must be.   10

I turned and looked back upward.
The whole sky was blue;
And the thick flakes floating at a pause
Were but frost knots on an airy gauze,
With the sun shining through.   15

CLEAR AND COLDER

Wind, the season-climate mixer,
In my Witches' Weather Primer
Says, to make this Fall Elixir
First you let the summer simmer,
Using neither spoon nor skimmer,   5

303

Till about the right consistence.
(This like fate by stars is reckoned,
None remaining in existence
Under magnitude the second.)

Then take some leftover winter   10
Far to north of the St. Lawrence.
Leaves to strip and branches splinter,
Bring on wind. Bring rain in torrents—
Colder than the season warrants.

Dash it with some snow for powder.   15
If this seems like witchcraft rather,
If this seems a witches' chowder
(All my eye and Cotton Mather!),

Wait and watch the liquor settle.
I could stand whole dayfuls of it.   20
Wind she brews a heady kettle.
Human beings love it—love it.
Gods above are not above it.

UNHARVESTED

A scent of ripeness from over a wall.
And come to leave the routine road
And look for what had made me stall,
There sure enough was an apple tree
That had eased itself of its summer load,   5
And of all but its trivial foliage free,
Now breathed as light as a lady's fan.
For there there had been an apple fall

As complete as the apple had given man.
The ground was one circle of solid red.   10

May something go always unharvested!
May much stay out of our stated plan,
Apples or something forgotten and left,
So smelling their sweetness would be no theft.

THERE ARE ROUGHLY ZONES

We sit indoors and talk of the cold outside.
And every gust that gathers strength and heaves
Is a threat to the house. But the house has long been tried.
We think of the tree. If it never again has leaves,
We'll know, we say, that this was the night it died.   5
It is very far north, we admit, to have brought the peach.
What comes over a man, is it soul or mind—
That to no limits and bounds he can stay confined?
You would say his ambition was to extend the reach
Clear to the Arctic of every living kind.   10
Why is his nature forever so hard to teach
That though there is no fixed line between wrong and right,
There are roughly zones whose laws must be obeyed?
There is nothing much we can do for the tree tonight,
But we can't help feeling more than a little betrayed   15
That the northwest wind should rise to such a height
Just when the cold went down so many below.
The tree has no leaves and may never have them again.
We must wait till some months hence in the spring to know.
But if it is destined never again to grow,   20
It can blame this limitless trait in the hearts of men.

A TRIAL RUN

I said to myself almost in prayer,
It will start hair-raising currents of air
When you give it the livid metal-sap.
It will make a homicidal roar.
It will shake its cast stone reef of floor.   5
It will gather speed till your nerves prepare
To hear it wreck in a thunderclap.
But stand your ground,
As they say in war.
It is cotter-pinned, it is bedded true.   10
Everything its parts can do
Has been thought out and accounted for.
Your least touch sets it going round,
And when to stop it rests with you.

NOT QUITE SOCIAL

Some of you will be glad I did what I did,
And the rest won't want to punish me too severely
For finding a thing to do that though not forbid
Yet wasn't enjoined and wasn't expected, clearly.

To punish me overcruelly wouldn't be right   5
For merely giving you once more gentle proof
That the city's hold on a man is no more tight
Than when its walls rose higher than any roof.

You may taunt me with not being able to flee the earth.
You have me there, but loosely, as I would be held.   10
The way of understanding is partly mirth.
I would not be taken as ever having rebelled.

306

And anyone is free to condemn me to death—
If he leaves it to nature to carry out the sentence.
I shall will to the common stock of air my breath   15
And pay a death tax of fairly polite repentance.

PROVIDE, PROVIDE

The witch that came (the withered hag)
To wash the steps with pail and rag
Was once the beauty Abishag,

The picture pride of Hollywood.
Too many fall from great and good   5
For you to doubt the likelihood.

Die early and avoid the fate.
Or if predestined to die late,
Make up your mind to die in state.

Make the whole stock exchange your own!   10
If need be occupy a throne,
Where nobody can call *you* crone.

Some have relied on what they knew,
Others on being simply true.
What worked for them might work for you.   15

No memory of having starred
Atones for later disregard
Or keeps the end from being hard.

Better to go down dignified
With boughten friendship at your side   20
Than none at all. Provide, provide!

TEN MILLS

I. PRECAUTION

I never dared be radical when young
For fear it would make me conservative when old.

II. THE SPAN OF LIFE

The old dog barks backward without getting up.
I can remember when he was a pup.

III. THE WRIGHTS' BIPLANE

This biplane is the shape of human flight.
Its name might better be First Motor Kite.
Its makers' name—Time cannot get that wrong,
For it was writ in heaven doubly Wright.

IV. EVIL TENDENCIES CANCEL

Will the blight end the chestnut?
The farmers rather guess not.
It keeps smoldering at the roots
And sending up new shoots
Till another parasite
Shall come to end the blight.

5

V. PERTINAX

Let chaos storm!
Let cloud shapes swarm!
I wait for form.

VI. WASPISH

On glossy wires artistically bent
He draws himself up to his full extent.
His natty wings with self-assurance perk.
His stinging quarters menacingly work.
Poor egotist, he has no way of knowing   5
But he's as good as anybody going.

VII. ONE GUESS

He has dust in his eyes and a fan for a wing,
A leg akimbo with which he can sing,
And a mouthful of dyestuff instead of a sting.

VIII. THE HARDSHIP OF ACCOUNTING

Never ask of money spent
Where the spender thinks it went.
Nobody was ever meant
To remember or invent
What he did with every cent.   5

IX. NOT ALL THERE

I turned to speak to God
About the world's despair;
But to make bad matters worse
I found God wasn't there.

God turned to speak to me   5
(Don't anybody laugh);
God found I wasn't there—
At least not over half.

X. IN DIVÉS' DIVE

It is late at night and still I am losing,
But still I am steady and unaccusing.

As long as the Declaration guards
My right to be equal in number of cards,

It is nothing to me who runs the Dive.   5
Let's have a look at another five.

THE VINDICTIVES

You like to hear about gold.
A king filled his prison room
As full as the room could hold
To the top of his reach on the wall
With every known shape of the stuff.   5
'Twas to buy himself off his doom.
But it wasn't ransom enough.
His captors accepted it all,
But didn't let go of the king.
They made him send out a call   10
To his subjects to gather them more.
And his subjects wrung all they could wring
Out of temple and palace and store.
But when there seemed no more to bring,
His captors convicted the king   15
Of once having started a war,
And strangled the wretch with a string.

But really that gold was not half
That a king might have hoped to compel—
Not a half, not a third, not a tithe.   20

310

The king had scarce ceased to writhe,
When hate gave a terrible laugh,
Like a manhole opened to Hell.
If gold pleased the conqueror, well,
That gold should be the one thing   25
The conqueror henceforth should lack.

They gave no more thought to the king.
All joined in the game of hide-gold.
They swore all the gold should go back
Deep into the earth whence it came.   30
Their minds ran on cranny and crack.
All joined in the maddening game.
The tale is still boastingly told
Of many a treasure by name
That vanished into the black   35
And put out its light for the foe.

That self-sack and self-overthrow,
That was the splendidest sack
Since the forest Germans sacked Rome
And took the gold candlesticks home.   40

One Inca prince on the rack,
And late in his last hour alive,
Told them in what lake to dive
To seek what they seemed so to want.
They dived and nothing was found.   45
He told them to dive till they drowned.
The whole fierce conquering pack
Hunted and tortured and raged.
There were suns of story and vaunt
They searched for into Brazil,   50
Their tongues hanging out unassuaged.

311

But the conquered grew meek and still.
They slowly and silently aged.
They kept their secrets and died,
Maliciously satisfied.   55
One knew of a burial hole
In the floor of a tribal cave,
Where under deep ash and charcoal
And cracked bones, human and beast,
The midden of feast upon feast,   60
Was coiled in its last resting grave
The great treasure wanted the most,
The great thousand-linked gold chain,
Each link of a hundredweight,
That once between post and post   65
(In-leaning under the strain),
And looped ten times back and forth,
Had served as a palace gate.
Some said it had gone to the coast,
Some over the mountains east,   70
Some into the country north,
On the backs of a single-file host,
Commanded by one sun-priest,
And raising a dust with a train
Of flashing links in the sun.   75
No matter what some may say.
(The saying is never done.)
There bright in the filth it lay
Untarnished by rust and decay.
And be all plunderers curst.   80

"The best way to hate is the worst.
'Tis to find what the hated need,
Never mind of what actual worth,

312

And wipe that out of the earth.
Let them die of unsatisfied greed,   85
Of unsatisfied love of display,
Of unsatisfied love of the high,
Unvulgar, unsoiled, and ideal.
Let their trappings be taken away.
Let them suffer starvation and die   90
Of being brought down to the real."

THE BEARER OF EVIL TIDINGS

The bearer of evil tidings,
When he was halfway there,
Remembered that evil tidings
Were a dangerous thing to bear.

So when he came to the parting   5
Where one road led to the throne
And one went off to the mountains
And into the wild unknown,

He took the one to the mountains.
He ran through the Vale of Cashmere,   10
He ran through the rhododendrons
Till he came to the land of Pamir.

And there in a precipice valley
A girl of his age he met
Took him home to her bower,   15
Or he might be running yet.

She taught him her tribe's religion:
How, ages and ages since,
A princess en route from China

To marry a Persian prince

Had been found with child; and her army
Had come to a troubled halt.
And though a god was the father
And nobody else at fault,

It had seemed discreet to remain there 25
And neither go on nor back.
So they stayed and declared a village
There in the land of the Yak.

And the child that came of the princess
Established a royal line, 30
And his mandates were given heed to
Because he was born divine.

And that was why there were people
On one Himalayan shelf;
And the bearer of evil tidings 35
Decided to stay there himself.

At least he had this in common
With the race he chose to adopt:
They had both of them had their reasons
For stopping where they had stopped. 40

As for his evil tidings,
Belshazzar's overthrow,
Why hurry to tell Belshazzar
What soon enough he would know?

IRIS BY NIGHT

One misty evening, one another's guide,
We two were groping down a Malvern side
The last wet fields and dripping hedges home.
There came a moment of confusing lights,
Such as according to belief in Rome   5
Were seen of old at Memphis on the heights
Before the fragments of a former sun
Could concentrate anew and rise as one.
Light was a paste of pigment in our eyes.
And then there was a moon and then a scene   10
So watery as to seem submarine;
In which we two stood saturated, drowned.
The clover-mingled rowan on the ground
Had taken all the water it could as dew,
And still the air was saturated too,   15
Its airy pressure turned to water weight.
Then a small rainbow like a trellis gate,
A very small moon-made prismatic bow,
Stood closely over us through which to go.
And then we were vouchsafed the miracle   20
That never yet to other two befell
And I alone of us have lived to tell.
A wonder! Bow and rainbow as it bent,
Instead of moving with us as we went
(To keep the pots of gold from being found),   25
It lifted from its dewy pediment
Its two mote-swimming many-colored ends
And gathered them together in a ring.
And we stood in it softly circled round
From all division time or foe can bring   30
In a relation of elected friends.

BUILD SOIL

A political pastoral

Why, Tityrus! But you've forgotten me.
I'm Meliboeus the potato man,
The one you had the talk with, you remember,
Here on this very campus years ago.
Hard times have struck me and I'm on the move.   5
I've had to give my interval farm up
For interest, and I've bought a mountain farm
For nothing down, all-out-doors of a place,
All woods and pasture only fit for sheep.
But sheep is what I'm going into next.   10
I'm done forever with potato crops
At thirty cents a bushel. Give me sheep.
I know wool's down to seven cents a pound.
But I don't calculate to sell my wool.
I didn't my potatoes. I consumed them.   15
I'll dress up in sheep's clothing and eat sheep.
The Muse takes care of you. You live by writing
Your poems on a farm and call that farming.
Oh, I don't blame you. I say take life easy.
I should myself, only I don't know how.   20
But have some pity on us who have to work.
Why don't you use your talents as a writer
To advertise our farms to city buyers,
Or else write something to improve food prices.
Get in a poem toward the next election.   25

Oh, Meliboeus, I have half a mind
To take a writing hand in politics.
Before now poetry has taken notice
Of wars, and what are wars but politics

316

Transformed from chronic to acute and bloody?   30

I may be wrong, but, Tityrus, to me
The times seem revolutionary bad.

The question is whether they've reached a depth
Of desperation that would warrant poetry's
Leaving love's alternations, joy and grief,   35
The weather's alternations, summer and winter,
Our age-long theme, for the uncertainty
Of judging who is a contemporary liar—
Who in particular, when all alike
Get called as much in clashes of ambition.   40
Life may be tragically bad, and I
Make bold to sing it so, but do I dare
Name names and tell you who by name is wicked?
Whittier's luck with Skipper Ireson awes me—
Many men's luck with Greatest Washington   45
(Who sat for Stuart's portrait, but who sat
Equally for the nation's Constitution).
I prefer to sing safely in the realm
Of types, composite and imagined people:
To affirm there is such a thing as evil   50
Personified, but ask to be excused
From saying on a jury "Here's the guilty."

I doubt if you're convinced the times are bad.

I keep my eye on Congress, Meliboeus.
They're in the best position of us all   55
To know if anything is very wrong.
I mean they could be trusted to give the alarm
If earth were thought about to change its axis,
Or a star coming to dilate the sun.
As long as lightly all their livelong sessions,   60

Like a yardful of schoolboys out at recess
Before their plays and games were organized,
They yelling mix tag, hide-and-seek, hopscotch,
And leapfrog in each other's way—all's well.
Let newspapers profess to fear the worst!   65
Nothing's portentous, I am reassured.

Is socialism needed, do you think?

We have it now. For socialism is
An element in any government.
There's no such thing as socialism pure—   70
Except as an abstraction of the mind.
There's only democratic socialism,
Monarchic socialism, oligarchic—
The last being what they seem to have in Russia.
You often get it most in monarchy,   75
Least in democracy. In practice, pure,
I don't know what it would be. No one knows.
I have no doubt like all the loves when
Philosophized together into one—
One sickness of the body and the soul.   80
Thank God our practice holds the loves apart,
Beyond embarrassing self-consciousness
Where natural friends are met, where dogs are kept,
Where women pray with priests. There is no love.
There's only love of men and women, love   85
Of children, love of friends, of men, of God:
Divine love, human love, parental love,
Roughly discriminated for the rough.

Poetry, itself once more, is back in love.

Pardon the analogy, my Meliboeus,   90

318

For sweeping me away. Let's see, where was I?

But don't you think more should be socialized
Than is?

What should you mean by socialized?

Made good for everyone—things like inventions—
Made so we all should get the good of them—   95
All, not just great exploiting businesses.

We sometimes only get the bad of them.
In your sense of the word ambition has
Been socialized—the first propensity
To be attempted. Greed may well come next.   100
But the worst one of all to leave uncurbed,
Unsocialized, is ingenuity:
Which for no sordid self-aggrandizement,
For nothing but its own blind satisfaction
(In this it is as much like hate as love),   105
Works in the dark as much against as for us.
Even while we talk some chemist at Columbia
Is stealthily contriving wool from jute
That when let loose upon the grazing world
Will put ten thousand farmers out of sheep.   110
Everyone asks for freedom for himself,
The man free love, the businessman free trade,
The writer and talker free speech and free press.
Political ambition has been taught,
By being punished back, it is not free: 115
It must at some point gracefully refrain.
Greed has been taught a little abnegation
And shall be more before we're done with it.
It is just fool enough to think itself

Self-taught. But our brute snarling and lashing taught it.
None shall be as ambitious as he can.
None should be as ingenious as he could,
Not if I had my say. Bounds should be set
To ingenuity for being so cruel
In bringing change unheralded on the unready.   125

I elect you to put the curb on it.

Were I dictator, I'll tell you what I'd do.

What should you do?

                     I'd let things take their course
And then I'd claim the credit for the outcome.

You'd make a sort of safety-first dictator.   130

Don't let the things I say against myself
Betray you into taking sides against me,
Or it might get you into trouble with me.
I'm not afraid to prophesy the future,
And be judged by the outcome, Meliboeus.   135
Listen and I will take my dearest risk.
We're always too much out or too much in.
At present from a cosmical dilation
We're so much out that the odds are against
Our ever getting inside in again.   140
But inside in is where we've got to get.
My friends all know I'm interpersonal.
But long before I'm interpersonal,
Away 'way down inside I'm personal.
Just so before we're international,   145
We're national and act as nationals.
The colors are kept unmixed on the palette,
Or better on dish plates all around the room,

320

So the effect when they are mixed on canvas
May seem almost exclusively designed.   150
Some minds are so confounded intermental
They remind me of pictures on a palette:
"Look at what happened. Surely some god *pinxit*.
Come look at my significant mud pie."
It's hard to tell which is the worse abhorrence,   155
Whether it's persons pied or nations pied.
Don't let me seem to say the exchange, the encounter,
May not be the important thing at last.
It well may be. We meet—I don't say when—
But must bring to the meeting the maturest,   160
The longest-saved-up, raciest, localest
We have strength of reserve in us to bring.

Tityrus, sometimes I'm perplexed myself
To find the good of commerce. Why should I
Have to sell you my apples and buy yours?   165
It can't be just to give the robber a chance
To catch them and take toll of them in transit.
Too mean a thought to get much comfort out of.
I figure that like any bandying
Of words or toys, it ministers to health.   170
It very likely quickens and refines us.

To market 'tis our destiny to go.
But much as in the end we bring for sale there,
There is still more we never bring or should bring;
More that should be kept back—the soil for instance,   175
In my opinion—though we both know poets
Who fall all over each other to bring soil
And even subsoil and hardpan to market.
To sell the hay off, let alone the soil,

Is an unpardonable sin in farming. 180
The moral is, make a late start to market.
Let me preach to you, will you, Meliboeus?

Preach on. I thought you were already preaching.
But preach and see if I can tell the difference.

Needless to say to you, my argument 185
Is not to lure the city to the country.
Let those possess the land, and only those,
Who love it with a love so strong and stupid
That they may be abused and taken advantage of
And made fun of by business, law, and art; 190
They still hang on. That so much of the earth's
Unoccupied need not make us uneasy.
We don't pretend to complete occupancy.
The world's one globe, human society
Another softer globe that slightly flattened 195
Rests on the world, and clinging slowly rolls.
We have our own round shape to keep unbroken.
The world's size has no more to do with us
Than has the universe's. We are balls,
We are round from the same source of roundness. 200
We are both round because the mind is round,
Because all reasoning is in a circle.
At least that's why the universe is round.

If what you're preaching is a line of conduct,
Just what am I supposed to do about it? 205
Reason in circles?

                    No, refuse to be
Seduced back to the land by any claim
The land may seem to have on man to use it.
Let none assume to till the land but farmers.

I only speak to you as one of them.   210
You shall go to your run-out mountain farm,
Poor castaway of commerce, and so live
That none shall ever see you come to market—
Not for a long, long time. Plant, breed, produce,
But what you raise or grow, why, feed it out,   215
Eat it or plow it under where it stands,
To build the soil. For what is more accursed
Than an impoverished soil, pale and metallic?
What cries more to our kind for sympathy?
I'll make a compact with you, Meliboeus,   220
To match you deed for deed and plan for plan.
Friends crowd around me with their five-year plans
That Soviet Russia has made fashionable.
You come to me and I'll unfold to you
A five-year plan I call so not because   225
It takes ten years or so to carry out,
Rather because it took five years at least
To think it out. Come close, let us conspire—
In self-restraint, if in restraint of trade.
You will go to your run-out mountain farm   230
And do what I command you. I take care
To command only what you meant to do
Anyway. That is my style of dictator.
Build soil. Turn the farm in upon itself
Until it can contain itself no more,   235
But sweating-full, drips wine and oil a little.
I will go to my run-out social mind
And be as unsocial with it as I can.
The thought I have, and my first impulse is
To take to market—I will turn it under.   240
The thought from that thought—I will turn it under.
And so on to the limit of my nature.

We are too much out, and if we won't draw in
We shall be driven in. I was brought up
A state-rights free-trade Democrat. What's that?   245
An inconsistency. The state shall be
Laws to itself, it seems, and yet have no
Control of what it sells or what it buys.
Suppose someone comes near me who in rate
Of speech and thinking is so much my better   250
I am imposed on, silenced and discouraged.
Do I submit to being supplied by him
As the more economical producer,
More wonderful, more beautiful producer?
No. I unostentatiously move off   255
Far enough for my thought-flow to resume.
Thought product and food product are to me
Nothing compared to the producing of them.
I sent you once a song with the refrain:

    Let me be the one   260
    To do what is done—

My share at least, lest I be empty-idle.
Keep off each other and keep each other off.
You see the beauty of my proposal is
It needn't wait on general revolution.   265
I bid you to a one-man revolution—
The only revolution that is coming.
We're too unseparate out among each other—
With goods to sell and notions to impart.
A youngster comes to me with half a quatrain   270
To ask me if I think it worth the pains
Of working out the rest, the other half.
I am brought guaranteed young prattle poems
Made publicly in school, above suspicion

Of plagiarism and help of cheating parents.   275
We congregate embracing from distrust
As much as love, and too close in to strike
And be so very striking. Steal away,
The song says. Steal away and stay away.
Don't join too many gangs. Join few if any.   280
Join the United States and join the family—
But not much in between unless a college.
Is it a bargain, Shepherd Meliboeus?

Probably, but you're far too fast and strong
For my mind to keep working in your presence.   285
I can tell better after I get home,
Better a month from now when cutting posts
Or mending fence it all comes back to me
What I was thinking when you interrupted
My life-train logic. I agree with you   290
We're too unseparate. And going home
From company means coming to our senses.

TO A THINKER

The last step taken found your heft
Decidedly upon the left.
One more would throw you on the right.
Another still—you see your plight.
You call this thinking, but it's walking.   5
Not even that, it's only rocking,
Or weaving like a stabled horse:
From force to matter and back to force,
From form to content and back to form,
From norm to crazy and back to norm,   10
From bound to free and back to bound,

From sound to sense and back to sound.
So back and forth. It almost scares
A man the way things come in pairs.
Just now you're off democracy   15
(With a polite regret to be)
And leaning on dictatorship;
But if you will accept the tip,
In less than no time, tongue and pen,
You'll be a democrat again.   20
A reasoner and good as such,
Don't let it bother you too much
If it makes you look helpless, please,
And a temptation to the tease.
Suppose you've no direction in you,   25
I don't see but you must continue
To use the gift you do possess,
And sway with reason more or less.
I own I never really warmed
To the reformer or reformed.   30
And yet conversion has its place
Not halfway down the scale of grace.
So if you find you must repent
From side to side in argument,
At least don't use your mind too hard,   35
But trust my instinct—I'm a bard.

A MISSIVE MISSILE

Someone in ancient Mas d'Azil
Once took a little pebble wheel
And dotted it with red for me,
And sent it to me years and years—
A million years to be precise—   5

326

Across the barrier of ice:
Two round dots and a ripple streak,
So vivid as to seem to speak.
But what imperfectly appears
Is whether the two dots were tears,   10
Two teardrops, one for either eye,
And the wave line a shaken sigh.
But no, the color used is red.
Not tears but drops of blood instead.
The line must be a jagged blade.   15
The sender must have had to die,
And wanted someone now to know
His death was sacrificial-votive.
So almost clear and yet obscure.
If only anyone were sure   20
A motive then was still a motive.
O you who bring this to my hand,
You are no common messenger
(Your badge of office is a spade).
It grieves me to have had you stand   25
So long for nothing. No reply—
There is no answer, I'm afraid,
Across the icy barrier
For my obscure petitioner.
Suppose his ghost is standing by   30
Importunate to give the hint
And be successfully conveyed.
How anyone can fail to see
Where perfectly in form and tint
The metaphor, the symbol lies!   35
Why will I not analogize?
(I do too much in some men's eyes.)
Oh, slow uncomprehending me,

Enough to make a spirit moan
Or rustle in a bush or tree. 40
I have the ocher-written flint,
The two dots and the ripple line.
The meaning of it is unknown,
Or else I fear entirely mine,
All modern, nothing ancient in't, 45
Unsatisfying to us each.
Far as we aim our signs to reach,
Far as we often make them reach,
Across the soul-from-soul abyss,
There is an aeon-limit set 50
Beyond which they are doomed to miss.
Two souls may be too widely met.
That sad-with-distance river beach
With mortal longing may beseech;
It cannot speak as far as this. 55

A Witness Tree

: 1942 :

BEECH

Where my imaginary line
Bends square in woods, an iron spine
And pile of real rocks have been founded.
And off this corner in the wild,
Where these are driven in and piled,   5
One tree, by being deeply wounded,
Has been impressed as Witness Tree
And made commit to memory
My proof of being not unbounded.
Thus truth's established and borne out,   10
Though circumstanced with dark and doubt—
Though by a world of doubt surrounded.

—The Moodie Forester

SYCAMORE

Zaccheus he
Did climb the tree
Our Lord to see.

—The New England Primer

THE SILKEN TENT

She is as in a field a silken tent
At midday when a sunny summer breeze
Has dried the dew and all its ropes relent,
So that in guys it gently sways at ease,

331

And its supporting central cedar pole,
That is its pinnacle to heavenward
And signifies the sureness of the soul,
Seems to owe naught to any single cord,
But strictly held by none, is loosely bound
By countless silken ties of love and thought
To everything on earth the compass round,
And only by one's going slightly taut
In the capriciousness of summer air
Is of the slightest bondage made aware.

ALL REVELATION

A head thrusts in as for the view,
But where it is it thrusts in from
Or what it is it thrusts into
By that Cyb'laean avenue,
And what can of its coming come,

And whither it will be withdrawn,
And what take hence or leave behind,
These things the mind has pondered on
A moment and still asking gone.
Strange apparition of the mind!

But the impervious geode
Was entered, and its inner crust
Of crystals with a ray cathode
At every point and facet glowed
In answer to the mental thrust.

Eyes seeking the response of eyes
Bring out the stars, bring out the flowers,

Thus concentrating earth and skies
So none need be afraid of size.
All revelation has been ours.   20

HAPPINESS MAKES UP IN HEIGHT
FOR WHAT IT LACKS IN LENGTH

O stormy, stormy world,
The days you were not swirled
Around with mist and cloud,
Or wrapped as in a shroud,
And the sun's brilliant ball   5
Was not in part or all
Obscured from mortal view—
Were days so very few
I can but wonder whence
I get the lasting sense   10
Of so much warmth and light.
If my mistrust is right
It may be altogether
From one day's perfect weather,
When starting clear at dawn   15
The day swept clearly on
To finish clear at eve.
I verily believe
My fair impression may
Be all from that one day   20
No shadow crossed but ours
As through its blazing flowers
We went from house to wood
For change of solitude.

COME IN

As I came to the edge of the woods,
Thrush music—hark!
Now if it was dusk outside,
Inside it was dark.

Too dark in the woods for a bird   5
By sleight of wing
To better its perch for the night,
Though it still could sing.

The last of the light of the sun
That had died in the west   10
Still lived for one song more
In a thrush's breast.

Far in the pillared dark
Thrush music went—
Almost like a call to come in   15
To the dark and lament.

But no, I was out for stars:
I would not come in.
I meant not even if asked,
And I hadn't been.   20

I COULD GIVE ALL TO TIME

To Time it never seems that he is brave
To set himself against the peaks of snow
To lay them level with the running wave,
Nor is he overjoyed when they lie low,
But only grave, contemplative and grave.   5

334

What now is inland shall be ocean isle,
Then eddies playing round a sunken reef
Like the curl at the corner of a smile;
And I could share Time's lack of joy or grief
At such a planetary change of style.   10

I could give all to Time except—except
What I myself have held. But why declare
The things forbidden that while the Customs slept
I have crossed to Safety with? For I am There,
And what I would not part with I have kept.   15

CARPE DIEM

Age saw two quiet children
Go loving by at twilight,
He knew not whether homeward,
Or outward from the village,
Or (chimes were ringing) churchward.   5
He waited (they were strangers)
Till they were out of hearing
To bid them both be happy.
"Be happy, happy, happy,
And seize the day of pleasure."   10
The age-long theme is Age's.
'Twas Age imposed on poems
Their gather-roses burden
To warn against the danger
That overtaken lovers   15
From being overflooded
With happiness should have it
And yet not know they have it.
But bid life seize the present?

335

It lives less in the present   20
Than in the future always,
And less in both together
Than in the past. The present
Is too much for the senses,
Too crowding, too confusing—   25
Too present to imagine.

THE WIND AND THE RAIN

I

That far-off day the leaves in flight
Were letting in the colder light.
A season-ending wind there blew
That, as it did the forest strew,
I leaned on with a singing trust   5
And let it drive me deathward too.
With breaking step I stabbed the dust,
Yet did not much to shorten stride.
I sang of death—but had I known
The many deaths one must have died   10
Before he came to meet his own!
Oh, should a child be left unwarned
That any song in which he mourned
Would be as if he prophesied?
It were unworthy of the tongue   15
To let the half of life alone
And play the good without the ill.
And yet 'twould seem that what is sung
In happy sadness by the young,
Fate has no choice but to fulfill.   20

II

Flowers in the desert heat
Contrive to bloom
On melted mountain water led by flume
To wet their feet.
But something in it still is incomplete.   25
Before I thought the wilted to exalt
With water I would see them water-bowed.
I would pick up all ocean less its salt,
And though it were as much as cloud could bear
Would load it onto cloud,   30
And rolling it inland on roller air,
Would empty it unsparing on the flower
That past its prime lost petals in the flood
(Who cares but for the future of the bud?),
And all the more the mightier the shower   35
Would run in under it to get my share.

'Tis not enough on roots and in the mouth,
But give me water heavy on the head
In all the passion of a broken drouth.

And there is always more than should be said.   40

As strong is rain without as wine within,
As magical as sunlight on the skin.

I have been one no dwelling could contain
When there was rain;
But I must forth at dusk, my time of day,   45
To see to the unburdening of skies.
Rain was the tears adopted by my eyes
That have none left to stay.

THE MOST OF IT

He thought he kept the universe alone;
For all the voice in answer he could wake
Was but the mocking echo of his own
From some tree-hidden cliff across the lake.
Some morning from the boulder-broken beach   5
He would cry out on life, that what it wants
Is not its own love back in copy speech,
But counter-love, original response.
And nothing ever came of what he cried
Unless it was the embodiment that crashed   10
In the cliff's talus on the other side,
And then in the far-distant water splashed,
But after a time allowed for it to swim,
Instead of proving human when it neared
And someone else additional to him,   15
As a great buck it powerfully appeared,
Pushing the crumpled water up ahead,
And landed pouring like a waterfall,
And stumbled through the rocks with horny tread,
And forced the underbrush—and that was all.   20

NEVER AGAIN WOULD BIRDS' SONG
BE THE SAME

He would declare and could himself believe
That the birds there in all the garden round
From having heard the daylong voice of Eve
Had added to their own an oversound,
Her tone of meaning but without the words.   5
Admittedly an eloquence so soft
Could only have had an influence on birds

338

When call or laughter carried it aloft.
Be that as may be, she was in their song.
Moreover her voice upon their voices crossed   10
Had now persisted in the woods so long
That probably it never would be lost.
Never again would birds' song be the same.
And to do that to birds was why she came.

THE SUBVERTED FLOWER

She drew back; he was calm:
"It is this that had the power."
And he lashed his open palm
With the tender-headed flower.
He smiled for her to smile,   5
But she was either blind
Or willfully unkind.
He eyed her for a while
For a woman and a puzzle.
He flicked and flung the flower,   10
And another sort of smile
Caught up like fingertips
The corners of his lips
And cracked his ragged muzzle.
She was standing to the waist   15
In goldenrod and brake,
Her shining hair displaced.
He stretched her either arm
As if she made it ache
To clasp her—not to harm;   20
As if he could not spare
To touch her neck and hair.
"If this has come to us

339

And not to me alone——"
So she thought she heard him say;   25
Though with every word he spoke
His lips were sucked and blown
And the effort made him choke
Like a tiger at a bone.
She had to lean away.   30
She dared not stir a foot,
Lest movement should provoke
The demon of pursuit
That slumbers in a brute.
It was then her mother's call   35
From inside the garden wall
Made her steal a look of fear
To see if he could hear
And would pounce to end it all
Before her mother came.   40
She looked and saw the shame:
A hand hung like a paw,
An arm worked like a saw
As if to be persuasive,
An ingratiating laugh   45
That cut the snout in half,
An eye become evasive.
A girl could only see
That a flower had marred a man,
But what she could not see   50
Was that the flower might be
Other than base and fetid:
That the flower had done but part,
And what the flower began
Her own too meager heart   55

Had terribly completed.
She looked and saw the worst.
And the dog or what it was,
Obeying bestial laws,
A coward save at night,   60
Turned from the place and ran.
She heard him stumble first
And use his hands in flight.
She heard him bark outright.
And oh, for one so young   65
The bitter words she spit
Like some tenacious bit
That will not leave the tongue.
She plucked her lips for it,
And still the horror clung.   70
Her mother wiped the foam
From her chin, picked up her comb,
And drew her backward home.

WILLFUL HOMING

It is getting dark and time he drew to a house,
But the blizzard blinds him to any house ahead.
The storm gets down his neck in an icy souse
That sucks his breath like a wicked cat in bed.

The snow blows on him and off him, exerting force   5
Downward to make him sit astride a drift,
Imprint a saddle, and calmly consider a course.
He peers out shrewdly into the thick and swift.

Since he means to come to a door he will come to a door,
Although so compromised of aim and rate   10

He may fumble wide of the knob a yard or more,
And to those concerned he may seem a little late.

A CLOUD SHADOW

A breeze discovered my open book
And began to flutter the leaves to look
For a poem there used to be on Spring.
I tried to tell her "There's no such thing!"

For whom would a poem on Spring be by?   5
The breeze disdained to make reply;
And a cloud shadow crossed her face
For fear I would make her miss the place.

THE QUEST OF THE PURPLE-FRINGED

I felt the chill of the meadow underfoot,
But the sun overhead;
And snatches of verse and song of scenes like this
I sung or said.

I skirted the margin alders for miles and miles   5
In a sweeping line.
The day was the day by every flower that blooms,
But I saw no sign.

Yet further I went to be before the scythe,
For the grass was high;   10
Till I saw the path where the slender fox had come
And gone panting by.

Then at last and following him I found—
In the very hour

When the color flushed to the petals it must have been— 15
The far-sought flower.

There stood the purple spires with no breath of air
Nor headlong bee
To disturb their perfect poise the livelong day
'Neath the alder tree.   20

I only knelt and putting the boughs aside
Looked, or at most
Counted them all to the buds in the copse's depth
That were pale as a ghost.

Then I arose and silently wandered home,   25
And I for one
Said that the fall might come and whirl of leaves,
For summer was done.

THE DISCOVERY OF THE MADEIRAS

A rhyme of Hakluyt

A stolen lady was coming on board,
But whether stolen from her wedded lord
Or from her own self against her will
Was not set forth in the lading bill.
A stolen lady was all it said.   5
She came down weakly and blindly led
To the darkening, windy village slip.
She would not look at the fateful ship.
Her lover to make the ordeal swift
Had to give her the final lift   10
And force her farewell step off shore.
The way she clung to him the more
Seemed to argue perhaps she went

343

Not entirely without consent.
But with no companion of womankind 15
To leave the English law behind
And sail for some vague Paphian bourn
Began already to seem forlorn.

It did more distance up and down,
Their little stormy ship, than on. 20
Now it took a fitful run;
Now standing cracked its sail and spun;
Now stood upon its bulging prow
Till the pirate sailors made a vow
Of where they would go on pilgrimage 25
If God would spare them to die of age.
When the clap of two converging waves
Failed to crush their barrel staves
Or the wind to snap their walking stick,
They laughed as if they had turned a trick. 30

This was no lady's time of year.
For long the lady would disappear,
And might be rolling dead below
For all the crew were let to know.
But when the ocean's worst had passed 35
She was carried out beside the mast,
Where all day long she lay and dozed.
Or she and her lover would sit opposed
And darkly drink each other's eyes
With faint headshakings, no more wise. 40
The most he asked her eyes to grant
Was that in what she does not want
A woman wants to be overruled.
Or was the instinct in him fooled?

He knew not, neither of them knew. 45
They could only say like any two,
"You tell me and I'll tell you."

Sometimes, with her permissive smile,
He left her to her thoughts awhile
And went to lean against the rail, 50
And let the captain tell him a tale.
(He had to keep the captain's favor.)
The ship it seemed had been a slaver.
And once they had shipped a captive pair
Whose love was such they didn't care 55
Who took in them onlooker's share.
Well, when at length the fever struck
That spoils the nigger-trader's luck
The man was among the first it took.
"Throw him over alive," they said, 60
"Before the thing has time to spread.
You've got to keep the quarters clean."
But the girl fought them and made a scene.
She was a savage jungle cat
It was easy to be angry at; 65
Which put the thought into someone's head
Of the ocean bed for a marriage bed.
Some Tom said to Dick or Harry:
"Apparently these two ought to marry.
We get plenty funerals at sea. 70
How for a change would a wedding be?—
Or a combination of the two,
How would a funeral-wedding do?
It's gone so far she's probably caught
Whatever it is the nigger's got." 75
They bound them naked so they faced

345

With a length of cordage about the waist.
Many lovers have been divorced
By having what is free enforced.
But presence of love these had in death   80
To kiss and drink each other's breath
Before they were hurled from the slaver's deck.
They added clasps about the neck
And went embraced to the cold and dark
To be their own marriage feast for the shark.   85

When after talk with other men
A man comes back to a woman again
He tells her as much of blood and dirt
As he thinks will do her not too much hurt.
"What was the pirate captain's chaff?   90
He laughed but he did not make you laugh.
The jest seemed his and the plaudits his.
I heard him shout 'What a thing it is!'
Some standing jest between you men?
Don't tell me if you don't want to, then."   95
Whereat in a moment of cross unruth
He thought, All right, if you want the truth!

"I don't believe it! It isn't true!
It never happened! Did it, you?"
Seeing no help in wings or feet   100
She withdrew back in self-retreat
Till her heart almost ceased to beat.
Her spirit faded as far away
As the living ever go yet stay.
And her thought was she had had her pay.   105

He said to the captain, "Give command,
And bring us to the nearest land;

346

And let us try an untossed place
And see if it will help her case."
They brought her to a nameless isle. 110
And the ship lay in the bay for a while
Waiting to see if she would mend;
But sailed and left them in the end.
Her lover saw them sail away,
But dared not tell her all one day. 115
For slowly even her sense of him
And love itself were growing dim.
He no more drew the smile he sought.
The story is she died of thought.

And when her lover was left alone 120
He stayed long enough to carve on stone
The name of the lady with his own
To be her only marriage lines.
And carved them round with a scroll of vines.
Then he gouged a clumsy sailing trough 125
From a fallen tree and pushing off
Safely made the African shore;
Where he fell a prisoner to the Moor.
But the Moor strangely enough believed
The tale of the voyage he had achieved, 130
And sent him to the King to admire.
He came at last to his native shire.
The island he found was verified.
And the bay where his stolen lady died
Was named for him instead of her. 135
But so is history like to err.
And soon it is neither here nor there
Whether time's rewards are fair or unfair.

THE GIFT OUTRIGHT

The land was ours before we were the land's.
She was our land more than a hundred years
Before we were her people. She was ours
In Massachusetts, in Virginia,
But we were England's, still colonials,   5
Possessing what we still were unpossessed by,
Possessed by what we now no more possessed.
Something we were withholding made us weak
Until we found out that it was ourselves
We were withholding from our land of living,   10
And forthwith found salvation in surrender.
Such as we were we gave ourselves outright
(The deed of gift was many deeds of war)
To the land vaguely realizing westward,
But still unstoried, artless, unenhanced,   15
Such as she was, such as she would become.

TRIPLE BRONZE

The Infinite's being so wide
Is the reason the Powers provide
For inner defense my hide.
For next defense outside

I make myself this time   5
Of wood or granite or lime
A wall too hard for crime
Either to breach or climb.

Then a number of us agree
On a national boundary.   10

348

And that defense makes three
Between too much and me.

OUR HOLD ON THE PLANET

We asked for rain. It didn't flash and roar.
It didn't lose its temper at our demand
And blow a gale. It didn't misunderstand
And give us more than our spokesman bargained for;
And just because we owned to a wish for rain,   5
Send us a flood and bid us be damned and drown.
It gently threw us a glittering shower down.
And when we had taken that into the roots of grain,
It threw us another and then another still,
Till the spongy soil again was natal wet.   10
We may doubt the just proportion of good to ill.
There is much in nature against us. But we forget:
Take nature altogether since time began,
Including human nature, in peace and war,
And it must be a little more in favor of man,   15
Say a fraction of one percent at the very least,
Or our number living wouldn't be steadily more,
Our hold on the planet wouldn't have so increased.

TO A YOUNG WRETCH
(Boethian)

As gay for you to take your father's ax
As take his gun—rod—to go hunting—fishing.
You nick my spruce until its fiber cracks,
It gives up standing straight and goes down swishing.
You link an arm in its arm and you lean   5
Across the light snow homeward smelling green.

349

I could have bought you just as good a tree
To frizzle resin in a candle flame,
And what a saving 'twould have meant to me.
But tree by charity is not the same   10
As tree by enterprise and expedition.
I must not spoil your Christmas with contrition.

It is your Christmases against my woods.
But even where, thus, opposing interests kill,
They are to be thought of as opposing goods   15
Oftener than as conflicting good and ill;
Which makes the war god seem no special dunce
For always fighting on both sides at once.

And though in tinsel chain and popcorn rope
My tree, a captive in your window bay,   20
Has lost its footing on my mountain slope
And lost the stars of heaven, may, oh, may
The symbol star it lifts against your ceiling
Help me accept its fate with Christmas feeling.

THE LESSON FOR TODAY

If this uncertain age in which we dwell
Were really as dark as I hear sages tell,
And I convinced that they were really sages,
I should not curse myself with it to hell,
But leaving not the chair I long have sat in   5
I should betake me back ten thousand pages
To the world's undebatably dark ages,
And getting up my medieval Latin,
Seek converse common cause and brotherhood
(By all that's liberal—I should, I should)   10

With poets who could calmly take the fate
Of being born at once too early and late,
And for these reasons kept from being great.
Yet singing but Dione in the wood
And *ver aspergit terram floribus*   15
They slowly led old Latin verse to rhyme
And to forget the ancient lengths of time,
And so began the modern world for us.

    I'd say, O Master of the Palace School,
You were not Charles' nor anybody's fool: 20
Tell me as pedagogue to pedagogue,
You did not know that since King Charles did rule
You had no chance but to be minor, did you?
Your light was spent perhaps as in a fog
That at once kept you burning low and hid you.   25
The age may very well have been to blame
For your not having won to Virgil's fame.
But no one ever heard you make the claim.
You would not think you knew enough to judge
The age when full upon you. That's my point.   30
We have today and I could call their name
Who know exactly what is out of joint
To make their verse and their excuses lame.
They've tried to grasp with too much social fact
Too large a situation. You and I   35
Would be afraid if we should comprehend
And get outside of too much bad statistics,
Our muscles never could again contract:
We never could recover human shape,
But must live lives out mentally agape   40
Or die of philosophical distention.
That's how we feel—and we're no special mystics.

We can't appraise the time in which we act.
But for the folly of it, let's pretend
We know enough to know it for adverse.   45
One more millennium's about to end.
Let's celebrate the event, my distant friend,
In publicly disputing which is worse,
The present age or your age. You and I
As schoolmen of repute should qualify   50
To wage a fine scholastical contention
As to whose age deserves the lower mark,
Or should I say the higher one, for dark.
I can just hear the way you make it go:
There's always something to be sorry for,   55
A sordid peace or an outrageous war.
Yes, yes, of course. We have the same convention.
The groundwork of all faith is human woe.
It was well worth preliminary mention.
There's nothing but injustice to be had,   60
No choice is left a poet, you might add,
But how to take the curse, tragic or comic.
It was well worth preliminary mention.
But let's go on to where our cases part,
If part they do. Let me propose a start.   65
(We're rivals in the badness of our case,
Remember, and must keep a solemn face.)
Space ails us moderns: we are sick with space.
Its contemplation makes us out as small
As a brief epidemic of microbes   70
That in a good glass may be seen to crawl
The patina of this the least of globes.
But have we there the advantage after all?
You were belittled into vilest worms
God hardly tolerated with his feet;   75

Which comes to the same thing in different terms.
We both are the belittled human race,
One as compared with God and one with space.
I had thought ours the more profound disgrace;
But doubtless this was only my conceit.   80
The cloister and the observatory saint
Take comfort in about the same complaint.
So science and religion really meet.

I can just hear you call your Palace class:
Come learn the Latin *eheu* for alas.   85
You may not want to use it and you may.
O paladins, the lesson for today
Is how to be unhappy yet polite.
And at the summons Roland, Olivier,
And every sheepish paladin and peer,   90
Being already more than proved in fight,
Sits down in school to try if he can write
Like Horace in the true Horatian vein,
Yet like a Christian disciplined to bend
His mind to thinking always of the end.   95
Memento mori and obey the Lord.
Art and religion love the somber chord.
Earth's a hard place in which to save the soul,
And could it be brought under state control,
So automatically we all were saved,   100
Its separateness from Heaven could be waived;
It might as well at once be kingdom-come.
(Perhaps it will be next millennium.)

But these are universals, not confined
To any one time, place, or human kind.   105
We're either nothing or a God's regret.

353

As ever when philosophers are met,
No matter where they stoutly mean to get,
Nor what particulars they reason from,
They are philosophers, and from old habit   110
They end up in the universal Whole
As unoriginal as any rabbit.

 One age is like another for the soul.
I'm telling you. You haven't said a thing,
Unless I put it in your mouth to say.   115
I'm having the whole argument my way—
But in your favor—please to tell your King—
In having granted you all ages shine
With equal darkness, yours as dark as mine.
I'm liberal. You, you aristocrat,   120
Won't know exactly what I mean by that.
I mean so altruistically moral
I never take my own side in a quarrel.
I'd lay my hand on his hand on his staff,
Lean back and have my confidential laugh,   125
And tell him I had read his Epitaph.

 It sent me to the graves the other day.
The only other there was far away
Across the landscape with a watering pot
At his devotions in a special plot.   130
And he was there resuscitating flowers
(Make no mistake about its being bones);
But I was only there to read the stones
To see what on the whole they had to say
About how long a man may think to live,   135
Which is becoming my concern of late.
And very wide the choice they seemed to give;

354

The ages ranging all the way from hours
To months and years and many, many years.
One man had lived one hundred years and eight.   140
But though we all may be inclined to wait
And follow some development of state,
Or see what comes of science and invention,
There is a limit to our time extension.
We all are doomed to broken-off careers,   145
And so's the nation, so's the total race.
The earth itself is liable to the fate
Of meaninglessly being broken off.
(And hence so many literary tears
At which my inclination is to scoff.)   150
I may have wept that any should have died
Or missed their chance, or not have been their best,
Or been their riches, fame, or love denied;
On me as much as any is the jest.
I take my incompleteness with the rest.   155
God bless himself can no one else be blessed.

    I hold your doctrine of *Memento Mori*.
And were an epitaph to be my story
I'd have a short one ready for my own.
I would have written of me on my stone: 160
I had a lover's quarrel with the world.

TIME OUT

It took that pause to make him realize
The mountain he was climbing had the slant
As of a book held up before his eyes
(And was a text albeit done in plant).
Dwarf cornel, goldthread, and *Maianthemum*,   5

He followingly fingered as he read,
The flowers fading on the seed to come;
But the thing was the slope it gave his head:
The same for reading as it was for thought,
So different from the hard and level stare   10
Of enemies defied and battles fought.
It was the obstinately gentle air
That may be clamored at by cause and sect,
But it will have its moment to reflect.

TO A MOTH SEEN IN WINTER

Here's first a gloveless hand warm from my pocket,
A perch and resting place 'twixt wood and wood,
Bright-black-eyed silvery creature, brushed with brown,
The wings not folded in repose, but spread.
(Who would you be, I wonder, by those marks   5
If I had moths to friend as I have flowers?)
And now pray tell what lured you with false hope
To make the venture of eternity
And seek the love of kind in wintertime?
But stay and hear me out. I surely think   10
You make a labor of flight for one so airy,
Spending yourself too much in self-support.
Nor will you find love either, nor love you.
And what I pity in you is something human,
The old incurable untimeliness,   15
Only begetter of all ills that are.
But go. You are right. My pity cannot help.
Go till you wet your pinions and are quenched.
You must be made more simply wise than I
To know the hand I stretch impulsively   20
Across the gulf of well-nigh everything

May reach to you, but cannot touch your fate.
I cannot touch your life, much less can save,
Who am tasked to save my own a little while.

A CONSIDERABLE SPECK

(*Microscopic*)

A speck that would have been beneath my sight
On any but a paper sheet so white
Set off across what I had written there.
And I had idly poised my pen in air
To stop it with a period of ink,   5
When something strange about it made me think.
This was no dust speck by my breathing blown,
But unmistakably a living mite
With inclinations it could call its own.
It paused as with suspicion of my pen,   10
And then came racing wildly on again
To where my manuscript was not yet dry;
Then paused again and either drank or smelt—
With loathing, for again it turned to fly.
Plainly with an intelligence I dealt.   15
It seemed too tiny to have room for feet,
Yet must have had a set of them complete
To express how much it didn't want to die.
It ran with terror and with cunning crept.
It faltered: I could see it hesitate;   20
Then in the middle of the open sheet
Cower down in desperation to accept
Whatever I accorded it of fate.
I have none of the tenderer-than-thou
Collectivistic regimenting love   25
With which the modern world is being swept.

357

But this poor microscopic item now!
Since it was nothing I knew evil of
I let it lie there till I hope it slept.

I have a mind myself and recognize   30
Mind when I meet with it in any guise.
No one can know how glad I am to find
On any sheet the least display of mind.

THE LOST FOLLOWER

As I have known them passionate and fine,
The gold for which they leave the golden line
Of lyric is a golden light divine,
Never the gold of darkness from a mine.

The spirit plays us strange religious pranks   5
To whatsoever god we owe the thanks.
No one has ever failed the poet ranks
To link a chain of money-metal banks.

The loss to song, the danger of defection
Is always in the opposite direction.   10
Some turn in sheer, in Shelleyan dejection
To try if one more popular election

Will give us by shortcut the final stage
That poetry with all its golden rage
For beauty on the illuminated page   15
Has failed to bring—I mean the Golden Age.

And if this may not be (and nothing's sure),
At least to live ungolden with the poor,
Enduring what the ungolden must endure.
This has been poetry's great anti-lure.   20

358

The Muse mourns one who went to his retreat
Long since in some abysmal city street,
The bride who shared the crust he broke to eat,
As grave as he about the world's defeat.

With such it has proved dangerous as friend   25
Even in a playful moment to contend
That the millennium to which you bend
In longing is not at a progress-end

By grace of state-manipulated pelf,
Or politics of Ghibelline or Guelph,   30
But right beside you booklike on a shelf,
Or even better godlike in yourself.

He trusts my love too well to deign reply.
But there is in the sadness of his eye
Something about a kingdom in the sky   35
(As yet unbrought to earth) he means to try.

NOVEMBER

We saw leaves go to glory,
Then almost migratory
Go part way down the lane,
And then to end the story
Get beaten down and pasted   5
In one wild day of rain.
We heard "'Tis over" roaring.
A year of leaves was wasted.
Oh, we make a boast of storing,
Of saving and of keeping,   10
But only by ignoring
The waste of moments sleeping,

359

The waste of pleasure weeping,
By denying and ignoring
The waste of nations warring.   15

THE RABBIT-HUNTER

Careless and still
The hunter lurks
With gun depressed,
Facing alone
The alder swamps   5
Ghastly snow-white.
And his hound works
In the offing there
Like one possessed,
And yelps delight   10
And sings and romps,
Bringing him on
The shadowy hare
For him to rend
And deal a death   15
That he nor it
(Nor I) have wit
To comprehend.

A LOOSE MOUNTAIN

(Telescopic)

Did you stay up last night (the Magi did)
To see the star shower known as Leonid
That once a year by hand or apparatus
Is so mysteriously pelted at us?
It is but fiery puffs of dust and pebbles,   5

No doubt directed at our heads as rebels
In having taken artificial light
Against the ancient sovereignty of night.
A fusillade of blanks and empty flashes,
It never reaches earth except as ashes   10
Of which you feel no least touch on your face
Nor find in dew the slightest cloudy trace.
Nevertheless it constitutes a hint
That the loose mountain lately seen to glint
In sunlight near us in momentous swing   15
Is something in a Balearic sling
The heartless and enormous Outer Black
Is still withholding in the Zodiac
But from irresolution in his back
About when best to have us in our orbit,   20
So we won't simply take it and absorb it.

IT IS ALMOST THE YEAR TWO THOUSAND

To start the world of old
We had one age of gold
Not labored out of mines,
And some say there are signs
The second such has come,   5
The true Millennium,
The final golden glow
To end it. And if so
(And science ought to know)
We well may raise our heads   10
From weeding garden beds
And annotating books
To watch this end deluxe.

IN A POEM

The sentencing goes blithely on its way
And takes the playfully objected rhyme
As surely as it keeps the stroke and time
In having its undeviable say.

ON OUR SYMPATHY WITH
THE UNDER DOG

First under up and then again down under,
We watch a circus of revolving dogs
No senator dares in to kick asunder,
Lest both should bite him in the toga-togs.

A QUESTION

A voice said, Look me in the stars
And tell me truly, men of earth,
If all the soul-and-body scars
Were not too much to pay for birth.

BOEOTIAN

I love to toy with the Platonic notion
That wisdom need not be of Athens Attic,
But well may be Laconic, even Boeotian.
At least I will not have it systematic.

THE SECRET SITS

We dance round in a ring and suppose,
But the Secret sits in the middle and knows.

362

AN EQUALIZER

It is as true as Caesar's name was Kaiser
That no economist was ever wiser
(Though prodigal himself and a despiser
Of capital, and calling thrift a miser).
And when we get too far apart in wealth,   5
'Twas his idea that for the public health,
So that the poor won't have to steal by stealth,
We now and then should take an equalizer.

A SEMI-REVOLUTION

I advocate a semi-revolution.
The trouble with a total revolution
(Ask any reputable Rosicrucian)
Is that it brings the same class up on top.
Executives of skillful execution   5
Will therefore plan to go halfway and stop.
Yes, revolutions are the only salves,
But they're one thing that should be done by halves.

ASSURANCE

The danger not an inch outside
Behind the porthole's slab of glass
And double ring of fitted brass
I trust feels properly defied.

AN ANSWER

But Islands of the Blessèd, bless you, son,
I never came upon a blessèd one.

TRESPASS

No, I had set no prohibiting sign,
And yes, my land was hardly fenced.
Nevertheless the land was mine:
I was being trespassed on and against.

Whoever the surly freedom took   5
Of such an unaccountable stay
Busying by my woods and brook
Gave me a strangely restless day.

He might be opening leaves of stone,
The picture book of the trilobite,   10
For which the region round was known,
And in which there was little property right.

'Twas not the value I stood to lose
In specimen crab in specimen rock,
But his ignoring what was whose   15
That made me look again at the clock.

Then came his little acknowledgment:
He asked for a drink at the kitchen door,
An errand he may have had to invent,
But it made my property mine once more.   20

A NATURE NOTE

Four or five whippoorwills
Have come down from their native ledge
To the open country edge
To give us a piece of their bills.

364

Two in June were a pair—   5
You'd say sufficiently loud,
But this was a family crowd,
A full-fledged family affair.

All out of time pell-mell!
I wasn't in on the joke,   10
Unless it was coming to folk
To bid us a mock farewell.

I took note of when it occurred,
The twenty-third of September,
Their latest that I remember,   15
September the twenty-third.

OF THE STONES OF THE PLACE

I farm a pasture where the boulders lie
As touching as a basketful of eggs,
And though they're nothing anybody begs,
I wonder if it wouldn't signify

For me to send you one out where you live   5
In wind-soil to a depth of thirty feet,
And every acre good enough to eat,
As fine as flour put through a baker's sieve.

I'd ship a smooth one you could slap and chafe,
And set up like a statue in your yard,   10
An eolith palladium to guard
The West and keep the old tradition safe.

Carve nothing on it. You can simply say
In self-defense to quizzical inquiry:

"The portrait of the soul of my Gransir Ira.
It came from where he came from anyway."

NOT OF SCHOOL AGE

Around bend after bend,
It was blown woods and no end.
I came to but one house,
I made but the one friend.

At the one house a child was out   5
Who drew back at first in doubt,
But spoke to me in a gale
That blew so he had to shout.

His cheek smeared with apple sand,
A part apple in his hand,   10
He pointed on up the road
As one having war-command.

A parent, his gentler one,
Looked forth on her small son
And wondered with me there   15
What now was being done.

His accent was not good.
But I slowly understood.
Something where I could go—
He couldn't but I could.   20

He was too young to go,
Not over four or so.
Well, would I please go to school,
And the big flag they had—you know

The big flag: the red—white—
And blue flag, the great sight—
He bet it was out today,
And would I see if he was right?

A SERIOUS STEP LIGHTLY TAKEN

Between two burrs on the map
Was a hollow-headed snake.
The burrs were hills, the snake was a stream,
And the hollow head was a lake.

And the dot in *front* of a name   5
Was what should be a town.
And there might be a house we could buy
For only a dollar down.

With two wheels low in the ditch
We left our boiling car   10
And knocked at the door of a house we found,
And there today we are.

It is turning three hundred years
On our cisatlantic shore
For family after family name.   15
We'll make it three hundred more

For our name farming here,
Aloof yet not aloof,
Enriching soil and increasing stock,
Repairing fence and roof;   20

A hundred thousand days
Of front-page paper events,

A half a dozen major wars,
And forty-five presidents.

THE LITERATE FARMER AND
THE PLANET VENUS

*A dated popular-science medley on a mysterious light
recently observed in the western sky at evening*

My unexpected knocking at the door
Started chairs thundering on the kitchen floor,
Knives and forks ringing on the supper plates,
Voices conflicting like the candidates.
A mighty farmer flung the house door wide,   5
He and a lot of children came outside,
And there on an equality we stood.
That's the time knocking at a door did good.

   "I stopped to compliment you on this star
You get the beauty of from where you are.   10
To see it so, the bright and only one
In sunset light, you'd think it was the sun
That hadn't sunk the way it should have sunk,
But right in heaven was slowly being shrunk
So small as to be virtually gone,   15
Yet there to watch the darkness coming on—
Like someone dead permitted to exist
Enough to see if he was greatly missed.
I didn't see the sun set. Did it set?
Will anybody swear that isn't it?   20
And will you give me shelter for the night?
If not, a glass of milk will be all right."

   "Traveler, I'm glad you asked about that light.

Your mind mistrusted there was something wrong,
And naturally you couldn't go along   25
Without inquiring if 'twas serious.
'Twas providential you applied to us,
Who were just on the subject when you came.
There is a star that's Serious by name
And nature too, but this is not the same.   30
This light's been going on for several years,
Although at times we think it disappears.
You'll hear all sorts of things. You'll meet with them
Will tell you it's the star of Bethlehem
Above some more religion in a manger.   35
But put that down to superstition, Stranger.
What's a star doing big as a baseball?
Between us two it's not a star at all.
It's a new patented electric light,
Put up on trial by that Jerseyite   40
So much is being now expected of,
To give developments the final shove
And turn us into the next specie folks
Are going to be, unless these monkey jokes
Of the last fifty years are all a libel,   45
And Darwin's proved mistaken, not the Bible.
I s'pose you have your notions on the vexed
Question of what we're turning into next."

    "As liberals we're willing to give place
To any demonstrably better race,   50
No matter what the color of its skin.
(But what a human race the white has been!)
I heard a fellow in a public lecture
On Pueblo Indians and their architecture
Declare that if such Indians inherited   55

369

The cóndemned world the legacy was merited.
So far as he, the speaker, was concerned
He had his ticket bought, his passage earned,
To take the *Mayflower* back where he belonged,
Before the Indian race was further wronged.   60
But come, enlightened as in talk you seem,
You don't believe that that first-water gleam
Is not a star?"

          "Believe it? Why, I know it.
Its actions any cloudless night will show it.
You'll see it be allowed up just so high,   65
Say about halfway up the western sky,
And then get slowly, slowly pulled back down.
You might not notice if you've lived in town,
As I suspect you have. A town debars
Much notice of what's going on in stars.   70
The idea is no doubt to make one job
Of lighting the whole night with one big blob
Of electricity in bulk the way
The sun sets the example in the day."

   "Here come more stars to character the skies,   75
And they in the estimation of the wise
Are more divine than any bulb or arc,
Because their purpose is to flash and spark,
But not to take away the precious dark.
We need the interruption of the night   80
To ease attention off when overtight,
To break our logic in too long a flight,
And ask us if our premises are right."

   "Sick talk, sick talk, sick sentimental talk!
It doesn't do you any good to talk.   85
I see what *you* are: can't get you excited

With hopes of getting mankind unbenighted.
Some ignorance takes rank as innocence.
Have it for all of me and have it dense.
The slave will never thank his manumitter;   90
Which often makes the manumitter bitter."

"In short, you think that star a patent medicine
Put up to cure the world by Mr. Edison."

"You said it—that's exactly what it is.
My son in Jersey says a friend of his   95
Knows the old man, and nobody's so deep
In incandescent lamps and ending sleep.
The old man argues science cheapened speed.
A good cheap anti-dark is now the need.
Give us a good cheap twenty-four-hour day,   100
No part of which we'd have to waste, I say,
And who knows where we can't get! Wasting time
In sleep or slowness is the deadly crime.
He gave up sleep himself some time ago,
It puffs the face and brutalizes so.   105
You take the ugliness all so much dread,
Called getting out of the wrong side of bed.
That is the source perhaps of human hate
And well may be where wars originate.
Get rid of that and there'd be left no great   110
Of either murder or war in any land.
You know how cunningly mankind is planned:
We have one loving and one hating hand.
The loving's made to hold each other like,
While with the hating other hand we strike.   115
The blow can be no stronger than the clutch,
Or soon we'd bat each other out of touch,
And the fray wouldn't last a single round.

And still it's bad enough to badly wound,
And if our getting up to start the day 120
On the right side of bed would end the fray,
We'd hail the remedy. But it's been tried
And found, he says, a bed has no right side.
The trouble is, with that receipt for love,
A bed's got no right side to get out of. 125
We can't be trusted to the sleep we take,
And simply must evolve to stay awake.
He thinks that chairs and tables will endure,
But beds—in less than fifty years he's sure
There will be no such piece of furniture. 130
He's surely got it in for cots and beds.
No need for us to rack our common heads
About it, though. We haven't got the mind.
It best be left to great men of his kind
Who have no other object than our good. 135
There's a lot yet that isn't understood.
Ain't it a caution to us not to fix
No limits to what rose in rubbing sticks
On fire to scare away the pterodix
When man first lived in caves along the creeks?" 140

"Marvelous world in nineteen-twenty-six."

Steeple Bush

: 1947 :

A YOUNG BIRCH

The birch begins to crack its outer sheath
Of baby green and show the white beneath,
As whosoever likes the young and slight
May well have noticed. Soon entirely white
To double day and cut in half the dark   5
It will stand forth, entirely white in bark,
And nothing but the top a leafy green—
The only native tree that dares to lean,
Relying on its beauty, to the air.
(Less brave perhaps than trusting are the fair.)   10
And someone reminiscent will recall
How once in cutting brush along the wall
He spared it from the number of the slain,
At first to be no bigger than a cane,
And then no bigger than a fishing pole,   15
But now at last so obvious a bole
The most efficient help you ever hired
Would know that it was there to be admired,
And zeal would not be thanked that cut it down
When you were reading books or out of town.   20
It was a thing of beauty and was sent
To live its life out as an ornament.

SOMETHING FOR HOPE

At the present rate it must come to pass,
And that right soon, that the meadowsweet

And steeple bush, not good to eat,
Will have crowded out the edible grass.

Then all there is to do is wait   5
For maple, birch, and spruce to push
Through meadowsweet and steeple bush
And crowd them out at a similar rate.

No plow among these rocks would pay.
So busy yourself with other things   10
While the trees put on their wooden rings
And with long-sleeved branches hold their sway.

Then cut down the trees when lumber grown,
And there's your pristine earth all freed
From lovely blooming but wasteful weed   15
And ready again for the grass to own.

A cycle we'll say of a hundred years.
Thus foresight does it and laissez-faire,
A virtue in which we all may share
Unless a government interferes.   20

Patience and looking away ahead,
And leaving some things to take their course.
Hope may not nourish a cow or horse,
But *spes alit agricolam* 'tis said.

ONE STEP BACKWARD TAKEN

Not only sands and gravels
Were once more on their travels,
But gulping muddy gallons
Great boulders off their balance
Bumped heads together dully   5

And started down the gully.
Whole capes caked off in slices.
I felt my standpoint shaken
In the universal crisis.
But with one step backward taken　　　　　10
I saved myself from going.
A world torn loose went by me.
Then the rain stopped and the blowing,
And the sun came out to dry me.

DIRECTIVE

Back out of all this now too much for us,
Back in a time made simple by the loss
Of detail, burned, dissolved, and broken off
Like graveyard marble sculpture in the weather,
There is a house that is no more a house　　　　　5
Upon a farm that is no more a farm
And in a town that is no more a town.
The road there, if you'll let a guide direct you
Who only has at heart your getting lost,
May seem as if it should have been a quarry—　　　　　10
Great monolithic knees the former town
Long since gave up pretense of keeping covered.
And there's a story in a book about it:
Besides the wear of iron wagon wheels
The ledges show lines ruled southeast-northwest,　　　　　15
The chisel work of an enormous Glacier
That braced his feet against the Arctic Pole.
You must not mind a certain coolness from him
Still said to haunt this side of Panther Mountain.
Nor need you mind the serial ordeal　　　　　20

Of being watched from forty cellar holes
As if by eye pairs out of forty firkins.
As for the woods' excitement over you
That sends light rustle rushes to their leaves,
Charge that to upstart inexperience.   25
Where were they all not twenty years ago?
They think too much of having shaded out
A few old pecker-fretted apple trees.
Make yourself up a cheering song of how
Someone's road home from work this once was,   30
Who may be just ahead of you on foot
Or creaking with a buggy load of grain.
The height of the adventure is the height
Of country where two village cultures faded
Into each other. Both of them are lost.   35
And if you're lost enough to find yourself
By now, pull in your ladder road behind you
And put a sign up CLOSED to all but me.
Then make yourself at home. The only field
Now left's no bigger than a harness gall.   40
First there's the children's house of make-believe,
Some shattered dishes underneath a pine,
The playthings in the playhouse of the children.
Weep for what little things could make them glad.
Then for the house that is no more a house,   45
But only a belilaced cellar hole,
Now slowly closing like a dent in dough.
This was no playhouse but a house in earnest.
Your destination and your destiny's
A brook that was the water of the house,   50
Cold as a spring as yet so near its source,
Too lofty and original to rage.
(We know the valley streams that when aroused

Will leave their tatters hung on barb and thorn.)
I have kept hidden in the instep arch   55
Of an old cedar at the waterside
A broken drinking goblet like the Grail
Under a spell so the wrong ones can't find it,
So can't get saved, as Saint Mark says they mustn't.
(I stole the goblet from the children's playhouse.)   60
Here are your waters and your watering place.
Drink and be whole again beyond confusion.

TOO ANXIOUS FOR RIVERS

Look down the long valley and there stands a mountain
That someone has said is the end of the world.
Then what of this river that having arisen
Must find where to pour itself into and empty?
I never saw so much swift water run cloudless.   5
Oh, I have been often too anxious for rivers
To leave it to them to get out of their valleys.
The truth is the river flows into the canyon
Of Ceasing-to-Question-What-Doesn't-Concern-Us,
As sooner or later we have to cease somewhere.   10
No place to get lost like too far in the distance.
It may be a mercy the dark closes round us
So broodingly soon in every direction.
The world as we know is an elephant's howdah;
The elephant stands on the back of a turtle;   15
The turtle in turn on a rock in the ocean.
And how much longer a story has science
Before she must put out the light on the children
And tell them the rest of the story is dreaming?
"You children may dream it and tell it tomorrow."   20

Time was we were molten, time was we were vapor.
What set us on fire and what set us revolving,
Lucretius the Epicurean might tell us
'Twas something we knew all about to begin with
And needn't have fared into space like his master   25
To find 'twas the effort, the essay of love.

AN UNSTAMPED LETTER
IN OUR RURAL LETTER BOX

Last night your watchdog barked all night,
So once you rose and lit the light.
It wasn't someone at your locks.
No, in your rural letter box
I leave this note without a stamp   5
To tell you it was just a tramp
Who used your pasture for a camp.
There, pointed like the pip of spades,
The young spruce made a suite of glades
So regular that in the dark   10
The place was like a city park.
There I elected to demur
Beneath a low-slung juniper
That like a blanket to my chin
Kept some dew out and some heat in,   15
Yet left me freely face to face
All night with universal space.
It may have been at two o'clock
That under me a point of rock
Developed in the grass and fern,   20
And as I woke afraid to turn

Or so much as uncross my feet,
Lest having wasted precious heat
I never should again be warmed,
The largest firedrop ever formed   25
From two stars' having coalesced
Went streaking molten down the west.
And then your tramp astrologer
From seeing this undoubted stir
In Heaven's firm-set firmament,   30
Himself had the equivalent,
Only within. Inside the brain
Two memories that long had lain
Now quivered toward each other, lipped
Together, and together slipped;   35
And for a moment all was plain
That men have thought about in vain.
Please, my involuntary host,
Forgive me if I seem to boast.
'Tis possible you may have seen,   40
Albeit through a rusty screen,
The same sign Heaven showed your guest.
Each knows his own discernment best.
You have had your advantages.
Things must have happened to you, yes,   45
And have occurred to you no doubt,
If not indeed from sleeping out,
Then from the work you went about
In farming well—or pretty well.
And it is partly to compel   50
Myself, *in forma pauperis,*
To say as much I write you this.

TO AN ANCIENT

Your claims to immortality were two.
The one you made, the other one you grew.
Sorry to have no name for you but You.

We never knew exactly where to look,
But found one in the delta of a brook,   5
One in a cavern where you used to cook.

Coming on such an ancient human trace
Seems as expressive of the human race
As meeting someone living, face to face.

We date you by your depth in silt and dust   10
Your probable brute nature is discussed.
At which point we are totally nonplussed.

You made the eolith, you grew the bone,
The second more peculiarly your own,
And likely to have been enough alone.   15

You make me ask if I would go to time
Would I gain anything by using rhyme?
Or aren't the bones enough I live to lime?

FIVE NOCTURNES

I. THE NIGHT LIGHT

She always had to burn a light
Beside her attic bed at night.
It gave bad dreams and broken sleep,
But helped the Lord her soul to keep.

Good gloom on her was thrown away.   5
It is on me by night or day,
Who have, as I suppose, ahead
The darkest of it still to dread.

II. WERE I IN TROUBLE

Where I could think of no thoroughfare,
Away on the mountain up far too high,
A blinding headlight shifted glare
And began to bounce down a granite stair,
Like a star fresh fallen out of the sky.   5
And I away in my opposite wood
Am touched by that unintimate light
And made feel less alone than I rightly should,
For traveler there could do me no good
Were I in trouble with night tonight.   10

III. BRAVADO

Have I not walked without an upward look
Of caution under stars that very well
Might not have missed me when they shot and fell?
It was a risk I had to take—and took.

IV. ON MAKING CERTAIN ANYTHING HAS HAPPENED

I could be worse employed
Than as watcher of the void,
Whose part should be to tell
What star if any fell.

383

Suppose some seed-pearl sun   5
Should be the only one;
Yet still I must report
Some cluster one star short.

I should justly hesitate
To frighten church or state   10
By announcing a star down
From, say, the Cross or Crown.

To make sure what star I missed
I should have to check on my list
Every star in sight.   15
It might take me all night.

V. IN THE LONG NIGHT

I would build my house of crystal,
With a solitary friend,
Where the cold cracks like a pistol
And the needle stands on end.

We would pour oil on the ingle   5
And for want of books recite.
We would crawl out filing single
To observe the Northern Light.

If Etookashoo and Couldlooktoo
The Esquimaux should call,   10
There would be fish raw and cooked too
And enough drink oil for all.

As one rankly warm insider
To another I would say,

We can rest assured on eider   15
There will come another day.

A MOOD APART

Once down on my knees to growing plants
I prodded the earth with a lazy tool
In time with a medley of sotto chants;
But becoming aware of some boys from school
Who had stopped outside the fence to spy,   5
I stopped my song and almost heart,
For any eye is an evil eye
That looks in onto a mood apart.

THE FEAR OF GOD

If you should rise from Nowhere up to Somewhere,
From being No one up to being Someone,
Be sure to keep repeating to yourself
You owe it to an arbitrary god
Whose mercy to you rather than to others   5
Won't bear too critical examination.
Stay unassuming. If for lack of license
To wear the uniform of who you are,
You should be tempted to make up for it
In a subordinating look or tone,   10
Beware of coming too much to the surface
And using for apparel what was meant
To be the curtain of the inmost soul.

THE FEAR OF MAN

As a girl no one gallantly attends
Sets forth for home at midnight from a friend's—
She tries to make it in one catch of breath,
And this is not because she thinks of death.
The city seems in-toppling from a height,   5
But she can trust it not to fall tonight.
(It will be taken down before it falls.)
There scarcely is a light in all its walls,
Except beside a safe inside a bank
(For which assurance Mammon is to thank).   10
But there are little streetlights she should trust,
So jewel-steady in the wind and dust.
Her fear is being spoken by the rude
And having her exposure misconstrued.
May I in my brief bolt across the scene   15
Not be misunderstood in what I mean.

A STEEPLE ON THE HOUSE

What if it should turn out eternity
Was but the steeple on our house of life
That made our house of life a house of worship?
We do not go up there to sleep at night.
We do not go up there to live by day.   5
Nor need we ever go up there to live.
A spire and belfry coming on the roof
Means that a soul is coming on the flesh.

INNATE HELIUM

Religious faith is a most filling vapor.
It swirls occluded in us under tight

Compression to uplift us out of weight—
As in those buoyant bird bones thin as paper,
To give them still more buoyancy in flight.   5
Some gas like helium must be innate.

THE COURAGE TO BE NEW

I hear the world reciting
The mistakes of ancient men,
The brutality and fighting
They will never have again.

Heartbroken and disabled   5
In body and in mind,
They renew talk of the fabled
Federation of Mankind.

But they're blessed with the acumen
To suspect the human trait   10
Was not the *basest* human
That made them militate.

They will tell you more as soon as
You tell them what to do
With their ever breaking newness   15
And their courage to be new.

IOTA SUBSCRIPT

Seek not in me the big I capital,
Nor yet the little dotted in me seek.
If I have in me any I at all,
'Tis the iota subscript of the Greek.

So small am I as an attention beggar.   5
The letter you will find me subscript to
Is neither alpha, eta, nor omega,
But upsilon which is the Greek for you.

THE MIDDLENESS OF THE ROAD

The road at the top of the rise
Seems to come to an end
And take off into the skies.
So at the distant bend

It seems to go into a wood,   5
The place of standing still
As long the trees have stood.
But say what Fancy will,

The mineral drops that explode
To drive my ton of car   10
Are limited to the road.
They deal with near and far,

But have almost nothing to do
With the absolute flight and rest
The universal blue   15
And local green suggest.

ASTROMETAPHYSICAL

Lord, I have loved Your sky,
Be it said against or for me,
Have loved it clear and high,
Or low and stormy;

Till I have reeled and stumbled   5
From looking up too much,
And fallen and been humbled
To wear a crutch.

My love for every Heaven
O'er which You, Lord, have lorded,   10
From number One to Seven,
Should be rewarded.

It may not give me hope
That when I am translated
My scalp will in the cope   15
Be constellated.

But if that seems to tend
To my undue renown,
At least it ought to send
Me up, not down.   20

SKEPTIC

Far star that tickles for me my sensitive plate
And fries a couple of ebon atoms white,
I don't believe I believe a thing you state.
I put no faith in the seeming facts of light.

I don't believe I believe you're the last in space,   5
I don't believe you're anywhere near the last,
I don't believe what makes you red in the face
Is after explosion going away so fast.

The universe may or may not be very immense.
As a matter of fact there are times when I am apt   10

To feel it close in tight against my sense
Like a caul in which I was born and still am wrapped.

TWO LEADING LIGHTS

I never happened to contrast
The two in the celestial cast
Whose prominence has been so vast.
The Sun is satisfied with days.
He never has in any phase   5
That I have heard of shone at night.
And yet he is a power of light
And could in one burst overwhelm
And dayify the darkest realm
By right of eminent domain.   10
He has the greatness to refrain.
The Moon for all her light and grace
Has never learned to know her place.
The notedest astronomers
Have set the dark aside for hers.   15
But there are many nights, though clear,
She doesn't bother to appear.
Some lunatic or lunar whim
Will bring her out, diminished dim,
To set herself beside the Sun,   20
As Sheba came to Solomon.
It may be charitably guessed
Comparison is not her quest.
Some rumor of his wishing ring
That changes winter into spring   25
Has brought her merely visiting,
An irresponsible divinity
Presuming on her femininity.

A ROGERS GROUP

How young and unassuming
They waited in the street,
With babies in their arms
And baggage at their feet.

A trolley car they hailed   5
Went by with clanging gong
Before they guessed the corner
They waited on was wrong.

And no one told them so
By way of traveler's aid,   10
No one was so far touched
By the Rogers Group they made.

ON BEING IDOLIZED

The wave sucks back and with the last of water
It wraps a wisp of seaweed round my legs,
And with the swift rush of its sandy dregs
So undermines my barefoot stand I totter,
And did I not take steps would be tipped over   5
Like the ideal of some mistaken lover.

A WISH TO COMPLY

Did I see it go by,
That Millikan mote?
Well, I said that I did.
I made a good try.
But I'm no one to quote.   5

If I have a defect
It's a wish to comply
And see as I'm bid.
I rather suspect
All I saw was the lid   10
Going over my eye.
I honestly think
All I saw was a wink.

A CLIFF DWELLING

There sandy seems the golden sky
And golden seems the sandy plain.
No habitation meets the eye
Unless in the horizon rim,
Some halfway up the limestone wall,   5
That spot of black is not a stain
Or shadow, but a cavern hole,
Where someone used to climb and crawl
To rest from his besetting fears.
I see the callus on his sole,   10
The disappearing last of him
And of his race starvation slim,
Oh, years ago—ten thousand years.

IT BIDS PRETTY FAIR

The play seems out for an almost infinite run.
Don't mind a little thing like the actors fighting.
The only thing I worry about is the sun.
We'll be all right if nothing goes wrong with the lighting.

BEYOND WORDS

That row of icicles along the gutter
Feels like my armory of hate;
And you, you . . . you, you utter. . . .
You wait!

A CASE FOR JEFFERSON

Harrison loves my country too,
But wants it all made over new.
He's Freudian Viennese by night.
By day he's Marxian Muscovite.
It isn't because he's Russian Jew.   5
He's Puritan Yankee through and through.
He dotes on Saturday pork and beans.
But his mind is hardly out of his teens:
With him the love of country means
Blowing it all to smithereens   10
And having it all made over new.

LUCRETIUS VERSUS THE LAKE POETS

"Nature I loved; and next to Nature, Art."

Dean, adult education may seem silly.
What of it, though? I got some willy-nilly
The other evening at your college deanery.
And grateful for it (let's not be facetious!)
For I thought Epicurus and Lucretius   5
By Nature meant the Whole Goddam Machinery.
But you say that in college nomenclature
The only meaning possible for Nature
In Landor's quatrain would be Pretty Scenery.

Which makes opposing it to Art absurd   10
I grant you—if you're sure about the word.
God bless the Dean and make his deanship plenary.

HAEC FABULA DOCET

A Blindman by the name of La Fontaine,
Relying on himself and on his cane,
Came tap-tap-tapping down the village street,
The apogee of human blind conceit.
Now just ahead of him was seen to yawn   5
A trench where water pipes were laying on.
The Blindman might have found it with his ferrule,
But someone overanxious at his peril
Not only warned him with a loud command
But ran against him with a staying hand.   10
Enraged at what he could but think officious,
The Blindman missed him with a blow so vicious
He gave his own poor iliac a wrench
And plunged himself head foremost in the trench:
Where with a glee no less for being grim   15
The workmen all turned to and buried him.

Moral

The moral is, it hardly need be shown,
All those who try to go it sole alone,
Too proud to be beholden for relief,
Are absolutely sure to come to grief.   20

ETHEREALIZING

A theory if you hold it hard enough
And long enough gets rated as a creed:

394

Such as that flesh is something we can slough
So that the mind can be entirely freed.
Then when the arms and legs have atrophied,   5
And brain is all that's left of mortal stuff,
We can lie on the beach with the seaweed
And take our daily tide baths smooth and rough.
There once we lay as blobs of jellyfish
At evolution's opposite extreme.   10
But now as blobs of brain we'll lie and dream,
With only one vestigial creature wish:
Oh, may the tide be soon enough at high
To keep our abstract verse from being dry.

WHY WAIT FOR SCIENCE

Sarcastic Science, she would like to know,
In her complacent ministry of fear,
How we propose to get away from here
When she has made things so we have to go
Or be wiped out. Will she be asked to show   5
Us how by rocket we may hope to steer
To some star off there, say, a half light-year
Through temperature of absolute zeró?
Why wait for Science to supply the how
When any amateur can tell it now?   10
The way to go away should be the same
As fifty million years ago we came—
If anyone remembers how that was.
I have a theory, but it hardly does.

ANY SIZE WE PLEASE

No one was looking at his lonely case;
So, like a half-mad outpost sentinel,
Indulging an absurd dramatic spell,
Albeit not without some shame of face,
He stretched his arms out to the dark of space   5
And held them absolutely parallel
In infinite appeal. Then saying "Hell,"
He drew them in for warmth of self-embrace.
He thought if he could have his space all curved,
Wrapped in around itself and self-befriended,   10
His science needn't get him so unnerved.
He had been too all out, too much extended.
He slapped his breast to verify his purse
And hugged himself for all his universe.

AN IMPORTER

Mrs. Someone's been to Asia.
What she brought back would amaze ye.
Bamboos, ivories, jades, and lacquers,
Devil-scaring firecrackers,
Recipes for tea with butter,   5
Sacred rigmaroles to mutter,
Subterfuge for saving faces,
A developed taste in vases,
Arguments too stale to mention
'Gainst American invention—   10
Most of all the mass production
Destined to prove our destruction.
What are telephones, skyscrapers,
Safety razors, Sunday papers

But the silliest evasion 15
Of the truths we owe an Asian?
But the best of her exhibit
Was a prayer machine from Tibet
That by brook power in the garden
Kept repeating Pardon, pardon; 20
And as picturesque machinery
Beat a sundial in the scenery—
The most primitive of engines
Mass-producing with a vengeance.
Teach those Asians mass production? 25
Teach your grandmother egg suction.

THE PLANNERS

If anything should put an end to This,
I'm thinking the unborn would never miss
What they had never had of vital bliss.
No burst of nuclear phenomenon
That put an end to what was going on 5
Could make much difference to the dead and gone.
Only a few of those even in whose day
It happened would have very much to say.
And anyone might ask them who were *they*.
Who *would* they be? The guild of social planners 10
With the intention blazoned on their banners
Of getting one more chance to change our manners?
These anyway might think it was important
That human history should not be shortened.

NO HOLY WARS FOR THEM

States strong enough to do good are but few.
Their number would seem limited to three.
Good is a thing that they, the great, can do,
But puny little states can only be.
And being good for these means standing by   5
To watch a war in nominal alliance,
And when it's over watch the world's supply
Get parceled out among the winning giants.
God, have You taken cognizance of this?
And what on this is Your divine position?   10
That nations like the Cuban and the Swiss
Can never hope to wage a Global Mission.
No Holy Wars for them. The most the small
Can ever give us is a nuisance brawl.

BURSTING RAPTURE

I went to the physician to complain,
The time had been when anyone could turn
To farming for a simple way to earn;
But now 'twas there as elsewhere, any gain
Was made by getting science on the brain;   5
There was so much more every day to learn,
The discipline of farming was so stern,
It seemed as if I couldn't stand the strain.
But the physician's answer was, "There, there,
What you complain of, all the nations share.   10
Their effort is a mounting ecstasy
That when it gets too exquisite to bear
Will find relief in one burst. You shall see.
That's what a certain bomb was sent to be."

U. S. 1946 KING'S X

Having invented a new Holocaust,
And been the first with it to win a war,
How they make haste to cry with fingers crossed,
King's X—no fairs to use it anymore!

THE INGENUITIES OF DEBT

These I assume were words so deeply meant
They cut themselves in stone for permanent
Like trouble in the brow above the eyes:
TAKE CARE TO SELL YOUR HORSE BEFORE HE DIES
THE ART OF LIFE IS PASSING LOSSES ON.   5
The city saying it was Ctesiphon,
Which may a little while by war and trade
Have kept from being caught with the decayed,
Infirm, worn-out, and broken on its hands;
But judging by what little of it stands,   10
Not even the ingenuities of debt
Could save it from its losses being met.
Sand has been thrusting in the square of door
Across the tessellation of the floor,
And only rests, a serpent on its chin,   15
Content with contemplating, taking in,
Till it can muster breath inside a hall
To rear against the inscription on the wall.

THE BROKEN DROUGHT

The prophet of disaster ceased to shout.
Something was going right outside the hall.
A rain, though stingy, had begun to fall

That rather hurt his theory of the drought
And all the great convention was about.   5
A cheer went up that shook the mottoed wall.
He did as Shakespeare says, you may recall,
Good orators *will* do when they are out.
Yet in his heart he was unshaken sure
The drought was one no spit of rain could cure.   10
It was the drought of deserts. Earth would soon
Be uninhabitable as the moon.
What for that matter had it ever been?
Who advised man to come and live therein?

TO THE RIGHT PERSON

In the one state of ours that is a shire,
There is a District Schoolhouse I admire
As much as anything for situation.
There are few institutions standing higher
This side the Rockies in my estimation—   5
Two thousand feet above the ocean level.
It has two entries for coeducation.
But there's a tight-shut look to either door
And to the windows of its fenestration,
As if to say mere learning was the devil   10
And this school wasn't keeping anymore,
Unless for penitents who took their seat
Upon its doorsteps as at mercy's feet
To make up for a lack of meditation.

"An Afterword" from
Complete Poems
: 1949 :

TAKE SOMETHING LIKE A STAR

O Star (the fairest one in sight),
We grant your loftiness the right
To some obscurity of cloud—
It will not do to say of night,
Since dark is what brings out your light.　　5
Some mystery becomes the proud.
But to be wholly taciturn
In your reserve is not allowed.
Say something to us we can learn
By heart and when alone repeat.　　10
Say something! And it says, "I burn."
But say with what degree of heat.
Talk Fahrenheit, talk Centigrade.
Use language we can comprehend.
Tell us what elements you blend.　　15
It gives us strangely little aid,
But does tell something in the end.
And steadfast as Keats' Eremite,
Not even stooping from its sphere,
It asks a little of us here.　　20
It asks of us a certain height,
So when at times the mob is swayed
To carry praise or blame too far,
We may take something like a star
To stay our minds on and be staid.　　25

FROM PLANE TO PLANE

Neither of them was better than the other.
They both were hired. And though Pike had the advantage
Of having hoed and mowed for fifty years,
Dick had of being fresh and full of college.
So if they fought about equality   5
It was on an equality they fought.

"Your trouble is not sticking to the subject,"
Pike said with temper. And Dick longed to say,
"Your trouble is bucolic lack of logic,"
But all he did say was, "What *is* the subject?"   10

"It's whether these professions really work.
Now take the Doctor—"

                    They were giving corn
A final going over with the hoe
Before they turned from everything to hay.
The wavy upflung pennons of the corn   15
Were loose all round their legs—you couldn't say
How many thousand of them in an acre.
Every time Dick or Pike looked up, the Doctor
With one foot on the dashboard of his buggy
Was still in sight like someone to depend on.   20
Nowhere but on the Bradford Interval
By the Connecticut could anyone
Have stayed in sight so long as an example.

"—Taking his own sweet time as if to show
He don't mind having lost a case," Pike said;   25
And when he caught Dick looking once too often,
"Hoeing's too much like work for Dick," he added.
"Dick wishes he could swap jobs with the Doctor.

404

Let's holler and ask him if he won't prescribe
For all humanity a complete rest   30
From all this wagery. But what's the use
Of asking any sympathy of him?
That class of people don't know what work *is*—
More than they know what courage is that claim
The moral kind's as brave as facing bullets."   35

Dick told him to be fairer to the Doctor:
"He looks to me like going home successful,
Full of success, with that foot on the dashboard,
As a small self-conferred reward of virtue.
I get you when you hoe out to the river,   40
Then pick your hoe up, maybe shoulder it,
And take your walk of recreation back
To curry favor with the dirt some more.
Isn't it pretty much the same idea?
You said yourself you weren't avoiding work.   45
You'd bet you got more work done in a day,
Or at least in a lifetime, by that method."

"I wouldn't hoe both ways for anybody!"

"And right you are. You do the way we do
In reading, don't you, Bill?—at every line end   50
Pick up our eyes and carry them back idle
Across the page to where we started from.
The other way of reading back and forth,
Known as boustrophedon, was found too awkward."

Pike grunted rather grimly with misgiving   55
At being thus expounded to himself
And made of by a boy; then having reached
The river bank, quit work defiantly,
As if he didn't care who understood him,

And started his march back again discoursing: 60
"A man has got to keep his extrication.
The important thing is not to get bogged down
In what he has to do to earn a living.
What's more, I hate to keep afflicting weeds.
I like to give my enemies a truce."   65

"Be careful how you use your influence.
If I decided to become a doctor,
You'd be to blame for furnishing the reasons."

"I thought you meant to be an Indian Chief—
You said the second coming of Tecumseh.   70
Remember how you envied General Sherman.
William Tecumseh Sherman. Why Tecumseh?"
(He tried to imitate Dick's tone of voice.)
"You wished your middle name had been Tecumseh."

"I think I'll change my mind."

                         "You're saying that   75
To bother me by siding with the Doctor.
You've got no social conscience, as they say,
Or you'd feel differently about the classes.
You can't claim *you're* a social visionary."

"I'm saying it to argue his idea's   80
The same as your idea, only more so.
And I suspect it may be more and more so
The further up the scale of work you go.
You could do worse than boost me up to see."

"It isn't just the same, and someday, schoolboy,   85
I'll show you why it isn't—not today.
Today I want to talk about the sun.
May as expected was a disappointment,

And June was not much better, cold and rainy.
The sun then had his longest day in heaven,   90
But no one from the feeling would have guessed
His presence was particularly there.
He only stayed to set the summer on fire,
Then fled for fear of getting stuck in lava
In case the rocks should melt and run again.   95
Everyone has to keep his extrication."

"That's what the Doctor's doing, keeping his.
That's what I have to do in school, keep mine
From knowing more than I know how to think with.
You see it in yourself and in the sun;   100
Yet you refuse to see it in the Doctor."

"All right, let's harmonize about the Doctor.
He may be some good, in a manner of speaking.
I own he does look busy when the sun
Is in the sign of Sickness in the winter   105
And everybody's being sick for Christmas.
Then's when his Morgan lights out throwing snowballs
Behind her at the dashboard of his pung."

"But Cygnus isn't in the Zodiac,"
Dick longed to say, but wasn't sure enough   110
Of his astronomy. (He'd have to take
A half course in it next year.) And besides,
Why give the controversy a relapse?

They were both bent on scuffling up
Alluvium so pure that when a blade   115
To their surprise rang once on stone all day
Each tried to be the first at getting in
A superstitious cry for farmers' luck—

A rivalry that made them both feel kinder.

And so to let Pike seem to have the palm 120
With grace and not too formal a surrender
Dick said, "You've been a lesson in work wisdom
To work with, Bill. But you won't have my thanks.
I like to think the sun's like you in that—
Since you bring up the subject of the sun. 125
This would be my interpretation of him.
He bestows summer on us and escapes
Before our realizing what we have
To thank him for. He doesn't want our thanks.
He likes to turn his back on gratitude 130
And avoid being worshiped as a god.
Our worship was a thing he had too much of
In the old days in Persia and Peru.
Shall I go on or have I said enough—
To convey my respect for your position?" 135

"I guess so," Pike said, innocent of Milton.
"That's where I reckon Santa Claus comes in—
To be our parents' pseudonymity
In Christmas giving, so they can escape
The thanks and let him catch it as a scapegoat. 140
And even he, you'll notice, dodges off
Up chimney to avoid the worst of it.
We all know his address, Mount Hecla, Iceland.
So anyone can write to him who has to;
Though they do say he doesn't open letters. 145
A Santa Claus was needed. And there *is* one."

"So I have heard and do in part believe it,"
Dick said, to old Pike innocent of Shakespeare.

In the Clearing

: 1962 :

POD OF THE MILKWEED

Calling all butterflies of every race
From source unknown but from no special place
They ever will return to all their lives,
Because unlike the bees they have no hives,
The milkweed brings up to my very door   5
The theme of wanton waste in peace and war
As it has never been to me before.
And so it seems a flower's coming out
That should if not be talked then sung about.
The countless wings that from the infinite   10
Make such a noiseless tumult over it
Do no doubt with their color compensate
For what the drab weed lacks of the ornate.
For drab it is its fondest must admit.
And yes, although it is a flower that flows   15
With milk and honey, it is bitter milk,
As anyone who ever broke its stem
And dared to taste the wound a little knows.
It tastes as if it might be opiate.
But whatsoever else it may secrete,   20
Its flowers' distilled honey is so sweet
It makes the butterflies intemperate.
There is no slumber in its juice for them.
One knocks another off from where he clings.
They knock the dyestuff off each other's wings—   25
With thirst on hunger to the point of lust.
They raise in their intemperance a cloud

411

Of mingled butterfly and flower dust
That hangs perceptibly above the scene.
In being sweet to these ephemerals   30
The sober weed has managed to contrive
In our three hundred days and sixty-five
One day too sweet for beings to survive.
Many shall come away as struggle-worn
And spent and dusted off of their regalia,   35
To which at daybreak they were freshly born,
As after one-of-them's proverbial failure
From having beaten all day long in vain
Against the wrong side of a windowpane.

But waste was of the essence of the scheme.   40
And all the good they did for man or god
To all those flowers they passionately trod
Was leave as their posterity one pod
With an inheritance of restless dream.
He hangs on upside down with talon feet   45
In an inquisitive position odd
As any Guatemalan parakeet.
Something eludes him. Is it food to eat?
Or some dim secret of the good of waste?
He almost has it in his talon clutch.   50
Where have those flowers and butterflies all gone
That science may have staked the future on?
He seems to say the reason why so much
Should come to nothing must be fairly faced.

AWAY!

Now I out walking
The world desert,

And my shoe and my stocking
Do me no hurt.

I leave behind   5
Good friends in town.
Let them get well-wined
And go lie down.

Don't think I leave
For the outer dark   10
Like Adam and Eve
Put out of the Park.

Forget the myth.
There is no one I
Am put out with   15
Or put out by.

Unless I'm wrong
I but obey
The urge of a song:
"I'm—bound—away!"   20

And I may return
If dissatisfied
With what I learn
From having died.

A CABIN IN THE CLEARING

For Alfred Edwards

MIST.   I don't believe the sleepers in this house
Know where they are.

SMOKE.   They've been here long enough
To push the woods back from around the house
And part them in the middle with a path.

MIST.   And still I doubt if they know where they are.   5
And I begin to fear they never will.
All they maintain the path for is the comfort
Of visiting with the equally bewildered.
Nearer in plight their neighbors are than distance.

SMOKE.   I am the guardian wraith of starlit smoke   10
That leans out this and that way from their chimney.
I will not have their happiness despaired of.

MIST.   No one—not I—would give them up for lost
Simply because they don't know where they are.
I am the damper counterpart of smoke,   15
That gives off from a garden ground at night
But lifts no higher than a garden grows.
I cotton to their landscape. That's who I am.
I am no further from their fate than you are.

SMOKE.   They must by now have learned the native tongue.
Why don't they ask the Red Man where they are?

MIST.   They often do, and none the wiser for it.
So do they also ask philosophers
Who come to look in on them from the pulpit.
They will ask anyone there is to ask—   25
In the fond faith accumulated fact
Will of itself take fire and light the world up.
Learning has been a part of their religion.

SMOKE.   If the day ever comes when they know who
They are, they may know better where they are.   30
But who they are is too much to believe—

414

Either for them or the onlooking world.
They are too sudden to be credible.

MIST.   Listen, they murmur talking in the dark
On what should be their daylong theme continued.   35
Putting the lamp out has not put their thought out.
Let us pretend the dewdrops from the eaves
Are you and I eavesdropping on their unrest—
A mist and smoke eavesdropping on a haze—
And see if we can tell the bass from the soprano.   40

   Than smoke and mist who better could appraise
   The kindred spirit of an inner haze?

CLOSED FOR GOOD

Much as I own I owe
The passers of the past
Because their to and fro
Has cut this road to last,
I owe them more today   5
Because they've gone away

And come not back with steed
And chariot to chide
My slowness with their speed
And scare me to one side.   10
They have found other scenes
For haste and other means.

They leave the road to me
To walk in saying naught
Perhaps but to a tree   15
Inaudibly in thought,
"From you the road receives

415

A priming coat of leaves.

"And soon for lack of sun,
The prospects are in white   20
It will be further done,
But with a coat so light
The shape of leaves will show
Beneath the brush of snow."

And so on into winter   25
Till even I have ceased
To come as a foot printer,
And only some slight beast
So mousy or so foxy
Shall print there as my proxy.   30

AMERICA IS HARD TO SEE

Columbus may have worked the wind
A new and better way to Ind
And also proved the world a ball,
But how about the wherewithal?
Not just for scientific news   5
Had the Queen backed him to a cruise.

Remember he had made the test
Finding the East by sailing West.
But had he found it? Here he was
Without one trinket from Ormuz   10
To save the Queen from family censure
For her investment in his venture.

There had been something strangely wrong
With every coast he tried along.

416

He could imagine nothing barrener. 15
The trouble was with him the mariner.
He wasn't off a mere degree;
His reckoning was off a sea.

And to intensify the drama
Another mariner, da Gama, 20
Came just then sailing into port
From the same general resort,
And with the gold in hand to show for
His claim it was another Ophir.

Had but Columbus known enough 25
He might have boldly made the bluff
That better than da Gama's gold
He had been given to behold
The race's future trial place,
A fresh start for the human race. 30

He might have fooled Valladolid.
I was deceived by what he did.
If I had had my chance when young
I should have had Columbus sung
As a god who had given us 35
A more than Moses' exodus.

But all he did was spread the room
Of our enacting out the doom
Of being in each other's way,
And so put off the weary day 40
When we would have to put our mind
On how to crowd but still be kind.

For these none-too-apparent gains
He got no more than dungeon chains

And such small posthumous renown
(A country named for him, a town,
A holiday) as, where he is,
He may not recognize for his.

They say his flagship's unlaid ghost
Still probes and dents our rocky coast
With animus approaching hate,
And for not turning out a strait,
He has cursed every river mouth
From fifty North to fifty South.

Someday our navy, I predict,
Will take in tow this derelict
And lock him through Culebra Cut,
His eyes as good (or bad) as shut
To all the modern works of man
And all we call American.

America is hard to see.
Less partial witnesses than he
In book on book have testified
They could not see it from outside—
Or inside either for that matter.
We know the literary chatter.

Columbus, as I say, will miss
All he owes to the artifice
Of tractor-plow and motor-drill.
To naught but his own force of will,
Or at most some Andean quake,
Will he ascribe this lucky break.

High purpose makes the hero rude;
He will not stop for gratitude.

But let him show his haughty stern   75
To what was never his concern
Except as it denied him way
To fortune-hunting in Cathay.

He will be starting pretty late.
He'll find that Asiatic state   80
Is about tired of being looted
While having its beliefs disputed.
His can be no such easy raid
As Cortez on the Aztecs made.

ONE MORE BREVITY

I opened the door so my last look
Should be taken outside a house and book.
Before I gave up seeing and slept
I said I would see how Sirius kept
His watchdog eye on what remained   5
To be gone into if not explained.
But scarcely was my door ajar,
When past the leg I thrust for bar
Slipped in to be my problem guest,
Not a heavenly dog made manifest,   10
But an earthly dog of the carriage breed;
Who, having failed of the modern speed,
Now asked asylum—and I was stirred
To be the one so dog-preferred.
He dumped himself like a bag of bones,   15
He sighed himself a couple of groans,
And head to tail then firmly curled
Like swearing off on the traffic world.
I set him water, I set him food.

He rolled an eye with gratitude   20
(Or merely manners it may have been),
But never so much as lifted chin.
His hard tail loudly smacked the floor
As if beseeching me, "Please, no more;
I can't explain—tonight at least."   25
His brow was perceptibly trouble-creased.
So I spoke in terms of adoption thus:
"Gustie, old boy, Dalmatian Gus,
You're right, there's nothing to discuss.
Don't try to tell me what's on your mind,   30
The sorrow of having been left behind,
Or the sorrow of having run away.
All that can wait for the light of day.
Meanwhile feel obligation-free.
Nobody has to confide in me."   35
'Twas too one-sided a dialogue,
And I wasn't sure I was talking dog.
I broke off baffled. But all the same,
In fancy I ratified his name,
Gustie—Dalmatian Gus, that is—   40
And started shaping my life to his,
Finding him in his right supplies
And sharing his miles of exercise.

Next morning the minute I was about
He was at the door to be let out   45
With an air that said, "I have paid my call.
You mustn't feel hurt if now I'm all
For getting back somewhere or further on."
I opened the door and he was gone.
I was to taste in little the grief   50
That comes of dogs' lives being so brief,

420

Only a fraction of ours at most.
He might have been the dream of a ghost
In spite of the way his tail had smacked
My floor so hard and matter-of-fact.   55
And things have been going so strangely since,
I wouldn't be too hard to convince,
I might even claim, he was Sirius
(Think of presuming to call him Gus),
The star itself—Heaven's greatest star,   60
Not a meteorite, but an avatar—
Who had made an overnight descent
To show by deeds he didn't resent
My having depended on him so long,
And yet done nothing about it in song.   65
A symbol was all he could hope to convey,
An intimation, a shot of ray,
A meaning I was supposed to seek,
And finding, wasn't disposed to speak.

ESCAPIST—NEVER

He is no fugitive—escaped, escaping.
No one has seen him stumble looking back.
His fear is not behind him but beside him
On either hand to make his course perhaps
A crooked straightness yet no less a straightness.   5
He runs face forward. He is a pursuer.
He seeks a seeker who in his turn seeks
Another still, lost far into the distance.
Any who seek him seek in him the seeker.
His life is a pursuit of a pursuit forever.   10
It is the future that creates his present.
All is an interminable chain of longing.

FOR JOHN F. KENNEDY
HIS INAUGURATION

Gift outright of "The Gift Outright"

(With some preliminary history in rhyme)

Summoning artists to participate
In the august occasions of the state
Seems something artists ought to celebrate.
Today is for my cause a day of days.
And his be poetry's old-fashioned praise   5
Who was the first to think of such a thing.
This verse that in acknowledgment I bring
Goes back to the beginning of the end
Of what had been for centuries the trend;
A turning point in modern history.   10
Colonial had been the thing to be
As long as the great issue was to see
What country'd be the one to dominate
By character, by tongue, by native trait,
The new world Christopher Columbus found.   15
The French, the Spanish, and the Dutch were downed
And counted out. Heroic deeds were done.
Elizabeth the First and England won.
Now came on a new order of the ages
That in the Latin of our founding sages   20
(Is it not written on the dollar bill
We carry in our purse and pocket still?)
God nodded His approval of as good.
So much those heroes knew and understood—
I mean the great four, Washington,   25
John Adams, Jefferson, and Madison—
So much they knew as consecrated seers

422

They must have seen ahead what now appears:
They would bring empires down about our ears
And by the example of our Declaration   30
Make everybody want to be a nation.
And this is no aristocratic joke
At the expense of negligible folk.
We see how seriously the races swarm
In their attempts at sovereignty and form.   35
They are our wards we think to some extent
For the time being and with their consent,
To teach them how Democracy is meant.
"New order of the ages" did we say?
If it looks none too orderly today,   40
'Tis a confusion it was ours to start
So in it have to take courageous part.
No one of honest feeling would approve
A ruler who pretended not to love
A turbulence he had the better of.   45
Everyone knows the glory of the twain
Who gave America the aeroplane
To ride the whirlwind and the hurricane.
Some poor fool has been saying in his heart
Glory is out of date in life and art.   50
Our venture in revolution and outlawry
Has justified itself in freedom's story
Right down to now in glory upon glory.
Come fresh from an election like the last,
The greatest vote a people ever cast,   55
So close yet sure to be abided by,
It is no miracle our mood is high.
Courage is in the air in bracing whiffs
Better than all the stalemate an's and ifs.
There was the book of profile tales declaring   60

423

For the emboldened politicians daring
To break with followers when in the wrong,
A healthy independence of the throng,
A democratic form of right divine
To rule first answerable to high design.   65
There is a call to life a little sterner,
And braver for the earner, learner, yearner.
Less criticism of the field and court
And more preoccupation with the sport.
It makes the prophet in us all presage   70
The glory of a next Augustan age
Of a power leading from its strength and pride,
Of young ambition eager to be tried,
Firm in our free beliefs without dismay,
In any game the nations want to play.   75
A golden age of poetry and power
Of which this noonday's the beginning hour.

THE GIFT OUTRIGHT

The land was ours before we were the land's.
She was our land more than a hundred years
Before we were her people. She was ours
In Massachusetts, in Virginia,
But we were England's, still colonials,
Possessing what we still were unpossessed by,
Possessed by what we now no more possessed.
Something we were withholding made us weak
Until we found out that it was ourselves
We were withholding from our land of living,
And forthwith found salvation in surrender.
Such as we were we gave ourselves outright
(The deed of gift was many deeds of war)

424

To the land vaguely realizing westward,
But still unstoried, artless, unenhanced,
Such as she was, such as she would become.

ACCIDENTALLY ON PURPOSE

The Universe is but the Thing of things,
The things but balls all going round in rings.
Some of them mighty huge, some mighty tiny,
All of them radiant and mighty shiny.

They mean to tell us all was rolling blind   5
Till accidentally it hit on mind
In an albino monkey in a jungle,
And even then it had to grope and bungle,

Till Darwin came to earth upon a year
To show the evolution how to steer.   10
They mean to tell us, though, the Omnibus
Had no real purpose till it got to us.

Never believe it. At the very worst
It must have had the purpose from the first
To produce purpose as the fitter bred: 15
We were just purpose coming to a head.

Whose purpose was it? His or Hers or Its?
Let's leave that to the scientific wits.
Grant me intention, purpose, and design—
That's near enough for me to the Divine.   20

And yet for all this help of head and brain
How happily instinctive we remain,
Our best guide upward further to the light,
Passionate preference such as love at sight.

425

A NEVER NAUGHT SONG

There was never naught,
There was always thought.
But when noticed first
It was fairly burst
Into having weight.   5
It was in a state
Of atomic One.
Matter was begun—
And in fact complete,
One and yet discrete   10
To conflict and pair.
Everything was there,
Every single thing
Waiting was to bring,
Clear from hydrogen   15
All the way to men.
It is all the tree
It will ever be,
Bole and branch and root
Cunningly minute.   20
And this gist of all
Is so infra-small
As to blind our eyes
To its every guise
And so render nil   25
The whole Yggdrasill.
Out of coming-in
Into having been!
So the picture's caught
Almost next to naught   30
But the force of thought.

VERSION

Once there was an Archer,
And there was a minute
When He shot a shaft
On a New Departure.
Then He must have laughed: 5
Comedy was in it.
For the game He hunted
Was the non-existence
Of the Phoenix pullet
(The Μὴ ὄν of Plato),   10
And the shaft got blunted
On her non-resistance,
Like a dum-dum bullet—
Did in fact get splattered
Like a ripe tomato.   15
That's how matter mattered.

A CONCEPT SELF-CONCEIVED

The latest creed that has to be believed
And entered in our childish catechism
Is that the All's a concept self-conceived,
Which is no more than good old Pantheism.

Great is the reassurance of recall.   5
Why go on further with confusing voice
To say God's either All or over all?
The rule is, never give a child a choice.

[FORGIVE, O LORD...]

Forgive, O Lord, my little jokes on Thee
And I'll forgive Thy great big one on me.

KITTY HAWK

Back there in 1953 with the Huntington Cairnses
(A skylark for them in three-beat phrases)

PART ONE

PORTENTS, PRESENTIMENTS,
AND PREMONITIONS

Kitty Hawk, O Kitty,
There was once a song,
Who knows but a great
Emblematic ditty,
I might well have sung   5
When I came here young
Out and down along
Past Elizabeth City
Sixty years ago.
I was, to be sure,   10
Out of sorts with Fate,
Wandering to and fro
In the earth alone,
You might think too poor-
Spirited to care   15
Who I was or where
I was being blown
Faster than my tread—
Like the crumpled, better-

428

Left-unwritten letter   20
I had read and thrown.
Oh, but not to boast,
Ever since Nag's Head
Had my heart been great,
Not to claim elate,   25
With a need the gale
Filled me with to shout
Summary riposte
To the dreary wail
There's no knowing what   30
Love is all about.
Poets know a lot.
Never did I fail
Of an answer back
To the zodiac   35
When in heartless chorus
Aries and Taurus,
Gemini and Cancer
Mocked me for an answer.
It was on my tongue   40
To have up and sung
The initial flight
I can see now might—
Should have been—my own
Into the unknown,   45
Into the sublime
Off these sands of Time
Time had seen amass
From his hourglass.
Once I told the Master,   50
Later when we met,
I'd been here one night

As a young Alastor
When the scene was set
For some kind of flight   55
Long before he flew it.
Just supposing I—
I had beat him to it.
What did men mean by
THE original?   60
Why was it so very,
Very necessary
To be first of all?
How about the lie
That he wasn't first?   65
I was glad he laughed.
There was such a lie
Money and maneuver
Fostered overlong
Until Herbert Hoover   70
Raised this tower shaft
To undo the wrong.
Of all crimes the worst
Is to steal the glory
From the great and brave,   75
Even more accursed
Than to rob the grave.
But the sorry story
Has been long redressed.
And as for my jest   80
I had any claim
To the runway's fame
Had I only sung,
That is all my tongue.
I can't make it seem   85

More than that my theme
Might have been a dream
Of dark Hatteras
Or sad Roanoke,
One more fond alas   90
For the seed of folk
Sowed in vain by Raleigh,
Raleigh of the cloak,
And some other folly.

Getting too befriended,   95
As so often, ended
Any melancholy
Götterdämmerung
That I might have sung.
I fell in among   100
Some kind of committee
From Elizabeth City,
Each and every one
Loaded with a gun
Or a demijohn.   105
(Need a body ask
If it was a flask?)
Out to kill a duck
Or perhaps a swan
Over Currituck.   110
This was not their day
Anything to slay
Unless one another.
But their lack of luck
Made them no less gay,   115
No, nor less polite.
They included me

431

Like a little brother
In their revelry—
All concern to take   120
Care my innocence
Should at all events
Tenderly be kept
For good gracious' sake.
And if they were gentle   125
They were sentimental.
One drank to his mother
While another wept.
Something made it sad
For me to break loose   130
From the need they had
To make themselves glad
They were of no use.
Manners made it hard,
But that night I stole   135
Off on the unbounded
Beaches where the whole
Of the Atlantic pounded.
There I next fell in
With a lone coast guard   140
On midnight patrol,
Who as of a sect
Asked about my soul
And where-all I'd been.
Apropos of sin,   145
Did I recollect
How the wreckers wrecked
Theodosia Burr
Off this very shore?
'Twas to punish her,   150

432

But her father more—
We don't know what for:
There was no confession.
Things they think she wore
Still sometimes occur   155
In someone's possession
Here at Kitty Hawk.
We can have no notion
Of the strange devotion
Burr had for his daughter: 160
He was too devoted.
So it was in talk
We prolonged the walk,
On one side the ocean,
And on one a water   165
Of the inner sound;
"And the moon was full,"
As the poet said
And I aptly quoted.
And its being full   170
And right overhead,
Small but strong and round,
By its tidal pull
Made all being full.
Kitty Hawk, O Kitty,   175
Here it was again
In the selfsame day,
I at odds with men
Came upon their pity,
Equally profound   180
For a son astray
And a daughter drowned.

433

PART TWO

When the chance went by
For my Muse to fly
From this Runway Beach   185
As a figure of speech
In a flight of words,
Little I imagined
Men would treat this sky
Someday to a pageant   190
Like a thousand birds.
Neither you nor I
Ever thought to fly.
Oh, but fly we did,
Literally fly.   195
That's because though mere
Lilliputians we're
What Catullus called
Somewhat (*aliquid*).
Mind you, we are mind.   200
We are not the kind
To stay too confined.
After having crawled
Round the place on foot
And done yeoman share   205
Of just staying put,
We arose from there
And we scaled a plane
So the stilly air
Almost pulled our hair   210
Like a hurricane.

Then I saw it all.

Pulpiteers will censure

Our instinctive venture
Into what they call   215
The material
When we took that fall
From the apple tree.
But God's own descent
Into flesh was meant   220
As a demonstration
That the supreme merit
Lay in risking spirit
In substantiation.
Westerners inherit   225
A design for living
Deeper into matter—
Not without due patter
Of a great misgiving.
All the science zest   230
To materialize
By on-penetration
Into earth and skies
(Don't forget the latter
Is but further matter)   235
Has been West-Northwest.
If it was not wise,
Tell me why the East
Seemingly has ceased
From its long stagnation   240
In mere meditation.
What is all the fuss
To catch up with us?
Can it be to flatter
Us with emulation?   245

Spirit enters flesh

435

And for all it's worth
Charges into earth
In birth after birth
Ever fresh and fresh.   250
We may take the view
That its derring-do
Thought of in the large
Was one mighty charge
On our human part   255
Of the soul's ethereal
Into the material.
In a running start,
As it were from scratch,
On a certain slab   260
Of (we'll say) basalt
In or near Moab
With intent to vault
In a vaulting match,
Never mind with whom   265
(No one, I presume,
But ourselves—mankind,
In a love and hate
Rivalry combined)—
'Twas a radio   270
Voice that said, "Get set
In the alphabet,
That is, A B C,
Which someday should be
Rhymed with 1 2 3   275
On a college gate."
Then the radio
Region voice said, "Go,
Go you on to know

436

More than you can sing.   280
Have no hallowing fears
Anything's forbidden
Just because it's hidden.
Trespass and encroach
On successive spheres   285
Without self-reproach."
Then for years and years
And for miles and miles
'Cross the Aegean Isles,
Athens, Rome, France, Britain,   290
Always West-Northwest,
As have I not written,
Till the so-long-kept
Purpose was expressed
In the leap we leapt.   295
And the radio
Cried, "The Leap—The Leap!"
It belonged to US,
Not our friends the Russ,
To have run the event   300
To its full extent
And have won the crown,
Or let's say the cup,
On which with a date
Is the inscription, though,   305
"Nothing can go up
But it must come down."
Earth is still our fate.
The uplifted sight
We enjoyed at night   310
When instead of sheep
We were counting stars,

437

Not to go to sleep,
But to stay awake
For good gracious' sake,   315
Naming stars to boot
To avoid mistake,
Jupiter and Mars,
Just like Pullman cars,
'Twas no vain pursuit.   320
Some have preached and taught
All there was to thought
Was to master Nature
By some nomenclature.
But if not a law   325
'Twas an end foregone
Anything we saw
And thus fastened on
With an epithet,
We would see to yet—   330
We would want to touch,
Not to mention clutch.

TALK ALOFT

Someone says the Lord
Says our reaching toward
Is its own reward.   335
One would like to know
Where God says it, though.

We don't like that much.

Let's see where we are.
What's that sulphur blur   340
Off there in the fog?
Go consult the log.

It's some kind of town,
But it's not New York.
We're not very far   345
Out from where we were.
It's still Kitty Hawk.

We'd have got as far
Even at a walk.

Don't you crash me down.   350
Though our kiting ships
Prove but flying chips
From the science shop
And when motors stop
They may have to drop   355
Short of anywhere,
Though our leap in air
Prove as vain a hop
As the hop from grass
Of a grasshopper,   360
Don't discount our powers;
We have made a pass
At the infinite,
Made it, as it were,
Rationally ours,   365
To the most remote
Swirl of neon-lit
Particle afloat.
Ours was to reclaim
What had long been faced   370
As a fact of waste
And was waste in name.

That's how we became,

Though an earth so small,
Justly known to fame   375
As the Capital
Of the universe.
We make no pretension
Of projecting ray
We can call our own   380
From this ball of stone,
None I don't reject
As too new to mention.
All we do's reflect
From our rocks, and yes,   385
From our brains no less.
And the better part
Is the ray we dart
From this head and heart,
The *mens animi*.   390

Till we came to be
There was not a trace
Of a thinking race
Anywhere in space.
We know of no world   395
Being whirled and whirled
Round and round the rink
Of a single sun
(So as not to sink),
Not a single one   400
That has thought to think.

THE HOLINESS OF WHOLENESS

Pilot, though at best your

440

Flight is but a gesture,
And your rise and swoop,
But a loop the loop,   405
Lands on someone hard
In his own backyard
From no higher heaven
Than a bolt of levin,
I don't say retard.   410
Keep on elevating.
But while meditating
What we can't or can
Let's keep starring man
In the royal role.   415
It will not be his
Ever to create
One least germ or coal.
Those two things we can't.
But the comfort is   420
In the covenant
We may get control,
If not of the whole,
Of at least some part
Where not too immense,   425
So by craft or art
We can give the part
Wholeness in a sense.
The becoming fear
That becomes us best   430
Is lest habit-ridden
In the kitchen midden
Of our dump of earning
And our dump of learning

441

We come nowhere near   435
Getting thought expressed.

THE MIXTURE MECHANIC

This wide flight we wave
At the stars or moon
Means that we approve
Of them on the move.   440
Ours is to behave
Like a kitchen spoon
Of a size Titanic
To keep all things stirred
In a blend mechanic,   445
Saying That's the tune,
That's the pretty kettle!
Matter mustn't curd,
Separate and settle.
Action is the word.   450

Nature's never quite
Sure she hasn't erred
In her vague design
Till on some fine night
We two come in flight   455
Like a king and queen
And by right divine,
Waving scepter-baton,
Undertake to tell her
What in being stellar   460
She's supposed to mean.

God of the machine,
Peregrine machine,

Some still think is Satan,
Unto you the thanks   465
For this token flight,
Thanks to you and thanks
To the brothers Wright,
Once considered cranks
Like Darius Green   470
In their hometown, Dayton.

AUSPEX

Once in a California Sierra
I was swooped down upon when I was small,
And measured, but not taken after all,
By a great eagle bird in all its terror.

Such auspices are very hard to read.   5
My parents when I ran to them averred
I was rejected by the royal bird
As one who would not make a Ganymede.

Not find a barkeep unto Jove in me?
I have remained resentful to this day   10
When any but myself presumed to say
That there was anything I couldn't be.

THE DRAFT HORSE

With a lantern that wouldn't burn
In too frail a buggy we drove
Behind too heavy a horse
Through a pitch-dark limitless grove.

443

And a man came out of the trees 5
And took our horse by the head
And reaching back to his ribs
Deliberately stabbed him dead.

The ponderous beast went down
With a crack of a broken shaft. 10
And the night drew through the trees
In one long invidious draft.

The most unquestioning pair
That ever accepted fate
And the least disposed to ascribe 15
Any more than we had to to hate,

We assumed that the man himself
Or someone he had to obey
Wanted us to get down
And walk the rest of the way. 20

ENDS

Loud talk in the overlighted house
That made us stumble past.
Oh, there had once been night the first,
But this was night the last.

Of all the things he might have said, 5
Sincere or insincere,
He never said she wasn't young,
And hadn't been his dear.

Oh, some as soon would throw it all
As throw a part away.   10
And some will say all sorts of things,
But some mean what they say.

PERIL OF HOPE

It is right in there
Betwixt and between
The orchard bare
And the orchard green,

When the boughs are right   5
In a flowery burst
Of pink and white,
That we fear the worst.

For there's not a clime
But at any cost   10
Will take that time
For a night of frost.

QUESTIONING FACES

The winter owl banked just in time to pass
And save herself from breaking window glass.
And her wings straining suddenly aspread
Caught color from the last of evening red
In a display of underdown and quill   5
To glassed-in children at the windowsill.

DOES NO ONE AT ALL
EVER FEEL THIS WAY IN THE LEAST?

O ocean sea, for all your being vast,
Your separation of us from the Old
That should have made the New World newly great
Would only disappoint us at the last
If it should not do anything foretold   5
To make us different in a single trait.

This though we took the Indian name for maize
And changed it to the English name for wheat.
It seemed to comfort us to call it corn.
And so with homesickness in many ways   10
We sought however crudely to defeat
Our chance of being people newly born.

And now, O sea, you're lost by aeroplane.
Our sailors ride a bullet for a boat.
Our coverage of distance is so facile   15
It makes us to have had a sea in vain.
Our moat around us is no more a moat,
Our continent no more a moated castle.

Grind shells, O futile sea, grind empty shells
For all the use you are along the strand.   20
I cannot hold you innocent of fault.
Spring water in our mountain bosom swells
To pour fresh rivers on you from the land,
Till you have lost the savor of your salt.

I pick a dead shell up from where the kelp   25
Lies in a windrow, brittle-dry and black,
And holding it far forward for a symbol

446

I cry, "Do work for women—all the help
I ask of you. Grind this I throw you back
Into a lady's finger ring or thimble."   30

The ocean had been spoken to before.
But if it had no thought of paying heed
To taunt of mine I knew a place to go
Where I need listen to its rote no more,
Nor taste its salt, nor smell its fish and weed,   35
Nor be reminded of them in a blow—

So far inland the very name of ocean
Goes mentionless except in baby-school
When teacher's own experiences fail her
And she can only give the class a notion   40
Of what it is by calling it a pool
And telling them how Sinbad was a sailor.

THE BAD ISLAND—EASTER

(Perhaps so called because it may have risen once)

That primitive head
So ambitiously vast,
Yet so rude in its art,
Is as easily read
For the woes of the past   5
As a clinical chart.
For one thing alone,
The success of the lip
So scornfully curled,
Has that tonnage of stone   10
Been brought in a ship

447

Halfway round the world.

They were days on that stone.
They gave it the wedge
Till it flaked from the ledge.   15
Then they gave it a face.
Then with tackle unknown
They stood it in place
On a cliff for a throne.
They gave it a face   20
Of what was it? Scorn
Of themselves as a race
For having been born?
And then having first
Been cajoled and coerced   25
Into being beruled?
By what stratagem
Was their cynical throng
So cozened and fooled
And jollied along?   30
Were they told they were free
And persuaded to see
Something in it for them?
Well they flourished and waxed
By executive guile,   35
By fraud and by force,
Or so for a while;
Until overtaxed
In nerve and resource
They started to wane.   40
They emptied the aisle
Except for a few
That can but be described

As a vile residue,
And a garrulous too.   45
They were punished and bribed;
All was in vain,
Nothing would do.
Some mistake had been made
No book can explain,   50
Some change in the law
That nobody saw
Except as a gain.
But one thing is sure,
Whatever kultur   55
They were made to parade,
What heights of altrur-
ian thought to attain,
Not a trace of it's left
But the gospel of sharing,   60
And that has decayed
Into a belief
In being a thief
And persisting in theft
With cynical daring.   65

OUR DOOM TO BLOOM

"Shine, perishing republic."

ROBINSON JEFFERS

Cumaean Sibyl, charming Ogress,
What are the simple facts of Progress
That I may trade on with reliance
In consultation with my clients?
The Sibyl said, "Go back to Rome   5

449

And tell your clientele at home
That if it's not a mere illusion
All there is to it is diffusion—
Of coats, oats, votes, to all mankind.
In the Surviving Book we find   10
That liberal, or conservative,
The state's one function is to give.
The bud must bloom till blowsy blown
Its petals loosen and are strown;
And that's a fate it can't evade   15
Unless 'twould rather wilt than fade."

THE OBJECTION TO BEING STEPPED ON

At the end of the row
I stepped on the toe
Of an unemployed hoe.
It rose in offense
And struck me a blow   5
In the seat of my sense.
It wasn't to blame
But I called it a name.
And I must say it dealt
Me a blow that I felt   10
Like malice prepense.
You may call me a fool,
But *was* there a rule
The weapon should be
Turned into a tool?   15
And what do we see?
The first tool I step on
Turned into a weapon.

A-WISHING WELL

A poet would a-wishing go,
And he wished love were thus and so.
"If but it were," he said, said he,
"And one thing more that may not be,
This world were good enough for me."   5
I quote him with respect verbatim.
Some quaint dissatisfaction ate him.
I would give anything to learn
The one thing more of his concern.
But listen to me register   10
The one thing more I wish there were.
As a confirmed astronomer
I'm always for a better sky.
(I don't care how the world gets by.)
I'm tempted to let go restraint,   15
Like splashing phosphorescent paint,
And fill the sky as full of moons
As circus day of toy balloons.
That ought to make the Sunday Press.
But that's not like me. On much less   20
And much, much easier to get,
From childhood has my heart been set.
Some planets, the unblinking four,
Are seen to juggle moons galore.
A lot would be a lot of fun.   25
But all I ask's an extra one.
Let's get my incantation right:
"I wish I may, I wish I might"
Give earth another satellite.
Where would we get another? Come,   30
Don't you know where new moons are from?

When clever people ask me where
I get a poem, I despair.
I'm apt to tell them in New York
I think I get it via stork   35
From some extinct old chimney pot.
Believe the Arcadians or not,
They claim they recollect the morn
When unto Earth her first was born.
It cost the Earth as fierce a pang   40
As Keats (or was it Milton?) sang
It cost her for Enormous Caf.
It came near splitting her in half.
'Twas torn from her Pacific side.
All the sea water in one tide   45
And all the air rushed to the spot.
Believe the Arcadians or not,
They saved themselves by hanging on
To a plant called the silphion,
Which has for its great attribute   50
It can't be pulled up by the root.
Men's legs and bodies in the gale
Streamed out like pennants swallow-tail.
Most of them let go and were gone.
But there was this phenomenon: 55
Some of them gave way at the wrist
Before they gave way at the fist.
In branches of the silphion
Is sometimes found a skeleton
Of desperately clutching hand   60
Science has failed to understand.
One has been lately all the talk
In the museum of Antioch.
That's how it was from the Pacific.

It needn't be quite so terrific   65
To get another from the Atlantic.
It needn't be quite so gigantic
As coming from a lesser ocean.
Good liberals will object my notion
Is too hard on the human race.   70
That's something I'm prepared to face.
It merely would entail the purge
That the just-pausing Demiurge
Asks of himself once in so often
So the firm firmament won't soften.   75
I am assured at any rate
Man's practically inexterminate.
Someday I must go into that.
There's always been an Ararat
Where someone someone else begat   80
To start the world all over at.

HOW HARD IT IS TO KEEP
FROM BEING KING WHEN
IT'S IN YOU AND IN THE SITUATION

The King said to his son: "Enough of this!
The Kingdom's yours to finish as you please.
I'm getting out tonight. Here, take the crown."

But the Prince drew away his hand in time
To avoid what he wasn't sure he wanted.   5
So the crown fell and the crown jewels scattered.
And the Prince answered, picking up the pieces,
"Sire, I've been looking on, and I don't like
The looks of empire here. I'm leaving with you."

So the two making good their abdication   10
Fled from the palace in the guise of men.
But they had not walked far into the night
Before they sat down weary on a bank
Of dusty weeds to take a drink of stars.
And eyeing one he only wished were his,   15
Rigel, Bellatrix, or else Betelgeuse,
The ex-King said, "Yon star's indifference
Fills me with fear I'll be left to my fate:
I needn't think I have escaped my duty,
For hard it is to keep from being King   20
When it's in you and in the situation.
Witness how hard it was for Julius Caesar.
He couldn't keep himself from being King.
He had to be stopped by the sword of Brutus.
Only less hard was it for Washington.   25
My crown shall overtake me, you will see;
It will come rolling after us like a hoop."

"Let's not get superstitious, Sire," the Prince said.
"We should have brought the crown along to pawn."

"You're right," the ex-King said, "we'll need some money. 30
How would it be for you to take your father
To the slave auction in some marketplace
And sell him into slavery? My price
Should be enough to set you up in business—
Or making verse if that is what you're bent on.   35
Don't let your father tell you what to be."

The ex-King stood up in the marketplace
And tried to look ten thousand dollars' worth.
To the first buyer coming by who asked
What good he was he boldly said, "I'll tell you: 40

I know the *Quint*essence of many things.
I know the *Quint*essence of food, I know
The *Quint*essence of jewels, and I know
The *Quint*essence of horses, men, and women."

The eunuch laughed: "Well, that's a lot to know.   45
And here's a lot of money. Who's the taker?
This larrikin? All right. You come along.
You're off to Xanadu to help the cook.
I'll try you in the kitchen first on food
Since you put food first in your repertory.   50
It seems you call quint*essence* *quint*essence."

"I'm a Rhodes scholar—that's the reason why.
I was at college in the Isle of Rhodes."

The slave served his novitiate dishwashing.
He got his first chance to prepare a meal   55
One day when the chief cook was sick at heart.
(The cook was temperamental like the King.)
And the meal made the banqueters exclaim
And the Great King inquire whose work it was.

"A man's out there who claims he knows the secret,   60
Not of food only but of everything,
Jewels and horses, women, wine, and song."

The King said grandly, "Even as we are fed
See that our slave is also. He's in favor.
Take notice, Haman, he's in favor with us."   65

There came to court a merchant selling pearls,
A smaller pearl he asked a thousand for,
A larger one he asked five hundred for.
The King sat favoring one pearl for its bigness,
And then the other for its costliness   70

455

(He seems to have felt limited to one),
Till the ambassadors from Punt or somewhere
Shuffled their feet as if to hint respectfully,
"The choice is not between two pearls, O King,
But between peace and war as we conceive it.   75
We are impatient for your royal answer."
No estimating how far the entente
Might have deteriorated had not someone
Thought of the kitchen slave and had him in
To put an end to the King's vacillation.   80

And the slave said, "The small one's worth the price,
But the big one is worthless. Break it open.
My head for it—you'll find the big one hollow.
Permit me." And he crushed it under his heel
And showed them it contained a live teredo.   85

"But tell us how you knew," Darius cried.

"Oh, from my knowledge of its *quint*essence.
I told you I knew the *quint*essence of jewels.
But anybody could have guessed in this case,
From the pearl's having its own native warmth,   90
Like flesh, there must be something living in it."

"Feed him another feast of recognition."

And so it went with triumph after triumph
Till on a day the King, being sick at heart
(The King was temperamental like his cook,   95
But nobody had noticed the connection),
Sent for the ex-King in a private matter.
"You say you know the inwardness of men,
As well as of your hundred other things.
Dare to speak out and tell me about myself.   100

What ails me? Tell me. Why am I unhappy?"

"You're not where you belong. You're not a King
Of royal blood. Your father was a cook."

"You die for that."

               "No, you go ask your mother."

His mother didn't like the way he put it,   105
"But yes," she said, "someday I'll tell you, dear.
You have a right to know your pedigree.
You're well descended on your mother's side,
Which is unusual. So many Kings
Have married beggar maids from off the streets.   110
Your mother's folks——"

                He stayed to hear no more,
But hastened back to reassure his slave
That if he had him slain it wouldn't be
For having lied but having told the truth.
"At least you ought to die for wizardry.   115
But let me into it and I will spare you.
How did you know the secret of my birth?"

"If you had been a King of royal blood,
You'd have rewarded me for all I've done
By making me your minister-vizier,   120
Or giving me a nobleman's estate.
But all you thought of giving me was food.
I picked you out a horse called Safety Third,
By Safety Second out of Safety First,
Guaranteed to come safely off with you   125
From all the fights you had a mind to lose.
You could lose battles, you could lose whole wars,
You could lose Asia, Africa, and Europe,

No one could get you: you would come through smiling.
You lost your army at Mosul. What happened?   130
You came companionless, but you came home.
Is it not true? And what was my reward?
This time an all-night banquet, to be sure,
But still food, food. Your one idea was food.
None but a cook's son could be so food-minded.   135
I knew your father must have been a cook.
I'll bet you anything that's all as King
You think of for your people—feeding them."

But the King said, "Haven't I read somewhere
There is no act more kingly than to give?"   140

"Yes, but give character and not just food.
A King must give his people character."

"They can't have character unless they're fed."

"You're hopeless," said the slave.

                              "I guess I am;
I am abject before you," said Darius.   145
"You know so much, go on, instruct me further.
Tell me some rule for ruling people wisely,
In case I should decide to reign some more.
How shall I give a people character?"

"Make them as happy as is good for them.   150
But that's a hard one, for I have to add:
Not without consultation with their wishes;
Which is the crevice that lets Progress in.
If we could only stop the Progress somewhere,
At a good point for pliant permanence,   155
Where Madison attempted to arrest it.
But no, a woman has to be her age,

A nation has to take its natural course
Of Progress round and round in circles
From King to Mob to King to Mob to King   160
Until the eddy of it eddies out."

"So much for Progress," said Darius meekly.
"Another word that bothers me is Freedom.
You're good at maxims. Say me one on Freedom.
What has it got to do with character?   165
My satrap Tissaphernes has no end
Of trouble with it in his Grecian cities
Along the Aegean coast. That's all they talk of."

"Behold my son in rags here with his lyre,"
The ex-King said. "We're in this thing together.   170
He is the one who took the money for me
When I was sold—and small reproach to him.
He's a good boy. 'Twas at my instigation.
I looked on it as a Carnegie grant
For him to make a poet of himself on   175
If such a thing is possible with money.
Unluckily it wasn't money enough
To be a test. It didn't last him out.
And he may have to turn to something else
To earn a living. I don't interfere.   180
I want him to be anything he has to.
He has been begging through the Seven Cities
Where Homer begged. He'll tell you about Freedom.
He writes free verse, I'm told, and he is thought
To be the author of the Seven Freedoms: 185
Free Will, Trade, Verse, Thought, Love, Speech, Coinage.
(You ought to see the coins done in Cos.)
His name is Omar. I as a Rhodes scholar
Pronounce it Homer with a Cockney rough.

Freedom is slavery some poets tell us.   190
Enslave yourself to the right leader's truth,
Christ's or Karl Marx', and it will set you free.
Don't listen to their play of paradoxes.
The only certain freedom's in departure.
My son and I have tasted it and know.   195
We feel it in the moment we depart
As fly the atomic smithereens to nothing.
The problem for the King is just how strict
The lack of liberty, the squeeze of law
And discipline should be in school and state   200
To insure a jet departure of our going
Like a pip shot from 'twixt our pinching fingers."

"All this facility disheartens me.
Pardon my interruption; I'm unhappy.
I guess I'll have the headsman execute me   205
And press your father into being King."

"Don't let him fool you: he's a King already.
But though almost all-wise, he makes mistakes.
I'm not a free-verse singer. He was wrong there.
I claim to be no better than I am.   210
I write real verse in numbers, as they say.
I'm talking not free verse but blank verse now.
Regular verse springs from the strain of rhythm
Upon a meter, strict or loose iambic.
From that strain comes the expression *strains of music*. 215
The tune is not that meter, not that rhythm,
But a resultant that arises from them.
Tell them Iamb, Jehovah said, and meant it.
Free verse leaves out the meter and makes up
For the deficiency by church intoning.   220
Free verse, so called, is really cherished prose,

460

Prose made of, given an air by church intoning.
It has its beauty, only I don't write it.
And possibly my not writing it should stop me
From holding forth on Freedom like a Whitman— 225
A Sandburg. But permit me in conclusion:
Tell Tissaphernes not to mind the Greeks.
The freedom they seek is by politics,
Forever voting and haranguing for it.
The reason artists show so little interest 230
In public freedom is because the freedom
They've come to feel the need of is a kind
No one can give them—they can scarce attain—
The freedom of their own material:
So, never at a loss in simile, 235
They can command the exact affinity
Of anything they are confronted with.
This perfect moment of unbafflement,
When no man's name and no noun's adjective
But summons out of nowhere like a jinni. 240
We know not what we owe this moment to.
It may be wine, but much more likely love—
Possibly just well-being in the body,
Or respite from the thought of rivalry.
It's what my father must mean by departure, 245
Freedom to flash off into wild connections.
Once to have known it, nothing else will do.
Our days all pass awaiting its return.
You must have read the famous valentine
Pericles sent Aspasia in absentia: 250

> For God himself the height of feeling free
> Must have been His success in simile
> When at sight of you He thought of me.

Let's see, where are we? Oh, we're in transition,
Changing an old King for another old one.   255
What an exciting age it is we live in—
With all this talk about the hope of youth
And nothing made of youth. Consider me,
How totally ignored I seem to be.
No one is nominating me for King.   260
The headsman has Darius by the belt
To lead him off the Asiatic way
Into oblivion without a lawyer.
But that is as Darius seems to want it.
No fathoming the Asiatic mind.   265
And father's in for what we ran away from.
And superstition wins. He blames the stars,
Aldebaran, Capella, Sirius
(As I remember they were summer stars
The night we ran away from Ctesiphon),   270
For looking on and not participating.
(Why are we so resentful of detachment?)
But don't tell me it wasn't his display
Of more than royal attributes betrayed him.
How hard it is to keep from being King   275
When it's in you and in the situation.
And that is half the trouble with the world
(Or more than half I'm half inclined to say)."

LINES WRITTEN IN DEJECTION
ON THE EVE OF GREAT SUCCESS

I once had a cow that jumped over the moon,
Not onto the moon but over.

I don't know what made her so lunar a loon;
All she'd been having was clover.

That was back in the days of my godmother Goose.   5
But though we are goosier now,
And all tanked up with mineral juice,
We haven't caught up with my cow.

POSTSCRIPT

But if over the moon I had wanted to go
And had caught my cow by the tail,   10
I'll bet she'd have made a melodious low
And put her foot in the pail;

Than which there is no indignity worse.
A cow did that once to a fellow
Who rose from the milking stool with a curse   15
And cried, "I'll larn you to bellow."

He couldn't lay hands on a pitchfork to hit her
Or give her a stab of the tine,
So he leapt on her hairy back and bit her
Clear into her marrow spine.   20

No doubt she would have preferred the fork.
She let out a howl of rage
That was heard as far away as New York
And made the papers' front page.

He answered her back, "Well, who begun it?"   25
That's what at the end of a war
We always say—not who won it,
Or what it was foughten for.

THE MILKY WAY IS A COWPATH

On wings too stiff to flap
We started to exult
In having left the map
On journey the penult.

But since we got nowhere,   5
Like small boys we got mad
And let go at the air
With everything we had.

Incorrigible Quidnuncs,
We *would* see what would come   10
Of pelting heaven with chunks
Of crude uranium.

At last in self-collapse
We owned up to our wife
The Milky Way perhaps   15
Was woman's way of life.

Our un-outwitted spouse
Replied she had as soon
Believe it was the cow's
That overshot the moon.   20

The parabolic curve
Of her celestial track,
As any might observe,
Might never bring her back.

The famous foster nurse   25
Of man and womankind
Had for the universe
Left trivia behind;

And gone right on astray
Through let-down pasture bars   30
Along the Milky Way
A-foraging on stars,

Perennial as flowers,
To where as some allege
This universe of ours   35
Has got a razor edge;

And if she don't take care
She'll get her gullet cut,
But that is no affair
Of anybody's but—   40

The author of these words,
Whose lifelong unconcern
Has been with flocks and herds
For what they didn't earn.

SOME SCIENCE FICTION

The chance is the remotest
Of its going much longer unnoticed
That I'm not keeping pace
With the headlong human race.

And some of them may mind   5
My staying back behind
To take life at a walk
In philosophic talk;

Though as yet they only smile
At how slow I do a mile,   10

With tolerant reproach
For me as an Old Slow Coach.

But I know them what they are:
As they get more nuclear
And more bigoted in reliance   15
On the gospel of modern science,

For them my loitering around
At less than the speed of sound
Or even the speed of light
Won't seem unheretical quite.   20

They may end by banishing me
To the penal colony
They are thinking of pretty soon
Establishing on the moon.

With a can of condensed air   25
I could go almost anywhere,
Or rather submit to be sent
As a noble experiment.

They should try one wastrel first
On a landscape so accursed   30
To see how long they should wait
Before they make it a state.

*   *   *

ENVOI TO HYDE THE CASTAWAY
OF CROW ISLAND

I made this you to beguile
With some optimism for Christmas
On your isle that would be an isle   35
But isn't because of an isthmus.

466

QUANDARY

Never have I been sad or glad
That there was such a thing as bad.
There had to be, I understood,
For there to have been any good.
It was by having been contrasted   5
That good and bad so long had lasted.
That's why discrimination reigns.
That's why we need a lot of brains
If only to discriminate
'Twixt what to love and what to hate.   10
To quote the oracle of Delphi,
Love thou thy neighbor as thyself, aye,
And hate him as thyself thou hatest.
There quandary is at its greatest.
We learned from the forbidden fruit   15
For brains there is no substitute.
"Unless it's sweetbreads," you suggest
With innuendo I detest.
You drive me to confess in ink:
Once I was fool enough to think   20
That brains and sweetbreads were the same,
Till I was caught and put to shame,
First by a butcher, then a cook,
Then by a scientific book.
But 'twas by making sweetbreads do   25
I passed with such a high I.Q.

A REFLEX

Hear my rigmarole.
Science stuck a pole
Down a likely hole
And he got it bit.
Science gave a stab   5
And he got a grab.
That was what he got.
"Ah," he said, "Qui vive,
Who goes there, and what
ARE we to believe?   10
That there is an It?"

IN A GLASS OF CIDER

It seemed I was a mite of sediment
That waited for the bottom to ferment
So I could catch a bubble in ascent.
I rode up on one till the bubble burst,
And when that left me to sink back reversed   5
I was no worse off than I was at first.
I'd catch another bubble if I waited.
The thing was to get now and then elated.

FROM IRON

TOOLS AND WEAPONS

To Ahmed S. Bokhari

Nature within her inmost self divides
To trouble men with having to take sides.

[FOUR-ROOM SHACK...]

Four-room shack aspiring high
With an arm of scrawny mast
For the visions in the sky
That go blindly pouring past.
In the ear and in the eye   5
What you get is what to buy.
Hope you're satisfied to last.

[BUT OUTER SPACE...]

But outer Space,
At least this far,
For all the fuss
Of the populace,
Stays more popular   5
Than populous.

ON BEING CHOSEN POET OF VERMONT

Breathes there a bard who isn't moved
When he finds his verse is understood
And not entirely disapproved
By his country and his neighborhood?

[WE VAINLY WRESTLE...]

We vainly wrestle with the blind belief
That aught we cherish
Can ever quite pass out of utter grief
And wholly perish.

[IT TAKES ALL SORTS...]

It takes all sorts of in- and outdoor schooling
To get adapted to my kind of fooling.

[IN WINTER IN THE WOODS...]

In winter in the woods alone
Against the trees I go.
I mark a maple for my own
And lay the maple low.

At four o'clock I shoulder ax,   5
And in the afterglow
I link a line of shadowy tracks
Across the tinted snow.

I see for Nature no defeat
In one tree's overthrow   10
Or for myself in my retreat
For yet another blow.

A Masque of Reason

: 1945 :

A MASQUE OF REASON

A fair oasis in the purest desert.
A man sits leaning back against a palm.
His wife lies by him looking at the sky.

MAN.   You're not asleep?

WIFE.   No, I can hear you. Why?

MAN.   I said the incense tree's on fire again.   5

WIFE.   You mean the Burning Bush?

MAN.   The Christmas Tree.

WIFE.   I shouldn't be surprised.

MAN.   The strangest light!

WIFE.   There's a strange light on everything today.

MAN.   The myrrh tree gives it. Smell the rosin burning?
The ornaments the Greek artificers   10
Made for the Emperor Alexius,
The Star of Bethlehem, the pomegranates,
The birds, seem all on fire with Paradise.
And hark, the gold enameled nightingales
Are singing. Yes, and look, the Tree is troubled.   15
Someone's caught in the branches.

WIFE.   So there is.
He can't get out.

MAN.   He's loose! He's out!

473

WIFE.   It's God.
I'd know Him by Blake's picture anywhere.
Now what's He doing?

MAN.   Pitching throne, I guess,
Here by our atoll.

WIFE.   Something Byzantine.   20

*(The throne's a plywood flat, prefabricated,
That God pulls lightly upright on its hinges
And stands beside, supporting it in place.)*

Perhaps for an Olympic Tournament,
Or Court of Love.

MAN.   More likely Royal Court—   25
Or Court of Law, and this is Judgment Day.
I trust it is. Here's where I lay aside
My varying opinion of myself
And come to rest in an official verdict.
Suffer yourself to be admired, my love,   30
As Waller says.

WIFE.   Or not admired. Go over
And speak to Him before the others come.
Tell Him He may remember you: you're Job.

GOD.   Oh, I remember well: you're Job, my Patient.
How are you now? I trust you're quite recovered,   35
And feel no ill effects from what I gave you.

JOB.   Gave me in truth: I like the frank admission.
I am a name for being put upon.
But, yes, I'm fine, except for now and then
A reminiscent twinge of rheumatism.   40
The letup's heavenly. You perhaps will tell us

474

If that is all there is to be of Heaven,
Escape from so great pains of life on earth
It gives a sense of letup calculated
To last a fellow to Eternity.   45

GOD.   Yes, by and by. But first a larger matter.
I've had you on my mind a thousand years
To thank you someday for the way you helped me
Establish once for all the principle
There's no connection man can reason out   50
Between his just deserts and what he gets.
Virtue may fail and wickedness succeed.
'Twas a great demonstration we put on.
I should have spoken sooner had I found
The word I wanted. You would have supposed   55
One who in the beginning *was* the Word
Would be in a position to command it.
I have to wait for words like anyone.
Too long I've owed you this apology
For the apparently unmeaning sorrow   60
You were afflicted with in those old days.
But it was of the essence of the trial
You shouldn't understand it at the time.
It had to seem unmeaning to have meaning.
And it came out all right. I have no doubt   65
You realize by now the part you played
To stultify the Deuteronomist
And change the tenor of religious thought.
My thanks are to you for releasing me
From moral bondage to the human race.   70
The only free will there at first was man's,
Who could do good or evil as he chose.
I had no choice but I must follow him

475

With forfeits and rewards he understood—
Unless I liked to suffer loss of worship. 75
I had to prosper good and punish evil.
You changed all that. You set me free to reign.
You are the Emancipator of your God,
And as such I promote you to a saint.

JOB. You hear Him, Thyatira: we're a saint. 80
Salvation in our case is retroactive.
We're saved, we're saved, whatever else it means.

JOB'S WIFE. Well, after all these years!

JOB.   This is my wife.

JOB'S WIFE. If You're the deity I assume You are
(I'd know You by Blake's picture anywhere)— 85

GOD. The best, I'm told, I ever have had taken.

JOB'S WIFE. —I have a protest I would lodge with You.
I want to ask You if it stands to reason
That women prophets should be burned as witches,
Whereas men prophets are received with honor. 90

JOB. Except in their own country, Thyatira.

GOD. You're not a witch?

JOB'S WIFE.   No.

GOD.   Have you ever been one?

JOB. Sometimes she thinks she has and gets herself
Worked up about it. But she really hasn't—
Not in the sense of having to my knowledge 95
Predicted anything that came to pass.

JOB'S WIFE. The Witch of Endor was a friend of mine.

476

GOD.   You wouldn't say she fared so very badly.
I noticed when she called up Samuel
His spirit had to come. Apparently   100
A witch was stronger than a prophet there.

JOB'S WIFE.   But she was burned for witchcraft.

GOD.   That is not
Of record in my Note Book.

JOB'S WIFE.   Well, she was.
And I should like to know the reason why.

GOD.   There you go asking for the very thing   105
We've just agreed I didn't have to give.—

> (*The throne collapses. But He picks it up
> And this time locks it up and leaves it.*)

Where has she been the last half hour or so?
She wants to know why there is still injustice.   110
I answer flatly: That's the way it is,
And bid my will avouch it like Macbeth.
We may as well go back to the beginning
And look for justice in the case of Segub.

JOB.   Oh, Lord, let's not go *back* to anything.   115

GOD.   Because your wife's past won't bear looking into?—
In our great moment what did you do, Madam?
What did you try to make your husband say?

JOB'S WIFE.   No, let's not live things over. I don't care.
I stood by Job. I may have turned on You.   120
Job scratched his boils and tried to think what he
Had done or not done to or for the poor.
The test is always how we treat the poor.
It's time the poor were treated by the state

477

In some way not so penal as the poorhouse.   125
That's one thing more to put on Your agenda.
Job hadn't done a thing, poor innocent.
I told him not to scratch: it made it worse.
If I said once I said a thousand times,
Don't scratch! And when, as rotten as his skin,   130
His tents blew all to pieces, I picked up
Enough to build him every night a pup tent
Around him so it wouldn't touch and hurt him.
I did my wifely duty. I should tremble!
All You can seem to do is lose Your temper   135
When reason-hungry mortals ask for reasons.
Of course, in the abstract high singular
There isn't any universal reason;
And no one but a man would think there was.
You don't catch women trying to be Plato.   140
Still there must be lots of unsystematic
Stray scraps of palliative reason
It wouldn't hurt You to vouchsafe the faithful.
You thought it was agreed You needn't give them.
You thought to suit Yourself. I've not agreed   145
To anything with anyone.

JOB.   There, there,
You go to sleep. God must await events,
As well as words.

JOB'S WIFE.   I'm serious. God's had
Aeons of time and still it's mostly women
Get burned for prophecy, men almost never.   150

JOB. God needs time just as much as you or I
To get things done. Reformers fail to see that.—
She'll go to sleep. Nothing keeps her awake

But physical activity, I find.
Try to read to her and she drops right off. 155

GOD. She's beautiful.

JOB. Yes, she was just remarking
She now felt younger by a thousand years
Than the day she was born.

GOD. That's about right,
I should have said. You got your age reversed
When time was found to be a space dimension 160
That could, like any space, be turned around in?

JOB. Yes, both of us: we saw to that at once.
But, God, I have a question too to raise.
(My wife gets in ahead of me with hers.)
I need some help about this reason problem 165
Before I am too late to be got right
As to what reasons I agree to waive.
I'm apt to string along with Thyatira.
God knows—or rather, You know (God forgive me)
I waived the reason for my ordeal—but— 170
I have a question even there to ask—
In confidence. There's no one here but her,
And she's a woman: she's not interested
In general ideas and principles. 174

GOD. What are her interests, Job?

JOB. Witch-women's rights.
Humor her there or she will be confirmed
In her suspicion You're no feminist.
You have it in for women, she believes.
Kipling invokes You as Lord God of Hosts.
She'd like to know how You would take a prayer 180

479

That started off Lord God of Hostesses.

GOD. I'm charmed with her.

JOB.   Yes, I could see You were.
But to my question. I am much impressed
With what You say we have established,
Between us, You and I.

GOD.   I make you see?   185
It would be too bad if Columbus-like
You failed to see the worth of your achievement.

JOB. You call it mine.

GOD.   We groped it out together.
Any originality it showed
I give you credit for. My forte is truth,   190
Or metaphysics, long the world's reproach
For standing still in one place true forever;
While science goes self-superseding on.
Look at how far we've left the current science
Of Genesis behind. The wisdom there, though,   195
Is just as good as when I uttered it.
Still, novelty has doubtless an attraction.

JOB. So it's important who first thinks of things?

GOD. I'm a great stickler for the author's name.
By proper names I find I do my thinking.   200

JOB'S WIFE. God, who invented earth?

JOB.   What, still awake?

GOD. Any originality it showed
Was of the Devil. He invented Hell,
False premises that are the original

480

Of all originality, the sin   205
That felled the angels, Wolsey should have said.
As for the earth, we groped that out together,
Much as your husband, Job, and I together
Found out the discipline man needed most
Was to learn his submission to unreason;   210
And that for man's own sake as well as mine,
So he won't find it hard to take his orders
From his inferiors in intelligence
In peace and war—especially in war.

JOB.   So he won't find it hard to take his war.   215

GOD.   You have the idea. There's not much I can tell you.

JOB.   All very splendid. I am flattered proud
To have been in on anything with You.
'Twas a great demonstration if You say so.
Though incidentally I sometimes wonder   220
Why it had had to be at my expense.

GOD.   It had to be at somebody's expense.
Society can never think things out:
It has to see them acted out by actors,
Devoted actors at a sacrifice—   225
The ablest actors I can lay my hands on.
Is that your answer?

JOB.   No, for I have yet
To ask my question. We disparage reason.
But all the time it's what we're most concerned with.
There's will as motor and there's will as brakes.   230
Reason is, I suppose, the steering gear.
The will as brakes can't stop the will as motor
For very long. We're plainly made to go.

481

We're going anyway and may as well
Have some say as to where we're headed for;   235
Just as we will be talking anyway
And may as well throw in a little sense.
Let's do so now. Because I let You off
From telling me Your reason, don't assume
I thought You had none. Somewhere back   240
I knew You had one. But this isn't it
You're giving me. You say we groped this out.
But if You will forgive me the irreverence,
It sounds to me as if You thought it out,
And took Your time to it. It seems to me   245
An afterthought, a long-long-after-thought.
I'd give more for one least beforehand reason
Than all the justifying ex-post-facto
Excuses trumped up by You for theologists.
The front of being answerable to no one   250
I'm with You in maintaining to the public.
But, Lord, we showed them what. The audience
Has all gone home to bed. The play's played out.
Come, after all these years—to satisfy me.
I'm curious. And I'm a grown-up man: 255
I'm not a child for You to put me off
And tantalize me with another "Oh, because."
You'd be the last to want me to believe
All Your effects were merely lucky blunders.
That would be unbelief and atheism.   260
The artist in me cries out for design.
Such devilish ingenuity of torture
Did seem unlike You, and I tried to think
The reason might have been some other person's.
But there is nothing You are not behind.   265
I did not ask then, but it seems as if

482

Now after all these years You might indulge me.
Why did You hurt me so? I am reduced
To asking flatly for the reason—outright.   269

GOD.   I'd tell you, Job——

JOB.   All right, don't tell me, then,
If you don't want to. I don't want to know.
But what is all this secrecy about?
I fail to see what fun, what satisfaction
A God can find in laughing at how badly
Men fumble at the possibilities   275
When left to guess forever for themselves.
The chances are when there's so much pretense
Of metaphysical profundity
The obscurity's a fraud to cover nothing.
I've come to think no so-called hidden value's   280
Worth going after. Get down into things,
It will be found there's no more given there
Than on the surface. If there ever was,
The crypt was long since rifled by the Greeks.
We don't know where we are, or who we are.   285
We don't know one another; don't know You;
Don't know what time it is. We don't know, don't we?
Who says we don't? Who got up these misgivings?
Oh, we know well enough to go ahead with.
I mean we seem to know enough to act on.   290
It comes down to a doubt about the wisdom
Of having children—after having had them,
So there is nothing we can do about it
But warn the children they perhaps should have none.
You could end this by simply coming out   295
And saying plainly and unequivocally
Whether there's any part of man immortal.

483

Yet You don't speak. Let fools bemuse themselves
By being baffled for the sake of being.
I'm sick of the whole artificial puzzle.   300

JOB'S WIFE.   You won't get any answers out of God.

GOD.   My kingdom, what an outbreak!

JOB'S WIFE.   Job is right.
Your kingdom, yes, Your kingdom come on earth.
Pray tell me what does that mean? Anything?
Perhaps that earth is going to crack someday   305
Like a big egg and hatch a heaven out
Of all the dead and buried from their graves.
One simple little statement from the throne
Would put an end to such fantastic nonsense;
And, too, take care of twenty of the four   310
And twenty freedoms on the party docket.
Or is it only four? My extra twenty
Are freedoms from the need of asking questions.
(I hope You know the game called twenty questions.)
For instance, is there such a thing as Progress?   315
Job says there's no such thing as Earth's becoming
An easier place for man to save his soul in.
Except as a hard place to save his soul in,
A trial ground where he can try himself
And find out whether he is any good,   320
It would be meaningless. It might as well
Be Heaven at once and have it over with.

GOD.   Two pitching on like this tend to confuse me.
One at a time, please. I will answer Job first.
I'm going to tell Job why I tortured him,   325
And trust it won't be adding to the torture.
I was just showing off to the Devil, Job,

484

As is set forth in Chapters One and Two.
(*Job takes a few steps pacing.*) Do you mind?
(*God eyes him anxiously.*)

JOB.   No. No, I mustn't.   330
'Twas human of You. I expected more
Than I could understand and what I get
Is almost less than I can understand.
But I don't mind. Let's leave it as it stood.
The point was it was none of my concern.   335
I stick to that. But talk about confusion!—
How is that for a mix-up, Thyatira?—
Yet I suppose what seems to us confusion
Is not confusion, but the form of forms,
The serpent's tail stuck down the serpent's throat,   340
Which is the symbol of eternity
And also of the way all things come round,
Or of how rays return upon themselves,
To quote the greatest Western poem yet.
Though I hold rays deteriorate to nothing: 345
First white, then red, then ultrared, then out.

GOD.   Job, you must understand my provocation.
The tempter comes to me and I am tempted.
I'd had about enough of his derision
Of what I valued most in human nature.   350
He thinks he's smart. He thinks he can convince me
It is no different with my followers
From what it is with his. Both serve for pay.
Disinterestedness never did exist,
And if it did, it wouldn't be a virtue.   355
Neither would fairness. You have heard the doctrine.
It's on the increase. He could count on no one:
That was his lookout. I could count on you.

485

I wanted him forced to acknowledge so much.
I gave you over to him, but with safeguards.   360
I took care of you. And before you died
I trust I made it clear I took your side
Against your comforters in their contention
You must be wicked to deserve such pain.
That's Browning and sheer Chapel Non-conformism.   365

JOB.   God, please, enough for now. I'm in no mood
For more excuses.

GOD.   What I mean to say:
Your comforters were wrong.

JOB.   Oh, that committee!

GOD.   I saw you had no fondness for committees.
Next time you find yourself pressed onto one   370
For the revision of the Book of Prayer
Put that in if it isn't in already:
Deliver us from committees. 'Twill remind me.
I would do anything for you in reason.

JOB.   Yes, yes.

GOD.   You don't seem satisfied.

JOB.   I am.   375

GOD.   You're pensive.

JOB.   Oh, I'm thinking of the Devil.
You must remember he was in on this.
We can't leave him out.

GOD.   No. No, we don't need to.
We're too well off.

JOB.   Someday we three should have

A good old get-together celebration. 380

GOD. Why not right now?

JOB.   We can't without the Devil.

GOD. The Devil's never very far away.
He too is pretty circumambient.
He has but to appear. He'll come for me,
Precipitated from the desert air.— 385
Show yourself, son.—I'll get back on my throne
For this I think. I find it always best
To be upon my dignity with him.

            (*The Devil enters like a sapphire wasp*
            That flickers mica wings. He lifts a hand 390
            To brush away a disrespectful smile.
            Job's wife sits up.)

JOB'S WIFE.   Well, if we aren't all here,
Including me, the only Dramatis
Personae needed to enact the problem.

JOB. We've waked her up.

JOB'S WIFE.   I haven't been asleep. 395
I've heard what you were saying—every word.

JOB. What did we say?

JOB'S WIFE.   You said the Devil's in it.

JOB. She always claims she hasn't been asleep.—
And what else did we say?

JOB'S WIFE.   Well, what led up—
Something about—(*The three men laugh.*) 400
—The Devil's being God's best inspiration.

487

JOB.   Good, pretty good.

JOB'S WIFE.   Wait till I get my Kodak.—
Would you two please draw in a little closer?
No—no, that's not a smile there. That's a grin.
Satan, what ails you? Where's the famous tongue,   405
Thou onetime Prince of Conversationists?
This is polite society you're in,
Where good and bad are mingled every which way,
And ears are lent to any sophistry
Just as if nothing mattered but our manners.   410
You look as if you either hoped or feared
You were more guilty of mischief than you are.
Nothing has been brought out that for my part
I'm not prepared for or that Job himself
Won't find a formula for taking care of.   415

SATAN.   Like the one Milton found to fool himself
About his blindness.

JOB'S WIFE.   Oh, he speaks! He *can* speak!
That strain again! Give me excess of it!
As dulcet as a pagan temple gong!
He's twitting us.—Oh, by the way, you haven't   420
By any chance a Lady Apple on you?
I saw a boxful in the Christmas market.
How I should prize one personally from you.

GOD.   Don't *you* twit. He's unhappy. Church neglect
And figurative use have pretty well   425
Reduced him to a shadow of himself.

JOB'S WIFE.   *That* explains why he's so diaphanous
And easy to see through. But where's he off to?
I thought there were to be festivities

488

Of some kind. We could have charades.   430

GOD.   He has his business he must be about.
Job mentioned him, and so I brought him in,
More to give his reality its due
Than anything.

JOB'S WIFE.   He's very real to me
And always will be.—Please don't go. Stay, stay   435
But to the evensong, and having played
Together we will go with you along.
There are who won't have had enough of you
If you go now.—Look how he takes no steps!
He isn't really going, yet he's leaving.   440

JOB.   (*Who has been standing dazed with new ideas*)
He's on that tendency that like the Gulf Stream,
Only of sand, not water, runs through here.
It has a rate distinctly different
From the surrounding desert; just today   445
I stumbled over it and got tripped up.

JOB'S WIFE.   Oh, yes, that tendency!—Oh, do come off it.
Don't let it carry you away. I hate
A tendency. The minute you get on one
It seems to start right off accelerating.   450
Here, take my hand.

> (*He takes it and alights*
> *In three quick steps as off an escalator.*
> *The tendency, a long, long narrow strip*
> *Of middle-aisle church carpet, sisal hemp,*
> *Is worked by hands invisible, offstage.*)   455

I want you in my group beside the throne—
Must have you. There, that's just the right arrangement.

489

Now someone can light up the Burning Bush
And turn the gold enameled artificial birds on.
I recognize them. Greek artificers   460
Devised them for Alexius Comnenus.
They won't show in the picture. That's too bad.
Neither will I show. That's too bad moreover.
Now if you three have settled anything
You'd as well smile as frown on the occasion.   465

(Here endeth Chapter Forty-three of Job.)

A Masque of Mercy

: 1947 :

A MASQUE OF MERCY

A bookstore late at night. The Keeper's wife
Pulls down the window curtain on the door
And locks the door. One customer, locked in,
Stays talking with the Keeper at a showcase.
The Keeper's wife has hardly turned away   5
Before the door's so violently tried
It makes her move as if to reinforce it.

JESSE BEL.   You can't come in! (*Knock, knock*) The store
is closed!

PAUL.   Late, late, too late, you cannot enter now.

JESSE BEL.   We can't be always selling people things.   10
He doesn't go.

KEEPER.   You needn't be so stern.
Open enough to find out who it is.

JESSE BEL.   Keeper, you come and see. Or you come, Paul.
Our second second-childhood case tonight.
Where do these senile runaways escape from?   15
Wretchedness in a stranger frightens me
More than it touches me.

PAUL.   You may come in.

FUGITIVE.   (*Entering hatless in a whirl of snow*)
God's after me!

JESSE BEL.   You mean the Devil is.

FUGITIVE.   No, God.

493

JESSE BEL.   I never heard of such a thing.   20

FUGITIVE.   Haven't you heard of Thompson's "Hound
of Heaven"?

PAUL.   "I fled Him, down the nights and down the days;
I fled Him, down the arches of the years."

KEEPER.   This is a bookstore—not a sanctuary.

JESSE BEL.   I thought you just now said it was a gift shop.

KEEPER.   Don't you be bitter about it. I'm not bitter.   26

FUGITIVE.   Well, I could use a book.

KEEPER.   What book?

FUGITIVE.   A Bible.

KEEPER.   To find out how to get away from God?
Which is what people use it for too often—
And why we wouldn't have one in the store.   30
We don't believe the common man should read it.
Let him seek his religion in the Church.

JESSE BEL.   Keeper, be still.—Pay no attention to him.
He's being a religious snob for fun.
The name his mother gave him is to blame   35
For Keeper's levity: My Brother's Keeper.
She didn't do it to him to be quaint,
But out of politics. She told me so.
She was left over from the Brook Farm venture.

KEEPER.   Why is God after you?—to save your soul?   40

FUGITIVE.   No, make me prophesy.

JESSE BEL.   And—you—just—won't?

494

FUGITIVE.   Haven't you noticed anything (hear that!)
Since I came in?

KEEPER.   Hear what? That army truck?

FUGITIVE.   Look, I don't need the Bible to consult.
I just thought if you had a copy handy,   45
I could point out my sort of passport in it.
There is a story you may have forgotten
About a whale.

KEEPER.   Oh, you mean *Moby Dick*
By Rockwell Kent that everybody's reading.
Trust me to help you find the book you want.   50

JESSE BEL.   Keeper, be still. He knows what book he wants.
He said the Bible.

FUGITIVE.   I should hate to scare you
With the suspicion at this hour of night
That I might be a confidence impostor.
I'm Jonas Dove—if that is any help.   55

PAUL.   Which is the same as saying Jonah, Jonah—
Ah, Jonah, Jonah—twice—reproachfully.

FUGITIVE.   Spare me the setting of my fate to music.
How did you know that way to break my heart?
Who are you?

PAUL.   Who are *you?*

JONAH.   I think you know,   60
You seem so ready at translating names.
Unless I'm much mistaken in myself
This is the seventh time I have been sent
To prophesy against the city evil.

KEEPER.   What have you got against the city?

JONAH.   *He* knows.
We have enough against it, haven't we?   66
Cursed be the era that congested it.

KEEPER.   Come, come, you talk like an agrarian.
The city is all right. To live in one
Is to be civilized, stay up and read   70
Or sing and dance all night and see sunrise
By waiting up instead of getting up.
The country's only useful as a place
To rest at times from being civilized.
You take us two, we're losers in this store,   75
So losers in the city, but we're game:
We don't go back on grapes we couldn't reach.
We blame ourselves. We're good sports, aren't we, Bel?

JESSE BEL.   I'm not a sport and don't pretend I am one.—
It's only fair to Keeper to inform you   80
His favorite reading is seed catalogues.
When he gets too agrarian for me
I take to drink—at least I take *a* drink.

         (*She has her own glass in a vacant chair.*)

PAUL.   She'll take to drink and see how we like that.   85

KEEPER.   Bel is a solitary social drinker.
She doesn't mind not offering a drink
To anyone around when she is drinking.

JESSE BEL.   We're poor—that's why. My man can't
   earn a living.

KEEPER.   Is it just any city you're against?   90

JONAH.   Yes, but New York will do as an example.

496

KEEPER.   Well, you're as good as in New York this minute—
Or bad as in New York.

JONAH.   I know I am.
That was where my engagement was to speak
This very night. I had the hall all hired,   95
The audience assembled. There I was
Behind the scenes, ordained and advertised
To prophesy, and full of prophecy,
Yet could not bring myself to say a word.
I left light shining on an empty stage   100
And fled to you. But you receive me not.

KEEPER.   Yes, we do too, with sympathy, my friend.
Your righteous indignation fizzled out,
Or else you were afraid of being mobbed
If what you had to say was disagreeable.   105

JESSE BEL.   Your courage failed. The saddest thing in life
Is that the best thing in it should be courage.
Them is my sentiments, and, Mr. Flood,
Since you propose it, I believe I will.

JONAH.   Please, someone understand.

PAUL.   I understand.   110

JONAH.   These others don't.

PAUL.   You don't yourself entirely.

JONAH.   What don't I understand? It's easy enough.
I'm in the Bible, all done out in story.
I've lost my faith in God to carry out
The threats He makes against the city evil.   115
I can't trust God to be unmerciful.

KEEPER.   You've lost your faith in God? How wicked of you.

497

JESSE BEL.   You naughty kitten, you shall have no pie.

PAUL.   Keeper's the kind of Unitarian
Who having by elimination got   120
From many gods to Three, and Three to One,
Thinks why not taper off to none at all,
Except as father putative to sort of
Legitimize the brotherhood of man,
So we can hang together in a strike.   125

KEEPER.   Now we are hearing from the Exegete.
You don't know Paul: he's in the Bible too.
He is the fellow who theologized
Christ almost out of Christianity.
Look out for him.

PAUL.   "Look out for me" is right.   130
I'm going to tell you something, Jonas Dove.
I'm going to take the nonsense out of you
And give you rest, poor Wandering Jew.

JONAH.   I'm not
The Wandering Jew—I'm who I say I am,
A prophet with the Bible for credentials.   135

PAUL.   I never said you weren't. I recognized you.
You are the universal fugitive—
Escapist, as we say—though you are not
Running away from Him you think you are,
But from His mercy-justice contradiction.   140
Mercy and justice are a contradiction.
But here's where your evasion has an end.
I have to tell you something that will spoil
Indulgence in your form of melancholy
Once and for all. I'm going to make you see   145

How relatively little justice matters.

JONAH. I see what you are up to: robbing me
Of my incentive—canceling my mission.

PAUL. I am empowered to excuse you from it.

JONAH. You! Who are you? I asked you once before. 150

JESSE BEL. He is our analyst.

JONAH.   Your analyst?

KEEPER. Who keeps our bookstore annals.

JESSE BEL.   Stop it, Keeper.—
An analyst's the latest thing in doctors.
He's mine. That's what he is (you asked)—my doctor.
I'm sick.

JONAH. Of what?

JESSE BEL.   Oh, everything, I guess.   155
The doctors say the trouble with me is
I'm not in love. I didn't love the doctor
I had before. That's why I changed to Paul—
To try another.

PAUL.   Jesse Bel's a girl
Whose cure will lie in getting her idea   160
Of the word love corrected. She got off
To a bad start it seems in the wrong school
Of therapy.

JESSE BEL. I don't love Paul—as yet.

JONAH. How about loving God?

JESSE BEL.   You make me shrug.—
And I don't love you either, do I, Keeper?   165

499

KEEPER. Don't lay your hand on me to say it, shameless.
Let me alone.

JESSE BEL.   I'm sick. Joe's sick. The world's sick.
I'll take to drink—at least I'll take *a* drink.

JONAH.   My name's not Joe. I don't like what she says.
It's Greenwich Village cocktail-party talk—   170
Big-city talk. I'm getting out of here.
"I'm—bound—away!" (*He quotes it to the tune.*)

PAUL.   Oh, no, you're not. You're staying here tonight.—
You locked the door, Bel. Let me have the key.

(*He goes and takes it from the door himself.*)   175

JONAH.   Then I'm a prisoner?

PAUL.   You are tonight.
We take it you were sent in here for help.
And help you're going to get.

JONAH.   I'll break your door down.
Always the same when I set out in flight.
I take the first boat. God puts up a storm   180
That someone in the crew connects with me.
The sailors throw me overboard for luck,
Or, as you might say, throw me to the whale—
For me to disagree with him and get spit out
Right back in the same trouble I was in.   185
You're modern; so the whale you throw me to
Will be some soulless lunatic asylum—
For me to disagree with any science
There may be there and get spit out again.

JESSE BEL.   You poor, poor swallowable little man.   190

PAUL.   If you would take the hands out of your hair

500

And calm yourself. Be sane! I hereby hold
Your forearms in the figure of a cross
The way it rested two points on the ground
At every station but the final one. 195

JONAH. What good is that?

PAUL. I'll make you see what good.

JONAH. I *am* sick, as she says. Nothing exhausts me
Like working myself up to prophesy
And then not prophesying. (*He sits down.*) 199

JESSE BEL. Can you interpret dreams? I dreamed last night
Someone took curved nail-scissors and snipped off
My eyelids so I couldn't shut my eyes
To anything that happened anymore.

JONAH. She's had some loss she can't accept from God—
Is that it? Some Utopian belief— 205
Or child, and this is motherly resentment?

JESSE BEL. You look so sleepless.—If he'd promise us
To go straight home, we wouldn't keep him, would we?—
Where are you staying—anywhere in town?

JONAH. Under the bandstand in Suburban Park. 210

JESSE BEL. Why, what a story. At this time of year
There's not a footprint to it in the snow.

PAUL. Jonah, I'm glad, not sad, to hear you say
You can't trust God to be unmerciful.
There you have the beginning of all wisdom. 215

KEEPER. One minute, may I, Paul?—before we leave
Religion for these philosophic matters.
That's the right style of coat for prophecy

501

You're sporting there. I'll bet you're good at it.
Shall it be told we had a prophet captive   220
And let him get off without prophesying?
Let's have some prophecy. What form of ruin
(For ruin I assume was what it was)
Had you in mind to visit on the city,
Rebellion, pestilence, invasion?

JONAH.   Earthquake   225
Was what I thought of.

KEEPER.   Have you any grounds,
Or undergrounds, for confidence in earthquake?

JONAH. It's good geology—the Funday Fault,
A fracture in the rocks beneath New York
That only needs a finger touch from God   230
To spring it like a deadfall and the fault
In nature would wipe out all human fault.
(*He stops to listen.*) That's a mighty storm,
And we are shaken. But it isn't earthquake.
Another possibility I thought of—   235

> (*He stops to listen and his unspoken thought,*
> *Projected from the lantern of his eyes,*
> *Is thrown in script, as at Belshazzar's feast,*
> *On the blank curtain on the outer door.*)

—Was Babel: everyone developing   240
A language of his own to write his book in,
And one to cap the climax by combining
All language in a one-man tongue-confusion.

> (*He starts to speak, but stops again to listen.*
> *The writing on the screen must change too fast*   245
> *For any but the rapidest eye readers.*)

502

Suspicion of the income-tax returns,
A question who was getting the most out
Of business, might increase into a madness.
The mob might hold a man up in the streets   250
And tear his clothes off to examine him
To find if there were pockets in his skin,
As in a smuggler's at the diamond fields,
Where he was hoarding more than they enjoyed.

PAUL.   We can all see what's passing in your mind.   255
(I won't have Keeper calling it religion.)
It's a hard case. It's got so prophecy
Is a disease of your imagination.
You're so lost in the virtuosity
Of getting up good ruins, you've forgotten   260
What the sins are men ought to perish for.

JONAH.   You wrong me.

KEEPER.   Well then, name a single sin.

JONAH.   Another possibility I thought of——

JESSE BEL.   There he goes off into another trance.

KEEPER.   You stick to earthquake, you have something
      there—   265
Something we'll know we're getting when we get it.

PAUL.   (Taking a walk off down the store distressed)
Keeper, I'll turn on you if you keep on.

KEEPER.   If I were in your place, though, Mr. Prophet,
I'd want to be more certain I was called,   270
Before I undertook so delicate
A mission as to have to tell New York
'Twas in for an old-fashioned shaking down

503

Like the one Joshua gave Jericho.
You wouldn't want the night clubs laughing at you.   275

JESSE BEL.   Or *The New Yorker*.

KEEPER.   When was the last time
You heard from God—I mean had orders from Him?

JONAH.   I'm hearing from Him now, did you but notice.
Don't any of you hear a sound?

KEEPER.   The storm!
Merely the windows rattling in the storm.   280
Trucks going by to war. A war is on.

JONAH.   That is no window. That's a showcase rattling.
That is your antiques rattling on a shelf.

JESSE BEL.   You're doing it.

JONAH.   I'm not. How could I be?

JESSE BEL.   You're doing something to our minds.

JONAH.   I'm not.—
Don't *you* feel something?

PAUL.   Leave me out of this.   286

(*He leans away in tolerant distaste.*)

JONAH.   And here come all your Great Books tumbling
   down!
You see the Lord God is a jealous God!
He wrote one book. Let there be no more written.   290
How are their volumes fallen!

KEEPER.   Only one!

JONAH.   Hold on there. Leave that open where it lies.

504

Be careful not to lose the place. Be careful.
Please let me have it.

JESSE BEL.　　　　　Read us what it says.

JONAH.　Look, will you look! God can't put words in
my mouth.　　　　　　　　　　　　　　　　295
My tongue's my own, as True Thomas used to say.

KEEPER.　So you've been Bohning up on Thomism too.

JONAH.　Someone else read it.

KEEPER.　　　　　　　No, you read it to us.
And if it's prophecy, we'll see what happens.　　299

JONAH.　Nothing would happen. That's the thing of it.
God comes on me to doom a city for Him.
But oh, no, not for Jonah. I refuse
To be the bearer of an empty threat.
He may be God, but me, I'm only human:
I shrink from being publicly let down.　　　　305

JESSE BEL.　Is this the love of God you preached to me?

JONAH.　There's not the least lack of the love of God
In what I say. Don't be so silly, woman.
His very weakness for mankind's endearing.
I love and fear Him. Yes, but I fear for Him.　　310
I don't see how it can be to His interest,
This modern tendency I find in Him
To take the punishment out of all failure
To be strong, careful, thrifty, diligent,
Anything we once thought we had to be.　　　315

KEEPER.　You know what lets us off from being careful?
The thing that did what you consider mischief,
That ushered in this modern lenience,

505

Was the discovery of fire insurance.
The future state is springing even now   320
From the discovery that loss from failure,
By being spread out over everybody,
Can be made negligible.

PAUL.   What's your book?
What's this?

JONAH.   Don't lose the place.

PAUL.   Old Dana Lyle,
Who reconciled the Pentateuch with science.   325

JONAH.   Where shall I start in? Where my eyes fell first?
It seems to be a chapter head in meter.

JESSE BEL.   It's too big for him. Help him hold it up.

JONAH.   Someone else read it.

KEEPER.   No, you asked for it.

JESSE BEL.   Come on, or we'll begin to be afraid.   330

JONAH.   Well, but remember this is unofficial:
"The city's grotesque iron skeletons
Would knock their drunken penthouse heads together
And cake their concrete dirt off in the streets."
Then further down it seems to start from where   335
The city is admittedly an evil:
"O city on insecure rock pedestal,
So knowing—and yet needing to be told
The thought that added cubits to your height
Would better have been taken to your depth."   340
(*A whole shelf cascades down.*) Here come some more.
The folly crashes and the dust goes up.

(When the dust settles it should be apparent
Something has altered in the outer door.)   344

JESSE BEL.   Mercy, for mercy's sake!

KEEPER.   Bel wants some mercy.—
Kneel to your doctor. He dispenses mercy.—
You're working it, old man. Don't be discouraged.

JONAH.   This isn't it. I haven't prophesied.
This is God at me in my skulking place,
Trying to flush me out. That's all it is.   350

KEEPER.   It's nothing but the Lending Library.
All secondhand. Don't get excited, folks;
The one indecency's to make a fuss
About our own or anybody's end.

JONAH.   It's nothing I brought on by words of mine.   355

KEEPER.   You know, there may have been a small temblor.
If so, it will be in tomorrow's paper.

PAUL.   Now if we've had enough of sacrilege,
We can go back to where we started from.
Let me repeat: I'm glad to hear you say   360
You can't trust God to be unmerciful.
What would you have God if not merciful?

JONAH.   Just, I would have Him just before all else,
To see that the fair fight is really fair.
Then he could enter on the stricken field   365
After the fight's so definitely done
There can be no disputing who has won—
Then he could enter on the stricken field
As Red Cross Ambulance Commander-in-Chief
To ease the more extremely wounded out   370

507

And mend the others up to go again.

PAUL.   I thought as much. You have it all arranged,
Only to see it shattered every day.
You should be an authority on Mercy.
That book of yours in the Old Testament   375
Is the first place in literature, I think,
Where Mercy is explicitly the subject.
I say you should be proud of having beaten
The Gospels to it. After doing Justice justice
Milton's pentameters go on to say,   380
But Mercy first and last shall brightest shine—
Not only last, but first, you will observe;
Which spoils your figure of the ambulance.

KEEPER.   Paul only means you make too much of justice.
There's some such thing and no one will deny it—   385
Enough to bait the trap of the ideal
From which there can be no escape for us
But by our biting off our adolescence
And leaving it behind us in the trap.

JONAH.   Listen, ye! It's the proletariat!   390
A revolution's coming down the street!
Lights out, I say, so's to escape attention.

   (He snaps one bulb off. Paul snaps on another.)

JESSE BEL.   You needn't shout like that, you wretched man.
There's nothing coming on us, is there, Paul?   395
We've had about enough of these sensations.
It's a coincidence, but we were on
The subject of the workers' revolution
When you came in. We're revolutionists.
Or Keeper is a revolutionist.   400
Paul almost had poor Keeper in a corner

508

Where he would have to quit his politics
Or be a Christian.—Paul, I wish you'd say
That over. I shall have to retail it
To some of Keeper's friends that come in here,   405
A bunch of small-time revolutionaries.—
Paul makes it come out so they look like Christians.
How they'll like that. Paul said conservatives—
You say it, Paul.

PAUL.   You mean about success,
And how by its own logic it concentrates   410
All wealth and power in too few hands?
The rich in seeing nothing but injustice
In their impoverishment by revolution
Are right. But 'twas intentional injustice.
It was their justice being mercy-crossed.   415
The revolution Keeper's bringing on
Is nothing but an outbreak of mass mercy,
Too long pent up in rigorous convention—
A holy impulse towards redistribution.
To set out to homogenize mankind   420
So that the cream could never rise again
Required someone who laughingly could play
With the idea of justice in the courts,
Could mock at riches in the right it claims
To count on justice to be merely just.   425
But we are talking over Jonah's head,
Or clear off what we know his interests are.
Still, not so far off, come to think of it.
There is some justice, even as Keeper says.
The thing that really counts, though, is the form   430
Of outrage—violence—that breaks across it.
The very sleep we sleep is an example.

509

So that because we're always starting fresh
The best minds are the best at premises.
And the most sacred thing of all's abruption. 435
And if you've got to see your justice crossed
(And you've got to), which will you prefer
To see it, evil-crossed or mercy-crossed?

KEEPER. We poets offer you another: star-crossed.
Of star-crossed, mercy-crossed, or evil-crossed 440
I choose the star-crossed as a star-crossed lover.

JONAH. I think my trouble's with the crisises
Where mercy-crossed to me seemed evil-crossed.

KEEPER. Good for you, Jonah. That's what I've been
saying.
For instance, when to purify the Itzas 445
They took my love and threw her down a well.

JESSE BEL. If it is me in my last incarnation
He's thinking of, it wasn't down a well,
But in a butt of malmsey I was drowned.

JONAH. Why do you call yourself a star-crossed lover? 450

KEEPER. Not everything I say is said in scorn.
Some people want you not to understand them,
But I want you to understand me wrong.

JONAH. I noticed how he just now made you out
A revolutionary—which of course you can't be. 455

KEEPER. Or not at least the ordinary kind.
No revolution I brought on would aim
At anything but change of personnel.
The Andrew Jackson slogan of *Væ Victis*
Or "Turn the rascals out" would do for me. 460

PAUL.   Don't you be made feel small by all this posing.
Both of them caught it from Bel's favorite poet,
Who in his favorite pose as poet-thinker
(His was the doctrine of the Seven Poses)
Once charged the Nazarene with having brought   465
A darkness out of Asia that had crossed
Old Attic grace and Spartan discipline
With violence. The Greeks were hardly strangers
To the idea of violence. It flourished,
Persisting from old Chaos in their myth,   470
To embroil the very gods about their spheres
Of influence. It's been a commonplace
Ever since Alexander Greeced the world.
'Twere nothing new if that were all Christ brought.
Christ came to introduce a break with logic   475
That made all other outrage seem as child's play:
The Mercy on the Sin against the Sermon.
Strange no one ever thought of it before Him.
'Twas lovely and its origin was love.   479

KEEPER.   We know what's coming now.

PAUL.   You say it, Keeper,
If you have learned your lesson. Don't be bashful.

KEEPER.   Paul's constant theme. The Sermon on the Mount
Is just a frame-up to insure the failure
Of all of us, so all of us will be
Thrown prostrate at the Mercy Seat for Mercy.   485

JESSE BEL.   Yes, Paul, you do say things like that sometimes.

PAUL.   You all have read the Sermon on the Mount.
I ask you all to read it once again.

511

(They put their hands together like a book
And hold it up nearsightedly to read.)

KEEPER AND
JESSE BEL. We're reading it.

PAUL.   Well, now you've got it read,
What do you make of it?

JESSE BEL.   The same old nothing.

KEEPER. A beautiful impossibility.

PAUL. Keeper, I'm glad you think it beautiful.

KEEPER. An irresistible impossibility.
A lofty beauty no one can live up to,
Yet no one turn from trying to live up to.

PAUL. Yes, spoken so we can't live up to it,
Yet so we'll have to weep because we can't.
Mercy is only to the undeserving.
But such we all are made in the sight of God.

> "Oh, what is a king here,
> And what is a boor?
> Here all starve together,
> All dwarfed and poor."

Here we all fail together, dwarfed and poor.
Failure is failure, but success is failure.
There is no better way of having it.
An end you can't by any means achieve,
And yet can't turn your back on or ignore,
That is the mystery you must accept.—
Do you accept it, Master Jonas Dove?

JONAH. What do you say to it, My Brother's Keeper?

512

KEEPER.   I say I'd rather be lost in the woods
Than found in church.

JONAH.   That doesn't help me much.   515

KEEPER.   Our disagreement when we disagree, Paul,
Lies in our different approach to Christ,
Yours more through Rome, mine more through Palestine.—
But let's be serious about Paul's offer.
His irresistible impossibility,   520
His lofty beauty no one can live up to,
Yet no one turn away from or ignore—
I simply turn away from it.

PAUL.   You Pagan!

KEEPER.   Yes, call me Pagan, Paul, as if you meant it.
I won't deceive myself about success   525
By making failure out of equal value.
Any equality they may exhibit's
In making fools of people equally.

PAUL.   But you—what is your answer, Jonas Dove?

JONAH.   You ask if I see yonder shining gate,   530
And I reply I almost think I do,
Beyond this great door you have locked against me,
Beyond the storm, beyond the universe.

PAUL.   Yes, Pilgrim now instead of runaway,
Your fugitive escape become a quest.   535

KEEPER.   Don't let him make you see too bright a gate
Or you will come to with a foolish feeling.
When a great tide of argument sweeps in
My small fresh-water spring gets drowned of course.
But when the brine goes back, as go it must,   540

I can count on my source to spring again,
Not even brackish from its salt experience.
No true source can be poisoned.

JONAH.   Then that's all.
You've finished. I'm dismissed. I want to run
Toward what you make me see beyond the world.   545
Unlock the door for me.

KEEPER.   Not that way out.

JONAH.   I'm all turned round.

PAUL.   There is your way prepared.

JONAH.   That's not my door.

KEEPER.   No, that's another door.
Your exit door's become a cellar door.

            (*The door here opens darkly of itself.*)   550

JONAH.   You mean I'm being sent down in the cellar?

PAUL.   You must make your descent like everyone.

KEEPER.   Go if you're going.

JONAH.   Who is sending me?
Whose cellar is it, yours or the apostle's?   554

KEEPER.   It is the cellar to my store.—What ho, down there!
My dungeoneers, come fetch us.—No one answers.
There's not much we can do till Martin gets here.—
Don't let me scare you. I was only teasing.
It is the cellar to my store, but not my cellar.
Jesse has given Paul the rent of it   560
To base his campaign on to save the world.

JESSE BEL.   Something's the matter, everyone admits.

514

On the off-chance it may be lack of faith,
I have contributed the empty cellar
To Paul to see what he can do with it   565
To bring faith back. I'm only languidly
Inclined to hope for much. Still what we need
Is something to believe in, don't we, Paul?

KEEPER.   By something to believe in, Jesse means
Something to be fanatical about,   570
So as to justify the orthodox
In saving heretics by slaying them,
Not on the battlefield, but down in cellars.
That way's been tried too many times for me.
I'd like to see the world tried once without it.   575

JESSE BEL.   The world seems crying out for a Messiah.

KEEPER.   Haven't you heard the news? We already have one,
And of the Messianic race, Karl Marx.

JESSE BEL.   Light, bring a light!

KEEPER.   Awh, there's no lack of
   light, you—
A light that falls diffused over my shoulder   580
And is reflected from the printed page
And bed of world-flowers so as not to blind me.
If even the face of man's too bright a light
To look at long directly (like the sun),
Then how much more the face of truth must be.   585
We were not given eyes or intellect
For all the light at once the source of light—
For wisdom that can have no counterwisdom.
In our subscription to the sentiment
Of one God, we provide He shall be one   590

Who can be many Gods to many men,
His church on earth a Roman Pantheon;
Which is our greatest hope of rest from war.
Live and let live, believe and let believe.
'Twas said the lesser gods were only traits   595
Of the one awful God. Just so the saints
Are God's white light refracted into colors.

JESSE BEL.   Let's change the subject, boys, I'm getting
   nervous.

KEEPER.   Nervous is all the great things ever made you.
But to repeat and get it through your head: 600
We have all the belief that's good for us.
Too much all-fired belief and we'd be back
Down burning skeptics in the cellar furnace
Like Shadrach, Meshach, and Abednego.

JONAH.   What's all this talk of slaying down in cellars— 605
So sinister? You spoke to someone down there.

KEEPER.   My friends and stokers, Jeffers and O'Neill.
They fail me. Now I'm teasing you again.
There's no one down there getting tortured, save
A penitent perhaps, self-thrown on Mercy.   610

JONAH.   I heard a deep groan—maybe out of him.
What's really down there?

PAUL.   Just an oubliette,
Where you must lie in self-forgetfulness
On the wet flags before a crucifix
I have had painted on the cellar wall   615
By a religious Aztec Indian.

JONAH.   Then it's not lethal—to get rid of me?
Have they been down?

PAUL.   Not in the proper spirit.
These two are stubborn children, as you see.
Their case is not so simple. You are good.   620

JONAH.   I am your convert. Tell me what I think.
My trouble has been with my sense of justice.
And you say justice doesn't really matter.

PAUL.   Does it to you as greatly as it did?

JONAH.   I own the need of it had somewhat faded   625
Even before I came in here tonight.

PAUL.   Well then!

JONAH.   And that's what I'm to meditate?

PAUL.   Meditate nothing. Learn to contemplate.
Contemplate glory. There will be a light.
Contemplate Truth until it burns your eyes out.   630

JONAH.   I don't see any staircase.

KEEPER.   There are stairs.

PAUL.   Some lingering objection holds you back.

JONAH.   If what you say is true, if winning ranks
The same with God as losing, how explain
Our making all this effort mortals make?   635

KEEPER.   Good for you, Jonah. That's what I've been saying.

JONAH.   You'll tell me sometime. All you say has greatness.
Yet your friend here can't be quite disregarded.

KEEPER.   I say we keep him till we wring some more
Naïveness about Justice out of him,   640
As once the Pharaoh did it out of Sekhti
By having him whipped every day afresh

517

For clamoring for justice at the gate,
Until the scribes had taken down a bookful
For distribution to his bureaucrats.   645

JONAH.   I'm going now. But don't you push me off.

KEEPER.   I was supporting you for fear you'd faint
From disillusionment. You've had to take it.

> (*Jonah steps on the threshold as the door*
> *Slams in his face. The blow and the repulse*   650
> *Crumple him on the floor. Keeper and Paul*
> *Kneel by him. Bel stands up beside her chair*
> *As if to come, but Keeper waves her off.*)

JONAH.   I think I may have got God wrong entirely.

KEEPER.   All of us get each other pretty wrong.   655

JESSE BEL.   Now we have done it, Paul. What did he say?

JONAH.   I should have warned you, though, my sense of
   justice
Was about all there ever was to me.
When that fades I fade—every time I fade.
Mercy on me for having thought I knew.   660

JESSE BEL.   What did he say? I can't hear what he says.

PAUL.   Mercy on him for having asked for justice.

KEEPER.   Die saying that, old-fashioned sapient,
You poor old sape, if I may coin the slang.
We like you, don't we, Paul? (*Paul takes his wrist.*)   665

JESSE BEL.   (*Still standing off*) We've all grown fond of you.

PAUL.   We've all grown fond of you. (*Paul says it louder,*
But Jonah gives no sign of having heard.)

518

KEEPER.   Who said, "Too late, you cannot enter now"?

JESSE BEL.   He was rejected for his reservations!   670

KEEPER.   (*Still on his knees, he sits back on his heels.*)
But one thing more before the curtain falls.—
(*The curtain starts to fall.*) Please hold the curtain.—
All Paul means, and I wish the dead could hear me—
All you mean, Paul, I think——

JESSE BEL.   Will you stand there   675
And let that tell you what you think, like that?

PAUL.   Suffer a friend to try to word you better.

JESSE BEL.   Oh, there's to be a funeral oration.
And we're an orator. Get up. Stand up
For what you think your doctor thinks, why don't you?   680
Don't wear your pants out preaching on your knees.
Save them to say your prayers on.—What's the matter?

KEEPER.   (*He doesn't rise, but looks at her a moment.*)
Lady, at such a time, and in the Presence!—
I won't presume to tell Bel where to go.   685
But if this prophet's mantle fell on me
I should dare say she would be taken care of.
We send our wicked enemies to Hell,
Our wicked friends we send to Purgatory.
But Bel gets some things right—and she was right—   690

JESSE BEL.   (*She startles at the sudden note of kindness.*)
I *am* right, then?

KEEPER.   —In glorifying courage.
Courage is of the heart by derivation,
And great it is. But fear is of the soul.

519

And I'm afraid. (*The bulb lights sicken down.*   695
The cellar door swings wide and slams again.)

PAUL.   The fear that you're afraid with is the fear
Of God's decision lastly on your deeds.
That is the Fear of God whereof 'tis written.

KEEPER.   But not the fear of punishment for sin   700
(I have to sin to prove it isn't that).
I'm no more governed by the fear of Hell
Than by the fear of the asylum, jail, or poorhouse,
The basic three the state is founded on.
But I'm too much afraid of God to claim   705
I have been fighting on the angels' side.
That is for Him and not for me to say.
For me to say it would be irreligious.
(Sometimes I think you are too sure you have been.)
And I can see that the uncertainty   710
In which we act is a severity,
A cruelty, amounting to injustice
That nothing but God's mercy can assuage.
I can see that, if that is what you mean.
Give me a hand up, if we are agreed.   715

PAUL.   Yes, there you have it at the root of things.
We have to stay afraid deep in our souls
Our sacrifice—the best we have to offer,
And not our worst nor second best, our best,
Our very best, our lives laid down like Jonah's,   720
Our lives laid down in war and peace—may not
Be found acceptable in Heaven's sight.
And that they may be is the only prayer
Worth praying. May my sacrifice
Be found acceptable in Heaven's sight.   725

520

KEEPER. Let the lost millions pray it in the dark!
My failure is no different from Jonah's.
We both have lacked the courage in the heart
To overcome the fear within the soul
And go ahead to any accomplishment.   730
Courage is what it takes and takes the more of
Because the deeper fear is so eternal.
And if I say we lift him from the floor
And lay him where you ordered him to lie
Before the cross, it is from fellow-feeling,   735
As if I asked for one more chance myself
To learn to say (*He moves to Jonah's feet.*)
Nothing can make injustice just but mercy.

Curtain

Bibliographical
&
Textual Notes

EDITOR'S STATEMENT

This edition follows basically the organization of *Complete Poems of Robert Frost* (1949), with the addition of *In the Clearing* (1962), which has been placed in sequence immediately before *A Masque of Reason* and *A Masque of Mercy*, thus allowing the two *Masques* to stand together at the end of the overall collection, as in *Complete Poems*.

The bibliographical and textual notes are arranged according to the order within this volume of the elements to which they relate. Entries for individual poems are prefixed by a citation giving, first, the page on which the poem appears or begins, then, its title; thereafter are included: 1) reference to any initial authorized appearance (or *"1st"*) which preceded publication of the poem in one of RF's books of new poetry, 2) reflection, by the year of any such publication, of the poem's inclusion by RF within his major selected and collected editions, 3) line-by-line specification of such textual variance as may exist among the printed sources referred to, 4) indication of changes introduced by the present editor that constitute departures from the copy-texts, and 5) provision of other information deemed to be of special pertinence.

The documentation herein of divergent readings is intended to reproduce published versions only, without attempting to trace, in a period that is still too early for doing so comprehensively, manuscript and typescript variants. (The texts the poet personally committed to publication are incident mainly to first appearances (*"1st"*s) of his poems in periodicals and elsewhere and to appearances within his own books of new verse and his volumes of selected and collected poetry. In the making of textual comparisons first printings or issues have been consistently used.) Differences of a substantive character have been identified (as VARIANTS) within the notes, but variations resulting from obvious and inconsequential typographical errors, as well as those involving differing punctuation and alternate spelling, have generally not been cited.

Based on what is known of RF's attention to the proofs of his books in the latter years of his life, *Complete Poems* and *In the Clearing* have been chosen as possessing prime textual authority and are followed in *The Poetry of Robert Frost*. Departures have, however, been made from these copy-texts, both for the correction of errors and for achieving greater textual clarity. All editorial changes have been recorded (as EMENDATIONS) in the notes except those associated with standardizing the employment of double quote-marks for the setting off of quotations and single quotes for quotations within quotations. Although an effort has been made to normalize spelling, in order to attain a degree of uniformity for the volume as a whole and to conform to present-day usage, no attempt has been made to impose upon the text strict consistency in capitalization, since to do so would risk occasional conflict with the poet's intentions of emphasis or with other of his deliberate stylistic practices.

Abbreviations which have been adopted for the designation of RF's principal works are:

ABW — *A Boy's Will* (London: David Nutt, 1913)
NOB — *North of Boston* (London: David Nutt, 1914)
MI — *Mountain Interval* (New York: Henry Holt, 1916)
NH — *New Hampshire* (New York: Henry Holt, 1923)
WRB — *West-Running Brook* (New York: Henry Holt, 1928)
AFR — *A Further Range* (New York: Henry Holt, 1936)
AWT — *A Witness Tree* (New York: Henry Holt, 1942)
AMOR — *A Masque of Reason* (New York: Henry Holt, 1945)

SB   — *Steeple Bush* (New York: Henry Holt, 1947)
AMOM— *A Masque of Mercy* (New York: Henry Holt, 1947)
ITC   — *In the Clearing* (New York: Holt, Rinehart and
                Winston, 1962)
1923   — *Selected Poems* (New York: Henry Holt, 1923)
1928   — *Selected Poems* (New York: Henry Holt, 1928)
1930   — *Collected Poems* (New York: Henry Holt, 1930)
1934   — *Selected Poems* (New York: Henry Holt, 1934)
1936   — *Selected Poems* (London: Jonathan Cape, 1936)
1939   — *Collected Poems* (New York: Henry Holt, 1939)
1946   — *The Poems* (New York: Modern Library, 1946)
1949   — *Complete Poems* (New York: Henry Holt, 1949)
1954   — *Aforesaid* (New York: Henry Holt, 1954)
1955   — *Selected Poems* (London: Penguin Books, 1955)
1963   — *Selected Poems* (New York: Holt, Rinehart and
                Winston, 1963)

The following is a sample entry for one of the poems of this collection:

> 266 THE ARMFUL: *1st* in *The Nation*, February 8, 1928; in *1930, 1934, 1936, 1939, 1949, 1963*; VARIANT   5 I should care] one would like *1st*; EMENDATIONS   1 *(as 1st)* seize] seize,   3 —],

Citing "The Armful" as on page two hundred and sixty-six, the entry indicates: that the poem first appeared in *The Nation* of February 8, 1928; that (besides its presence in *West-Running Brook*) it was included in the selected and collected editions identified by the years given; that within the several publications referred to one textual variant occurred—in line five what now reads "I should care" read "one would like" in the first appearance; and that the present editor has made two emendations—in the first line a comma

527

has been deleted, so that (as was the case in the first appearance) the reading is "seize" where the copy-text read "seize," and in line three a dash has been substituted for a comma which existed in the copy-text.

With further regard to the noting of editorial emendations, a notation such as —] or ;] indicates that the punctuation given before the bracket has been inserted where the copy-text had no punctuation at all. If more than one identical change has been made within a line, but one notation is given; thus ,] signifies that a comma *or commas* have been supplied. The use of -] always means that a hyphen has been provided editorially to join what in the copy-text were separate words, while in those instances where a hyphen has been entered within what was a single word in the copy-text both the new and old forms are given in full; accordingly, "far-distant" emended from "far distant" is noted simply as -] while "small-time" for "smalltime" is small-time] smalltime when represented in the notes.

E. C. L.

Dartmouth College
August 1969

NOTES

1 THE PASTURE: originally included in *NOB* as the introductory poem of that book, "The Pasture" appears as such with respect to the total contents of the present volume, in extension of a provision made by RF for his collected editions, *1930* and *1939*, and for his *Complete Poems, 1949*; it was also placed by RF as the initial poem in each of the editions of his *Selected Poems* and in his *Poems, 1946*; in *1923, 1928, 1930, 1934, 1936, 1939, 1946, 1949, 1955, 1963*; EMENDATIONS 4 and 8 *(as 1923, 1928, 1934, 1936)* shan't] sha'n't

A BOY'S WILL
(London: David Nutt, 1913)

In its original form the table of contents for *A Boy's Will* specified a division of the book into three numbered sections and included, also, a gloss for each of the poems except two, "Going for Water" and "Reluctance":

PART I

INTO MY OWN   *The youth is persuaded that he will be rather more than less himself for having forsworn the world.*

GHOST HOUSE   *He is happy in society of his choosing.*

MY NOVEMBER GUEST   *He is in love with being misunderstood.*

LOVE AND A QUESTION   *He is in doubt whether to admit real trouble to a place beside the hearth with love.*

A LATE WALK   *He courts the autumnal mood.*

STARS   *There is no oversight of human affairs.*

STORM FEAR   *He is afraid of his own isolation.*

WIND AND WINDOW FLOWER   *Out of the winter things he fashions a story of modern love.*

TO THE THAWING WIND   *He calls on change through the violence of the elements.*

A PRAYER IN SPRING   *He discovers that the greatness of love lies not in forward-looking thoughts;*

FLOWER GATHERING   *nor yet in any spur it may be to ambition.*

PART II

PART III

When RF's *Collected Poems* was published in 1930 three poems ("Asking for Roses," "In Equal Sacrifice," and "Spoils of the Dead") were omitted from the representation of *A Boy's Will* therein, while one poem ("In Hardwood Groves") was added. The 1934 edition of *A Boy's Will* included "Asking for Roses" but not "In Equal Sacrifice," "Spoils of the Dead," or "In Hardwood Groves." *Collected Poems* of 1939 and *Complete Poems* in 1949 both followed the contents that had been established for *A Boy's Will* by the 1930 collected edition, as does the present volume.

A Boy's Will was dedicated: TO E. M. F.

5 INTO MY OWN: *1st* as "Into Mine Own" in *New England Magazine*, May 1909; in *1923, 1928, 1930, 1934, 1936, 1939, 1946, 1949, 1955, 1963*; VARIANTS   5 withheld] deterred, *1st*   8 wheel pours] wheels pour *1st*   11 who should] those who *1st*   12 held] hold *1st*

5 GHOST HOUSE: *1st* in *The Youth's Companion*, March 15, 1906; in *1930, 1939, 1946, 1949, 1955, 1963*; VARIANTS   12 that] the *1st*   29 how] so *1st*; EMENDATIONS   4 falls] falls,   26 —],   27 —],—

6 MY NOVEMBER GUEST: *1st* in *The Forum*, November 1912; in *1923, 1928, 1930, 1934, 1936, 1939, 1946, 1949, 1954, 1955, 1963*; VARIANTS   4 the bare, the] both bare and *1st*   8 are] have *1st*   10 silver] silvered *1st*   11 desolate, deserted trees] fallen, bird-forsaken breeze *1st*

7 LOVE AND A QUESTION: in *1930, 1939, 1946, 1949, 1954, 1955, 1963*; VARIANT   1 Stranger] stranger *ABW*; EMENDATION   10 With,] With

8 A LATE WALK: *1st* in *The Pinkerton Critic* (Pinkerton Academy, Derry, New Hampshire), October 1910; in *1930, 1939, 1949, 1963*; EMENDATION   13 ,]

9 STARS: in *1930, 1939, 1946, 1949*; EMENDATION   8 —],—

9 STORM FEAR: in *1923, 1928, 1930, 1934, 1936, 1939, 1946, 1949, 1955, 1963*; EMENDATIONS   3 -]   12 —],—

10 WIND AND WINDOW FLOWER: in *1930, 1939, 1949*; EMENDATIONS   2 *(as ABW, 1930, 1939)* ,] .   9 *(as ABW, 1930, 1939)* ,]   11 by] by,

11 TO THE THAWING WIND: in *1923, 1928, 1930, 1934, 1936, 1939, 1946, 1949, 1955, 1963*; VARIANTS   4 steam] stream *1946*   8 ice will] ices *ABW*

12 A PRAYER IN SPRING: in *1930, 1939, 1946, 1949, 1955, 1963*; EMENDATION   12 -]

12 FLOWER-GATHERING: in *1923, 1928, 1930, 1934, 1936, 1939, 1946, 1949*; EMENDATION   2 glow] glow,

13 ROSE POGONIAS: in *1930, 1939, 1946, 1949, 1963;*
EMENDATIONS   7 —] ,—   15 color] color,   22 hours] hours,

14 WAITING: in *1930, 1939, 1946, 1949, 1963;*   VARIANT
2 among] along *1949, 1963;* EMENDATIONS   2 *(as ABW, 1930, 1939,
1946)* among] along   26 absent,] absent

15 IN A VALE: in *1930, 1939, 1949*

16 A DREAM PANG: in *1930, 1939, 1949;* EMENDATION   9 all,] all

16 IN NEGLECT: in *1930, 1939, 1946, 1949, 1955, 1963*

17 THE VANTAGE POINT: in *1923, 1928, 1930, 1934,
1939, 1946, 1949, 1963;* VARIANTS   Title The] A *1923, 1928,
1934*   8 are] are most *1923, 1928, 1934;* EMENDATION
11 sunburned] sun-burned

17 MOWING: in *1923, 1928, 1930, 1934, 1936, 1939,
1946, 1949, 1955, 1963*

18 GOING FOR WATER: in *1923, 1928, 1930, 1934, 1936,
1939, 1946, 1949*

19 REVELATION: in *1923, 1928, 1930, 1934, 1936, 1939, 1946,
1949, 1955, 1963;* VARIANTS   4 really find us] find us really *ABW,
1928, 1930, 1934, 1939, 1946* finds us really *1936*   5 'Tis] A *1923*

19 THE TRIAL BY EXISTENCE: *1st* in *The Independent,*
October 11, 1906; in *1930, 1939, 1949, 1955, 1963;* VARIANTS
50 strife] life *1st*   61 taken] ta'en *1st;* EMENDATIONS   12 *(as 1st)*
pasturewise] pasture-wise   14 —] ;—   17 *(as 1st)* cliff top] cliff-top
32 His] his

22 THE TUFT OF FLOWERS: *1st* in *The Derry Enterprise*
(Derry, New Hampshire), March 9, 1906; in *1923, 1928, 1930,
1934, 1936, 1939, 1946, 1949, 1954, 1955, 1963;* VARIANTS
7 had gone his way] was vanished, too *1st*   8 be] work *1st*   been]
worked *1st*   9 be] work *1st*   11 swift] close *1st*   12 bewildered]
'wildered *1st, ABW*   17 eye] one *1st*   21 eye] eyes *1st*
(*1st, ABW, 1923, 1928, 1930, 1934, 1939, 1946 have following*
24 *a couplet:* I left my place to know them by their name, / Finding
them butterfly weed when I came.)   31 wakening birds around]
birds' awakening sound *1st*   34 worked] was *1st*   37 dreaming,

532

as it were] it seemed to me *1st*   38 thought] life *1st*; EMENDATION
8 *(as 1923, 1928, 1934, 1936)* —] ,—

23 PAN WITH US: in *1930, 1939, 1949*; EMENDATIONS
1 —] ,—   3 —] ,—   12 ,]   28 sunburned] sun-burned   29 .] —

24 THE DEMIURGE'S LAUGH: in *1930, 1939, 1946, 1949,
1955, 1963*

25 NOW CLOSE THE WINDOWS: in *1930, 1939, 1949*

25 IN HARDWOOD GROVES: *1st* as "The Same Leaves" in
The Dearborn Independent, December 18, 1926; as noted above,
not in *ABW*; in *1930, 1939, 1949*; VARIANTS   9 *must* be] must
first be *1st*   flowers and] flowers, then *1st*; EMENDATION   2 ,]

26 A LINE-STORM SONG: *1st* in *New England Magazine,*
October 1907; in *1930, 1939, 1946, 1949, 1955*; VARIANT
13 crushed] hushed *1st*; EMENDATIONS   3 *(as 1st)* -]   4 hoofprints]
hoof-prints   23 ,]   29 *(as 1st)* ,]

27 OCTOBER: *1st* in *The Youth's Companion,* October 3, 1912; in
1923, 1928, 1930, 1934, 1936, 1939, 1946, 1949, 1955, 1963

28 MY BUTTERFLY: *1st,* subtitled "An Elegy," in *The
Independent,* November 8, 1894 (the poem having also been
included in 1894 in RF's privately printed *Twilight*); in *1930, 1939,
1949*; VARIANTS   8 scarce] not *ABW*   13 thy] the *1st, ABW*
19 regret] two tears *1st*   land] fields *1st*   22 Thou didst not know]
And didst thou think *1st (wherein* 24 *ends with a question mark)*
23 That fate had] Fate had not *1st*   25 Nor yet did I.] 'Twas
happier to die *1st*   (*1st has following* 25 *a line:* And let the days
blow by.)   26 And there were other] These were the unlearned
1st   (*1st has following* 30, *which therein ends with a comma, a line:*
Jealous of immortality.)   34 and the dreaming fond;] and *1st*
42 thy] your *1st*   43 broken] withered *1st*   44 thou art] you are
1st; EMENDATIONS   5 —]   27 His] his   *(as 1st)* ,] :   28 He] he
29 Him] him

29 RELUCTANCE: *1st* in *The Youth's Companion,* November 7,
1912; in *1923, 1928, 1930, 1934, 1936, 1939, 1946, 1949, 1954,
1955, 1963*; VARIANTS   13 lie] are *1st*   20 Was] Seemed
1st; EMENDATION   16 witch hazel] witch-hazel

533

NORTH OF BOSTON
(London: David Nutt, 1914)

Issuance at New York by Henry Holt and Company of a quantity of English sheets of *North of Boston* (the volume having a cancel title page dated 1914 and a binding distinct from the English ones) was followed during 1915 by publication of the firm's own editions of both *North of Boston* and *A Boy's Will*. Thus began an association between RF and Holt, as his principal publisher, which was to continue thereafter throughout the poet's lifetime.

North of Boston originally carried on the page after its table of contents the following statement: *Mending Wall* takes up the theme where *A Tuft of Flowers* in *A Boy's Will* laid it down.

Dedication: TO E. M. F. THIS BOOK OF PEOPLE

As noted elsewhere, "The Pasture," which was originally used as the introductory poem in *North of Boston*, appears as such for the overall contents of the present volume, this in continuance of a feature of RF's 1930 and 1939 collected editions and his *Complete Poems* (1949). In their original handling within *North of Boston* both "The Pasture" and the final poem, "Good Hours," were set in italic, rather than roman.

33 MENDING WALL: in *1923, 1928, 1930, 1934, 1936, 1939, 1946, 1949, 1955, 1963*; VARIANT 7 on a] on NOB; EMENDATIONS 2 it] it, 3 ,] ; 38 ,]

34 THE DEATH OF THE HIRED MAN: in *1923, 1928, 1930, 1934, 1936, 1939, 1946, 1949, 1954, 1955, 1963*; VARIANTS 105 saw it] saw NOB, *1923, 1928, 1934, 1936* 109 some] the NOB, *1923, 1928, 1934, 1936* 128 doesn't] didn't NOB, *1923, 1928, 1930, 1934, 1936, 1939, 1946* 136 he had] he'd had NOB, *1923, 1928, 1934, 1936* 144 anybody. Worthless though he is,] anyone. He won't be made ashamed NOB, *1923, 1928, 1934, 1936* 145 He won't be made ashamed to please his brother] To please his brother, worthless though he is NOB, *1923, 1928, 1934, 1936*; EMENDATIONS 1 ,] 3 tiptoe] tip-toe 28 pocket money—] pocket-money,— 35 barn door] barn-door 73 -] 80 ,] 87 *(as NOB, 1923, 1928, 1934)* ——] — 107 harplike] harp-like 130 ,] 164 her—] her,

40 THE MOUNTAIN: in *1923, 1928, 1930, 1934, 1936, 1939,*

1946, 1949, 1954, 1955, 1963; VARIANTS   92 around] round *1923,*
1928, 1934, 1936   94 ever you can] you can ever *NOB;*
EMENDATIONS   17 oxen,] oxen   60 —] .   103 *(as NOB, 1923,*
1928, 1930, 1934, 1936, 1939) .]   106 *(as NOB, 1923, 1928, 1934)* ——] −

44 A HUNDRED COLLARS: *1st* in *Poetry and Drama,* December
1913; in *1923, 1928, 1930, 1934, 1936, 1939, 1946, 1949, 1955, 1963;*
VARIANTS   7 And sees old friends he somehow can't get near]
Never for more. Old friends—he can't get near them *1st (wherein
the preceding line ends with a comma)*   10 as] while *1st*   14 up]
down *1st*   21 lamps] lights *1st*   27 beds, of course, you understand]
beds you understand, of course *1st*   40 went] vanished *1st*
41 *Lay*fayette] *Lafayette 1st*   45 don't] can't *1st*   (46 *and* 47 *not
in 1st)*   48 I'll ask you later] I want to ask you *1st*   forget it]
forget *1st*   49 Lafe and] Lafe, then *1st*   50 Naked] Unclad *1st*
51 light] lamp-light *1st*   58 blamed it on] thought it was *1st*
63 fourteen] fifteen *1st*   Fourteen] Fifteen *1st*   64 fourteen]
fifteen *1st*   65 come to think I must have back] now I think of it,
I have *1st*   66 fourteen] fifteen *1st*   67 them all. You ought to
have] them. Some one ought to use *1st*   68 They're yours and
welcome; let me send them to you.—] I'll send them to you—hang
me if I don't! *1st*   74 a pillow] two pillows *1st*   80 'My man' is it?]
'My man, my man.' *1st*   84 fourteen] fifteen *1st*   86 ninety]
eighty *1st*   88 carry] have *1st*   I can] You'll let me *1st*   89 Where]
Who *1st*   to] for *1st*   Stay still.] For me? *1st*   93 Will you
believe me if I put it there] Shall I convince you, if I leave it there, *1st*
95 so, Mister Man] that, anyway *1st*   96 ninety] eighty *1st*
101 Now we are getting on together—talking.] We're getting on
together. Now we're talking! *1st   (1st has following* 101 *a line:*
I've been collecting for it all my life.)   103 find] find out *1st*
people] folks *1st*   113 I says] says I *1st*   122 You drive around? It
must be pleasant work.] It must be pleasant, driving round the
country. *1st*   128 near] round *1st*   130 Everything's shut sometimes]
Everything may be shut *1st*   133 get] seem *1st*   135 maple trees]
apple-trees *1st* apple trees *NOB, 1923, 1928, 1934, 1936   (1st has*
143 *and* 144 *transposed in order and altered textually:* Whether I
have an errand there or not, / As if she had some sort of curvature.)
150 are] might be *1st (wherein* "Oh, *at the end of* 150 *is not present
and the succeeding line begins with quotes)*   157 No] Oh *1st*

535

158 Here's looking at you, then.—] Well, now I'm leaving you. *1st*
(159 *not in 1st*) 160 I'm gone] I am out *1st* 167 really I—I]
really—I *1923, 1928, 1934, 1936* 175 scared people] a scared man
1st 176 in] through *1st*; EMENDATIONS (*interlinear space entered
after* 13 *as in 1st*) 20 (*as 1st, NOB, 1923, 1928, 1934*) ——] –
68 —] 79 ,] 91 (*as 1st*) ,] 154 —] 157 (*as 1st, NOB, 1923,
1928, 1934*) ——] – (*comma after second* no *of* 157 *broken in
1949 and left out through error in 1963*) 158 ,] 170 (*as 1st*) ,]
174 (*as 1st*) ,] 176 —] 177 —]

51 HOME BURIAL: in *1923, 1928, 1930, 1934, 1936, 1939,
1946, 1949, 1954, 1955, 1963;* VARIANT 71 how to speak] how
NOB, 1923, 1928, 1934, 1936; EMENDATIONS 7 ?] 10 (*as
1923, 1928, 1934, 1936*) ?] , 13 help,] help 30 (*as NOB,
1923, 1928, 1934*) ——] – 31 ,] 32 (*as NOB, 1923, 1928, 1930,
1934, 1936, 1939, 1946, 1955*) banister] bannister 36 —] 37 —]
47 ,] 50 womenfolk] women-folk 66 (*as NOB, 1923, 1928, 1934*)
——] – 91 :] . 96 (*as 1923, 1928, 1934, 1936*) ?] . 110 (*as
1923, 1928, 1934, 1936*) ?] . 113 (*as NOB, 1923, 1928, 1934*) ——] –

55 THE BLACK COTTAGE: in *1928, 1930, 1934, 1936, 1939, 1946,
1949, 1955, 1963;* VARIANTS 26 the war] war *NOB, 1928, 1934, 1936*
103 I] I *1928, 1934, 1936* 120 loosely] closely *1928, 1934, 1936;*
EMENDATIONS 13 windowsill] window-sill 19 (*as 1928, 1934,
1936*) West] west 22 haircloth] hair-cloth 27 (*as 1928, 1934,
1936*) knelt,] knelt 36 went,] went 54 ,] 72 ,] 85
When,] When 92 ,] 101 ,] 102 Good-night] Good-night,
123 sandstorm] sand storm (*interlinear space entered after* 124 *as in
NOB, 1928, 1934, 1936*) 125 (*as NOB, 1928, 1934, 1936*) "]

59 BLUEBERRIES: in *1923, 1928, 1930, 1934, 1936, 1939,
1946, 1949, 1955, 1963;* VARIANTS 2 Patterson's] Mortenson's
NOB, 1923, 1928, 1934, 1936 28 Patterson] Mortenson *NOB,
1923, 1928, 1934, 1936* 58 Not] No *1949, 1955, 1963* 81
Pattersons'] Mortensons' *NOB, 1923, 1928, 1934, 1936;*
EMENDATIONS 24 ,] 29 ,] 58 (*as NOB, 1923, 1928, 1930, 1934,
1936, 1939, 1946*) Not] No 67 (*as 1923, 1928, 1934, 1936*) once,]
once 97 (*as NOB, 1923, 1928, 1934, 1936*) shan't] sha'n't

62 A SERVANT TO SERVANTS: in *1923, 1928, 1930, 1934, 1936,
1939, 1946, 1949, 1955;* EMENDATIONS 7 ,] 22 Straightaway]

Straight away   115 —] ,—   135 ,]   137 (as NOB, 1923, 1928,
1930, 1934, 1936, 1939) —]   141 ,]   143 catchall] catch-all   155
window views] window-views   171 (as NOB) course] course,   176
(as NOB, 1923, 1928, 1934, 1936) shan't] sha'n't

68 AFTER APPLE-PICKING: in 1923, 1928, 1930, 1934, 1936,
1939, 1946, 1949, 1955, 1963

69 THE CODE: 1st as "The Code—Heroics" in Poetry, February
1914; in 1923, 1928, 1930, 1934, 1936, 1939, 1946, 1949, 1955, 1963;
VARIANTS 2 cocks of hay] haycocks up 1st   10 is] was 1st, 1923
just now said] said just now 1st   13 more than] nearly 1st
18 would take time, of course,] had to take his time 1st   23 better or
faster] faster or better 1st   35 big's] big as 1st   52 a] the 1st   says]
said 1st   53 well] right 1st   54 jag] take 1st catch NOB, 1928, 1934,
1936   60 those] these NOB, 1928, 1934, 1936   71 right] just 1st
81 mopping] mopping the 1st   85 ye] you 1st   93 or] else 1st
98 Against the stove] Stuck in the oven 1st, NOB, 1923, 1928, 1934,
1936   99 clean disgusted from behind] mad in back, and so
disgusted 1st   103 my just] just my 1st   105 meet] face 1st   108
his] the 1st   111 don't know] can't say 1st   say] tell 1st;
EMENDATIONS 20 (as 1st) is] is   30 (as 1st) ,]   31 (as 1st) ,]   35
(as 1st, NOB, 1923, 1928, 1930, 1934, 1936, 1939, 1955) .]
56 ,]   66 "Let her come"?] Let her come?   87 (as 1st) ,]

73 THE GENERATIONS OF MEN: in 1930, 1939, 1946, 1949, 1963;
VARIANTS 33 hear] to hear NOB   128 used to use] used NOB; EMENDA-
TIONS 8 byroad] by-road   20 -]   22 ,]   (interlinear space deleted after
35 as in NOB)   39 -]   (interlinear space entered after 44)   53 ,]   78
(as NOB) ——] −   80 :] ,   mine] mine,   (] 81)]   88 ,]   93 The-
Seven-Caves-that-We-Came-Out-of] The Seven Caves that We Came
out of   97 (as NOB) ——] −   101 —] ,   102 ,]   104 —] ,—
106 ;] ,   107 ,]   111 ?—] ,   120 forever] for ever   122 ,]
123 ,]   150 (as NOB) ——] −   158 (as NOB) ——] −   159 (as
NOB) ——] −   161 ,]   163 doorsill] door-sill   170 (as NOB)
——] −   186 ones,] ones   194 (as NOB) ——] −

81 THE HOUSEKEEPER: 1st in The Egoist, January 15, 1914; in
1930, 1939, 1946, 1949; VARIANTS 16 other. I know what:] other
on the road. 1st   19 good] help 1st   23 I'm] I am 1st   (1st has
following 27, which therein ends with an ellipsis and no close quote,

two lines: I know she isn't holding out for terms, / Nothing like that. I gave that up this morning.") 36 I] I'd *1st* 40 live] have lived *1st* 43 don't just] just don't *1st* 70 up his mind] his mind up *1st* 87 That's] There's *1st* 92 after all] in a way *1st* 106 look] see *1st* (*1st has following* 112, *which therein ends with a dash, a line*: Better than what we have to keep them in.) 114 farm] place *1st* 115 One thing] That's what *1st* 116 say] claim *1st* 117 don't complain] doesn't mind *1st* 118 our] the *1st* 119 You never saw] I guess you've seen *1st* 122 in] and *1st* (135 *not in 1st, wherein the preceding line ends with a period*) 137 say] *say 1st* 141 sell, they're worth as much to keep] someone else, they are to him *1st* 142 all expense, though] mostly outgo *1st* 145 Here you] Here we *1st* 150 been] *been 1st* 164 one. You needn't] one that's blind. Don't *1st* (*1st has following* 166, *which therein has no close quote, a line*: John's a good man to save, it seems to me.") 171 She's let] She lets *1st* 177 worse than that] even worse *1st* 185 what she's] what's she *NOB* who, but] who, *NOB* 197 him] John *1st* (205 *not in 1st, wherein a line of seven periods is in its place*) 207 he] John *1st*; EMENDATIONS 90 Why] "Why (*as 1st*) married?] married," 91 Why] "Why (*as 1st*) ?—] ?" 107 besides,] besides 143 (*as 1st*) —], 162 (*as NOB*)——] — 185 ——?] — 207 (*as 1st*) ?], 208 —] 209 —]

89 THE FEAR: *1st* in *Poetry and Drama*, December 1913; in *1930, 1939, 1946, 1949, 1955, 1963*; VARIANTS 67 came from well along the road] seemed to come from far away *1st* (80 *not in 1st, NOB, wherein the preceding line ends with a close quote*) 93 struck, it] struck it, *1st, NOB*; EMENDATIONS 1 -] 7 .], 8 —] 13 (*as NOB*)——] — 31 (*as 1st, NOB*) ——] — 35 (*as NOB, 1930*) .] 41 (*as 1st, NOB*)——] — 47 (*as 1st, NOB*) shan't] sha'n't 63 ,] 74 -] 81 (*as 1st, NOB*)——] — 85 (*as 1st, NOB*)——] — 90 —]

92 THE SELF-SEEKER: in *1923, 1928, 1930, 1934, 1936, 1939, 1949*; VARIANTS 56 I'm] And I'm *NOB, 1923, 1928, 1934, 1936* 160 what] that *NOB, 1923, 1928, 1930, 1934, 1936, 1939* 196 folks's] folkses *NOB, 1930, 1939* folkses' *1923, 1928, 1934, 1936* 227 try to] try *1923, 1928, 1934, 1936*; EMENDATIONS 3 or] or, 14 blessèd] blessed 17 ,] 27 wheel pit] wheel-pit 31 wheel pit] wheel-pit 35 kite string] kite-string 38 ,] 48 —] 55 ,] 70 ;],

538

86 *Cypripedium*] *Cyprepedium*   87 —]   92 ,]   95 ,]   96 . . .?] —
(*interlinear space deleted after* 96 *as in* 1923, 1928, 1934, 1936)
(*line break and comma introduced in* 105)   111 ,]   148 ,]
154 Floating] floating   155 sinus] *sinus*   172 —]   173 —]
188 useful,] useful   —]   192 —]   193 —]   205 (*as* NOB, 1923,
1928, 1934) ——] —   207 ,]   (*as* 1923, 1928, 1934) ——] —
217 (*as* NOB, 1923, 1928, 1934) ——] —   224 —]

101 THE WOOD-PILE: in 1923, 1928, 1930, 1934, 1936, 1939,
1946, 1949, 1954, 1955, 1963; VARIANT   5 through] down NOB;
EMENDATION   32 ,]

102 GOOD HOURS: in 1930, 1939, 1946, 1949

MOUNTAIN INTERVAL
(New York: Henry Holt, 1916)

In its original form the table of contents for *Mountain Interval* empha-
sized six titles by including them in full capitals, rather than in small
capitals as the others appeared. The six were "Christmas Trees," "In
the Home Stretch," "Birches," "The Hill Wife" (followed by the
names, in small capitals, of the five individual poems that make up
"The Hill Wife" group), "The Bonfire," and "Snow." As in the case of
North of Boston before it, *Mountain Interval* had its opening poem,
"The Road Not Taken," and its concluding one, "The Sound of the
Trees," in italic, instead of roman, type.

When the 1930 *Collected Poems* was published "The Exposed
Nest" was moved from its original location within the book (between
"A Girl's Garden" and " 'Out, Out—' ") to a position immediately
after "An Old Man's Winter Night," and two poems ("Locked Out"
and "The Last Word of a Bluebird") were added. Both 1939's *Collected
Poems* and *Complete Poems* of 1949 followed the 1930 arrangement
for *Mountain Interval,* as does the present volume.

Mountain Interval was dedicated: TO YOU WHO LEAST NEED
REMINDING that before this interval of the South Branch under black
mountains, there was another interval, the Upper at Plymouth, where
we walked in spring beyond the covered bridge; but that the first inter-
val of all was the old farm, our brook interval, so called by the man
we had it from in sale.

105 THE ROAD NOT TAKEN: *1st* in *The Atlantic Monthly*, August 1915; in *1923, 1928, 1930, 1934, 1936, 1939, 1946, 1949, 1954, 1955, 1963*; VARIANT   13 kept] marked *1st*; EMENDATION 9 ,]

105 CHRISTMAS TREES: in *1930, 1939, 1946, 1949, 1963*; EMENDATIONS   7 ,]   8 ,]   21 ,]   23 —] ,   *(interlinear space entered after* 32)   49 —] ,   53 *(as MI, 1930, 1939, 1946)* -] 56 *(as MI, 1930, 1939)* ,]

108 AN OLD MAN'S WINTER NIGHT: in *1923, 1928, 1930, 1934, 1936, 1939, 1946, 1949, 1954, 1955, 1963*; VARIANTS   6 what it was] the need *1930, 1939, 1946*   10 here] there *MI, 1923, 1928, 1930, 1934, 1936, 1939, 1946*   26 keep] fill *MI, 1930*; EMENDATIONS 11 —] ;—   18 —] ,   19 —] , ,]

109 THE EXPOSED NEST: as noted above, originally in a different location within the contents of *MI*; in *1930, 1939, 1949*; EMENDATIONS   14 cutter bar] cutter-bar   24 ,]

110 A PATCH OF OLD SNOW: in *1930, 1939, 1949*; EMENDATION 1 ,]

110 IN THE HOME STRETCH: *1st* in *The Century*, July 1916; in *1923, 1928, 1930, 1934, 1939, 1949*; VARIANTS 46 besides] beside *1st, MI*   56 went] gone *1st*   60 much] much for me *1st, MI, 1923, 1928, 1934*   82 tramping] trampling *1st* 107 bow] speech *1st*   128 Its] It's *MI, 1923, 1928, 1930, 1934, 1939, 1949*   196 To] And *1st*   202 The fire got out] Out got the fire *1st*; EMENDATIONS   32 mowing field] mowing-field   37 —] 49 *(as 1st, MI, 1923, 1928, 1930, 1934, 1939)* —] -   54 —] 78 *(as 1st, MI, 1923, 1928, 1930, 1934, 1939)* ,] .   *(interlinear space entered after* 94 *as in 1st)   (interlinear space entered after* 98 *as in 1st, MI, 1928, 1934)   (interlinear space entered after* 110 *as in 1st, MI)*   118 ten] Ten   128 *(as 1st)* Its] It's   157 *(as MI, 1928, 1934)*——] —   189 ,]

118 THE TELEPHONE: *1st* in *The Independent*, October 9, 1916; in *1930, 1939, 1946, 1949, 1955, 1963*; VARIANTS   15 What] *What MI*   17 *Someone*] Some one *1st*; EMENDATION   8 windowsill] window sill

118 MEETING AND PASSING: in *1930, 1939, 1949;* EMENDATION 14 ,]

119 HYLA BROOK: in *1923, 1928, 1930, 1934, 1936, 1939, 1946, 1949, 1954, 1955;* EMENDATIONS 1 (*as MI, 1923, 1928, 1930, 1934, 1936, 1939, 1946*) .] 6 sleigh bells] sleigh-bells 7 jewelweed] jewel-weed 8 ,]

119 THE OVEN BIRD: in *1923, 1928, 1930, 1934, 1936, 1939, 1946, 1949, 1954, 1955, 1963;* EMENDATION 6 ,]

120 BOND AND FREE: in *1923, 1928, 1930, 1934, 1939, 1946, 1949, 1963*

121 BIRCHES: *1st* in *The Atlantic Monthly,* August 1915; in *1923, 1928, 1930, 1934, 1936, 1939, 1946, 1949, 1954, 1955, 1963;* VARIANTS 5 As ice storms do] Ice-storms do that *1st, MI, 1923, 1928, 1930, 1934, 1936, 1939, 1946 (wherein all of which appearances the preceding line ends with a period)* (*1st and MI have following* 22 *a line in parentheses:* Now am I free to be poetical?); EMENDATIONS 5 ice storms] ice-storms 11 snow crust] snow-crust 22 matter of fact] matter-of-fact ice storm] ice-storm (*as 1st, 1923, 1928, 1934, 1936*) ,]

123 PEA BRUSH: in *1930, 1939, 1946, 1949;* EMENDATION 2 ,]

123 PUTTING IN THE SEED: *1st* in *Poetry and Drama,* December 1914; in *1923, 1928, 1930, 1934, 1936, 1939, 1946, 1949, 1955, 1963;* VARIANTS 5 Soft] The *1st* 10 through] from *1st* 12 soil] ground *1st;* EMENDATION 6 (*as 1st*)),] ;)

124 A TIME TO TALK: *1st* in *The Prospect* (Plymouth Normal School, Plymouth, New Hampshire), June 1916; in *1923, 1928, 1930, 1934, 1936, 1939, 1946, 1949, 1955, 1963*

124 THE COW IN APPLE TIME: *1st* in *Poetry and Drama,* December 1914; in *1923, 1928, 1930, 1934, 1936, 1939, 1946, 1949, 1955;* VARIANT 8 spiked] pierced *1st*

125 AN ENCOUNTER: *1st* in *The Atlantic Monthly,* November 1916; in *1923, 1928, 1930, 1934, 1939, 1946, 1949, 1963;* VARIANTS 7 ever] had *1st* 22 I'm] *I'm 1st;* EMENDATION 6 (*as 1st*) overheated] over-heated

126 RANGE-FINDING: in *1923, 1928, 1930, 1934, 1936, 1939, 1946,*
1949, 1955, 1963; EMENDATIONS 2 groundbird's] ground bird's 6 ,]

126 THE HILL WIFE: collective title for five poems which first
appeared as a group in *The Yale Review*, April 1916 ("The Smile"
having previously been published, as noted below, in *Poetry and
Drama*, December 1914); EMENDATIONS *roman numerals have
been prefixed to the titles of the individual poems, as in the case of
the other poem groups in the present volume—*

126 I. LONELINESS: *1st* in *The Yale Review*, April 1916; in
1923, 1928, 1930, 1934, 1936, 1939, 1946, 1949, 1955, 1963

127 II. HOUSE FEAR: *1st* in *The Yale Review*, April 1916; in
1923, 1928, 1930, 1934, 1936, 1939, 1946, 1949, 1963; EMENDATIONS
3 ,] 6 ,] 8 indoor] in-door 9 house door] house-door

127 III. THE SMILE: *1st*, without subtitle, in *Poetry and Drama*,
December 1914; in *1923, 1928, 1930, 1934, 1936, 1939, 1946,
1949, 1963*

128 IV. THE OFT-REPEATED DREAM: *1st* in *The Yale Review*,
April 1916; in *1923, 1928, 1930, 1934, 1936, 1939, 1946, 1949, 1963*;
VARIANTS 5 The] His *1st* 9 It] He *1st* 12 the tree might] he
thought to *1st*; EMENDATION 3 *(as 1st)* window latch] window-latch

128 V. THE IMPULSE: *1st* in *The Yale Review*, April 1916; in
1923, 1928, 1930, 1934, 1936, 1939, 1946, 1949, 1963

129 THE BONFIRE: *1st* in *The Seven Arts*, November 1916; in
1930, 1939, 1946, 1949, 1963; VARIANTS 12 against] upon *1st*
(*1st has text of 18 and 19, without the final word of the latter,
in three lines*: And scare ourselves. Let wild fire loose / We will . . ."
/ "And scare you too?" the children said.) 34 with] to *1st* 39 around]
round *1st, MI* 45 the flame] that flame *1st, MI* 49 almost] *1st, MI*
76 Died not without] Rose till it made *1st* 77 and] or *1st* 94 wouldn't]
shouldn't *1st*; EMENDATIONS 18 ——] . . . 21 ,] 37 *(as 1st, MI,
1930, end of line damaged in 1939)* ;] 40 -] 41 (] 42 ,] 43)]
52 Bloodroot] Blood-root 107 —] ,— 113 uphill] up hill

133 A GIRL'S GARDEN: in *1930, 1939, 1949, 1963*; VARIANT
14 ideal] ideal *MI*; EMENDATIONS 31 *(as MI, 1930, 1939)*
corn,] corn 34 -] 45 . . . .] —

135 Locked Out: *1st* in *The Forge*, February *1917*; as noted above, not in *MI*; in *1930, 1939, 1949*; VARIANT 10 may have been to blame] always blamed myself *1st*

135 The Last Word of a Bluebird: as noted above, not in *MI*; in *1930, 1939, 1946, 1949, 1954, 1955*

136 "Out, Out—": *1st* in *McClure's*, July *1916*; in *1923, 1928, 1930, 1934, 1936, 1939, 1946, 1949, 1955, 1963*; VARIANTS 14 the word] that word *1st, MI* 15 knew what supper meant] could be hungry too *1st*; EMENDATION 20 ,]

137 Brown's Descent: in *1923, 1928, 1930, 1934, 1936, 1939, 1946, 1949*; VARIANTS (69 *through* 72 *not in 1923, wherein the preceding line ends with a period*); EMENDATIONS Subtitle *previously given over poem*: or, The Willy-Nilly Slide 8 -] 39 (*as 1923, 1928, 1934, 1936*)).] .) 46 road] road, 50 motorcars] motor-cars

140 The Gum-Gatherer: *1st* in *The Independent*, October 9, *1916*; in *1923, 1928, 1930, 1934, 1936, 1939, 1946, 1949, 1955, 1963*; VARIANT 3 And] And he *1st*; EMENDATIONS 2 downhill] down-hill 34 ,]

141 The Line-Gang: in *1930, 1939, 1946, 1949, 1955, 1963*; EMENDATIONS 7 (*as MI, 1930, 1939, 1946*) .] 12 ,]

142 The Vanishing Red: *1st* in *The Craftsman*, July *1916*; in *1930, 1939, 1946, 1949, 1963*; VARIANTS (*1st has in place of* 18 *two lines*: From a person who the less he attracted / Attention to himself you would have thought the better.); EMENDATIONS 6 —] ,— (*interlinear space entered after* 8 *as in MI*) 15 ,] 16 (*as 1st*) thumping,] thumping millstone,] millstone (*interlinear space entered after* 18 *as in MI*) 19 (*as 1st, MI, 1930, 1939, 1946*) wheel pit] wheel-pit 27 meal sack] meal-sack 28 meal sack] meal-sack 29 (*as 1st, MI, 1930, 1939, 1946*) wheel pit] wheel-pit

143 Snow: *1st* in *Poetry*, November *1916*; in *1923, 1928, 1930, 1934, 1936, 1939, 1946, 1949, 1955*; VARIANTS (*in the first printing of MI* 204 *was omitted and* 205 *was present twice*) 288 Gone] Come *MI* (*in 1st and MI* 319 *is given in quotes as a line of dialogue by Helen, rather than Fred, and quotation marks are*

543

entered appropriately in 318-320 *and an interlinear space is present before and after* 319) (*in 1923, 1928, 1934, and 1936 there is a break in the dialogue between* 319 *and* 320 *with appropriate close and open quotes to represent a change of speaker at that point*) (*in 1st a line break occurs in the latter part of* 324 *after the close quote*); EMENDATIONS   3 (*as 1st*) Coles,] Coles   4 ;] ,   5 ,]   7 pipestem] pipe-stem   22 uphill] up hill   29 (*as 1st, MI, 1923, 1928, 1934, 1936*) then,] then   36 —]   38 (*as 1st*) .] ,   42 (*as 1923, 1928, 1934*) ——] —   —]   51 (*as 1st*) —]   55 look] Look   (*as 1st, MI, 1923, 1928, 1930, 1934, 1936, 1939, 1946*) twelve,] twelve.   57 (*as 1st*) :] .   64 -]   78 ,]   108 Please?] please?   120 (*as 1st*) :] ;   123 (*as 1st*) ;] , (*as 1st*) ,]   166 windowpane] window-pane   179 windowsills] window-sills   181 words—] words.   190 (*as 1st*) snow-line] snowline   210 Good-night] good-night   221 snowstorms] snow-storms   230 ,]   233 (*as 1st*) why,] why   to,] to   246 table,] table   249 (*as 1st*) tongues] tongues,   267 (*as 1st*) —] .   294 ?—] ?   296 —]   302 ,]   304 ,]   —]   305 suppose?—she] suppose—?   She   324 (*as 1st*) ,]   329 and] And   330 answer.—] answer.   334 him,] him   339 to] To   342 (*as MI, 1923, 1928, 1934*) ——] —

156 THE SOUND OF TREES: *1st in Poetry and Drama,* December 1914; *in 1923, 1928, 1930, 1934, 1939, 1946, 1949, 1955, 1963;* VARIANT   Title The Sound of Trees] The Sound of the Trees *MI, 1928, 1930, 1934, 1939, 1946, 1949, 1955;* EMENDATION Title (*as 1st, 1923, 1963*) The Sound of Trees] The Sound of the Trees

NEW HAMPSHIRE
(New York: Henry Holt, 1923)

New Hampshire was the first of RF's books to have both a trade and a limited edition or issue. Thereafter each successive volume of new poetry was accorded such dual provision, as were the collected edition of 1930 and 1949's *Complete Poems.* (*Aforesaid* in 1954 was published solely in a limited edition, while the other collected and selected editions had trade editions only.) The limited *New Hampshire* consisted of three hundred and fifty numbered copies, signed by the author.

Dedication: *To* VERMONT AND MICHIGAN

The title page of *New Hampshire* carried a subtitle identifying the book as "A Poem with Notes and Grace Notes," and the volume was divided into three parts: the title poem itself, followed by the section called "Notes" (consisting of the poems "A Star in a Stoneboat" through "I Will Sing You One-O") and, finally, the section of "Grace Notes" (including the remaining thirty poems). As specified below, several elements of the title poem bore footnote references to poems of the "Notes" section, as did one line in "The Star-Splitter."

159 New Hampshire: in *1930, 1939, 1946, 1949, 1955, 1963;* emendations   40 turrets,] turrets   47 ,]   48 ,]   62 showcase,] show-case   64 President. (Pronounce] President (pronounce 66 .)]).   74 ,]   77 *(as NH)* Indians] Indians,   141 *(as NH)* fool's] fools'   144 showcase] show-case   *(interlinear space entered after 144)*   160 stem end] stem-end   blossom end] blossom-end 173 businesslike] business-like   businessmen] business men 177 Yokefellows] Yoke-fellows   sap yoke] sap-yoke   192 crossroads] cross-roads   200 laugh] laugh,   205 fear—] fear,—   207 exclaim] exclaim,   244 *(as NH, 1930, 1939, 1946)* Ireland] Ireland,   254 handbag] hand-bag   279 regime] régime   293 hound dogs] hound-dogs   294 ,]   304 lifelong] life-long   306 otherworldliness] other-worldliness   318 ,]   337 overfertile] over-fertile   345 logjam] log-jam   349 skipping] skipping,   371 " 'Nature] 'Nature blood';] blood;   380 overstepped] over-stepped   381 —] ;   383 foiled] foiled,   385 throne"—] throne.'   391 *(as NH, 1930, 1939)* .]   400 And] And,   409 ,]   410 ,]   *(As noted above, in NH several elements of this title poem bore footnote references to poems of the "Notes" section of the book. These references are as follows: from* sell *in* 7 Cf. page 37, "The Axe-helve."; *from the end of* 108 Cf. line 5, page 21, "A Star in a Stone-boat." *(the line cited being the poem's fifth line); from* style. *in* 125 Cf. page 56, "The Witch of Coös."; *from* quality *in* 148 Cf. line 31, page 25, "The Census-Taker;" line 26, page 27, "The Star-splitter;" and line 21, page 21, "A Star in a Stone-boat." *(the lines cited being the fifty-seventh, twenty-sixth, and twenty-first lines of the respective poems); from the end of* 164 Cf. page 49, "Wild Grapes."; *from the end of* 171 Cf. page 67, "A Fountain, a Bottle, a Donkey's Ears and Some Books."; *from* Marches. *in*

178 Cf. page 31, "Maple."; *from* Election *in* 195 Cf. page 61, "The Pauper Witch of Grafton."; *from the end of* 209 Cf. page 24, "The Census-taker."; *from the end of* 238 Cf. page 41, "The Grindstone."; *from the end of* 259 Cf. page 37, "The Axe-helve."; *from the end of* 266 Cf. page 27, "The Star-splitter."; *from the end of* 293 Cf. page 64, "The Pauper Witch of Grafton."; *from the end of* 299 Cf. line 27, page 50, "Wild Grapes." *(the line cited being the poem's fifty-third line); from the end of* 303 Cf. page 27, "The Star-splitter."; *from the end of* 345 Cf. page 44, "Paul's Wife."; *from the end of* 364 Cf. page 65, "An Empty Threat."; *and from the end of* 379 Cf. page 67, "A Fountain, a Bottle, a Donkey's Ears and Some Books.")

172 A STAR IN A STONEBOAT: *1st,* without dedication, in *The Yale Review,* January *1921;* in *1930, 1939, 1946, 1949, 1955, 1963;* VARIANT 11 besides] beside *1949, 1955, 1963;* EMENDATIONS Title Stoneboat] Stone-boat 4 stone-cold] stone cold 5 gold] gold, 11 *(as 1st, NH, 1930, 1939, 1946)* besides] beside 14 ant eggs] ant-eggs 16 tail] tail, 19 *(as 1st)* —] , 20 *(as 1st)* :] ; 26 stoneboat] stone-boat 40 ,] 48 —] , 53 ,]

174 THE CENSUS-TAKER: *1st* in *The New Republic,* April 6, *1921;* in *1930, 1939, 1946, 1949, 1963;* VARIANTS 50 This] The *1st* 58 is] be *1st;* EMENDATIONS 12 *(as 1st)* much,] much 45 straw-dust-covered] straw-dust covered 57 ,]

176 THE STAR-SPLITTER: *1st* in *The Century Magazine,* September *1923;* in *1930, 1939, 1946, 1949, 1955, 1963;* VARIANTS 6 frozen] hard *1st* 34 given] giving *1st* 55 one for Christmas gift] one's gift for Christmas *1st, NH, 1930, 1939, 1946* (95 *through* 99 *not in 1963);* EMENDATIONS 15 farming] farming, 18 *(as 1st)* lifelong] life-long *(interlinear space entered after* 21) 71 out,] out 75 stargazing] star-gazing 87 Star-Splitter] Star-splitter 89 ,] 92 *(as 1st)* ,] *(As noted above, in NH this poem bore a footnote reference to other poems of the "Notes" section of the book. This reference is: from* 86 Cf. page 21, "A Star in a Stone-boat;" and page 73, "I Will Sing You One-O.")

179 MAPLE: *1st* in *The Yale Review,* October *1921;* in *1930, 1939, 1949;* VARIANTS *(1st has following* 29 *(which therein ends*

without punctuation) a line: In a child's mind, he suddenly
perceived.) 36 he] he'd *1st* 41 her name over] over her name *1st*
44 her] the *1st* Its strangeness lay] She saw its strangeness *1st*
45 In having too much] Lay in its having *1st* 52 Her] The *1st*
60 still] yet *1930, 1939, 1949* 67 But] She *1st* the leaf back] back
the leaf *1st* 68 read] find *1st* 99 side] end *1st* 122 when he was]
when *1st* 126 on to a] to *1st* 139 maples] maple *1st* 163
meaning] a meaning *1st*; EMENDATIONS 3 *(as 1st)* ,] 7
M–A–P–L–E] M-A-P-L-E 23 *(as 1st) How*] How 60 *(as 1st, NH
—subsequently altered by RF to avoid, during the Prohibition era, the
possible whimsical misreading of "still" in the sense of a distillery for
the making of "home brew")* still] yet 65 ,] 76 *(as 1st, NH,
1930, 1939)* .] 79 pad] pad, 80 ,] 82 unshiplike] unship-like
116 *(as 1st)* life] life, 133 *(as 1st)* But] But, 138 sugarhouse]
sugar house

185 THE AX-HELVE: *1st* in *The Atlantic Monthly*, September
1917; in *1928, 1930, 1934, 1936, 1939, 1946, 1949, 1955*; VARIANT
44 with] 'mid *1st*; EMENDATIONS 8 *(as 1928, 1934, 1936)* chopping
block] chopping-block 24 *(as 1st)* -] 30 *(as 1st, NH, 1928, 1930,
1934, 1936, 1939, 1946)* ,] . *(interlinear space deleted after 54 as in
1st, 1928, 1934, 1936)* 78 eyehole] eye-hole 97 —] ,—
101 *(as 1st)* :] ;

188 THE GRINDSTONE: *1st* in *Farm and Fireside*, June 1921; in
1928, 1930, 1934, 1936, 1939, 1946, 1949, 1955, 1963; VARIANTS
40 gait] gate *1st, NH* 49 the] to *1st* 62 I'd welcome] I welcomed
1st; EMENDATIONS 10 *(as 1st)* ;] , 15 steel] steel, 27 *(as 1st,
NH, 1928, 1930, 1934, 1936, 1939, 1946)* ;] , 31 willpower]
will-power 41 hate] hate; 60 *(as 1928, 1934, 1936)* faster] faster,
66 *(as 1st, NH, 1928, 1930, 1934, 1936, 1939, 1946)* ,] .

191 PAUL'S WIFE: *1st* in *The Century Magazine*, November
1921; in *1930, 1939, 1946, 1949, 1954, 1955, 1963*; VARIANTS 14 is]
is *1st* 41 anything] any one *1st* 69 broad] long *1st* 137 not
from] not *1st* 157 speak] speak in *1st*; EMENDATIONS 11 —] ,—
37 hero] hero, 44 ,] 55 there] there, 64 -] 80 jackknife]
jack-knife 81 *(as 1st)* dugout] dug-out 87 jackknife] jack-knife
96 *(as 1st)* And] And, 101 *(as 1st)* ,] 110 *(as 1st)* log,] log 114
(as 1st) (] 115 *(as 1st)* .)] 117 waterlogged] water-logged

120 *(as 1st)* ,] 131 millpond] mill-pond 153 *(as 1st)* her] her,

196 WILD GRAPES : *1st* in *Harper's Magazine,* December 1920; in *1930, 1939, 1946, 1949, 1963;* VARIANT 17 as] of *1st;* EMENDATIONS 21 *(as 1st)* headdress] head-dress 39 treetop] tree-top 43 *(as 1st)* ,] 45 ,] 52 *(as 1st, NH, 1930, 1939, 1946)* which] which, 63 *(as 1st)* fox grapes] fox-grapes 75 .] ;

199 PLACE FOR A THIRD : *1st* in *Harper's Magazine,* July 1920; in *1930, 1939, 1949;* VARIANT 65 confused] confused up *1st;* EMENDATIONS 23 -] 27 *(as 1st, NH, 1930, 1939)* :] ; 40 ;] , 56 .] , *(interlinear space entered after 57 as in 1st)*

202 TWO WITCHES : collective title for two poems—

202 I. THE WITCH OF COÖS : *1st* in *Poetry,* January 1922; in *1930, 1934, 1936, 1939, 1946, 1949, 1954, 1955, 1963;* VARIANTS *(throughout 1st* MOTHER.] *The Mother* SON.] *The Son)* 5 could] *could 1st* 6 won't] *won't 1st* 8 I would have them know] you're to understand *1st* 15 could that] that could *1st* 53 a little] little *1st* 124 have] like *1st* 125 stay] *stay 1st* 141 was] was to *NH, 1930, 1934, 1936, 1939, 1946, 1949, 1954, 1955, 1963* 146 kept up] kept *NH, 1930, 1934, 1936, 1939, 1946, 1949, 1954, 1955, 1963;* 155 Lajway] Barre *1st;* EMENDATIONS 15 souls—] souls, 23 ,] 27 *(as 1st, NH)* ?] ! 40 cellar stairs] cellar-stairs 55 double doors] double-doors 81 button box] button-box 100 *(as 1st)* ,] 110 'The Wild Colonial Boy,'] *The Wild Colonial Boy,* 131 anymore] any more 141 *(in accordance with a note by RF for an intended change and as 1st)* was] was to 146 *(as 1st)* kept up] kept *(A note in 1st and NH dates poem: Circa 1922)*

207 II. THE PAUPER WITCH OF GRAFTON : *1st* in *The Nation,* April 13, 1921; in *1930, 1939, 1949, 1963;* EMENDATIONS 18 ,] 28 ,] 55 trademark] trade mark 65 ,] 97 snowberries] snow berries

210 AN EMPTY THREAT : in *1930, 1939, 1946, 1949, 1955, 1963;* EMENDATIONS 9 cross-legged] crosslegged 24 windbreak] wind-break 28 —] , 30 headshake] head shake 36 man,] man 48 —] 49 —] , 56 -]

212 A FOUNTAIN, A BOTTLE, A DONKEY'S EARS, AND SOME BOOKS : *1st* in *The Bookman,* October 1923; in *1930, 1939, 1949;*

VARIANTS (13 *not in 1st*) 17 shut you up] silence you *1st* (83 *not in 1st*) 89 uncomfortably] uncomfortable *1st* 95 heart of love] "heart of love" *1st* 127 kindness] awe *1st*; EMENDATIONS Title *(as 1st)* Ears,] Ears 2 someday] some day 5 -] 14 Someday] Some day 30 ——]— 31 *am*] am 64 Be ready,] 'Be ready,' for] 'for anything.] anything.' 80 windowsill] window sill 81 windowsill] window sill 93 *(as 1st)* packing case] packing-case, 96 ,] 111 wind] wind,

217 I WILL SING YOU ONE-O: *1st* in *The Yale Review,* October 1923; in *1930, 1939, 1949, 1955;* EMENDATIONS 26 *(as 1st, NH, 1930, 1939)* .] 35 en masse] *en masse* 74 ,] 75 ,]

220 FRAGMENTARY BLUE: *1st* in *Harper's Magazine,* July 1920; in *1928, 1930, 1934, 1939, 1946, 1949, 1955, 1963*

220 FIRE AND ICE: *1st* in *Harper's Magazine,* December 1920; in *1928, 1930, 1934, 1936, 1939, 1946, 1949, 1955, 1963;* VARIANT 7 say] know *1st*

221 IN A DISUSED GRAVEYARD: *1st* in *The Measure,* August 1923; in *1930, 1939, 1949, 1963;* EMENDATION 4 anymore] any more

221 DUST OF SNOW: *1st* as "A Favour" in *The London Mercury,* December 1920 (and immediately thereafter as "Snow Dust" in *The Yale Review,* January 1921); in *1928, 1930, 1934, 1936, 1939, 1946, 1949, 1954, 1955, 1963*

222 TO E. T.: *1st* in *The Yale Review,* April 1920; in *1930, 1939, 1946, 1949, 1955;* EMENDATIONS 1 ,] 3 ,] 4 see] see, you] you,

222 NOTHING GOLD CAN STAY: *1st* in *The Yale Review,* October 1923; in *1928, 1930, 1934, 1939, 1946, 1949, 1955, 1963*

223 THE RUNAWAY: *1st* in *The Amherst Monthly* (Amherst College), June 1918; in *1923, 1928, 1930, 1934, 1936, 1939, 1946, 1949, 1955, 1963;* VARIANTS 5 at] to *1st* he had to] we saw him *1st* 8 against the curtain of falling] across instead of behind the *1st* 9 "I think the] The *1st* of the] of the falling *1st* 10 isn't winter-broken] never saw it before *1st* 12 I doubt if even his mother could tell] He wouldn't believe when his mother told *1st* 13 He'd think] He thought *1st* 14 Where is his mother? He can't be out alone."] So this is something he has to bear alone *1st* 15 with] with a *1st, 1923, 1928, 1934, 1936* 16 And] He *1st* 17 And all his tail that isn't hair] Dilated nostrils, and tail held

straight *1st*   20 When] When all *1st*

223 THE AIM WAS SONG: *1st* in *The Measure*, March 1921; in *1930, 1939, 1946, 1949, 1955, 1963*

224 STOPPING BY WOODS ON A SNOWY EVENING: *1st* in *The New Republic*, March 7, 1923; in *1928, 1930, 1934, 1936, 1939, 1946, 1949, 1954, 1955, 1963*; VARIANT   5 My] The *1st*; EMENDATIONS 2 ,]   13 dark,] dark

225 FOR ONCE, THEN, SOMETHING: *1st* in *Harper's Magazine*, July 1920; in *1930, 1939, 1946, 1949, 1954, 1955, 1963*; EMENDATIONS   5 ,]

225 BLUE-BUTTERFLY DAY: *1st* in *The New Republic*, March 16, 1921; in *1930, 1939, 1946, 1949, 1963*

226 THE ONSET: *1st* in *The Yale Review*, January 1921; in *1928, 1930, 1934, 1936, 1939, 1946, 1949, 1954, 1955, 1963*; EMENDATION   18 downhill] down hill

226 TO EARTHWARD: *1st* in *The Yale Review*, October 1923; in *1928, 1930, 1934, 1936, 1939, 1946, 1949, 1954, 1955, 1963*; EMENDATIONS   5 *(as 1st, NH, 1928, 1930, 1934, 1936, 1939, 1946)* ,] 8 Downhill] Down hill   17 ,]

228 GOOD-BY AND KEEP COLD: *1st* in *Harper's Magazine*, July 1920; in *1928, 1930, 1934, 1936, 1939, 1946, 1949, 1955, 1963*; VARIANTS   2 the cold] cold *1st, NH, 1928, 1934, 1936*   22 nurtured] nourished *NH, 1928, 1934, 1936*

229 TWO LOOK AT TWO: in *1928, 1930, 1934, 1936, 1939, 1946, 1949, 1955*; EMENDATIONS   21 ,]   28 ,]

230 NOT TO KEEP: *1st* in *The Yale Review*, January 1917; in *1930, 1939, 1946, 1949*; VARIANTS   4 there] in her sight *1st, NH, 1930, 1939, 1946*   8 to look and ask] to ask *1st, NH, 1930, 1939, 1946*   9 is] was *1st*; EMENDATIONS   2 ....] ...   6 .—]—

231 A BROOK IN THE CITY: *1st* in *The New Republic*, March 9, 1921; in *1930, 1934, 1936, 1939, 1946, 1949*; VARIANT   23 The] These *1st*; EMENDATIONS   11 hearthstone] hearth-stone   18 ,]   22 ,]

232 THE KITCHEN CHIMNEY: *1st* in *The Measure*, August 1923; in *1930, 1939, 1946, 1949, 1963*; VARIANT   19 would serve] served

550

1s*t*; EMENDATION   6 apiece] a-piece

232 LOOKING FOR A SUNSET BIRD IN WINTER: in *1930*, *1939*, *1946*, *1949*, *1954*, *1955*, *1963*; EMENDATION   5 ,]

233 A BOUNDLESS MOMENT: *1st* in *The New Republic*, October 24, 1923; in *1930*, *1939*, *1949*; VARIANT   11 moved] walked *1st*; EMENDATIONS   5 *(as 1st)* Paradise-in-Bloom] Paradise-in-bloom 9 so,] so

234 EVENING IN A SUGAR ORCHARD: *1st* in *Whimsies* (University of Michigan), November 1921; in *1930*, *1939*, *1949*; VARIANTS   1 lull in] lull of *1st*   3 with a careful] in a quiet *1st* 13 a] one *1st*; EMENDATION   2 sugarhouse] sugar-house

234 GATHERING LEAVES: *1st* in *The Measure*, August 1923; in *1930*, *1939*, *1946*, *1949*, *1963*; EMENDATION   17 *(as 1st, NH, 1930, 1939, 1946)* ;] ,

235 THE VALLEY'S SINGING DAY: *1st* in *Harper's Magazine*, December 1920; in *1930*, *1939*, *1949*; EMENDATIONS   5 songbird] song-bird   10 overnight] over-night

236 MISGIVING: *1st* in *The Yale Review*, January 1921; in *1930*, *1939*, *1946*, *1949*, *1955*, *1963*; VARIANTS   6 had] have *1st*   9 his] the *1st*   16 me] *me 1st*; EMENDATIONS   13 *(as 1st)* ,]   14 *(as 1st)* ,]

237 A HILLSIDE THAW: *1st* in *The New Republic*, April 6, 1921; in *1928*, *1930*, *1934*, *1939*, *1949*; VARIANTS   23 six] eight *1st*   26 nine] ten *1st*; EMENDATIONS   13 —] ,—   16 —] ,

238 PLOWMEN: *1st* in *A Miscellany of American Poetry* 1920 (New York, 1920); in *1930*, *1939*, *1946*, *1949*; VARIANTS   1 A plow, they say,] I hear men say *1st*   2 no] though *1st*, NH, *1930*, *1939*, *1946*

238 ON A TREE FALLEN ACROSS THE ROAD: *1st*, without subtitle, in *Farm and Fireside*, October 1921; in *1930*, *1939*, *1946*, *1949*, *1955*, *1963*; VARIANTS   12 earth by the] by either *1st* 13 And, tired of aimless] This aimless earth now *1st*   14 Steer straight off after something into] And steer it a direction straight through *1st*

239 OUR SINGING STRENGTH: *1st* in *The New Republic*, May 2, 1923; in *1930*, *1939*, *1946*, *1949*, *1963*; VARIANTS   9 ground]

round *1st*   48 left] let *1st*; EMENDATIONS   35 *(as 1st)* underfoot]
under foot   41 ,]   52 nonetheless] none the less   53 *(as 1st)* wild
flowers] wildflowers

240 THE LOCKLESS DOOR: *1st* in *A Miscellany of American
Poetry 1920* (New York, 1920); in *1930, 1939, 1949, 1963*; VARIANT
15 whatever] whoever *1st*; EMENDATIONS   6 *(as 1st)* tiptoed]
tip-toed   9 *(as 1st, NH, 1930, 1939)* .]

241 THE NEED OF BEING VERSED IN COUNTRY THINGS: *1st* in
Harper's Magazine, December 1920; in *1928, 1930, 1934, 1936,
1939, 1946, 1949, 1954, 1955, 1963*

WEST-RUNNING BROOK
(New York: Henry Holt, 1928)

West-Running Brook was originally divided into six sections: I. Spring
Pools (being the first eleven poems), II. Fiat Nox ("Once by the
Pacific" through "Acquainted with the Night"), III. West-Running
Brook (the title poem itself), IV. Sand Dunes (from the poem of that
name through "The Flower Boat"), V. Over Back ("The Times Table"
through "The Birthplace"), and VI. My Native Simile (the final seven
poems).

When 1930's *Collected Poems* appeared three poems not previously
part of the contents of *West-Running Brook* were introduced therein
("The Lovely Shall Be Choosers," "What Fifty Said," and "The Egg
and the Machine"). The collected edition of 1939 and *Complete
Poems* (1949) both retained the 1930 additions to *West-Running
Brook*, as does the present volme.

The limited issuance of the book consisted of one thousand num-
bered copies, signed by RF.

Dedicated: To E. M. F.

245 SPRING POOLS: *1st* in *The Dearborn Independent*, April 23,
1927; in *1930, 1934, 1936, 1939, 1946, 1949, 1954, 1955, 1963*;
VARIANT   9 Let them] May well *1st (wherein the preceding line ends
without punctuation)*

245 THE FREEDOM OF THE MOON: in *1930, 1939, 1946, 1949*;
EMENDATION   8 later] later,

552

246 THE ROSE FAMILY: *1st* in *The Yale Review* and *The London Mercury*, July *1927*; in *1930, 1939, 1949*; VARIANT   6 plum] peach *The Yale Review*

246 FIREFLIES IN THE GARDEN: in *1930, 1939, 1946, 1949, 1955, 1963*; EMENDATIONS   2 flies] flies,   3 ,]   size] size,   4),])   5 starlike] star-like

246 ATMOSPHERE: *1st* as "Inscription for a Garden Wall" in *Ladies' Home Journal*, October *1928*; in *1930, 1939, 1946, 1949*

247 DEVOTION: in *1930, 1939, 1946, 1949, 1963*

247 ON GOING UNNOTICED: *1st* as "Unnoticed" in *The Saturday Review of Literature*, March 28, *1925*; in *1930, 1939, 1946, 1949, 1955, 1963*; VARIANTS   2 on] so *1st*   6 is] seems *1st*; EMENDATIONS   3 ,]   5 coralroot,] coral-root   (*as 1st*) know,] know   15 coralroot] coral-root   (*A note in WRB dates poem: 1901*)

247 THE COCOON: *1st* in *The New Republic*, February 9, *1927*; in *1930, 1939, 1949*; VARIANTS   12 want] long *1st*   15 gale] wind *1st*; EMENDATIONS   1 ,]   2 ways] ways,   3 new] new,   5 ,]   11 womenfolk] women-folk   15 (*as 1st*) —] ,—

248 A PASSING GLIMPSE: *1st* as "The Passing Glimpse" in *The New Republic*, April 21,*1926*; in *1930, 1939, 1946, 1949, 1955, 1963*; VARIANTS   5 flowers] kinds *1st*   7 Not] Nor *1st*   8 Not] Nor *1st*   12 Not in] In no *WRB*

249 A PECK OF GOLD: *1st* as "The Common Fate" in *The Yale Review*, July *1927*; in *1930, 1934, 1936, 1939, 1946, 1949, 1955, 1963*; EMENDATION   2 sea fog] sea-fog   (*A note in WRB dates poem: As of about 1880*)

249 ACCEPTANCE: in *1930, 1939, 1946, 1949, 1963*; VARIANTS   6 her] its *WRB*   8 his] its *WRB*

250 ONCE BY THE PACIFIC: *1st* in *The New Republic*, December 29, *1926*; in *1930, 1934, 1936, 1939, 1946, 1949, 1954, 1955, 1963*; VARIANT   8 shore] sand *1st*   (*A note in WRB dates poem: As of about 1880*)

250 LODGED: *1st* in *The New Republic*, February 6, *1924*; in *1930, 1939, 1946, 1949, 1955, 1963*; VARIANT   3 smote] struck *1st*

250 A MINOR BIRD: *1st* as "The Minor Bird" in *The Inlander*

(University of Michigan), January 1926; in *1930, 1939, 1946,*
1949, 1955, 1963; VARIANTS   5 must] may *1st*   7 of course] I own
1st   8 wanting to silence any] ever wanting to silence *1st*

251 BEREFT: *1st* in *The New Republic,* February 9, 1927; in
1930, 1934, 1939, 1946, 1949, 1955, 1963; VARIANTS   6 past] passed
1st   7 in] on *1st*   11 sinister in the] in the sinister *1st;*
EMENDATIONS   5 downhill] down hill   8 *(as 1st)* floor] floor,
(A note in WRB dates poem: As of about 1893)

251 TREE AT MY WINDOW: *1st* in *The Yale Review,* July 1927;
in *1930, 1934, 1936, 1939, 1946, 1949, 1954, 1955, 1963*

252 THE PEACEFUL SHEPHERD: *1st* in *The New York Herald
Tribune Books,* March 22, 1925; in *1930, 1939, 1946, 1949, 1955,
1963;* VARIANT   6 fear] think *1st;* EMENDATION   2 *(as 1st)* bars]
bars,

252 THE THATCH: in *1930, 1939, 1949;* EMENDATIONS
17 eaves] eaves,   35 onto] on to   *(A note in WRB dates poem:
As of 1914)*

254 A WINTER EDEN: *1st* in *The New Republic,* January 12,
1927; in *1930, 1939, 1946, 1949, 1954, 1955, 1963;* VARIANTS
1 garden] Eden *1st*   13 So near to paradise all pairing] Pairing in
all known paradises *1st;* EMENDATION   11 -]

254 THE FLOOD: *1st* as "Blood" in *The Nation,* February 8, 1928;
in *1930, 1939, 1946, 1949, 1955, 1963;* VARIANTS   10 implements of]
tools of trade and *1st*   11 but the] merely *1st;* EMENDATION   13 ,]

255 ACQUAINTED WITH THE NIGHT: *1st* in *The Virginia
Quarterly Review,* October 1928; in *1930, 1934, 1936, 1939, 1946,
1949, 1954, 1955, 1963;* VARIANT   7 stopped] hushed *1st;*
EMENDATION   11 *(as 1st)* height] height,

255 THE LOVELY SHALL BE CHOOSERS: *1st* in separate form
(New York, 1929), being a booklet in "The Poetry Quartos" series
published by Random House; as noted above, not in *WRB;* in *1930,
1939, 1946, 1949, 1954, 1955, 1963;* VARIANTS   6 *would*] would *1st*
24 they] *they 1st*   35 dare] dares *1st*   49 linger for her] stay and
hear a *1st;* EMENDATIONS   15 earrings] ear-rings   *(as 1st)* pearls,]
pearls   17 -]   24 well,] well   35 ,]

554

257 WEST-RUNNING BROOK: in *1930, 1934, 1936, 1939, 1946,*
1949, 1954, 1955, 1963; EMENDATIONS 2 West-Running]
West-running 3 West-Running] West-running 26 -] 30 you,]
you 35 —] ,— 47 ;] , 49 abyss's] abyss' 74 West-Running]
West-running

260 SAND DUNES: *1st* in *The New Republic,* December 15, 1926;
in *1930, 1939, 1946, 1949, 1955, 1963;* EMENDATIONS 2 *(as 1st)* die]
die, 6 town] town, 11 *(as 1st)* shape] shape,

261 CANIS MAJOR: *1st* as "On a Star-bright Night" in *The New
York Herald Tribune Books,* March 22, 1925; in *1930, 1934, 1936,
1939, 1946, 1949, 1963;* VARIANT 12 romps] roams *WRB;*
EMENDATION 1 *(as 1st, WRB, 1930, 1934, 1936, 1939, 1946)* ,] .

261 A SOLDIER: *1st* as "The Soldier" in *McCall's Magazine,*
May 1927; in *1930, 1934, 1936, 1939, 1946, 1949, 1954, 1955, 1963*

262 IMMIGRANTS: *1st* as fourth stanza of "The Return of the
Pilgrims" in George P. Baker's *The Pilgrim Spirit* (Boston, 1921);
in *1930, 1939, 1946, 1949, 1955, 1963;* VARIANTS 1 of] at *1st*
2 Have] Has *WRB* people] races *1st* 3 *Mayflower*] Mayflower
1st, WRB, 1930, 1939, 1946 4 her] their *1st, WRB* in to] to the
1st; EMENDATIONS 3 *(as 1st)* ,]

262 HANNIBAL: in *1930, 1939, 1946, 1949, 1955, 1963*

262 THE FLOWER BOAT: *1st* in *The Youth's Companion,* May
20, 1909; in *1930, 1939, 1946, 1949;* VARIANTS 6 of] with *1st*
growing] a-growing *1st* 9 judge] know *1st* 10 That all they ask
is rougher] She will brave but once more the Atlantic *1st* 11 And]
When *1st* master will] fisherman *1st;* EMENDATIONS 5 *(as 1st)* ,]
8 *(as 1st)* Georges Bank] George's bank (*A note in WRB records
poem as: Very early*)

263 THE TIMES TABLE: *1st* in *The New Republic,* February 9,
1927; in *1930, 1939, 1946, 1949, 1963;* VARIANTS 2 with] and *1st*
14 just] not *1st* a thing] thing *1st* 15 Nor] Or *1st* nor nobody]
or anyone *1st;* EMENDATIONS 5 water bar] water-bar 15 I] I,

263 THE INVESTMENT: in *1930, 1939, 1946, 1949, 1954, 1955,
1963*

264 THE LAST MOWING: in *1930*, *1939*, *1946*, *1949*, *1963*;
EMENDATIONS   1 Faraway] Far-away   16 O] oh

264 THE BIRTHPLACE: *1st* in *The Dartmouth Bema* (Dartmouth
College), June *1923*; in *1930*, *1934*, *1939*, *1946*, *1949*, *1955*, *1963*;
VARIANTS   3 built, enclosed] built beside *1st*   4 wall] rock *1st*   5
Subdued] Reduced *1st*   6 our] out *1st*

265 THE DOOR IN THE DARK: in *1930*, *1939*, *1949*; EMENDATIONS
1 dark] dark,   8 anymore] any more

265 DUST IN THE EYES: issued in broadside form as an
advertisement for *WRB*; in *1930*, *1939*, *1946*, *1949*, *1963*

266 SITTING BY A BUSH IN BROAD SUNLIGHT: in *1930*, *1934*,
1939, *1946*, *1949*, *1954*, *1955*, *1963*; EMENDATION   13 He] he

266 THE ARMFUL: *1st* in *The Nation*, February 8, 1928; in *1930*,
1934, *1936*, *1939*, *1949*, *1963*; VARIANT   5 I should care] one would
like *1st*; EMENDATIONS   1 *(as 1st)* seize] seize,   3 —],

267 WHAT FIFTY SAID: as noted above, not in *WRB*; in *1930*,
1939, *1946*, *1949*, *1963*

267 RIDERS: in *1930*, *1939*, *1946*, *1949*, *1955*, *1963*

268 ON LOOKING UP BY CHANCE AT THE CONSTELLATIONS:
in *1930*, *1934*, *1936*, *1939*, *1946*, *1949*, *1954*, *1955*, *1963*

268 THE BEAR: *1st* in *The Nation*, April 18, 1928; in *1930*, *1934*,
1936, *1939*, *1946*, *1949*, *1955*, *1963*; VARIANT   1 around] round *1st*;
EMENDATIONS   3 chokecherries] choke cherries   7 *(as 1st)* barbed
wire] barbed-wire   13 ,]   17 toenail] toe-nail   24 *(as 1st)* -]
27 *(as 1st)* shut] shut,   31 *(as 1st)* ,]

269 THE EGG AND THE MACHINE: as noted above, not in *WRB*;
1st as "The Walker" in *The Second American Caravan* (New York,
1928), edited by Alfred Kreymborg, Lewis Mumford, and Paul
Rosenfeld; in *1930*, *1939*, *1946*, *1949*, *1955*; VARIANTS   9 now, he
had himself to thank] now to throw it down the bank *1st*   20
turtle's] turtle *1st*   30 in its goggle glass] on its polished brass *1st*;
EMENDATIONS   2 *(as 1st)* ,]   7 ,]   13 *(as 1st)* ,]   14 *(as 1st)* ,]
25 *(as 1st)* leather,] leather   27 anymore] any more

A FURTHER RANGE
(New York: Henry Holt, 1936)

A Further Range was divided into six sections: Taken Doubly (the first fourteen poems, each having in the book's "Preface of Contents" an alternative title), Taken Singly ("Lost in Heaven" through "Provide, Provide"), Ten Mills (originally eleven in number, as noted below), The Outlands ("The Vindictives" through "Iris by Night"), Build Soil (both the poem of that title and "To a Thinker"), and Afterthought (the single poem "A Missive Missile").

Dedication: To E. F. for what it may mean to her that beyond the White Mountains were the Green; beyond both were the Rockies, the Sierras, and, in thought, the Andes and the Himalayas—range beyond range even into the realm of government and religion

The limited *A Further Range* consisted of eight hundred and three numbered copies, signed by the author.

273 A LONE STRIKER: *1st* as *The Lone Striker* in booklet form, being Number Eight of "The Borzoi Chap Books" (New York: Knopf, *1933*); in *1939, 1946, 1949, 1955, 1963*; EMENDATIONS 11 many-many-eyed] many, many eyed *(interlinear space deleted after 26 as in 1st)* 29 harplike] harp-like 56 ,] *(Subtitled in table of contents in AFR, 1939, 1949, 1955, and 1963 and also over poem in 1955: or, Without Prejudice to Industry)*

275 TWO TRAMPS IN MUD TIME: *1st* in *The Saturday Review of Literature*, October 6, *1934*; in *1939, 1946, 1949, 1954, 1955, 1963*; VARIANTS 9 oak] beech *1st, AFR, 1939, 1946* 26 turns to] fronts *1st, AFR, 1939, 1946* 66 living] life *1st*; EMENDATIONS 14 ,] 26 *(as 1st, AFR)* ,] 34 witching wand] witching-wand 46 *(as 1st, AFR)* ,]. 55 ax] ax, *(Subtitled in table of contents in AFR, 1939, 1949, 1955, and 1963 and also over poem in 1955: or, A Full-time Interest)*

277 THE WHITE-TAILED HORNET: *1st*, with subtitle "or Doubts About an Instinct," in *The Yale Review*, Spring *1936*; in *1939, 1946, 1949, 1954, 1955, 1963*; VARIANTS 19 stung] stings *1st* 20 rolled] rolls *1st* 21 would] will *1st* my explanations] an explanation *1st* 22 went] go *1st* 23 at] to *1st*

25 another] the other *1st*   40 scent] smell *1st*   (*1st has in place of*
55 *two lines*: That robs someone of what we want to keep, / I mean
our cherished fallibility.)   59 comparisons] comparison *1st*   63
comparisons were] comparison was *1st*; EMENDATION   20 heels]
heels,   (*Subtitled in table of contents in AFR, 1939, 1949, 1955,
and 1963 and also over poem in 1955: or, The Revision of Theories*)

279 A BLUE RIBBON AT AMESBURY: *1st in The Atlantic
Monthly*, April 1936; in *1939, 1946, 1949, 1955, 1963*; VARIANTS
5 honors] ribbons *1st*   8 style] shape *1st*   15 feeding at the] at the
feeding *1st*   23 past] of *1st*   24 And] Past *1st*   46 Yet] But *1st*
(*Subtitled in table of contents in AFR, 1939, 1949, 1955, and 1963
and also over poem in 1955: or, Small Plans Gratefully Heard Of*)

281 A DRUMLIN WOODCHUCK: *1st in The Atlantic Monthly*,
June 1936; in *1939, 1946, 1949, 1954, 1955, 1963*; EMENDATIONS
10 ,]   18 ,]   (*Subtitled in table of contents in AFR, 1939, 1949,
1955, and 1963 and also over poem in 1955: or, Be Sure to Locate*)

283 THE GOLD HESPERIDEE: *1st in Farm and Fireside*,
September 1921; in *1939, 1946, 1949*; VARIANTS   8 And turned] To
turn *1st*   24 growing] blowing *1st*   25 swung] shone *1st*
29 Would] Could *1st*   59 which] that *1st*; EMENDATIONS   24
pipestem,] pipe-stem   39 (*as 1st*) Under] Under,   41 (*as 1st, AFR,
1939*) .]   43 (*as 1st*) ,]   (*Subtitled in table of contents in AFR,
1939, and 1949: or, How to Take a Loss*)

285 IN TIME OF CLOUDBURST: *1st in The Virginia Quarterly
Review*, April 1936; in *1939, 1946, 1949, 1954, 1955, 1963*; VARIANTS
26 so endless a] the endless *1st*   27 Not] Never *1st*   (*Subtitled
in table of contents in AFR, 1939, 1949, 1955, and 1963 and also over
poem in 1955: or, The Long View*)

286 A ROADSIDE STAND: *1st in The Atlantic Monthly*, June
1936; in *1939, 1946, 1949*; VARIANT   31 ancient] old-fashioned *1st*;
EMENDATIONS   3 pled] plead   15 ,]   )]),   21 -]   25 ,]
26 anymore] any more   (*Subtitled in table of contents in AFR,
1939, and 1949: or, On Being Put Out of Our Misery*)

287 DEPARTMENTAL: *1st in The Yale Review*, Winter 1936;
in *1939, 1946, 1949, 1954, 1955, 1963*; VARIANTS   23 to] for *1st*

43 thoroughly] frightfully *1st*; EMENDATIONS   21 -]   35 ,]
(*Subtitled in table of contents in AFR, 1939, 1949, 1955, and 1963
and also over poem in 1955: or,* The End of My Ant Jerry)

289 THE OLD BARN AT THE BOTTOM OF THE FOGS: in *1939,
1949;* EMENDATIONS   6 that,] that   12 widespread] wide-spread
37 Prop-Locks] Prop-locks   41 was,] was   (*Subtitled in table of
contents in AFR, 1939, and 1949: or, Class Prejudice Afoot*)

290 ON THE HEART'S BEGINNING TO CLOUD THE MIND: *1st* in
Scribner's Magazine, April 1934; in *1939, 1946, 1949, 1955, 1963;*
VARIANTS   9 It] As it *1st*   10 Godforsaken] world-forsaken *1st*
14 knew] could tell *1st*   21 but] but I *1st*   31 And so] And *1st*
her] the lonely *1st*; EMENDATIONS   10 Godforsaken] God-forsaken
16 *(as 1st)* ;] :   38 *(as 1st, AFR, 1939)* ,]   39 *(as 1st)* one,] one
(*Subtitled in table of contents in AFR, 1939, 1949, 1955, and 1963
and also over poem in 1955: or,* From Sight to Insight)

292 THE FIGURE IN THE DOORWAY: *1st* in *The Virginia
Quarterly Review,* April 1936; in *1939, 1946, 1949, 1955;* VARIANTS
1 riding] speeding *1st*   4 oaks] oak *1st*   (*Subtitled in table of
contents in AFR, 1939, 1949, and 1955 and also over poem in 1955:
or, On Being Looked at in a Train*)

293 AT WOODWARD'S GARDENS: *1st* in *Poetry,* April 1936;
in *1939, 1946, 1949, 1955, 1963;* VARIANTS   12 laced] linked *1st*
22 flash of arm, a] flash, a monkey *1st*   26 though] but *1st*   (*1st has
33 on two lines, separated by interlinear space:* To answer for
themselves. / Who said it mattered—); EMENDATIONS   8 pinpoint]
pin-point   9 *(as 1st)* other,] other   24 *(as 1st)* -]   (*Sub-
titled in table of contents in AFR, 1939, 1949, 1955, and also over
poem in 1955: or, Resourcefulness Is More than Understanding*)

294 A RECORD STRIDE: *1st* in *The Atlantic Monthly,* May 1936;
in *1939, 1946, 1949, 1955, 1963;* EMENDATIONS   11 *(as AFR, 1939,
1946)* ,]   21 ,]   34 overelated] over-elated   (*Subtitled in table of
contents in AFR, 1939,1949, 1955, and 1963 and also over poem in
1955: or,* The United States Stated)

295 LOST IN HEAVEN: *1st* in *The Saturday Review of Literature,*
November 30, 1935; in *1939, 1946, 1949, 1963;* VARIANTS   11 O

559

opening] I warned the *1st (wherein the preceding line ends with a comma and close quote and the quote re-opens in the eleventh line in front of* by), AFR, *1939, 1946 (these three being as 1st, except that their preceding line ends with an exclamation mark and close quote)* Oh, opening *1949, 1963;* EMENDATIONS 4 *(as 1st)* sky-marks] skymarks 11 O] Oh,

296 DESERT PLACES: *1st* in *The American Mercury,* April 1934; in *1939, 1946, 1949, 1954, 1955, 1963;* VARIANT 14 where no human race is] void of human races *1st;* EMENDATION 9 *(as 1st)* ,]

296 LEAVES COMPARED WITH FLOWERS: *1st* in *The Saturday Review of Literature,* February 2, 1935; in *1939, 1946, 1949, 1955*

297 A LEAF-TREADER: *1st* in *The American Mercury,* October 1935; in *1939, 1946, 1949, 1955;* VARIANT 9 leaf to] leaves to *1st;* EMENDATIONS Title *(as 1st)* -] 12 *(as 1st)* ,]

298 ON TAKING FROM THE TOP TO BROADEN THE BASE: in *1939, 1949;* EMENDATION 11 ,]

299 THEY WERE WELCOME TO THEIR BELIEF: *1st* in *Scribner's Magazine,* August 1934; in *1939, 1946, 1949, 1963;* VARIANT 4 overimportant] over-confident *1st;* EMENDATION 11 *(as 1st)* ,]

299 THE STRONG ARE SAYING NOTHING: *1st* in *The American Mercury,* May 1936; in *1939, 1946, 1949, 1955, 1963;* VARIANTS 2 small] no *1st* 8 another] one still *1st* 13 farm to farm] man to man *1st* 14 cry] message *1st*

300 THE MASTER SPEED: *1st* as "Master Speed" in *The Yale Review,* Winter 1936; in *1939, 1946, 1949, 1963*

300 MOON COMPASSES: *1st* in *The Yale Review,* Autumn 1934; in *1939, 1946, 1949;* EMENDATION 5 ;] ,

301 NEITHER OUT FAR NOR IN DEEP: *1st* in *The Yale Review,* Spring 1934; in *1939, 1946, 1949, 1955, 1963;* VARIANT 9 The land may vary] Some say the land has *1st*

301 VOICE WAYS: *1st* in *The Yale Review,* Winter 1936; in *1939, 1946, 1949, 1955, 1963*

302 DESIGN: *1st* in *American Poetry 1922: A Miscellany* (New

York, 1922); in *1939, 1946, 1949, 1954, 1955, 1963*; VARIANT
7 like a] like *1st, AFR, 1939, 1946*

302 ON A BIRD SINGING IN ITS SLEEP: *1st* in *Scribner's Magazine,* December 1934; in *1939, 1946, 1949, 1955, 1963*; EMENDATIONS   4 *(as 1st)* ,] ;   9 ,]   11 *(as 1st)* ,]   12 *(as 1st)* ,]

303 AFTERFLAKES: *1st* in *The Yale Review,* Autumn 1934; in *1939, 1949*

303 CLEAR AND COLDER: *1st* in *Direction,* Autumn 1934; in *1939, 1949*; VARIANTS   10 take some leftover] from far reserves of *1st (wherein the succeeding line ends with a comma)*   11 to] from *1st*   15 Dash it with some] Even dashed with *1st (wherein the preceding line ends with a comma)*; EMENDATIONS   1 *(as 1st)* ,] 3 ,]   9 .)]);   10 leftover] left-over

304 UNHARVESTED: *1st* as "Ungathered Apples" in *The Saturday Review of Literature,* November 10, 1934; in *1939, 1946, 1949, 1963*; VARIANTS   (2 *and* 3 *not in 1st*)   4 was] stood *1st* (5 *not in 1st*)   6 And of] Of *1st*   7 Now breathed as] And breathing *1st*   8 For] And *1st*   12 May much stay] Much, much stays *1st*   14 So] To *1st*

305 THERE ARE ROUGHLY ZONES: in *1939, 1946, 1949, 1955, 1963*; EMENDATION   13 ?] .

306 A TRIAL RUN: *1st* in *The Atlantic Monthly,* June 1936; in *1939, 1946, 1949, 1955*; VARIANT   13 sets] set *1st*; EMENDATIONS 7 thunderclap] thunder-clap   8 ,]

306 NOT QUITE SOCIAL: *1st* in *The Saturday Review of Literature,* March 30, 1935; in *1939, 1946, 1949, 1955, 1963*; EMENDATIONS   4 ,]   10 loosely,] loosely   16 death tax] death-tax

307 PROVIDE, PROVIDE: *1st* in *The New Frontier,* September 1934; in *1939, 1946, 1949, 1954, 1955, 1963*; VARIANT   17 Atones] Makes up *1st*; EMENDATIONS   2 rag] rag,   13 ,] ;   17 *(as 1st)* disregard] disregard,

308 TEN MILLS: collective title for ten poems which first appeared as a group in *Poetry,* April 1936, wherein "The Wrights' Biplane" and "One Guess" were not, however, included, there being present there instead two couplets, "Assertive" and "Ring Around."

561

When *AFR* was published "Ring Around" (subsequently re-titled "The Secret Sits" and incorporated in *AWT*) was eliminated, "The Wrights' Biplane" and "One Guess" were added, and through error "Assertive" was retained, so that the "Ten Mills" group as it appeared in *AFR* consisted of eleven poems. "Assertive" first appeared as "By Myself" in Louis Untermeyer's *Rainbow in the Sky* (New York, 1935); also in *AFR* as lines 260-261 of "Build Soil." The order of the "Ten Mills" in *Poetry* was "Precaution," "The Span of Life," "Pertinax," "Assertive," "Tendencies Cancel," "Untried," "Money," "Ring Around," "Not All There," "In Dives' Dive." In *AFR* the order became "Precaution," "The Span of Life," "The Wrights' Biplane," "Assertive," "Evil Tendencies Cancel," "Pertinax," "Waspish," "One Guess," "The Hardship of Accounting," "Not All There," "In Divés' Dive." Both *1939* and *1946* follow *AFR*, but as collected in *1949* and subsequent editions the "Ten Mills" are—

308 I. PRECAUTION: *1st*, after incidental newspaper appearance, in *Poetry*, April 1936; in *1939, 1946, 1949, 1954, 1955, 1963*

308 II. THE SPAN OF LIFE: *1st* as "The Old Dog" in Untermeyer's *Rainbow in the Sky*; in *1939, 1946, 1949, 1955, 1963*; VARIANT 1 getting] looking *1st*

308 III. THE WRIGHTS' BIPLANE: in *1939, 1946, 1949, 1955, 1963*

308 IV. EVIL TENDENCIES CANCEL: *1st* as "Tendencies Cancel" in *Poetry*, April 1936; in *1939, 1946, 1949, 1955, 1963*; VARIANTS 1 end] kill *1st* 6 end] kill *1st*

308 V. PERTINAX: *1st* in *Poetry*, April 1936; in *1939, 1946, 1949, 1955, 1963*

309 VI. WASPISH: *1st* as "Untried" in *Poetry*, April 1936; in *1939, 1946, 1949, 1955, 1963*; EMENDATION 1 *(as 1st)* bent] bent,

309 VII. ONE GUESS: *1st* as "My What-Is-It" in Untermeyer's *Rainbow in the Sky*; in *1939, 1946, 1949, 1955, 1963*; VARIANTS 1 eyes and] eye, *1st* 2 A leg akimbo] An elegant leg *1st*; EMENDATION 3 dyestuff] dye stuff

309 VIII. THE HARDSHIP OF ACCOUNTING: *1st* as "Money" in *Poetry*, April 1936; in *1939, 1946, 1949, 1954, 1955, 1963*

309 IX. NOT ALL THERE: *1st* in *Poetry*, April 1936; in *1939, 1946, 1949, 1955, 1963*; EMENDATION 6 ;]

310 X. In Divés' Dive: *1st* in *Poetry*, April 1936; in *1939, 1946, 1949, 1955, 1963*; VARIANT 2 steady] patient *1st*

310 The Vindictives: in *1939, 1946, 1949, 1955, 1963*; EMENDATION 50 ,] (*A table-of-contents note in AFR, 1939, 1949, 1955, and 1963 associates the poem with*: The Andes)

313 The Bearer of Evil Tidings: *1st* in *The Yale Review*, Winter 1936; in *1939, 1946, 1949, 1955*; VARIANT 11 through the] through *1st, AFR*; EMENDATION 18 ,] (*A table-of-contents note in AFR, 1939, 1949, and 1955 associates the poem with*: The Himalayas)

315 Iris by Night: *1st* in *The Virginia Quarterly Review*, April 1936; in *1939, 1946, 1949, 1955, 1963*; VARIANTS 5 belief in] the tale at *1st* 6 seen of old] always seen *1st* (*1st has in place of* 16 *a line*: And unrelieved of any water-weight.); EMENDATIONS 24 (*as 1st*) went] went, 25 (*as 1st*)),]) 27 (*as 1st*) ends] ends, (*A table-of-contents note in AFR, 1939, 1949, 1955, and 1963 associates the poem with*: The Malverns (but these are only hills))

316 Build Soil: in *1939, 1946, 1949, 1955, 1963*; EMENDATIONS 44 —] . (*interlinear space entered after* 53) 60 livelong] live-long 61 yardful] yard full schoolboys] school boys 63 hopscotch] hop-scotch 64 leapfrog] leap frog —] ,— 72 ,] 73 ,] — —] , 81 ,] 86 :], 105 ,] 112 businessman] business man 143 ,] 145 ,] 153 god pinxit] God pinxit 155 ,] 173 ,] 175 ,] 176 —] ,— 187 land,] land 214 long, long] long long 215 why,] why 216 ,] 218 ,] 225 so] so, 241 (*as AFR, 1939*) .] 262 ,] 278 ,] (*A table-of-contents note in AFR, 1939, 1949, 1955, and 1963 records*: As delivered at Columbia University, May 31, 1932, before the National party conventions of that year)

325 To a Thinker: *1st* as "To a Thinker in Office" in *The Saturday Review of Literature*, January 11, 1936; in *1939, 1949*; VARIANT 3 One] Once *1st*; EMENDATIONS 16)]), 23 ,]

326 A Missive Missile: *1st* in *The Yale Review*, Autumn 1934; in *1939, 1946, 1949, 1955*; VARIANT 1 Someone in] Some son of *1st*

A WITNESS TREE
(New York: Henry Holt, 1942)

Following a page containing two short introductory poems ("Beech" and "Sycamore"), the contents of *A Witness Tree* was arranged in five sections: One or Two (including "The Silken Tent" through "The Discovery of the Madeiras"), Two or More ("The Gift Outright" through "The Lesson for Today"), Time Out (the poem of that title through "It Is Almost the Year Two Thousand"), Quantula ("In a Poem" through "An Answer"), and Over Back (being the last six poems of the book).

Besides the regular trade edition, a limited printing of seven hundred and thirty-five numbered copies, signed by RF, was issued.

The book was dedicated: TO K.M. FOR HER PART IN IT

331 BEECH: in *1946, 1949, 1963*

331 SYCAMORE: in *1946, 1949, 1963*

331 THE SILKEN TENT: *1st* in *The Virginia Quarterly Review,* Winter 1939; in *1946, 1949, 1954, 1955, 1963*

332 ALL REVELATION: *1st* as "Geode" in *The Yale Review,* Spring 1938; in *1946, 1949, 1954, 1955, 1963;* VARIANTS 3 Or] And *1st* 4 that] what *1st* 9 A] One *1st* 13 crystals] crystal *1st*

333 HAPPINESS MAKES UP IN HEIGHT FOR WHAT IT LACKS IN LENGTH: *1st* in *The Atlantic Monthly,* September 1938; in *1946, 1949, 1954, 1955, 1963;* VARIANTS 16 swept] went *1st* 22 its] the *1st*; EMENDATIONS 1 O] Oh, *(as 1st)* stormy,] stormy 15 *(as 1st)* dawn] dawn,

334 COME IN: *1st* in *The Atlantic Monthly,* February 1941; in *1946, 1949, 1954, 1955, 1963*

334 I COULD GIVE ALL TO TIME: *1st* in *The Yale Review,* Autumn 1941; in *1946, 1949, 1963;* VARIANT 12 held] thought *1st*

335 CARPE DIEM: *1st* in *The Atlantic Monthly,* September 1938; in *1946, 1949, 1954, 1955, 1963*

336 THE WIND AND THE RAIN: in *1946, 1949;* EMENDATIONS 4 ,] 19 ,] 30 onto] on to 33 flood] flood, 34 ,]

338 THE MOST OF IT: in *1946, 1949, 1954, 1955, 1963*;
EMENDATION   12 -]

338 NEVER AGAIN WOULD BIRDS' SONG BE THE SAME: in
1946, 1949, 1954, 1955, 1963

339 THE SUBVERTED FLOWER: in *1949, 1955, 1963*; EMENDA-
TIONS   12 fingertips] finger tips   24 ——] —   72 comb,] comb

341 WILLFUL HOMING: *1st* in *The Saturday Review of
Literature*, February 26, 1938, within Louis Untermeyer's "Play in
Poetry" (condensed from his then forthcoming book of that title); in
1946, 1949, 1955, 1963; VARIANTS   1 getting dark] growing late *1st*
3 storm] snow *1st*   an icy] a chilly *1st*   7 a course] his course *1st*
11 knob] latch *1st*; EMENDATION   7 *(as 1st)*,]

342 A CLOUD SHADOW: in *1946, 1949, 1963*

342 THE QUEST OF THE PURPLE-FRINGED: *1st* as "The Quest
of the Orchis" in *The Independent*, June 27, 1901; in *1946, 1949,
1963*; VARIANTS   2 overhead] o'erhead *1st*   9 to be before the
scythe] before the scythes should come *1st*   13 him] that *1st*
18 Nor] Or *1st*   24 That were pale] Pale *1st* *(wherein the preceding
line ends with a comma)*   25 silently] silent *1st*

343 THE DISCOVERY OF THE MADEIRAS: in *1949*; EMENDATIONS
Subtitle *Hakluyt*] HACKLUYT   7,]   21;],   28 staves] staves,
40 headshakings] head shakings   48,]   77.],   95,]   97 All]
'All   right,] right   !] !'   *(interlinear space entered after* 97)

348 THE GIFT OUTRIGHT: *1st* in *The Virginia Quarterly Review*,
Spring 1942; in *1946, 1949, 1954, 1955, 1963* *(appended to "For John
F. Kennedy His Inauguration")*; VARIANTS   9 found out that]
found *1st*, *AWT*, *1946*   16 would] might *1st*   *(A table-of-
contents note in AWT and 1949 records*: Read before the Phi Beta
Kappa Society at William and Mary College, December 5, 1941.)

348 TRIPLE BRONZE: *1st* in booklet form, as *Triple Plate*, being
RF's 1939 Christmas poem; in *1946, 1949, 1955, 1963*

349 OUR HOLD ON THE PLANET: *1st* in booklet form, being RF's
1940 Christmas poem; in *1946, 1949, 1955, 1963*; VARIANTS
3 And blow a gale. It didn't] It didn't blow a gale and *1st* *(wherein
the preceding line ends with a period)*   5 And just because] It didn't,

565

because *1st* *(wherein the preceding line ends with a period)* 11 to]
and *1st* 15 And it must be] It must be just *1st* (17 *in 1st appeared
as the thirteenth line therein, with variant phrasing*: The number of
people alive has been steadily more.) 18 Our] Or our *1st*;
EMENDATIONS 9 *(as 1st)* ,] 16 *(as 1st)* percent] per cent

349 To A YOUNG WRETCH: *1st*, without subtitle, in booklet form,
being RF's 1937 Christmas poem; in *1946, 1949, 1963*; VARIANTS
9 meant] been *1st* 15 opposing] conflicting *1st*; EMENDATIONS
14 where, thus,] where thus 19 rope] rope, 20 tree,] tree
(as 1st) bay,] bay (*Also in* The Saturday Review of Literature
for December 25, 1937.)

350 THE LESSON FOR TODAY: in *1946, 1949, 1955, 1963*;
VARIANT 64 go] get *AWT, 1946*; EMENDATIONS 5 in] in, 37
,] 40 agape] agape, 85 *eheu*] Eheu 96 *Memento mori*]
Memento mori 139 ,] 157 *Memento Mori*] Memento Mori
(*A table-of-contents note in AWT and 1949 and a footnote in 1963
record*: Read before the Phi Beta Kappa Society at Harvard
University, June 20, 1941.)

355 TIME OUT: *1st* in *The Virginia Quarterly Review*, Spring
1942; in *1946, 1949, 1963*; EMENDATIONS 5 goldthread] gold-thread
Maianthemum] maianthemum 13 ,] (*A table-of-contents note
in AWT and 1949 and a footnote in 1963 record*: Read before the
Phi Beta Kappa Society at William and Mary College, December
5, 1941.)

356 To A MOTH SEEN IN WINTER: *1st* in *The Virginia Quarterly
Review*, Spring 1942; in *1946, 1949, 1963*; EMENDATIONS 13 ,]
21 -] (*A table-of-contents note in AWT and 1949 records*: Read
before the Phi Beta Kappa Society at William and Mary College,
December 5, 1941. *A note at the end of the poem in 1st, AWT,
1946, 1949, and 1963 dates the poem*: Circa 1900)

357 A CONSIDERABLE SPECK: *1st*, without subtitle, in *The
Atlantic Monthly*, July 1939; in *1946, 1949, 1954, 1955, 1963*;
VARIANTS 14 loathing] horror *1st* 25 Collectivistic regimenting]
Political collectivistic *1st* 31 when] where *1st*; EMENDATION
5 *(as 1st)* ,]

358 THE LOST FOLLOWER: *1st* in *The Boston Herald*, September

566

13, 1936; in *1946, 1949, 1954, 1955, 1963*; VARIANTS 5 us] them *1st*
6 we] they *1st* 7 No] Not *1st* 9 loss] less *1st* 10 the] an *1st* 11
Some turn] Youth turns *1st* 25 such] him *1st* 26 a playful
moment] playful moments *1st* 30 or] and *1st*; EMENDATIONS 1
(as 1st) ,] 13 shortcut] short cut 21 *(as 1st)* Muse] muse 23 ,]
31 *(as 1st)* booklike] book-like 32 godlike] god-like 34 *(as 1st)*
eye] eye,

359 NOVEMBER: *1st* as "October" in *The Old Farmer's Almanac
1939* (Boston, 1938); in *1946, 1949, 1963* *(A note in AWT,
1946, 1949, and 1963 dates the poem: 1938)*

360 THE RABBIT-HUNTER: in *1946, 1949, 1963*; EMENDATION
Title -]

360 A LOOSE MOUNTAIN: in *1946, 1949, 1955*

361 IT IS ALMOST THE YEAR TWO THOUSAND: in *1946, 1949,
1955, 1963*; EMENDATION 13 deluxe] de luxe

362 IN A POEM: in *1949, 1963*; EMENDATION 1 way] way,

362 ON OUR SYMPATHY WITH THE UNDER DOG: in *1946, 1949,
1963*; EMENDATION 3 ,]

362 A QUESTION: in *1946, 1949, 1963*

362 BOEOTIAN: in *1946, 1949, 1955, 1963*

362 THE SECRET SITS: *1st* as "Ring Around" in *Poetry*, April
1936 (see note for "Ten Mills"); in *1946, 1949, 1954, 1955, 1963*

363 AN EQUALIZER: in *1949*; EMENDATION 4 ,]

363 A SEMI-REVOLUTION: in *1946, 1949, 1963*

363 ASSURANCE: in *1946, 1949, 1955*

363 AN ANSWER: in *1946, 1949, 1955, 1963*

364 TRESPASS: *1st* in *American Prefaces* (University of Iowa),
April 1939; in *1946, 1949, 1963*; VARIANT 8 me a] me *AWT, 1946,
1949, 1963*; EMENDATIONS 8 *(as 1st)* me a] me 10 *(as 1st)* picture
book] picture-book

364 A NATURE NOTE: *1st* as "A Nature Note On Whippoorwills"
in *The Coolidge Hill Gazette* (Cambridge, Massachusetts, amateur
journal), December 1938; in *1946, 1949*; VARIANTS 12 us] them

1st 13 I took note of] But I took note *1st* (14 *in 1st appeared* (*ending with a dash*) *as the fifteenth line and* 15 *as the fourteenth line therein*); EMENDATION 10 ,]

365 OF THE STONES OF THE PLACE: *1st* as "Rich in Stones" in *The Old Farmer's Almanac 1942* (Dublin, New Hampshire, 1941); in *1946, 1949, 1963*; VARIANT 5 one out] one *1st*; EMENDATIONS 2 basketful] basket full 15 (*as 1st*) Gransir] gransir

366 NOT OF SCHOOL AGE: in *1949*; EMENDATIONS 3 ,] 14 son] son, 25 :] , (*A note in AWT and 1949 dates the poem*: *1932*)

367 A SERIOUS STEP LIGHTLY TAKEN: in *1946, 1949, 1955, 1963*; EMENDATION 10 car] car,

368 THE LITERATE FARMER AND THE PLANET VENUS: *1st* in *The Atlantic Monthly*, March 1941; in *1946, 1949*; VARIANTS 56 cóndemned] damnèd *1st* 68 you've] you'd *1st*; EMENDATIONS 59 ,] 85 talk] walk 96 ,] 107 (*as 1st, AWT, 1946*) .] 108 hate] hate,

STEEPLE BUSH
(New York: Henry Holt, 1947)

The poems in *Steeple Bush* were set off in five sections: the first seven poems, followed by the "Five Nocturnes" group, then a section titled "A Spire and Belfry" ("A Mood Apart" through "Iota Subscript"), one called "Out and Away" ("The Middleness of the Road" through "Lucretius versus the Lake Poets"), and another designated "Editorials" (being the final twelve poems).

Dedication: FOR PRESCOTT · JOHN · ELINOR · LESLEY LEE [·] ROBIN AND HAROLD

The limited *Steeple Bush,* signed by the author and numbered, consisted of seven hundred and fifty-one copies.

375 A YOUNG BIRCH: *1st* in booklet form, being RF's 1946 Christmas poem; in *1949, 1954, 1955, 1963*; VARIANT 20 reading books] sick in bed *1st, SB*

375 SOMETHING FOR HOPE: *1st* in *The Atlantic Monthly,*

December 1946; in *1949, 1955, 1963*; VARIANTS   12 with] in *1st*
22 some things] somethings *SB*; EMENDATIONS   1 ,]   2 ,]
meadowsweet] meadow sweet   3 ,]   6 ,]   7 meadowsweet] meadow
sweet   18 -]   24 *(as 1st) spes alit agricolam*] spes alit agricolam
(*A note at the end of SB*: PAGE 4   "their wooden rings." Ripton
rings.)

376 ONE STEP BACKWARD TAKEN: *1st* in *The Book Collector's
Packet*, January 1946, within Ray Nash's "Robert Frost and His
Printers"; in *1949, 1955, 1963*; VARIANTS   9 universal] planetary *1st*
13 Then] But *1st*; EMENDATION   13 ,]

377 DIRECTIVE: *1st* in *The Virginia Quarterly Review*, Winter
1946; in *1949, 1954, 1955, 1963*; VARIANT   40 Now left's] You see
is *1st*; EMENDATIONS   15 -]   41 -]

379 TOO ANXIOUS FOR RIVERS: in *1949*; EMENDATIONS   9 -]
22 ,]

380 AN UNSTAMPED LETTER IN OUR RURAL LETTER BOX: *1st*
in booklet form, being RF's 1944 Christmas poem; in *1949*;
EMENDATIONS   1 ,]   8 ,]   33 *(as 1st)* lain] lain,   51 *in forma
pauperis*] in forma pauperis

382 TO AN ANCIENT: *1st* in *The Atlantic Monthly*, December
1946; in *1949, 1955, 1963*; EMENDATION   9 ,]

382 FIVE NOCTURNES: collective title for five poems, three of
which first appeared as a group, under the heading "Nocturnes," in
The Yale Review, Autumn 1946—

382 I. THE NIGHT LIGHT: *1st* in *The Yale Review*, Autumn
1946; in *1949, 1954, 1955, 1963*

383 II. WERE I IN TROUBLE: *1st* as "Were I in Trouble with
Night Tonight" in *The Yale Review*, Autumn 1946; in *1949, 1963*;
EMENDATION   4 ,]

383 III. BRAVADO: *1st* as "Bravery" in *The Yale Review*, Autumn
1946; in *1949, 1954, 1955, 1963*

383 IV. ON MAKING CERTAIN ANYTHING HAS HAPPENED:
1st in booklet form, being RF's 1945 Christmas poem; in *1949, 1955,
1963*; VARIANT   3 part] duty *1st*; EMENDATIONS   2 ,]   12 ,]

384 V. IN THE LONG NIGHT: *1st* in *Dartmouth in Portrait 1944* (Dartmouth College calendar: Hanover, *1943*); in *1949, 1963;* VARIANT   7 We would crawl out filing] Or would file out crawling *1st (wherein the preceding line ends with a semicolon);* EMENDATIONS 1 ,]   2 ,]   (*A note at the end of SB:* PAGE 21   Etookashoo and Couldlooktoo who accompanied Dr. Cook to the North Pole.)

385 A MOOD APART: *1st,* without title, (following an incidental, unauthorized appearance in an auction catalogue) in *Fifty Years of Robert Frost,* edited by Ray Nash (Dartmouth College Library exhibition catalogue: Hanover, *1944*); in *1949, 1954, 1955, 1963;* VARIANTS   1 to] to some *1st*   4 But] Till *1st*   8 mood] state *1st;* EMENDATION   8 onto] on to

385 THE FEAR OF GOD: in *1949, 1963;* EMENDATIONS   10 ,] 11 surface] surface,   (*A note at the end of SB:* PAGE 26   The Fear of God–Acknowledgment to the Papyrus Prisse)

386 THE FEAR OF MAN: in *1949, 1963;* EMENDATIONS   5 in-toppling] intoppling   8 ,]   11 streetlights] street lights   ,]   12 -]

386 A STEEPLE ON THE HOUSE: in *1949, 1955, 1963*

386 INNATE HELIUM: in *1949*

387 THE COURAGE TO BE NEW: initial two stanzas *1st* as "1946" in separate form, being a broadside printed for the dedication services of Orris C. Manning Memorial Park, Ripton, Vermont, July 28, 1946; in *1949, 1954, 1955, 1963;* EMENDATION   6 *(as 1st)* ,]   (*A note at the end of SB:* PAGE 30   The Courage to Be New[:] / No one cavils at their killing / And being killed for speed. / Then why be so unwilling / They should do as much for creed?)

387 IOTA SUBSCRIPT: in *1949, 1954, 1955, 1963*

388 THE MIDDLENESS OF THE ROAD: *1st* in *The Virginia Quarterly Review,* Winter 1946; in *1949, 1955, 1963*

388 ASTROMETAPHYSICAL: *1st* in *The Virginia Quarterly Review,* Winter 1946; in *1949;* VARIANTS   13 It may not give me] I should not dare to *1st*   19 it] you *1st;* EMENDATIONS   1 Your] your   10 You] you   11 ,]

389 SKEPTIC: in *1949, 1963*

570

390 Two LEADING LIGHTS: *1st* in *1944* Christmas booklet of Earle J. Bernheimer (California collector); in *1949*; VARIANTS 20 set] try *1st* 23 Comparison is not] Not power and glory are *1st* (*1st has following* 23 *two lines*: She doesnt hope to shine him down, / Or take away from his renown.) 24 his] the *1st* 25 That changes winter into] He turns to summon in the *1st*; EMENDATIONS 16 (*as 1st*),] 19,] 20,]

391 A ROGERS GROUP: *1st* in *The Atlantic Monthly*, December 1946; in *1949, 1963*

391 ON BEING IDOLIZED: in *1949, 1955, 1963*; EMENDATION 4,]

391 A WISH TO COMPLY: in *1949*

392 A CLIFF DWELLING: in *1949, 1963*; EMENDATION 10,]

392 IT BIDS PRETTY FAIR: in *1949, 1955, 1963*

393 BEYOND WORDS: in *1949, 1955*; EMENDATION 3....] ...

393 A CASE FOR JEFFERSON: in *1949, 1955, 1963*

393 LUCRETIUS VERSUS THE LAKE POETS: in *1949*; EMENDATIONS 2,] 4 let's] Let's

394 HAEC FABULA DOCET: *1st* in *The Atlantic Monthly*, December 1946; in *1949, 1955*; VARIANT (*1st has following* 20 *four lines headed* VARIANTLY, *being the same quatrain as cited in the note in SB quoted below, except that the first and third lines end with commas*); EMENDATIONS 8 (*as 1st*) overanxious] over anxious 9 command] command, 17 is,] is (*A note at the end of* SB: PAGE 51 Haec Fabula Docet–Alternatively[:] / The Moral is it hardly need be shown / All those who try to go it sole alone, / Or with the independence of Vermont / Are absolutely sure to come to want.)

394 ETHEREALIZING: *1st* in *The Atlantic Monthly*, April 1947; in *1949, 1954, 1955, 1963*

395 WHY WAIT FOR SCIENCE: *1st* as "Our Getaway" in *The New Hampshire Troubadour*, November 1946; in *1949, 1954, 1955, 1963*; VARIANTS 5 out. Will she be asked to] out; and to

what better *1st*   6 Us how by rocket we may hope] By whose
space-rocket we expect *1st*   7 To some star off there, say, a half]
A distance of not less than one *1st*; EMENDATIONS   1 Science,]
Science   7 ,]

396 ANY SIZE WE PLEASE: in *1949*; EMENDATIONS   1 ;] ,
2 So,] So   7 saying] saying,   Hell,] Hell   9 ,]

396 AN IMPORTER: *1st* as "The Importer" in *The Atlantic
Monthly*, April 1947; in *1949, 1955*; EMENDATIONS   10 —] ;
14 papers] papers,   24 -]

397 THE PLANNERS: *1st* in *The Atlantic Monthly*, December
1946; in *1949, 1955, 1963*

398 NO HOLY WARS FOR THEM: *1st* in *The Atlantic Monthly*,
April 1947; in *1949, 1955, 1963*; EMENDATIONS   3 they, the great,]
they the great   9 You] you   10 Your] your

398 BURSTING RAPTURE: in *1949*; EMENDATIONS   9 was,] was   10 ,]

399 U. S. 1946 KING'S X: *1st* in *The Atlantic Monthly*,
December 1946; in *1949, 1963*; EMENDATION   4 anymore] any more
(*A note at the end of* SB: PAGE 59   U S 1946 King's X—Recent
Riptonian)

399 THE INGENUITIES OF DEBT: *1st* in *The Atlantic Monthly*,
December 1946; in *1949, 1963*; EMENDATIONS   4 TAKE CARE TO
SELL YOUR HORSE BEFORE HE DIES] 'Take Care to Sell Your Horse
before He Dies   5 THE ART OF LIFE IS PASSING LOSSES ON.] The Art
of Life Is Passing Losses on.'   9 ;] ,   (*A note at the end of* SB:
PAGE 60   The Ingenuities of Debt–PreFranconian)

399 THE BROKEN DROUGHT: *1st* as "But He Meant It" in
The Atlantic Monthly, April 1947; in *1949, 1955*; VARIANT
13 that] the *1st*; EMENDATIONS   3 ,]

400 TO THE RIGHT PERSON: *1st*, with the subtitle "Fourteen
Lines," in *The Atlantic Monthly*, October 1946, at the end of RF's
"The Constant Symbol" (the introductory essay for his then
forthcoming Modern Library edition, *The Poems*); in *1946, 1949,
1955, 1963*; VARIANTS   3 much as] much for *1946*   10 learning]
knowledge *1st, 1946*; EMENDATIONS   8 (*as 1st, 1946*) -]   11
anymore] any more   (*as 1st, 1946*) ,]

572

"An Afterword" from COMPLETE POEMS
(New York: Henry Holt, 1949)

Following the text of *Steeple Bush,* and before that of *A Masque of Reason* and *A Masque of Mercy, Complete Poems* carried a section entitled "An Afterword," consisting of three poems: "Choose Something Like a Star" (the title of which was, as noted below, subsequently changed to "Take Something Like a Star"), "Closed for Good," and "From Plane to Plane." The second of these was in 1962 incorporated by RF as part of the contents of *In the Clearing,* and within the present volume the remaining two are included under the designation that was originally associated with all three poems in *Complete Poems.*

403 TAKE SOMETHING LIKE A STAR: *1st* as "Choose Something Like a Star" in RF's *Come In and Other Poems* (New York, 1943), compiled by Louis Untermeyer; in *1949, 1954, 1955, 1963;* VARIANTS   Title Take] Choose *1st, 1949, 1954, 1955*   24 take] choose *1st, 1949, 1954, 1955;* EMENDATIONS   Title *(as 1963)* Take] Choose   24 *(as 1963)* take] choose

404 FROM PLANE TO PLANE: *1st* in *What's New* (Abbott Laboratories, North Chicago, Illinois), December 1948; in *1949;* VARIANTS   10 *is*] is *1st*   41 your hoe up] up your hoe *1st*   147 believe it] believe *1st;* EMENDATIONS   24 —]   25 ;] ,   72 "] 74 "]   77 conscience,] conscience   85 someday] some day   103 ,] 148 ,]   Pike] Pike,

IN THE CLEARING
(New York: Holt, Rinehart and Winston, 1962)

The contents of *In the Clearing* was preceded, as an introductory element, by an excerpt from the poem "Kitty Hawk" (being lines 219-224 and 246-257, set without any indication of a break between the two segments and having one textual variation: Is for Was in line 254). The book had two titled units: Cluster of Faith (the five poems "Accidentally on Purpose" through that beginning "Forgive, O Lord") and Quandary (being the last ten poems of the volume).

Dedication: *Letters in prose to Louis Untermeyer, Sidney Cox, and John Bartlett for them to dispose of as they please; these to you in verse for keeps*

The limited *In the Clearing*, totaling fifteen hundred numbered copies, was signed by RF.

411 POD OF THE MILKWEED: *1st* as *From a Milkweed Pod* in booklet form, being RF's *1954* Christmas poem; in *1963*; EMENDATIONS 32 -] 34 -] 35 ,] 36 ,] 39 windowpane] window pane *(A note from the end of 54 in 1st, ITC, and 1963:* And shall be in due course.)

412 AWAY!: *1st* in booklet form, being RF's *1958* Christmas poem; in *1963*; VARIANT 19 urge] words *1st*; EMENDATIONS 20 "] "]

413 A CABIN IN THE CLEARING: *1st*, without dedication, in booklet form, being RF's *1951* Christmas poem; in *1963*; VARIANT 29 who] *who 1st*; EMENDATIONS *(periods entered after designation of speakers, as in 1963)* 15 ,] 42 ?].

415 CLOSED FOR GOOD: *1st* in booklet form, being RF's *1948* Christmas poem; in *1949, 1954, 1955, 1963*; VARIANTS *(1 through 6 not in ITC)* 7 And] They *ITC* 24 brush] spread *ITC (1st, 1949, 1954, and 1955 have following 30 an additional stanza:* How often is the case / I thus pay men a debt / For having left a place / And still do not forget / To pay them some sweet share / For having once been there.); EMENDATIONS *(1 through 6 restored, as in 1st, 1949, 1954, 1955, 1963)* 7 *(as 1st, 1949, 1954, 1955, 1963)* And] They 24 *(as 1st, 1949, 1954, 1955, 1963)* brush] spread

416 AMERICA IS HARD TO SEE: *1st* as "And All We Call American" in *The Atlantic Monthly*, June *1951*; in *1963*; VARIANTS 6 to] for *1st* 12 venture] future *1st* 23 And] But *1st* 31 Valladolid] them in Madrid *1st* 33 chance] way *1st* 48 for] as *1st*; EMENDATIONS 20 da] Da 27 da] Da 43 -] 47 ,] 55 Someday] Some day

419 ONE MORE BREVITY: *1st* in booklet form, being RF's *1953* Christmas poem; VARIANTS 38 baffled] puzzled *1st* 42 him in] him *1st* 45 was at] went to *1st* 46 With an air that said] As much as to say *1st* 47 feel] be *1st* 64 having depended on him] profiting by his virtue *1st* 65 And yet done nothing] Yet doing so little *1st* 69 wasn't disposed] was indisposed *1st*; EMENDATIONS

5 watchdog] watch-dog   24 ;], 　38 ,]　39 *(as 1st)* fancy] fancy,
40 —], 　56 ,]　59 *(as 1st)* ,]　60 —], 　61 —], 　*(A note*
from the end of 65 *in 1st and ITC:* But see "The Great Overdog"
and "Choose Something Like a Star," in which latter the star could
hardly have been a planet since fixity is of the essence of the piece.)

421 ESCAPIST—NEVER: *1st in The Massachusetts Review,*
Winter 1962; VARIANTS   10 pursuit forever.] pursuit *1st   (1st has*
following 10 *a line:* Of a pursuit of a pursuit forever.)

422 FOR JOHN F. KENNEDY HIS INAUGURATION: *1st in*
newspapers immediately following President Kennedy's Inauguration
of January 20, 1961—variously titled in the press but thereafter, in a
special book appearance, called "Dedication" with the present title
as a sub-element of that designation; in *1963;* VARIANTS   3 artists
ought] for us all *1st*　4 Today] This day *1st*　7 verse that in
acknowledgment] tribute verse to be his own *1st   (8 through* 10
not in 1st)   (11 through 18 *at a different point in 1st, as noted*
below)　19 Now came on a] Is about the *1st*　20 our] the *1st*
(21 and 22 *not in 1st)*　24 heroes] sages *1st*　25 I mean the great
four,] *(The mighty four of them were 1st, wherein the succeeding*
line ends with a close parenthesis　27 knew] saw *1st*　28 ahead what
now appears:] how in two hundred years *1st*　29 empires down] down
the world *1st*　30 And by] By *1st, wherein the line ends with a period*
31 Make everybody] It made the least tribe *1st   (1st has following* 31
three lines, the first being a slight variant of 39 *of ITC:* New order of the
ages did they say? / The newest thing in which they led the way / Is
in our very papers of the day. *1st thereafter has* 11 *through* 18 *of*
ITC, four lines of which include variants of ITC readings: 13
What] Which *1st*　14 by native] and native *1st*　15 The new
world Christopher Columbus] What Christopher Columbus first
had *1st*　17 And counted out. Heroic] They all were counted out:
the *1st, wherein the preceding line ends with a comma*　18 *is*
followed in 1st by seven lines, the fourth, fifth, and sixth being
variants of 41, 42, *and* 45 *of ITC:* Of what had been for centuries
the trend / This turned out the beginning of the end. / My verse
purports to be the guiding chart / To the o'erturning it was ours to
start / And in it have no unimportant part. / The turbulence we're
in the middle of / Is something we can hardly help but love.)

(32 *through* 48 *not in 1st, except for variants of* 39, 41, 42, *and* 45, *as noted above*) (54 *through* 77 *not in 1st, which ends with a line—following* 53–*which does not appear in ITC:* I sometimes think that all we ask is glory.); EMENDATIONS 23 His] his 24 —], 26 —],— 28 :], (*The text of "The Gift Outright" which was released to accompany the 1st of RF's Inaugural dedicatory verse contained an error in the eighth line, made reading* left *therein. Also, in saying the poem at the Inauguration RF substituted, at Mr. Kennedy's request,* will *for* would *in the final line.*) (*Following 1st, the dedicatory poem had several appearances in print, including revised and extended versions, prior to ITC.*)

425 ACCIDENTALLY ON PURPOSE: *1st* in booklet form, being RF's 1960 Christmas poem; VARIANT 13 Never] Don't you *1st*; EMENDATION 7 ,]

426 A NEVER NAUGHT SONG: in *1963*; EMENDATIONS 12 ,] 26 Yggdrasill] Yggdrasil

427 VERSION: incomplete as included in *ITC*, the poem as given in the present collection is based upon the texts of several variant holographs, particularly one within a copy of *ITC* in the Trinity College Library, Hartford, Connecticut (inscribed: "Version" corrected / R.F. / for Bacon Collamore); the ninth, tenth, and thirteenth through sixteenth lines have been drawn from manuscript and have been styled editorially to make them consistent with the handling of the text as published in *ITC*; in addition there are the following EMENDATIONS 1 ,] 8 non-existence] non-existence, 11 (*as RF-Collamore MS*) the] His 12 (*as RF-Collamore MS*) her] its ,].

427 A CONCEPT SELF-CONCEIVED: in *1963*

428 [FORGIVE, O LORD . . .]: *1st* as "The Preacher" in RF's *A Remembrance Collection of New Poems* (New York, 1959); in *1963*

428 KITTY HAWK: *1st*, with the subtitle date 1894, in booklet form, being RF's 1956 Christmas poem; in *1963*; VARIANTS (3 *not in 1st*) 4 Emblematic] A prophetic *1st* (7 *and* 8 *not in 1st*) (*1st has following* 9 *four lines*: It was then as though / I could hardly wait / To degravitate. / Habit couldn't hold me.) 14 think] say *1st* (*1st, wherein the preceding line ends with a*

period, has in place of 17 through 99 sixteen lines, the fourth, sixth, seventh, eighth, tenth, and thirteenth relating to 40, 46, 47, 49, 41, and 99 respectively in ITC: Still I must have known, / Something in me told me, / Flight would first be flown, / It is on my tongue / To say first be sprung, / Into the sublime / Off these sands of time / For his hour glass. / I felt in me wing / To have up and flung / An immortal fling. / I might well have soared, / I might well have sung, / Though my bent was toward / Little more, alas, / Than Cape Hatteras;) 100 I fell in] And I fell 1st (wherein the preceding line ends with a semicolon) 105 Or] And 1st (106 and 107 not in 1st) 114 But their lack] Being out 1st (1st, wherein the preceding line ends with a semicolon, has following 119 one line: Even at their height) 129 Something] All which 1st 132 themselves] someone 1st 163 the] our 1st 169 I aptly] right there I 1st (wherein the preceding line ends with a comma) (1st, wherein the preceding line ends with a comma, has following 169 two lines: That old laurel-crowned / Lord of a John Bull.) 170 And its] The Moon's 1st (175 not in 1st, at this point) 179 upon] twice on 1st (180 not in 1st) (1st, wherein the preceding line ends with a colon, has 181 and 182 transposed in order, slightly altered textually, and followed by thirteen lines, thus bringing the poem therein to an end as follows: For a daughter drowned, / For a son astray. / Kitty Hawk, O Kitty, / Know you no dismay, / But some time in some / Mood akin to pity / You would weep no less / For mankind's success / Than for their distress. / You'd be overcome / In the deathless scene / When that common scoff, / Poor Darius Green, / And his fool machine / Finally took off.); EMENDATIONS 19 -] 44 —] own] own— 69 overlong] over long 115 (as 1st) ,] 190 Someday] Some day 199 aliquid] aliquid 236 -] 258 ,] 259 ,] 265 whom] whom— 269)—] .) 273 is,] is 274 someday] some day 290 Athens, Rome, France,] Athens Rome France 291 -] 293 so-long-kept] so-long kept 305 inscription,] inscription 329 ,] 331 ,] 337 ,] 373 ,] 422 ,] 423 ,] 431 -] 445 ,] 468 ,] 471 hometown] home town (As noted above, lines 219 through 224 and 246 through 257, with one textual variant, appear in ITC as a frontispiece following the dedication page.) (Following 1st, a revised and greatly extended version, consisting of four hundred and thirty-two lines, appeared in The Atlantic Monthly, November 1957.)

443 Auspex: *1st* in Elizabeth Shepley Sergeant's *Robert Frost: The Trial by Existence* (New York, 1960); VARIANTS 1 California] Californian *1st* 4 its] his *1st* 7 I was] I'd been *1st* 9 unto Jove] to the gods *1st* 10 remained resentful to this] resented ever since that *1st*; EMENDATIONS 2 ,] 3 all,] all

443 The Draft Horse

444 Ends: in 1963

445 Peril of Hope: in 1963; VARIANTS 5 boughs are] orchard's *ITC* 7 pink and] all that's *ITC*; EMENDATIONS 5 (*as 1963*) boughs are] orchard's 7 (*as 1963*) pink and] all that's
(*An evidently incidental publication of a holograph draft of "Peril of Hope" appeared in* The Agnes Scott News (*Agnes Scott College, Decatur, Georgia), February 8, 1961.*)

445 Questioning Faces: *1st* as "Of a Winter Evening" in *The Saturday Review*, April 12, 1958; in 1963; VARIANT
3 wings straining suddenly aspread] wide wings strained suddenly at spread *1st*; EMENDATION 6 windowsill] window sill

446 Does No One at All Ever Feel This Way in the Least?: *1st* as *Does No One But Me at All Ever Feel This Way in the Least* in booklet form, being RF's 1952 Christmas poem; VARIANT 29 of you] of *you 1st*; EMENDATIONS 1 sea,] sea 23 ,] .
26 -] 28 ,] (*A note from the end of* 24 *in 1st and ITC: At this writing it seems pretty well accepted that any rivers added can only make the sea saltier.*) (*A note from the end of* 31 *in 1st and ITC:* By King Canute and Lord Byron among others.)

447 The Bad Island—Easter: *1st* in *The Times Literary Supplement*, September 17, 1954; EMENDATIONS 2 ,] 3 ,] 9 ,] 12 Halfway] Half way 26 beruled] be-ruled 54 ,]

449 Our Doom to Bloom: *1st*, without Robinson Jeffers quote, as *Doom to Bloom* in booklet form, being RF's 1950 Christmas poem; in 1963

450 The Objection to Being Stepped On: *1st* as *My Objection to Being Stepped On* in booklet form, being RF's 1957 Christmas poem; EMENDATION 4 offense] offence

451 A-Wishing Well: *1st* in booklet form, being RF's 1959

Christmas poem; VARIANT 80 someone someone] someone *1st*;
EMENDATIONS 3 were,] were 15 ,] 21 ,] 28 ,] 73 -]

453 How Hard It Is to Keep from Being King When It's
in You and in the Situation: *1st* in *Proceedings of the
American Academy of Arts and Letters and the National Institute of
Arts and Letters*, Second Series, Number One (1951); VARIANTS
16 Bellatrix, or else] Bellaterix, or *1st* 23 keep] stop *1st* 126 had]
have *1st* 169 here] there *1st* 194 freedom's in] freedom is *1st*
196 We feel it] The only freedom's *1st* (202 *not in 1st, wherein
the preceding line ends with a period and a close quote*) 253 at] at
the *1st* (*1st has in place of* 275 *and* 276 *one line*: It's hard for a
king to keep from being a king.) 278 Or more than half I'm half]
Exactly half I am *1st*; EMENDATIONS 8 on,] on 26 ;] ,
(*interlinear space entered after* 29 *as in 1st*) 32 marketplace]
market place 37 marketplace] market place 54 dishwashing]
dish-washing 57 (*as 1st*) .)]) (*interlinear space entered after* 62
as in 1st) 84 me." And] me"—and 88 (*as 1st*) quintessence]
quintessence 98 ,] 106 someday] some day 109 Kings] kings
111 ——] — 118 King] king 123 ,] 185 :] , 188 (*as 1st*)
scholar] Scholar 214 meter] metre 216 meter] metre 219
meter] metre 221 verse, so called,] verse so called 234 :] ; 247 ,]
(251 *through* 253 *in roman, as in 1st, rather than italic*) 252 His]
his 253 He] *he* 268 Sirius] Sirius, 270 ,] 275 King] king

462 Lines Written in Dejection on the Eve of Great
Success: *1st*, without the five "Postscript" stanzas, in RF's *A
Remembrance Collection of New Poems* (New York, 1959); in 1963;
VARIANTS Title of Great] of *1st* (*as noted*, 9-28 *and titling thereof
not in 1st*); EMENDATION 2 (*as 1st*) onto] on to

464 The Milky Way Is a Cowpath: EMENDATIONS 9
Quidnuncs] Quid-nuncs 22 ,] 23 ,] 41 ,]

465 Some Science Fiction: *1st*, without the concluding
quatrain and its titling, in booklet form, being RF's 1955 Christmas
poem; VARIANTS 11 With] And with *1st* 12 For me as an] Call
me the *1st* 17 around] round *1st* 20 unheretical] permissible *1st*
23 thinking of] thinking *1st* 24 Establishing] Of establishing *1st*
28 noble] social *1st* 29 wastrel] convict *1st* 30 accursed] accurst

1st; EMENDATION   36 (as early manuscripts and in accordance with a correctness of reference) of] it's   (Dedicatee: Edward Hyde Cox)

467 QUANDARY: 1st, prior to substantial revision, as "Somewhat Dietary" in The Massachusetts Review, Fall 1959; VARIANTS (1 through 6 not in 1st) (7 and 8 are variants of the third and fourth lines of 1st, which therein read: Because discrimination reigns / Is why there's such a need of brains.) (9 is a variant of the first line of 1st, which therein reads: We live but to discriminate) (10 appears as the second line of 1st) (11 through 14 not in 1st) (15 through 18 appear as the fifth through eighth lines of 1st) (19 is a slight variant of the ninth line of 1st, which therein ends without punctuation and is followed by a tenth line not in "Quandary": You want me to confess in ink / I did employ sweetbreads to think) (20 and 21 not in 1st) (22 appears as the eleventh line of 1st, which therein ends with a period and is followed by nine concluding lines not in "Quandary": I wasn't half as much to blame / As was my social science set, / My brothers of the Calumet, / The liberal progressive party / With whom, in being modern-arty, / Sweetbreads-for-brains, their slogan, had / A vogue amounting to a fad. / To sweetbreads on our club menu / They all ascribed my high I.Q.) (23 through 26 not in 1st) (Variant of 5 and 6 1st, as "The Old Pair," in The New-England Galaxy, Summer 1960.)

468 A REFLEX   468 IN A GLASS OF CIDER: EMENDATION   4 ,]

468 FROM IRON: 1st (following incidental, newspaper appearance), prefaced by the dedicatory text given below, as "The Sage," in RF's A Remembrance Collection of New Poems (New York, 1959); in 1963; VARIANT (1st has in place of subtitle and dedication six lines: This to the memory of my great friend / Ahmed Bokhari who had me down / from Vermont to view his lump of / purest iron ore at the United Nations / in the room for meditation on / Tools and Weapons.)

469 [FOUR-ROOM SHACK . . .]: in 1963

469 [BUT OUTER SPACE . . .]: 1st as "The Astronomer" in RF's A Remembrance Collection of New Poems (New York, 1959); VARIANTS   1 But outer] This Outer 1st   2 this] thus 1st   4

popul*ace*] populace *1st*   5 Stays] Seems *1st*   popu*lar*] popular *1st*
6 popul*ous*] populous *1st*

469 ON BEING CHOSEN POET OF VERMONT: *1st*, without title,
in newspapers immediately following RF's installation on July 22,
1961, as Poet Laureate of Vermont; in *1963*; VARIANTS   2 When he
finds] To know *1st*   3 not entirely disapproved] happily more or less
approved *1st*

469 [WE VAINLY WRESTLE . . .]

470 [IT TAKES ALL SORTS . . .]: *1st* as "The Poet" in RF's *A
Remembrance Collection of New Poems* (New York, 1959); in
1963; VARIANT   1 sorts] kinds *1st*; EMENDATION   1 -]

470 [IN WINTER IN THE WOODS . . .]: *1st* by RF in a holograph
facsimile, Amherst College, 1962; in *1963*; EMENDATION   5 ax,] axe

A MASQUE OF REASON
(New York: Henry Holt, 1945)

The limited edition, signed by the author, totaled eight hundred num-
bered copies.

473 A MASQUE OF REASON: in *1949, 1963*; VARIANT   269 the] a
AMOR; EMENDATIONS   *(periods entered after designation of
speakers, as 1963, and such designations, as 1963, given in roman small
capitals rather than italic capitals and lower case)*   41 letup's] let-up's
44 letup] let-up   80 Him] him   84 are] are—   89 ,]   97 Witch]
witch   106 —]   116 —]   147 ,]   152 —]   184 ,].   195
there,] there   208 ,]   246 long-long-after-thought] long long
afterthought   270 ——]—   me, then,] me then   281 ,]   304
mean?] mean.   325 ,]   328 Chapters] chapters   336 —]
337 —]   345 :],   346 ultrared] ultra red   354 ,]   358 lookout]
look out   370 onto] on to   385 —]   386 —]   392 *(as AMOR)*
here,] here.   398 —]   402 —]   407 ,]   408 every which way]
everywhichway   420 —]   432 ,]   435 —]   436 ,]   439 —]
443 sand,] sand   447 —]   455 ,]   *offstage*] off *stage*   466
Chapter Forty-three] *chapter forty-three*

581

A MASQUE OF MERCY
(New York: Henry Holt, 1947)

The limited edition of seven hundred and fifty-one numbered copies
was signed by RF.

493 A MASQUE OF MERCY: *1st* in *The Atlantic Monthly*, November 1947; in *1949*; VARIANTS   436 And] Now *1st*   437 you've] you
have *1st*; EMENDATIONS (*periods entered after designation of speakers, as 1st, and such designations given in roman small capitals rather than italic capitals and lower case*)   4 showcase] show case   21 "]
"]   33 —]   48 (*as 1st*) Moby Dick] Moby Dick   60 *you*] you
79 —]   84 (*as 1st*) .]   97 ,]   102 (*as 1st, AMOM*) do] do,   121
Three,] Three   137 —] ,   138 ,]   —] ,   139 ,]   152 —]   164 —
170 -]   172 "] !] .   "] (*as 1st*) .]   173 —]   175 (*as 1st*) .]   183 ,]
197 ,]   199 (*as 1st*) *down.*] *down*   201 -]   203 anymore] any
more   207 —]   208 home,] home.   (*as 1st*) we] We   —]
213 sad,] sad   233 (*as 1st*) .]   238 ,]   239 (*as 1st*) .]   246 (*as
1st*) .]   252 ,]   263 ——] —   269 place,] place   270 ,]   276 (*as
1st*) *The New Yorker*] THE NEW YORKER   282 showcase] show case
285 —]   287 (*as 1st*) .]   296 ,]   311 ,]   318 ,]   321 ,]   322 ,]
324 ,]   331 :] .   341 (*as 1st*) *down.*] *down*   344 (*as 1st*) .]
345 —]   346 —]   349 ,]   352 ;] ,   356 ,]   369 -]   376 ,]
379 justice] justice,   381 (*as 1st*) —] ,   393 (*as 1st*) *another.*]
another   403 —]   406 (*as 1st*) small-time] smalltime   —]
421 (*as 1st*) again] again.   428 ,]   429 ,]   430 ,]   437 ,]
439 (*as 1st*) .] ,   448 well,] well   459 *Væ Victis*] Vae Victis   462 ,]
463 -]   469 ,]   470 ,]   490 (*as 1st*) .]   492 (*as 1st, AMOM*) .]
496 ,]   498 (*as 1st*) it,] it   504 ,] .   509 ,]   511 —]   518 —]
521 ,]   539 (*as 1st*) -]   540 ,]   541 ,]   550 (*as 1st*) .]   555 —]
562 (*as 1st*) ,]   563 ,]   569 ,]   570 ,]   590 ,]   607 (*as 1st*)
O'Neill] O'Neil   609 ,]   610 ,]   619 ,]   643 ,]   653 (*as 1st*) .]
657 though,] though   665 (*as 1st*) .]   668 (*as 1st*) .]   669 ,]
"Too] too ,]   "]   671 ,]   (*as 1st*) .]   672 —]   673 (*as 1st*) *fall.*]
fall .—] —   674 —] ,   675 ——] —   676 ,]   683 (*as 1st*) .]
684 —]   691 (*as 1st*) .]   692 ,]   —]   696 (*as 1st*) .]   718 —] ,
721 —] ,   735 (*as 1st*) -]   737 (*as 1st*) .]

Index of
First Lines & Titles

585

586

589

594

595

603

607

The poetry, table of contents, and index have been set in Fairfield, the poems' titles in Fairfield Medium, Linotype faces by Rudolph Ruzicka, the designer of this volume. Matrices for the 8-point Fairfield figures fitted on 12-point body, used for the verse numbers, have been especially prepared for this book. The notes make use of both Fairfield and Fairfield Medium. Display lines of the title page and the section titles are in Monotype Bembo. Composition by Westcott & Thomson of Philadelphia; printed and bound at R. R. Donnelley, Harrisonburg, Virginia.

A NOTE ON THIS EDITION

The Poetry of Robert Frost: The Collected Poems is the only comprehensive volume of Frost's published verse: in it are the contents of all eleven of his individual books of poetry—from *A Boy's Will* (1913) to *In the Clearing* (1962), published during the year before he died. This work, the standard edition of Frost's poetry since its publication in 1969, is now available with the hope that the literary legacy of one of America's most famous poets will become more accessible to students, scholars, and indeed everyone who loves poetry.

The editor, Edward Connery Lathem, a Frost scholar and close friend of the poet's, has scrupulously annotated the more than 350 poems in the book. His notes include bibliographical information on the publication of the poems, as well as specification of textual changes Frost made over the years. This authoritative volume, *The Poetry of Robert Frost*, stands as a lasting tribute to a great figure in American life and literature.

"His death impoverishes us all; but he has bequeathed his nation a body of imperishable verse from which Americans will forever gain joy and understanding."

—*John F. Kennedy*